Let’s Agree on Poland

Let's Agree on Poland

A Case Study in Strategic Constitutional Design

Edited by

MACIEJ KISILOWSKI AND ANNA WOJCIUK

OXFORD
UNIVERSITY PRESS

OXFORD
UNIVERSITY PRESS

Great Clarendon Street, Oxford, OX2 6DP,
United Kingdom

Oxford University Press is a department of the University of Oxford.
It furthers the University's objective of excellence in research, scholarship,
and education by publishing worldwide. Oxford is a registered trade mark of
Oxford University Press in the UK and in certain other countries.

Published in the United States of America by Oxford University Press
198 Madison Avenue, New York, NY 10016, United States of America.

British Library Cataloguing in Publication Data
Data available

Library of Congress Control Number: 2025936600

ISBN 978–0–19–897956–2

DOI: 10.1093/oso/9780198979562.001.0001

Printed and bound by
CPI Group (UK) Ltd., Croydon, CR0 4YY

MIX
Paper | Supporting
responsible forestry
FSC® C013604
FSC www.fsc.org

The manufacturer's authorised representative in the EU for product safety is
Oxford University Press España S.A., Parque Empresarial San Fernando de Henares,
Avenida de Castilla, 2 – 28830 Madrid (www.oup.es/en or product.safety@oup.com).
OUP España S.A. also acts as importer into Spain of products made by the manufacturer.

Acknowledgements

Let's Agree on Poland is the product of eight years of dedicated work by a diverse group of individuals—members and friends of the Social Contract Incubator (IUS) association. Throughout this time, we have had the privilege of engaging with hundreds of people involved in public affairs, including experts, academics, journalists, local government officials, NGO activists, and politicians. From these conversations, we drew inspiration, exchanged ideas, and gained invaluable insights. Our sincere gratitude goes to all those who helped shape this project, offering diverse perspectives, refining its ideas, and contributing to its final form.

Developing a comprehensive blueprint for constitutional reform in a country of forty million people is, to say the least, an ambitious endeavor. For projects of far smaller scope, national and European institutions allocate multimillion-euro grants. Yet from the outset, we recognized that in the socio-political climate in which we operated, pursuing such an initiative with significant financial resources was simply not feasible. The Social Contract Incubator could offer only "sweat and tears"—a call for voluntary work in crafting an innovative power-sharing agreement for Poland, despite the real risk of resentment and criticism from those resistant to sharing power or opposed to the direction outlined in this book.

Despite these inherent challenges, nearly 130 dedicated Polish patriots responded to our call. These individuals, all busy already with commitments of their own, were willing to risk their established positions and public profiles to contribute. For intellectuals, seeing their thoughts reflected in the pages of a book is a source of professional and civic fulfillment. While we refrain from listing the many contributions of the IUS members and friends who are among the authors, we are deeply grateful for their involvement. Our true reward lies in your, Dear Reader's, interest in and passion for a democratic future—that of our country and yours.

We would, however, like to take this opportunity to acknowledge the immense contributions—particularly the intellectual and creative efforts—of those who, for various reasons, are not among the authors of the book, but whose support and engagement were pivotal.

Our gratitude goes to all IUS members, and especially to Magdalena Baran, Adam Czarnota, Bogusława Cimoszko-Skowroński, Szymon Gutkowski, Natalia Jarska, Mikołaj Jarski, Szymon Klocek, Michał Ludwikowski, Radomir Matczak, Agata Mazurowska-Rozdeiczer, Paweł Lisiewicz, Wojciech Sadurski, and Jan Wasilewski.

We would also like to thank Dariusz Baran, Dominik Batorski, Adam Białachowski, Marcin Bużański, Mikołaj Nikola Dragović, Piotr Górski, Witold

Grzesiak, Krzysztof Iszkowski, Stefan Kawalec, Joanna Lisiecka-Żurowska, Andrzej Lisiecki-Żurowski, Waldemar Maj, Renata Mieńkowska-Norkiene, Tadeusz Mroziuk, Hubert Norek, Patrycja Okuljar, Tomasz Pietrzykowski, Marcin Pilch, Jarosław Płuciennik, Krzysztof Stanowski, Jacek Szwarc, Kacper Wańczyk, Jerzy Wiśniewski, and Piotr Wojdat—for valuable ideas, involvement in the communication and promotion of the project, organizational assistance, and support in obtaining partners and funds.

We are deeply grateful to world-renowned scholars and authorities on constitutionalism, democratic processes, and public policies—to Kim Lane Scheppele, Bruce Ackerman, Peter Lindseth, Kalypso Nicolaidis, Wolf Linder, Richard Albert, Pola Cebulak, Grzegorz Ekiert, Peter Katzenstein, Filip Kostelka, Martin Krygier, Elżbieta Matynia, Andrew Moravcsik, Michał Rutkowski, Monika Nalepa, Grigore Pop-Eleches, Robert Post, Jan Zielonka, and Christina Zuber, who supported our project in many ways. These colleagues, as well as participants in seminars at the Department of Legal Studies of Central European University, Institute for European Studies at Cornell University, Transnational Democracy in the 21st Century Interdisciplinary Research Cluster at European University Institute, Gunzburg Center for European Studies at Harvard University, Transregional Center for Democratic Studies at the New School, and Liechtenstein Institute on Self-Determination at Princeton University, kindly, though of course sometimes critically, supported us with advice and motivated us as *Let's Agree on Poland* was being written.

We are also thankful to IUS's numerous friends and sympathetic observers. To those among them who, at various stages of this project, supported us with their full conviction. And also to those who—seeing in this project an opportunity for Poland, against the destructive logic of political conflict and despite their reservations about some of the proposed solutions—publicly engaged in a substantive discussion with us or otherwise gave the idea of a new social contract a chance. We are especially grateful to Arkadiusz Muś, Aleksander Bobko, Adam Bodnar, Jürg Burri, Edwin Bendyk, Władysław Teofil Bartoszewski, Krzysztof Borusowski, Barbara Brodzińska-Mirowska, Jacek Cichocki, Nadia Cristan, Mikołaj Chrzan, Jacek Dubois, Łukasz Dziedzic, Maciej A. Górecki, Sylwia Gregorczyk-Abram, Andrzej Herbet, Krzysztof Janik, Tomasz Janik, Igor Janke, Agnieszka Jędrzejczyk, Michał Federowicz, Rev. Sławomir Fundowicz, Grzegorz Gorzelak, Aleksander Grad, Paweł Graś, Ryszard Kalisz, Paulina Kieszkowska, Basil Kerski, Michał Kobosko, Michał Kolanko, Lidia Kołucka-Żuk, Hubert Kotarski, Karolina Klimiuk, Ryszard Koziołek, Jerzy Koźmiński, Renata and Arek Krasowski, Adam Krzysztoń, Przemysław Kubicki, Paweł Kukiz, Jarosław Kurski, Aldona Machnowska-Góra, Edward MacDonald, Tomasz Madras, Jarosław Makowski, Marta Makuch, Gabriela Masztafiak, Wojciech Maziarski, Patrycja Medowska, Łukasz Mikołajewski, Dariusz Mioduski, Małgorzata Mitura, Błażej Moder, Andrzej Morozowski, Małgorzata Niezabitowska, Władysław Ortyl, Grzegorz

Osiecki, Bożena Ostrowska, Jan Parys, Waldemar Pawlak, Waldemar Paś, Szymon Pękala, Piotr Pilch, Marcin Piróg, Michał Płociński, Karol Rajewski, Dariusz Rosiak, Magdalena Radwan-Röhrenschef, Magdalena Rigamonti, Michał Różycki, Andrzej Rzońca, Jarosław Sachajko, Chasper Sarrot, Ulrich Schwendimann, Natalia Skipietrow, Jacek Słoma, Konrad Stanglewicz, Paweł Swianiewicz, Franciszek Sterczewski, Jerzy Stępień, Agata Stremecka, Anna Streżyńska, Jacek Strojny, Adam Szłapka, Krzysztof Śmiszek, Małgorzata Tkacz-Janik, Piotr Trudnowski, Ola and Bartek Trzebiński, Marek Twaróg, Łukasz Warzecha, Michał Wawrykiewicz, Jan Wróbel, Michał Wróblewski, Artur Zawadowski, Hanna Zdanowska, Andrzej Zybertowicz, Jacek Żakowski, and Tomasz Żółciak.

We would like to thank the local government organizations, especially the Convent of the Marshals of voivodships. Our thanks also go to the institutions that supported us financially and organizationally, including in particular the Harvard Club of Poland, the Res Publica Foundation, the Foundation for Economic Freedom, and the Stefan Batory Foundation.

We are grateful to Julia Krzesicka, as well as to the researchers who supported the chapters on dream provinces with their expertise and deep knowledge of the regions: Agata Nijander-Dudzińska, Magdalena Olchanowska, and Krzysztof Stachura. Finally, we would like to thankOxford University Press and two anonymous reviewers of the book proposal for their openness to this non-standard project bringing together twenty-eight authors, four world-class international commentators, five fiction writers, and a number of fine translators and editors. In particular, we are grateful to Brian Stone and Lindsay Glick for their professionalism and patience in dealing with the unusual challenges and needs that this volume has presented.

Contents

Contributor Bios

EDITORS

Maciej Kisilowski is Associate Professor in law and strategy at Central European University. His research spans public law, management, and political economy. His academic work has appeared in *Business and Society* and *Law and Social Inquiry*, among others. He holds a JSD and LLM from Yale Law School, an MPA from Princeton, and an MBA from INSEAD, as well as a PhD and MA in law from Warsaw University. His commentary on populism, democracy, and the rule of law has been featured in *Politico*, *Financial Times*, *Project Syndicate*, and leading Austrian and Polish media outlets.

Anna Wojciuk is Associate Professor at the University of Warsaw, specializing in international relations with a focus on populist foreign policy. Her work has appeared in *Review of International Studies*, *Chinese Journal of International Politics*, and *European Political Science*. In 2018, she published the book *Empires of Knowledge in International Relations* with Routledge. She was a Fernand Braudel Fellow at the EUI (2017/18, 2024) and has held visiting positions at Harvard, Columbia, Cornell, and Sciences Po. She also contributes to leading media outlets, including *Foreign Policy* and *Politico*.

EXPERT AUTHORS

Ryszard Balicki is Associate Professor at the University of Wrocław, a constitutional lawyer, and since 2019 a member of the National Electoral Commission.

Maciej Bukowski is Assistant Professor at the University of Warsaw, a founder and president of the WISE-Europa think-tank, an economist, and former member of the Team of Strategic Advisors at the Chancellery of Prime Minister Donald Tusk (2008–14).

Agnieszka Chłoń-Domińczak is Associate Professor and Vice-Dean of the Warsaw School of Economics, economist, demographer, an expert on pension systems and health care, and former Deputy Minister of Labor and Social Policy.

Helena Chmielewska-Szlajfer is Associate Professor at Koźmiński University and a Visiting Fellow at the London School of Economics and Political Science. She received her PhD in Sociology from the New School for Social Research (2014). She is the author of *(Not) Kidding: Online Tabloid Politics* (Brill, 2024), *Reshaping Poland's Community after Communism: Ordinary Celebrations* (Palgrave, 2019), and *Kazimierz Kelles-Krauz: Marxism and Sociology* (Warsaw University Press, 2014; Brill, 2018). She studies everyday civic practices as well as news avoidance, disinformation, online politics, and populism, and is a regular contributor to major media outlets in Poland and abroad.

Paweł Dobrowolski is Director of the Stefan Jaracz Theater in Olsztyn, previously director of the Catholic art festival Nowe Epifanie, and co-creator of the *Let's Give Each Other a Sign of Peace* social campaign for LGBT + people in the Catholic Church.

Jakub Drożdż is a law graduate of the University of Warsaw and a PhD candidate at the University's Doctoral School, where he specializes in diplomacy. He is a manager with professional experience in NGOs and public administration, the latter since 2018. Jakub has held various roles at the Polish Ministry of Foreign Affairs, including at the Diplomatic Academy. He is also a former General Secretary of the Młoda Prawica (Youth Right) Association.

Antoni Dudek is Professor at the Cardinal Stefan Wyszyński University, and a historian, political scientist, and researcher of Poland's recent history. Since 2000 he is one of the founding members of the Institute of National Remembrance—an institution established to promote Polish history and prosecute crimes against the Polish nation.

Jacek Giedrojć is a partner and founder of Warsaw Equity Group, previously at Harvard Business School and Victoria University in Wellington. He holds a PhD from the Polish Academy of Sciences. He is an investor, sociologist, public intellectual (op-ed contributor for *Forbes, Gazeta Wyborcza*), and author of books on the social determinants of innovation.

Mirosław Granat is Professor at the Cardinal Stefan Wyszyński University, retired judge of the Constitutional Tribunal (2007–16), vice-president of the Polish Society of Constitutional Law, and a former member of the Legislative Council of the Prime Minister and the Program Council of the Sobieski Institute (an influential right-wing think tank).

Tomasz Grzegorz Grosse is Professor at the University of Warsaw, and an expert on European integration and regional development. He co-authored Poland's 1998 local government reform and represented the European Conservatives and Reformists and the European Committee of the Regions at the Conference on the Future of Europe. His recent publications include *Geoculture: The Relationship Between Geopolitics and Culture* (2023), *Sovereignty and the Political: A Study of European Integration* (2022), *Four Dimensions of Integration* (2021), and *Searching Geo-economics in Europe* (2014). He also edited *Fuel for Dominance: On the Economic Bases of Geopolitical Supremacy* (2020).

Jarosław Gwizdak is a barrister and former judge, former president of the District Court in Katowice, the first winner of the award for the most pro-citizen judge in Poland, and a public intellectual. An expert on the rule of law, he has been involved in defending the independence of Polish courts since 2018. He is a Policy Leadership Fellow at the European University Institute (2022). He has worked on judiciary reforms in Ukraine and Georgia. Since October 2024 he has been Minister of Justice Plenipotentiary for the Open Judiciary. Legal columnist for Poland's oldest daily, *Rzeczpospolita.* Member of the Board of the legal think-tank INPRIS—Institute for Law and Society. Lives in Katowice.

Mikołaj Herbst is a Professor at the University of Warsaw, economist, and expert in regional development, local government, finance, and educational policy. A former member of the Team of Strategic Advisors at the Chancellery of Prime Minister Donald Tusk (2008–2014).

Tomasz Kaczor PhD is an econometrician with experience in the financial and public sectors, currently at the e-Health Center of the National Health Fund, and from 2007 to 2018 chief economist of BGK (Polish state-owned development bank). He was Economist of the Year 2016 of the industry daily *Parkiet.*

Alicja Pacewicz, co-founder of the left-wing NGO Center for Civic Education, develops educational programs and trains teachers. In 2011 she was awarded by President Bronisław Komorowski the Officer's Cross of the Order of Polonia Restituta for opposition activities under communism.

Wojciech Przybylski is a political analyst who leads strategic foresight on EU affairs. He is editor-in-chief of *Visegrad Insight*; president of the Res Publica Foundation, a liberal think-tank; and an advisory board member at LSE IDEAS Ratiu Forum. He co-authored *Understanding Central Europe* (Routledge, 2017) and has been widely published in, among others, the *Journal of Democracy*, *Politico*, and *EUObserver*.

Arkadiusz Radwan is Associate Professor at the Vytautas the Great University in Kaunas; lawyer, founder, and president of the conservative Allerhand Institute in Cracow; previously deputy director of the Diplomatic Academy of the Ministry of Foreign Affairs; and Law and Justice candidate for judge of the Court of Justice of the European Union.

Łukasz Rozdeiczer, attorney, mediator, and arbitrator, and adjunct professor at Georgetown University, holds an LLM from Harvard University. He is vice-president of the Catholic Intelligentsia Club, vice-president of the Auschwitz-Birkenau Foundation, and founder and president of the Batna Group.

Jan Smoleński is Assistant Professor at the University of Warsaw; political scientist; and a researcher of democratic theory, federalism, and US politics. He holds a PhD from the New School for Social Research. He is a graduate of CEU, Fulbright scholar, and columnist for the left-wing magazine *Krytyka Polityczna.*

Jacek Sokołowski is Assistant Professor at the Jagiellonian University, lawyer, constitutional expert, collaborator of the conservative Jagiellonian Club in Cracow, and and author of popular books on Polish politics. He is a public intellectual popular on X (posting as Easy Rider), and a columnist for the center-right *Rzeczpospolita* and *DGP* dailies.

Leszek Stypułkowski is a board member of BGK (Polish Development Bank), founder of Index Copernicus, and an expert on innovation, science and higher education.

Sylwia Sysko-Romańczuk is Associate Professor at the Warsaw University of Technology, IESE Alumni Chapter board member in Poland, and an expert in technology transfer, commercialization, and digital transformation. She represents the Warsaw University of Technology in CESAER and is a member of the Task Force Innovation. Her research focuses on policy and strategies for advancing technology transfer and commercialization in business and industry. She also explores personalism in management. A former Deputy Minister of Education in the Law and Justice government (2005–7), she has experience as a supervisory board member of start-ups and listed companies.

Marek Tatała is an economist, a manager in the non-governmental organization sector, and president of the Economic Freedom Foundation (FWG)—the most dynamically developing classical liberal organization in Poland.

Artur Wołek is Professor at the Jesuit University Ignatianum in Cracow, an expert on political systems, co-author of the local government reform of 1998, and collaborator of the Center for Political Thought (*Ośrodek Myśli Politycznej*)—one of the most important conservative think-tanks in Poland.

Marcin Zieliński is President and chief economist of the Civic Development Forum (FOR), a classical liberal think-tank founded by Leszek Balcerowicz.

Fryderyk Zoll is Professor at the Jagiellonian University and the University of Osnabrück, and a member of numerous international institutions associating experts in the field of private and comparative law. He was awarded the Medal of Merit for the Justice System in 2013, and since 2015 has been co-organizer of the social movement Committee for the Defense of Democracy (KOD), defending the rule of law in Poland.

Michał Żabicki, a programmer and analyst, holds a PhD from the Jagiellonian University. He is a theoretical physicist by education (not practicing), and a researcher of complex systems. He is published in the left-wing press, including *Gazeta Wyborcza* and *Krytyka Polityczna.*

INTERNATIONAL COMMENTATORS

Wolf Linder is Professor Emeritus at the University of Bern, a political scientist, and an expert on comparative federalism, referendums, and Swiss democracy. His research focuses on decentralization and political power-sharing in young democracies. Linder co-authored *Swiss Democracy: Possible Solutions to Conflict in Multicultural Societies* (Palgrave, 2017) with Sean Mueller. He has published numerous books and articles in prestigious journals such as the *European Journal of Political Research* and the *Swiss Political Science Review*. Linder's work has had a significant impact on the study of democratic institutions and conflict resolution in multicultural societies.

Peter L. Lindseth is the Olimpiad S. Ioffe Professor of International and Comparative Law at the University of Connecticut School of Law. His research focuses on European integration, comparative administrative law, and legal history. His books include *Power and Legitimacy: Reconciling Europe and the Nation-State* (OUP, 2010) and several collective volumes on comparative administrative law. His articles have appeared in the *Columbia Law Review*, *Contemporary European History*, European Law Journal, *Revue française d'administration publique*, and *Yale Law Journal*, among other publications. He holds a BA and JD from Cornell, and a PhD in European history from Columbia.

Kalypso Nicolaidis is Professorial Chair of Global Affairs at the EUI School of Transnational Governance in Florence, where she directs the Transnational Democracy Programme, the Democratic Odyssey, the EUI democracy cluster, and the Global Peace Tech Hub. Her most recent book is *A Citizen's Guide to the Rule of Law: Why We Need to Fight for the Most Precious Human Inventions of All Time.*

Kim Lane Scheppele is Laurance S. Rockefeller Professor of Sociology and International Affairs at Princeton University and a faculty fellow at the University of Pennsylvania Law School. Her research spans the sociology of law, political sociology, comparative and historical sociology, sociology of knowledge, and human rights. She studies the rise and fall of constitutional government, focusing on post-1989 Eastern Europe and the enactment of new constitutions in Hungary and Russia. Her most recent book, *9/11 and the Rise of Global Anti-Terrorism Law: How the UN Security Council Rules the World* (with A. Vedaschi, CUP, 2021), addresses global legal shifts.

FICTIONALIZATION, LITERARY EDITING, AND TRANSLATION

Sylwia Chutnik is a writer, columnist, and activist with a PhD in cultural studies. She received the prestigious *Polityka* Passport award and has been nominated three times for the Nike Literary Award. A graduate of cultural studies, gender studies, and Polish–Jewish studies, she is an active publicist and social advocate. Chutnik lectures at the University of Warsaw and SWPS University, and is involved in curating literary festivals and initiatives. She contributes to *Polityka*, *Times of the Literature*, and various other platforms. Her work appears in both Polish and international publications, and she has received multiple literary and social awards.

Marta Kwaśnicka is a writer, literary critic, and editor with a PhD in history from the John Paul II Pontifical University in Cracow. She is the author of *Jadwiga*, a colorful biography of the Polish queen and Catholic saint, in which she skillfully reconstructs the spiritual and intellectual context of fourteenth-century Europe while vividly portraying Cracow's vibrant landscape. A winner of multiple literary awards, including the Dedals' Wings and Marek Nowakowski Literary Awards, Kwaśnicka has also published scholarly works, including two monographs on the eighteenth- and nineteenth-century history of the Jesuit Order. She lives in Cracow.

Karolina Lewestam is a writer, public intellectual, and former columnist for the center-right daily *Dziennik Gazeta Prawna*. She holds a PhD in philosophy from Boston University and is a member of the editorial board of Pismo. Lewestam has lectured at BU and the University of Warsaw and currently writes a monthly column for Pismo, covering culture, philosophy, and literature. She is also a bestselling author of children's books. Nominated for the Grand Press Award, Poland's most prestigious journalism prize, she remains active in cultural discourse. Lewestam resides in London.

Anna Merriman is an editor and former daily news journalist. She edits the English edition of national Polish arts and culture magazine *Przekrój*. Previously, she was an award-winning journalist for daily newspapers in Ohio, New Jersey, and New Hampshire, where she covered the criminal justice system and local government. She also served as an editor with *Vox*

Media, based out of Philadelphia, and taught writing at SWPS University in Warsaw. She currently lives in Warsaw with her cat, Bąbelek (Bubbles).

Agnes Monod-Gayraud is an author, editor, and translator based in London, specializing in non-fiction titles on science, nature, culture, and folklore. She has translated more than a dozen books from Polish into English, including *Earthlings* (Big Picture Press, 2024). In 2017, she received the Educational Writers' Award for *The Book of Bees* (Thames and Hudson/Abrams). Agnes is also the co-author of *Faedom*, an illustrated compendium of fairies and earth science (Big Picture Press, 2024). She is a freelance editor for *Astronomy & Astrophysics* and holds degrees from NYU and the University of Warsaw.

Piotr Siemion is a novelist, literary translator, and attorney. He received a PhD in humanities and a JD from Columbia University in New York. A Fulbright scholar, Siemion lived in the US and Canada from 1988 to 2000, where he translated works by William Butler Yeats, Tom Clancy, and Thomas Pynchon (for which he won the 1990 "Literature in the World" Award). He worked at Weil, Gotshal & Manges. A winner of several major literary awards in Poland, he currently resides in Warsaw.

Ziemowit Szczerek is a journalist, writer, and translator, and winner of the "Polityka" Passport, the Grand Prix of the Kryminalna Warszawa Festival, and the Silver Distinction of the Jerzy Żuławski Literary Award. Twice nominated for the prestigious Nike Literary Award, Szczerek is known for his gonzo-style explorations of Central and Eastern Europe. He is the author of *Mordor Will Come and Eat Us* and *The Triumphant Republic*, in which he blends history and fiction to examine the political and cultural intricacies of the region. His work deconstructs stereotypes and offers unconventional insights into the complexities of the post-Soviet space.

Jonathan Weber, a graduate of Glasgow University, has been providing professional freelance translation and proofreading services for almost thirty years. Initially immersed in market research, for the past decade and a half he has focused on sociological, philosophical, and economic texts. Born in London, raised in Scotland, and having spent most of his life in Warsaw, he now truly feels a European.

Kate Webster is a translator from Polish into English, specializing in literature, academic texts, and the arts. Her published translations include works of fiction, fantasy and reportage, as well as children's books and comics. Her work has been shortlisted for the Warwick Prize for Women in Translation (2024) and the Oxford-Weidenfeld Prize (2023), and longlisted for the International Booker Prize (2024). She is based in London.

Introduction

A Polarized Country in Need of a New Social Contract

Maciej Kisilowski and Anna Wojciuk

How to talk about the crisis

"This is perhaps the most important election of our lifetime. The very future of our democracy is at stake." How often have we heard such a dramatic call to action? In democracies old and new, worries about the survival of our constitutional systems have become the central theme of the political discourse. In the United States, three presidential elections have revolved around the spectacle of Donald J. Trump challenging mainstream democratic standards and the political establishment desperately trying to stave off his electoral advances. In France, three of the five presidential elections held in the past two decades involved runoffs with Trump's counterparts Jean-Marie and Marine Le Pen. In those two and many other countries, the democratic experience of an entire generation has resembled an at times apocalyptic struggle against supposed existential threats to the very continuation of the democratic form of governance.

In some nations, the politicians branded as villains in these struggles have eventually broken through mainstream cordons and risen to power. The home nation of this book's co-authors—Poland—is on that list. Writing about what happens next is not easy for us, the editors of this work by the most remarkably diverse group of contributors—intellectuals whose political leanings span from social democratic to very conservative.

Since 2017, when we started our work in a group of more than 130 Polish intellectuals, which we named the Social Contract Incubator—or IUS, which is the abbreviation of our Polish name—we have been following a few simple rules. For a start, each of us continued our work as a leftist, centrist, or conservative intellectual. In the context of Poland, this meant that we could all be active and passionate participants in the above-mentioned spectacle of the (real or imagined) democratic crisis. Many of us loudly protested the staunchly conservative government

Maciej Kisilowski and Anna Wojciuk, *Introduction* In: *Let's Agree on Poland*. Edited by: Maciej Kisilowski and Anna Wojciuk, Oxford University Press. © Maciej Kisilowski and Anna Wojciuk 2025.
DOI: 10.1093/oso/9780198979562.003.0001

of the Law and Justice party, known by its Polish acronym PiS, believing that it was leading Poland on a path to autocracy. Others, on the contrary, supported the government or at least viewed the alarm as wildly exaggerated and perhaps politically motivated. What we did agree on was that the "Polish–Polish war," a term coined with our typical national sarcasm, could not continue. Not when the historically unique period of geopolitical calm that our nation experienced after 1989 had ended so abruptly. Coming from our distinct ideological traditions, we also focused from the outset not on some elusive policy compromise, a "centrist" position that would satisfy no one, but rather on identifying an institutional arrangement that would allow "our" respective sides of the political game to continue to vigorously disagree and compete for voters' support, but within some mutually accepted rules of the game. The motto of our group, reflected in the structure of this book and proposed by one of our conservative members, became: "Agreed, we are different."

Our endeavors have indeed unfolded very much in the spirit of what Cass Sunstein called an "incompletely theorized agreement"[1]—a shared constitutional proposal that its various proponents support for different reasons. The intellectual task of determining the social, political, and economic *why* behind our proposal was never our objective. When the Polish edition of this volume was published in May 2023, quickly becoming an unlikely nonfiction bestseller and dubbed "the most important book on Polish politics since 1989" in the country's main opinion weekly, *Polityka*,[2] this absence of a deeper diagnosis was not too much of a problem: following decades of increasingly heated and high-stakes political conflict, every Pole intuitively understood what the "Polish–Polish war" meant, and why stopping it made sense.

For this international edition, however, we found it useful to place our efforts in a broader comparative context. But in doing so, we immediately encountered the challenge of creating a theoretical frame that would remain true to the spirit of our unusual exercise: a comparatively understandable diagnosis of the problem that Poland and, we believe, many other nations are facing—but a diagnosis that both a conservative and a progressive would consider fair. This is easier said than done. Lawyers and political scientists are too rarely ready to admit the degree to which our analytical work is influenced by our normative convictions. Even the labels that mainstream scholars use to describe right-wing leaders and movements are hardly neutral. Populists, far-, extreme- or radical right, authoritarians, autocrats, neo-fascists ... As individual scholars of liberal and centrist political persuasion, the authors of this introduction often describe modern radical right-wing movements in these terms. As organizers of a cross-ideological network,[3] we became used to seeing things from differing perspectives. And, perhaps, there is something analytically interesting in trying to describe the current democratic crisis in a way that engaged citizens on both sides of our political barricades can see as reasonably impartial. Let us try.

Conservative revolutionaries

Whatever you think about today's conservative movements that govern or have governed in the United States, Brazil, Poland, Israel, Britain, India, Slovakia, Hungary, Turkey, and Russia; joined coalition governments in Austria, Sweden, Finland, Italy, and the Netherlands; or contested power in France and Romania—indeed, regardless of whether you think these governments and movements even belong to one ideological family—we believe you may agree with the following statement: In the past few decades, in democracies old and young, something has changed about the preferred methods employed, respectively, by the right- and left-leaning political movements in pursuance of their political objectives.

Traditionally, parties on the right of the policy spectrum preferred preserving the status quo and slowing change.[4] We thus called them "conservatives." The parties on the left, by contrast, challenged that status quo. We called them "progressives." The progressive spectrum varied widely in its degree of radicalism. At the extreme, we had violent communist dictatorships. But even in the democratic world, progressives were bold. Bruce Ackerman, in a classic study, shows how the greatest liberal moments in American history—the Reconstruction, the New Deal, and the Civil Rights Era—were in fact audacious constitutional revolutions.[5] Most continental European lawyers will perhaps applaud the overall direction of these changes, their positive contribution to fundamental human rights, but may still shrug at how they failed to adhere to the formalist conditions for a proper Article V constitutional amendment. At the more mundane level, the progressive change occurred—to simmering right-wing dissatisfaction—through a relentless left-leaning push enacted through ordinary legislation and, increasingly, through a growing importance of international agreements as well as the secondary international law promulgated by supranational executive, legislative, and judicial bodies. In Europe, the key role here has been played by the European Union and the Council of Europe. Beyond the continent, we should note the impact of the World Trade Organization and, especially during the recent COVID pandemic, the World Health Organization.[6]

By the early twenty-first century, the change in social and economic realities had become so steady and all-encompassing that it was that change that was the new status quo. And that is when our right-wing compatriots began, quite rationally, to alter their preferred political strategy. In almost every society, right-wing parties began to adopt more revolutionary methods, historically associated with the Left. What emerged is a seeming contradiction of the conservative revolutionary. "Seeming" as, in a world dominated by constant change, stopping the progressive train and giving traditionalism a chance may indeed require revolutionary resolve.[7]

Note how this narrative can make sense even to a person deeply skeptical of the stern warnings about an impending democratic collapse. A committed democrat who is also sympathetic to the political agenda of conservative revolutionaries can simply point out that revolutions have always come in many shades and thus may not necessarily be undemocratic. To say that Jarosław Kaczyński, the leader of Poland's PiS party, belongs to the same ideological camp as Vladimir Putin might be viewed as a smear similar to the accusations branding Franklin Delano Roosevelt as a communist put forward by conservative free-market fundamentalists in the 1930s. For many conservatives, it is fundamentally dishonest to equate deep policy changes instituted within democratic systems, even when radical and risky, with brutal authoritarian regimes.

The worst-case scenario

But our story about conservative revolutionaries also squares well with what we could call the "worst-case scenario"—the political and scholarly narrative that sees conservative revolutionaries as inherently authoritarian.[8] Under this narrative, these revolutionaries will always, sooner or later, aim to weaken democracy understood in a very basic sense: as a constitutional order in which governments are chosen through competitive elections—in which, in the normal course of political life, ruling "parties lose elections."[9] The judiciary and other independent state institutions are then stuffed with partisan loyalists.[10] The security services start spying on,[11] or killing,[12] opposition leaders. Journalists get harassed, jailed, or murdered.[13] The media is turned into a propaganda machine.[14] Economic policy becomes focused on creating corrupt oligarchies supporting the ruling party.[15] And when, against all odds, the opposition parties manage to oust right-wing rulers from power, the latter use delaying tactics[16] or even outright violence[17] to thwart the transfer of power—which, in keeping with the definition we provided above, is the very essence of what democracy is about.

Moreover, under the worst-case scenario, once in office, conservative revolutionaries almost universally become more radical and anti-democratic. When he took over in the mid-2000s, Recep Tayyip Erdoğan was hailed as a model conservative Muslim democrat. By the late 2010s, thousands of journalists and opposition figures were languishing in Turkish jails. Upon taking power in 2016, Donald J. Trump surrounded himself with a number of right-leaning figures who nevertheless enjoyed cross-party respect, starting with his vice-president, former governor and congressman Mike Pence. When he returned to the White House in 2025, Trump initiated the most sweeping policy and institutional transformation since the New Deal—asserting expansive wartime powers to enable mass deportations without due process, seeking to dismantle birthright citizenship guaranteed by the Fourteenth Amendment, and launching political attacks on universities and law firms deemed ideologically noncompliant.

Looking at the worst-case scenario through the revolutionary lenses proposed here reveals a significant paradox. For if one really believes that the core program of conservative revolutionaries is about taking democracy apart, then one must conclude that in a number of modern democracies, large and highly mobilized minorities of voters—and sometimes outright majorities—are "democratically suicidal": they consistently support the systematic dismantling of the very political system in which they actively participate.[18]

Let us offer an alternative way to conceptualize this paradox. This volume looks at the challenges faced by our democracies from the perspective of Central Europe—a region which, to much fanfare, overcame communist dictatorships and declared its intention to join the democratic "West" in the early 1990s. It was largely in response to the constitutional transitions of the countries in our region that political scientists developed a rich set of conceptual tools to track when a nation truly "becomes" a democracy. In parallel to the above-mentioned procedural focus on the electoral transfer of power as the defining feature of a democratic system, a concept of "consolidated democracy" was proposed.[19] In accordance with that notion, democracy is "consolidated" only if the commitment to free and fair elections, and to potentially losing power through such elections, is "the only game in town." In the words of the view's famous proponent:

> Democracy is consolidated when under given political and economic conditions ... no one can imagine acting outside the democratic institutions, when all the losers want to do is to try again within the same institutions under which they have just lost.[20]

It is plain that the closer one is to the above-mentioned very harsh assessment of the governing practices—and governing ambitions—of conservative revolutionaries, the more one must conclude that a large number of modern democracies are no longer "consolidated."[21] If we believe that political movements enjoying the support of between a third and a half of the voters truly want to do away with a system of free and fair elections, then democracy is, plainly, no longer the only game in town. Yes, in most countries, the revolutionaries enjoy the support of a minority of the population.[22] But political scientists, at least since the classic work of Mancur Olson,[23] have pointed out the power of mobilized minorities. All successful revolutions were started by minority movements of passionate supporters.

Lawyers as counterrevolutionaries

Understanding modern right-wing parties as conservatively revolutionary also helps us make good sense of the role of legal scholars and practitioners in the political struggles of today—because the lawyers in our story act as typical counterrevolutionaries.[24] For progressive legal readers this claim may at first be difficult to accept, as counterrevolutionaries have historically been associated with causes that such readers may find quite objectionable. But while the goals and values of today's defenders of the rule of law differ from those of the enemies of earlier revolutions, the tactics employed are remarkably similar: to stop right-wing revolutionaries in their tracks and, when possible, aggressively reverse their policy and institutional changes.

The most explicit general statement of that program was outlined by András Sajó under his call for the "militant rule of law."[25] But it is the practical applications of the counterrevolutionary strategies that best shed light on the nature of the enterprise. In the EU context, multiple prominent legal academics and practitioners spearheaded an energetic effort to sanction Hungary or Poland for their non-compliance with Article 2 of the EU Treaty.[26] The article lists thirteen foundational values upon which the European Union is built, but the sanctions have focused disproportionally on the fifth one listed, namely the rule of law. That this value, traditionally associated with conservatism, is now the banner of predominantly progressive lawyers fighting with the Right aptly summarizes the historically paradoxical, but politically rational, reality of conservative revolution.[27]

Beyond the EU, there have also been attempts to use the legalistic approach to resist conservative revolutionaries. The 2024 decision of the Israeli Supreme Court, which declared an amendment to the country's Basic Law unconstitutional, brought renewed attention to the so-called Basic Structure Doctrine, under which a procedurally appropriate constitutional amendment can still be declared invalid if it violates some key unwritten tenets of the hitherto constitutional order. The anti-change nature of this doctrine is explicitly acknowledged by Rosalind Dixon and David Landau, who use the metaphor of a "speed bump" to describe the doctrine's effects.[28] As with their physical counterparts, legal speed bumps can irritate those who think they were placed in the wrong places, by illegitimate authorities or too inconsistently to have a measurable effect. But even if all those flaws are avoided, speed bumps, by their very nature, can at best slow down but never completely stop the conservative revolutionary agenda.

Most experts would also agree that the more defenders of democracy rely on legal speed bumps, the more the revolutionaries affected by them are strongly motivated to get better at circumvention. Kim Scheppele famously talks about "autocratic legalists"[29] who use formal legality to consolidate their power. The United States shows the end station of such legalism. Here, the conservative revolutionary managed to secure a majority on the Supreme Court made up of lawyers who just a decade earlier were called "radicals in robes."[30] Poland is a very similar case, to which we will turn soon.

Before then, however, let us point to perhaps the most significant limitation of the legalistic counterrevolutionary strategy. As Bruce Ackerman showed in the above-mentioned classic work on US constitutional history,[31] legal speed bumps have a peculiar side effect in that they can further legitimize a revolutionary. If, in response to legal pushback, a revolution falters (and revolutionaries go, perhaps, to jail), then the story is over. By now, however, in a handful of countries, the right-wing revolutionaries who gained power have encountered a stiff legal backlash and, eventually, been democratically ousted. The United States and Brazil can be given as such examples. Alas, in both cases the beaten revolutionary refused to concede defeat and, in fact, radicalized his agenda even further. And even so, the revolutionary has held on to the support of a large portion of the electorate. In 2024, Donald J. Trump completed his unlikely journey back to the White House by claiming victories in both the Electoral College and the popular vote.

Revolutions and counterrevolutions: A case study

To those two countries that experienced such unyielding conservative revolutionary pressure, we should add our own. Poland is unique, however, since it has experienced the full cycle of the conservative revolution that refuses to end, that declines to concede its defeat, not once but twice in the last two decades. It was just a year after Poland's triumphant 2004 EU accession that PiS first tried to establish an ultra-conservative "Fourth Polish Republic." This would have been the fourth when counting on from, first, the pre-modern Poland raided by its neighbors in the eighteenth century; second, the interwar Poland that was invaded by its neighbors in 1939; and third, the seemingly successful post-1989 third Republic.[32]

For two years, progressive Poles anxiously watched the increasingly hardball moves taken by the ruling government. But PiS governed in an unwieldy coalition. Early elections in 2007 brought to power Donald Tusk—a liberal highly regarded by European elites, who would later move on to chair the EU Council and be humorously described by the Danish Prime Minister, Lars Løkke Rasmussen, as "the good Donald" of the transatlantic world.[33]

That government, which ran Poland for eight years, attempted to address numerous problems. It shepherded Poland through the Great Recession; it organized a successful Euro football tournament in 2012; and it raised the retirement age. Yet one significant thing that the Polish liberals failed to do during this period was truly understand what had happened. Why, just a year after EU accession—perhaps the greatest geopolitical achievement in our country's rather sad history—did nearly 50 percent of Polish voters support a host of Euroskeptic or populist parties? This lack of serious intellectual effort to grasp the revolutionary signal sent by the voters came back to haunt the liberals, who lost again to PiS in 2015.

With lessons well learned from their previous stint in power, the revolution now proceeded much more swiftly and aggressively. Much has been written about this period, both academically and in international media. A number of this book's co-authors have contributed to this discussion, often from radically opposing standpoints. After another eight years, PiS was ousted once again.

This time, the counterrevolutionary nature of the progressive rule, and the legal community supporting it, became much more evident. The Tusk government swiftly took over key state institutions, including the public TV broadcaster and the prosecutor's office. A flurry of investigations into PiS's alleged illegalities and abuses of power followed. On the other side of the battle stood the Constitutional Tribunal,[34] staffed entirely by political allies of the deposed conservative revolutionaries. At the time of writing, we are witnessing a curious situation in which the liberal government is refusing to follow, or even to promulgate, the Tribunal's rulings—the very actions that, in other contexts, could be constructed as undermining the rule of law.

This conflict has not harmed support for the Right. In the June 2025 presidential election, PiS's candidate Karol Nawrocki scored an unexpected, narrow victory over Warsaw's liberal mayor, Rafał Trzaskowski. Nawrocki secured just under 51 percent of the vote, compared to Trzaskowski's 49.1 percent. As this book goes to press, it remains uncertain whether the Tusk government will endure the ultra-difficult cohabitation with a president who lacks executive authority but holds considerable power to obstruct the Cabinet's agenda—or whether it will collapse, triggering early elections and potentially paving the way for a Trump-style return of the Right to full control.

Crucially, however, the outcome itself changes little in the broader pattern we analyze in this volume. There is nothing unprecedented about Nawrocki's razor-thin victory. Over the past two decades, PiS has won the presidency in four out of five contests—yet always with narrow majorities, averaging under 52 percent.

Maybe voters are duped

If an exclusive reliance on legal counterrevolution is at best insufficient, and at worst may strengthen the resilience, resolve, and radicalism of conservative revolutionaries, why is it still the strategy of choice for liberals? The answer is largely that the liberal side lacks good alternatives to the New Right's stubborn surge. This is a strong claim given the vast literature, especially in political science, that deals with the topic. Let us, however, offer a concise survey to substantiate our critique. We should start with perhaps the most influential stream that advances what we may call the populist strategies argument. It views conservative revolutions as somewhat artificially manufactured by cynical politicians. These cunning "populists" manipulate the electorate, often by leveraging some less appealing features of the social media or the hyper-partisanship of cable and streaming TV stations. While the technologies used by populists may be new, the story of authoritarian demagogues duping "we the people" has been at the center of Western democratic consciousness at least since Adolf Hitler's rise to power following the 1932 general elections. Much of the literature on populist strategies makes the connection between present-day conservative revolutionaries and the traumatic experience of Nazism quite explicit.[35] Not surprisingly, conservatives find such normative equivalences particularly offensive.

The response of mainstream democratic forces suggested by the populist strategies literature is twofold. On the one hand, liberal politicians, journalists, academics, and other socially influential actors should be relentless in their unmasking of populist lies. On the other hand, populist schemers should never be allowed to reap political rewards of their mendacity. Mainstream political parties should cordon them off and refuse to govern with them, even if the only alternative is forming grand coalitions and democratic fronts of parties whose political platforms have very little in common.[36] The latter strategy was adopted by anti-PiS forces that formed an ideologically diverse coalition in Poland in 2023.

These prescriptions complement well the tactics developed by the legal scholars mentioned earlier. Both strands of the literature in fact suggest a reliance on counterrevolutionary measures, be it in the realm of legal norms or the informal norms of political propriety.[37] The advantage of the works on populist strategies is that they provide a clear response to the above-mentioned paradox of a democratically suicidal electorate. If the voters are bamboozled by authoritarian demagogues, they can unwittingly sign away their democratic freedoms.

But how does that explanation comport with the facts? We have already noted the steady and high support for conservative revolutionaries in Poland. Except for Hungary and Turkey, in few other European countries has "the New Right" (as of June 2025) been in power for about half of the past two decades. For the populist strategies argument to succeed, it would need to point to leadership or structural factors that make Polish voters particularly susceptible to "populist manipulation." And yet the search for such a "smoking gun" brings meager results. The leadership of the right-wing parties has been quite effective, but not outdoing similar leaders in other democracies in either skill or charisma.[38] The mainstream political elite, by contrast, has been quite professional and much less corrupt than in many other post-communist nations.[39] Mainstream parties, and especially the dominant centrist Civic Platform, have established structures, supported by public financing, which positioned them well to counter any mendacious populist messages.[40] Media, especially the printed press, has faced its share of disruption caused by the internet, but—before 2015—did not devolve into the hyper-partisanship of, say, the US cable news channels.[41] Indeed, it was the generally progressive bent of the media that motivated PiS to take close control over the public TV and radio broadcasters. That move, however, only happened after its stunning 2015 return to power. There are also no indications of Polish voters being particularly affected by a polarizing impact of social media.[42]

In view of this lack of long-term structural factors, the passage of time certainly does not work in favor of the populist strategies argument. The longer conservative revolutionaries remain as a major political force in our democracies, the harder it is for the trickery story to be viewed as descriptively accurate. In order to conceptually distinguish the political preference induced by populist lies and manipulation from the underlying "real" will of the people, we must establish a set of well-defined stimuli that, at a given moment, alter voters' behavior. The story of Hitler's electoral manipulation makes sense because his rise to power was swift and immediately followed by the establishment of a completely non-competitive dictatorship.

Today, we have simply witnessed too many electoral cycles in which modern conservative revolutionaries have been highly competitive to keep the story of a manipulated electorate conceptually sound. As was already mentioned, the revolutionary political movements in Poland have already taken hold of and lost power twice. Voters have had ample opportunity to thoroughly evaluate the revolutionaries' behavior—at the time of seeking power, when wielding it, and then when they lose it. In Poland, the eighteen months preceding the writing of this introduction have been particularly telling. In 2023, breaking PiS's above-mentioned hold on the public media was one of the first moves of the winning liberal coalition. Suddenly, public TV and radio began to report stories about PiS scandals and improprieties uncovered by the new government. And yet, as we have already mentioned, overall support for the conservative Right has not fallen. For the proponents of the populism argument, this raises the question: How long should we wait until we conclude that what a very large proportion of voters repeatedly expresses at the ballot box is what they really want?

Maybe it's the economy

This uncomfortable empirical reality motivates many political scientists to search for explanations that acknowledge the reality of the demand for conservative revolutionary politics. The most influential result of these inquiries can be called the materialist argument. Promoted among others by Dorothee Bohle,[43] John Judis,[44] and Barry Eichengreen,[45] it argues that contemporary rebellion against democracy stems from the accruing impact of neoliberal economic policies, with their recurring crises, growing inequality, and cascading side effects of globalization.[46] A special role in this explanatory account is attributed to the 2009 Global Financial Crisis and the Great Recession. This theory's proponents point especially to the sluggishness of the European response to the crisis and the resulting, painful, sovereign debt and currency crisis in the mid-2010s. The prescriptive conclusion is for policy elites to adopt a more Keynesian economic approach, to crack down on inequalities and other excesses of modern capitalism, and to expect voters to return to the mainstream democratic fold.

While the left-leaning contributors to this volume may somewhat disagree, the authors of this introduction see Poland as a powerful spoiler case for the materialist story. It would be difficult to find a nation more economically successful over the last several decades. Starting from a middle-income level in 1990, Polish real output, adjusted for purchasing power, had increased by more than 300 percent on per capita terms by 2015—and by 650 percent by 2023.[47] Even more unusually, despite this spectacular pace of growth, the country's income inequalities have generally been in line with the Western European average, with the 2015 Gini coefficient at 31.8.[48] This outcome makes Poland about as equal as, for instance, France.

Furthermore, the timing of the victories of right-wing revolutionaries makes the case for the materialist argument particularly hard. As was mentioned above, the first PiS triumph came in 2005. This was a year after Poland had joined the European Union and thus received unprecedentedly generous structural funds and agricultural subsidies.[49] The latter in particular benefited a large and traditionally poor rural population, which constitutes nearly 40 percent of the country (compared to 17 percent in France, and the EU average of 24 percent). The second PiS victory came in 2015. Again, the traditional materialist rationale seems oddly fitting. Uniquely in Europe, Poland largely avoided the Great Recession, and was frequently dubbed a "green island" in the red ocean of economic contraction. Since the country chose not to adopt the euro, it also did not suffer the consequences of the common currency's crisis.

In addition to not squaring well with the main version of the materialist argument, Poland also contravenes the streak that looks for the roots of revolutionary conservatism in relative psychological deprivation.[50] Of particular note here is that PiS's support base—the rural population—enjoys major tax privileges as compared to other professional groups. Polish farmers do not pay income taxes and benefit from an extremely preferential social security system. What we face here is, again, the question of a policy counter-factual: if the current system—under which the general population, including the urban lower-middle class and the poor, heavily subsidizes public services for the rural Poles—still produces "relative depravation" of the latter group, then which realistic policy setup would not?

Maybe it's xenophobia

If not economics, then perhaps xenophobia? The alternative explanation, which we call the diversity argument, is quickly gaining ground in the literature. Explicated thoroughly by Yascha Mounk[51] and Terry Smith,[52] and recently endorsed by Steven Levitsky and Daniel Ziblatt,[53] it posits that populism is the consequence of the trouble of unsuccessfully managing the challenges of a multiethnic and multiracial society. The associated policy solution is for liberal elites to, well, do better: pay more attention to how we can address white anxieties, and emphasize the gradual nature of the demographic change. The radical version of this prescription is to simply adopt some of the anti-immigrant policies advocated by conservative revolutionaries. This so-called far-right policy mainstreaming is becoming increasingly popular in Europe.[54] Indeed, in Poland, the liberal coalition that took over in 2023 surprised many human rights activists by choosing to continue PiS's hardline approach to refugees and economic migrants trying to illegally cross the country's border from Belarus.[55]

A growing body of literature tries to empirically evaluate whether mainstream political parties can win back some electoral support by replicating selected right-wing policies on issues such as migration.[56] Poland's experience with recent conservative revolutions undercuts the diversity argument at a more fundamental level, however. To begin with, our right-wing revolutionary politics emerged in one of the most ethnically, culturally, racially, and linguistically homogeneous mid-sized nations in Europe. Furthermore, our homogeneity exists against a unique historical background. Deep in the Polish cultural narrative is the understanding that our homogeneity is a relatively new phenomenon, emerging from the tragedy of the Holocaust and post-World War II mass resettlements. One of the key narratives inculcated into Polish children through public education is that, for nearly its entire history, Poland was in fact a highly diverse society, with Poles, Lithuanians, Ukrainians, and Germans, Catholics, Protestants, Orthodox, and Jews living side by side in an often uneasy coexistence. Until recently, this historical identity was corroborated by the elderly, who remembered the diverse pre-1939 Poland.

Poland is thus an example of a country where the diversity "experiment" described by Mounk and others actually took place for centuries before being abruptly (and tragically) stopped. Yet that newly found homogeneity has not made the country immune to the appeal of conservative revolutionaries. Indeed, complicating the story even further is that this diversity, including racial, began to increase under the right-wing PiS government. It is well known that PiS generously accepted millions of war refugees from Ukraine. But what is less known is that, faced with acute labor shortages, PiS increased migration—including from Asia, Africa, and the Middle East—even before the Russian invasion. This de facto openness oddly coexisted with strong anti-immigrant rhetoric—a point now often brought up by the even more conservative Konfederacja party. But it is plain that social tensions rooted in an experience of multiracial and multiethnic diversity could not have causally played a role in PiS's rise to political prominence, as this rise predated the increase in non-European migration of recent years.

Maybe it's history

Another theory, which we can call the argument of national decline, was discussed particularly in the wake of the Brexit referendum. Some scholars viewed the result as a sign of the inability of British society and its political elites to process post-imperial reality.[57] Similar claims were advanced in the context of Hungary, with right-wing populists preying on the lingering popular resentment about the significant territorial losses suffered by Hungary under the Treaty of Trianon of 1920.[58] When it comes to solutions, the literature in this stream often emphasizes the role of (progressive) education in establishing a more historically accurate view of the past. If voters, the argument goes, learn from a young age that our history was not as glorious as it may seem at first glance, they will be less interested in "making our nations great again." Indeed, a keen interest in the effects of education on voters' political behavior is shared by the conservatives. In the US, both the second Trump administration and governors of right-leaning states are attempting to reshape school and university curricula.[59]

We do not need to dig deep to show the limited applicability of the national decline argument to the case of Poland. Our country is living through one of the most successful periods in its history. Its rapid economic growth and consistently high military spending have led international commentators to talk of a new major European power.[60] More importantly, the perception of Poland's multi-faceted success is deeply embedded in the national psyche, especially against the strong sense of victimhood during earlier stages of our history. Unlike Hungarians, for instance, Poles view their post-World War II borders as "the most advantageous in our history," with no politically important actor ever expressing irredentist views.[61] Poles across the political spectrum are still largely united in maintaining a deep sense of pride in the role of "Solidarity" in toppling communism. Similar pride in the role of John Paul II has, in some demographic groups,[62] perhaps been undermined by the liberal accusations about the late Pope's role in covering up sexual abuse scandals—but this erosion largely occurred during, and not before, the second period of PiS rule (and thus could not have causally contributed to the polarization behind its 2005 and 2015 electoral successes). Neither the objective position of Poland nor the inter-subjective social sense of that position bear any traits of national decline that could breed resentment.[63]

Poland has also strongly debunked both liberal and conservative hopes for education, and especially revisionist historical education, serving as a magic bullet to shape future electoral preferences. In 1999, the country underwent a comprehensive educational reform. The new middle school system significantly decreased urban–rural educational disparities by bussing kids from fifth grade onwards to larger, better equipped—and more progressive—larger-town schools. A huge effort by experts and NGOs, often supported by Western funds, went into improving students' math and reading comprehension skills.[64] Between 2007 and 2015, the liberal government deepened the progressive tilt of the educational system, giving students more freedom to choose their individual educational paths. Importantly, students could now reduce the extent to which they studied Polish national history, and opt to learn more about cosmopolitan civilizational issues. The reforms were penned by global experts. In a 2014 New York Times bestseller, Amanda Ripley listed Poland, Finland, and South Korea as the countries with "the smartest kids in the world."[65]

A year later, voters—many of whom were products of the post-1999 school system—voted the right-wing PiS party into power. The abolition of the middle schools, and the return to the traditional, eight-grade-long primary school system, was one of the main points of PiS's policy platform, and one of its earliest decisions. One of this chapter's authors, who teaches at a Polish state university, remembers from this time undergraduate students sporting patriotic apparel featuring imposing Polish emblems and anti-communist symbols.

Like liberals in the late 1990s, the PiS government also saw schools and universities as among its main battlegrounds. Patriotic education became a mandatory subject. Conservative and Catholic academic journals were lavished with subsidies, and articles published in them were granted status equivalent to that enjoyed by articles in prestigious international journals such as *Nature*. Both the Ministry of Education and Science and the special Institute of National Remembrance vigorously opposed the academic research and study of Polish and international historians on the complicity of some Poles in the German persecution of Jews during World War II.

And yet, despite all these policies, it was the young generation of Polish voters that proved instrumental in the 2023 victory of the anti-PiS opposition. This time, a Polish university instructor would see young adults straight from PiS's ultraconservative school system proudly displaying LGBT rainbows, pro-abortion signs, or expletive-ridden calls for PiS to go away. It seems that both sides of the Polish–Polish war failed to get what they wanted from the education system.

Maybe it's the transition

The final stream of studies searching for the deeper roots of modern conservative revolutions focuses on the institutional weaknesses of transitioning democracies,[66] particularly in post-communist countries.[67] According to this view, countries such as Poland have never truly consolidated their democracy, and the regression to authoritarianism merely reflects the increasing risks inherent in a prolonged, unfinished transition.[68] The associated normative discussion is often tainted with an air of fatalism: only the passage of time will rid us of the legacies of the past. However, the more immediate democratic prescription is the appeal to political virtue. Recognizing the fragility of a young democracy, politicians should rise above short-term political gains and conduct themselves in a manner that gradually builds societal trust and engagement in the workings of the democratic system.[69]

The most obvious problem with this line of argument is that conservative revolutionaries are popular not only in post-communist countries such as our own, but also in some of the most historically established democracies, such as France and the United States.[70] The similarities between the policy platforms, preferred rhetoric, and modi operandi of the New Right movements in both old and new democracies make it difficult to substantiate the causal story that places long transitions at the center.[71]

Indeed, calls for the virtue and responsibility of the political elite, analogous to those made in the context of the literature on unfinished transition, are routinely posited in established Western democracies. Our survey has come full circle, as these calls are often part of the studies on populism that we reviewed earlier. In a recent influential volume, Larry Bartels uses Polish and Hungarian case studies to make a broad point about the need for a more honest and responsible political elite across the West.[72] Bartels' case selection evokes obvious enthusiasm among the authors of this introduction; after all, the very premise of this volume's English-language edition is that our country's predicament is representative of the challenges faced by many democracies, old and new alike. But that premise cannot be easily squared with the narrative of unfinished transition.[73]

Even if we somehow limit our attention to Eastern Europe, the narrative of unfinished transition faces serious empirical obstacles. After all, countries in the region have been subject to regular and comprehensive assessments of the progress in their democratic transitions—to a historically unprecedented extent. These evaluations come from two sources. The first includes the elaborate processes of candidacy and accession to the European Union and NATO. The second source comprises indices compiled regularly by institutions and scholars interested in keeping a comparative score of the transition process that, in a historically unusual way, was developing simultaneously in numerous countries with similar historical and institutional starting points. Perhaps the most influential of these comparative efforts has been Freedom House's Democracy Score, which—since the mid-2010s—has been ceding ground to a global indexing initiative, V-Dem.

The conclusion that a quick look at the history of these assessments leads to is unambiguous: the countries that experienced the most rapid regression were also among those previously assessed as the most advanced on their democratic path. Both Hungary and Poland were among the first Eastern European nations that qualified to join NATO and the EU. They were also among the leaders in quantitative indices. And yet, in 2023, the V-Dem Electoral Democracy Index of both Hungary and Poland is significantly below that of Bulgaria, Romania, and Croatia—countries that qualified for NATO and the EU membership much later (in Croatia's case, a full decade later).[74] In other words, proponents of the unfinished transition theory cannot merely claim an overall inflated perception of post-communist democratic consolidation; instead, they would need to establish that, in the case of Poland, it was for some reason particularly and uniquely inflated.[75]

Democratic versus moral legitimacy

Admittedly, our assessment of the extant literature is harsh. Scientific search for causes of complex political phenomena may take a long time. Perhaps scholars are still to identify the key drivers of modern conservative politics. A more complex, multivariate model might eventually emerge.[76] So why such a strong, critical claim?

We will back it with an even stronger one: All major arguments or theories regarding modern conservative revolutionary politics suffer from the same affliction—the problem we flagged at the very outset of this chapter. For all its methodological and disciplinary diversity, this literature shares subtle but deeply embedded twin normative assumptions about the nature of the phenomenon it tries to explain. Invariably, its starting point is, on the one hand, a strong belief in the moral illegitimacy of conservative revolutions, and on the other, a conviction about the fundamentally "righteous" inclinations of voters.

Like the politicians and media commentators quoted at the start of this chapter, political scientists construct right-wing revolutions as a threat, a political malady. At the same time, they refuse to accept that voters would, freely and willingly, support the perverted political platforms of the New Right. The search is always for some exogenous "reason" why people vote as they do. Critically, the choice of the potential reasons shows that the underlying electoral behavior is viewed as not only empirically but also normatively irregular. Whether it is political trickery, an empty stomach, white or male fragility, nationalist fantasies about forgone glory, or the inability to conclusively transit to the liberal order—all these narratives clearly serve a dual purpose: they not only positively explain voters' behavior, but also attempt to normatively excuse it. And, of course, the latter goal must be premised on the perception of conservative revolutions as morally corrupt; we look for excuses only if the behavior in question requires one. Most often, the extant literature tries to identify a "grievance"—real or manufactured—that pushes voters to the otherwise inexcusable right-leaning political choices.

This volume invites you to take another route. We believe that the search for the new progressive–conservative social contract—a set of stable democratic rules for our politically divided times—requires constitutional lawyers to acknowledge the other side of the normative coin. While we can continue to challenge the moral legitimacy of right-wing policy proposals, we must honestly concede that, in many countries, multiple ballot victories or near-victories scored by conservative revolutionaries amount to a democratically legitimate electoral signal. For the purpose of constitutional design, we must stop obsessively searching for excuses for why our compatriots are "erring" in their judgment, and look for institutional solutions that acknowledge both the strength and consistency of their preferences, our inability to convince them of their errors, and their corresponding failure to sway us.

That is how we treated past political movements that fought for comprehensive policy change. From the constitutional perspective, the starting point of our thinking about the civil rights, suffragist, or LGBT rights movements is their treatment as legitimate representations of the evolving will of the people. Granted, authors such as Bruce Ackerman have acknowledged that dissatisfaction with the status quo, and mobilization by charismatic political leaders, played an essential part in progressive movements. But those observations did not prevent him from viewing these movements as legitimate signals sent by "we the people."

To apply a similar logic to today's right-wing revolutions should emphatically not be understood as a call for progressive lawyers to morally acquiesce to the modern conservative agenda. Indeed, the authors of this introduction can honestly report that years of cooperative work with our conservative colleagues on a new constitutional settlement for our homeland did not alter our skepticism about the justifiability of key conservative postulates.[77] While we deeply appreciate our collaborators as colleagues, intellectuals, and human beings, our personal beliefs in impartial ethics, universal human rights, and individual liberty have not been diluted at the altar of some grand center-right "compromise." It is perhaps worth adding that, to our knowledge, our conservative collaborators likewise remain immune to our attempts at persuasion regarding liberal values.

In a particularly evocative passage of his magnum opus on American constitutional revolutions, Ackerman expertly captures the key distinction between moral and democratic legitimacy that we are striving to highlight here. He outlines a hypothetical scenario under which he sits on the US Supreme Court, while a determined voter-supported movement pushes for the establishment of a religious state. "While I hope that I would stick to my conviction that th[e] Christianity amendment was terribly wrong," he wrote, "I would uphold it as a fundamental part of the American Constitution."[78] An alternative course of action at which he points is for him to "resign my office and join in a campaign to convince the American people to change their mind."[79]

Ackerman's second strategy in particular shows that granting conservative revolutionaries their democratic legitimacy does not require liberal lawyers to sport a moral white flag. Indeed, we do not think that Ackerman's two options offer an exhaustive list. A fair-minded liberal democrat could also use one's judicial power to create a roadblock for the Christianity amendment. On Ackerman's own terms, such a judicial speed bump could play a legitimate, constructive role in the process of democratic constitution-making, in that it would test the revolutionaries' resolve and seriousness of commitment.

A smarter counterrevolution

We are thereby not advocating for liberals to make life easy for conservative revolutionaries.[80] What we are saying is that, if you want to have universally approved rules of the game, you need to acknowledge the existence of all the major teams playing. Indeed, the co-author of this introduction whose day job is to conduct research in international relations (IR) finds it puzzling that this simple fact is not more universally accepted within constitutional law. In IR, it is common to appreciate the need to attain stable institutional arrangements among actors that morally abhor each other.[81] Key international advances, such as the creation of the United Nations, or partial nuclear disarmament, or the Montreal Protocol that saved the Earth's ozone layer, were achieved between countries that viewed each other as fundamentally evil.

Indeed, the Cold War analogy deserves greater attention as we search for a way out of our democratic crisis. In particular, to the earlier mentioned list of political movements taken seriously by twentieth-century democracies we should prominently add leftist forces inspired by the rise of communism. There is no doubt that, in some cases, the post-World War II Left encountered hardball counterrevolutionary responses, not unlike the ones adopted by the constitutional lawyers of today. Diehard Soviet collaborators were jailed or even executed. But parallel to this strategy, the liberal West proved smart to adopt some socialist postulates. The massive expansion of the welfare state was no small concession from the standpoint of classic free-market liberals of the time. Likewise the acceptance of social-democratic parties ruling in most Western European democracies. These concessions were not made by the elites out of admiration for the Left. Indeed, much of the Western European establishment was as repulsed by the socialist agenda as liberal lawyers are today by the proposals of the conservative right. Rather, the accommodation of some leftist postulates was a pragmatic political strategy grounded in a somber view of reality.[82]

Most profoundly, many of the left-wing revolutionaries took the deal. Some did so out of pragmatism; it was better to secure concrete improvements for the working people than to chase the windmills of a comprehensive communist takeover. But, for many Western leftists, a liberal democratic state adopting certain socialist postulates was in truth preferrable to the communist utopia. Historical records show how successive eruptions of authoritarian violence in the Soviet bloc genuinely dampened the enthusiasm of the Western Left for the wholesale upending of liberal democracy.[83]

We notice a palpable current of similar worries among many supporters of today's conservative revolution. One can passionately believe in a society built on traditional, perhaps religious, values, or in the preservation of national, ethnic, and racial identities, yet still be worried, deep down, about whether their revolutionary leaders might take things too far. Even if liberals' comparisons of Donald Trump or Jarosław Kaczyński to Vladimir Putin seem fundamentally exaggerated, what if one day these leaders decide to push their concentration of executive power further than conservative voters anticipated or consented to? Far enough that it becomes difficult to reverse peacefully? Many conservatives share such concerns. The problem is that, given the current lines of political conflict, the only alternative to supporting the train of the conservative revolution, with its uncertain final destination, is lying on the tracks in the path of the full-speed progressive train.

The competing ecosystems

And here comes the limit of our analogy with the previous smart liberal democratic counterrevolution—that against the allure of communism. Marxist postulates were fundamentally of an economic nature, concerning the distribution of control over (and ultimately the fruits of) capital. The current conflict with conservative revolutionaries is chiefly about non-material goods: identity, tradition, and rights.

Why does that matter? For the simple reason that money—the thing that the Left wanted—is fungible. The smart liberal counterrevolutionary could simply adjust the balance between market exchange and governmental intervention. The word "simply" does not indicate that the effort was easy or inconsequential, only that—at the conceptual level—it could be accomplished in a straightforward manner by existing state institutions. Taxes were raised. Regulations became more pervasive. At some point, the outcome appeared to be good enough for moderate Marxists to abandon the revolutionary camp and join the liberal system.

The challenge we face today is that what both conservatives and progressives want is not easily divisible. Living in a traditional society cannot readily be achieved in a partial way. A collective identity happens mostly at the level of an ecosystem—a net of common understandings, norms, meanings, and social hierarchies that to liberals are often in conflict with basic equality.[84] Once a conservative partially concedes this ecosystem, for instance taking the principle that they will continue to be able to practice their faith or values in the confines of their homes or churches, they do not get a progressive–conservative "compromise"—they end up largely in a progressive ecosystem of diversity and multiculturalism.

We say "largely," because once the point of state-supported diversity is reached, the non-fungibility of cultural ecosystems starts being evident to progressives, too. In principle, in a liberal state people are free to practice their religious and other beliefs. But does that mean they can call homosexuals sinful, even if it clearly offends others? Can they ask schools to teach views contrary to scientific knowledge? Can religious symbols continue to be displayed in public spaces or manifested by people through their clothing choices? Should powerful state and social institutions tolerate the expression of views propounding the superiority of one's national values, or about the inherent advantages of patriarchal family structure? Should the state support monuments or other forms of commemoration of controversial past leaders?

If you answer "no" to these questions, then the ability of conservatives to continue with their traditional ways of life becomes illusory. And yet, if you respond in the affirmative, the ability of progressives to pursue their preferred good life is imperiled. Because much of what both conservatives and progressives want resides at the level of an ecosystem, the traditional democratic forms of compromise—"finding a middle ground" or "working across the aisle"—become genuinely less attractive to either side. And since, in the absence of an available compromise, the progressive side has generally been winning over the past couple of decades, it is rational for the conservatives to explore bolder, more revolutionary means to reverse the trend and achieve their political objectives.

It was this realization—that the essence of today's conservative–progressive clash lies in the competition between irreconcilable ecosystems—that brought our attention to political and constitutional geography. There is a rich body of literature that has long acknowledged the unique challenges faced by so-called plural societies divided along "objective"[85] lines of "linguistic, ethnic, religious, or cultural conflict."[86] In response to these challenges, the literature often postulates various power-sharing agreements,[87] often based on federalism and decentralization.

At the same time, the focus on "objective" differences rooted in language, ethnicity, or religion has, strangely enough, limited the scope of applicability of the institutional solutions proposed by this literature to a rather narrow set of national situations. We strongly believe that this self-imposed limitation is no longer justified. The case of Poland demonstrates to us that we are all plural societies now. For four interrelated reasons, today's ideological cleavages[88] between left-leaning progressive citizens and right-wing conservatives not only descriptively resemble the traditional "objective" differences; they should also normatively be managed in similar ways.

Why constitutional geography?

Consider the linguistic differences, say, between different cantons of Switzerland[89] or provinces of Canada. Just like the competing visions of society above, the preservation of a regional language can occur at the ecosystem level only. An offer for a German Swiss that they can still talk German at home, even though the dominant public exchanges would switch to English, would not be viewed as a sensible compromise between regional tradition and the requirements of post-modernity. They will continue to live in a German-speaking town only if most of their neighbors, as well as governing institutions, take the trouble to learn and speak German.

Furthermore, the difference between German-, French-, and Italian-speaking Swiss towns is similar to modern ideological differences in terms of the sheer force with which they impact individual lives. This was not always the case, largely because many progressive changes accrued over generations. Fortunately for human rights and elementary social cohesion, since World War II, conservatives have also shifted toward more liberal stances. There are few conservatives today who advocate for slavery, racial segregation, or the (re)criminalizing of interracial marriage or consensual homosexual intercourse. However, progressive change has massively outpaced these conservative shifts. As the growing literature on liberal urban culture has shown, the culture of a major Western metropolis is much more similar to that of counterpart urban centers in other countries (even when linguistic and national differences are factored in) than to the countryside immediately surrounding it.[90]

Third, like objective differences, ideological distinctions do not naturally fall into just two distinct categories. When we speak of "progressives" and "conservatives" in this volume, we should think of them as akin to linguistic or religious families. Christians, for instance, are keenly aware of the deep chasm between their belief system and that of Muslims. At the same time, within each family, there exist significant internal differences—Catholics, Orthodox, and Protestants within Christianity, or Shia and Sunnis within Islam. While ideological compromises may, in principle, be most difficult between such broad families, history has tragically shown that even within these traditions, seemingly irreconcilable conflicts have led to the deaths of millions.

This brings us to one of the most paradoxical aspects of winner-takes-all constitutional systems, which have emerged in many modern democracies. Although our societies would naturally divide into multiple "value clusters" or ecosystems, the political logic of top-down governance forces people into uneasy alignment within exactly *two* warring camps. This dynamic is a fundamental way in which our democratic structures fuel political polarization. If Switzerland, for example, were governed through a centralized, winner-takes-all system, it is likely that linguistic communities would be compelled into uncomfortable coalitions. A French–Italian bloc might form as a counterbalance to the perceived greater evil of German-speaking dominance.

The resulting conflagration of our multiple value systems, the inherent difficulty to compromise over values, and the strategic pressure to mobilize into two warring camps makes everybody unhappy. Just how much, we can see in the ugliness of the feuds between some feminists and advocates of the rights of nonbinary persons, between MAGA supporters and "never Trump" conservatives, or between progressives with different views on the State of Israel.

Fortunately, successful plural societies show a potential way out of this bind. In Switzerland, linguistic preferences are not only accommodated within geographically defined ecosystems but are also—fortuitously—clustered in a geographically cohesive manner. While causality is bidirectional, Swiss linguistic federalism functions, in part, because German-, French-, and Italian-speaking communities are concentrated in distinct regions.

The analogy to modern ideological divisions is well understood yet rarely pursued to its logical conclusion. In the United States, the concept of red and blue states is a staple of political discourse. In Britain, the Brexit referendum revealed notable regional divides—between London, Scotland, Wales, and Northern Ireland on one hand, and non-metropolitan England on the other. Similar regional distinctions shape political consciousness in many other countries. Overlapping these patterns is the growing recognition of the liberal shift in large cities. Yet, discussions on urban progressivism rarely situate it within a broader regional framework. Another flaw of the traditional "red/blue" categorization is that it serves the narrative of the binary winner-takes-all conflict for power at the center of American federal government. In reality, as any American knows, there are multiple shades of "red" and "blue." Yet, for strategic reasons, voters are compelled to align with broader ideological camps.

Constitutional geography: a case study

Poland, again, offers a perfect case study of the geographical distribution of ideological preferences. In all parliamentary elections since 1989, the country's southeastern regions (voivodships) have supported political parties with a significantly more conservative profile than the northwestern voivodships. Moreover, big cities voted more liberally than the surrounding countryside,[91] although mid-sized cities in the southeast were notably more conservative than those in the rest of the country. A particularly wide gap existed between the two largest, very progressive, cities—Warsaw and Cracow—both located in conservative regions, the former in the east and the latter in the south.

Behind this crude conservative–progressive distinction is the reality of the multitude of values that can easily be narrated in a way almost analogous to how we would talk about the reasons for the emergence of German-speaking Zurich or Italian-speaking Ticino. To keep it brief, let us start at the end of the eighteenth century, when Poland was partitioned and then occupied, for more than 120 years, by Prussia, Austria, and Russia. Figure 0.1 shows the eventual division (in the aftermath of the Napoleonic wars) against the country's present national borders and the borders between the current sixteen provinces. In each region, we indicate the summed results of PiS and the even more conservative Konfederacja in the recent 2023 elections, which ousted PiS from power.

While more data will be presented in the next chapter, it is already fairly clear that big differences in conservative support exist between the lands that, throughout the nineteenth century, were occupied by different powers. The parts under former Prussian (German) occupation are significantly more progressive than the lands of the former Catholic Habsburg Empire and the Russian Empire. A large body of academic literature discusses the numerous and persistent differences between these lands, ranging from the structure of farmland ownership to the density of railway networks.[92]

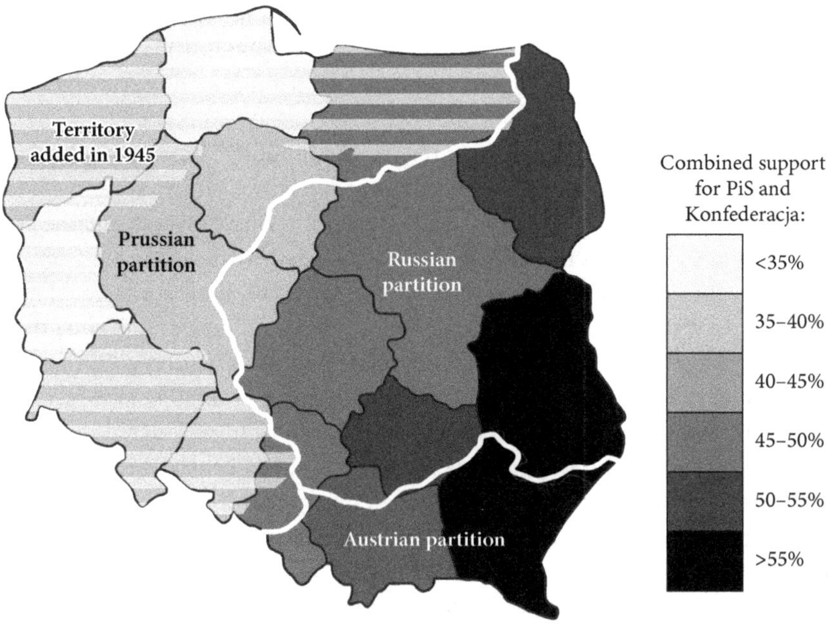

Figure 0.1 Support for revolutionary conservatives in the 2023 parliamentary election and Poland's history of foreign occupation and mass resettlements

Of particular note is the highlighted area in Northwestern Poland. This land was assigned to Poland by Stalin in his 1945 plan to radically shift the country's borders westward. Massive resettlement followed, during which local Germans were forcibly expelled while Polish settlers, themselves displaced from western Ukraine, Belarus, and Lithuania, as well as all other Polish regions, came to claim the emptied land and abandoned property.[93] The result was a remarkable social reinvention, which Polish literature and cinematography have compared to the US settlement of its western frontier.[94] Historically, a large share of residents of Poland's new western lands originated from some of the most conservative parts of pre-war Poland—from the depths of the former Russian and Austrian zones of occupation. Yet the experience of the resettlement, marked by the uprooting of traditional social, economic, and religious structures occurring alongside an aggressive communist revolution, clearly contributed to the creation of the most reliably progressive Polish regions.[95]

Normative geography

We have already noted how the above brief story of Poland's geographic ideological diversity sounds similar to a short description a Swiss would offer to explain their nation's linguistic differences. What we now want you to reflect on is how such a story differs from the above-mentioned theories of populist manipulations, or the various grievances that supposedly push voters in a conservative revolutionary direction.

On some level, elements of all these theories are bound to enter our geographic story: economic development, the experience of diversity, historically formed identities, institutions, the impact of post-1989 integration with the West, and the practice and models of political leadership (first provided by the occupying powers, and then by the Polish authorities who replaced them) all surely contributed to the provincial differences we observe today. What is different, however, is the normative positioning that we take when talking about political geography. Our account of geographic ideological differences does not revolve around a stern moral assessment of one group or another. We do not engage in a frantic search for a "solution" that will compel our compatriots to think, vote, and behave the way we want them to. Instead of picturing them as afflicted by a malady that a well-intentioned policy response could remedy, we examine the conservative–progressive political division through what cultural studies refer to as "thick descriptions"[96]—nuanced elucidations of historically conditioned and not easily alterable states of the world. This does not need to imply normative agnosticism; a Zurich resident can easily have strong opinions about the lifestyle of the Ticinesi. However, it does imply a certain modesty in our belief in the social engineering that can be effectively dispatched in response to this reality.

This "thickly descriptive" pragmatism is what we particularly value in the above-mentioned literature about liberal cities. Writers in this stream show convincingly how a collection of social, economic, technological, environmental, and cultural factors molds the political life of large urban centers in a decidedly progressive direction. What remains a puzzle for us is why this clear-eyed thinking should be limited to (liberal) cities only. In all the works of the genre, large cities are viewed as part of a local, not regional, level of governance. This may be accurate descriptively, although we should note the examples of Berlin, Vienna, or Hamburg—cities that possess the full rights of separate regions (Länder) within their respective decentralized constitutional structures. But viewing large cities as "localities" certainly does not make sense normatively. The average region in the EU has a population of a little over 1.8 million, while the median US state has about 4.5 million inhabitants. It is therefore clear that large cities, such as Warsaw (1.7 million population) or Houston, Texas (with a metropolitan population of 7.1 million), should be viewed as the equivalents of regions, and not localities, for the purposes of constitutional design. That framing would, in turn, put the cultures and political aspirations of liberal cities on a par with those of more conservative, less urbanized regions. Why did the "city localism" genre not take this route? "How Cities Can Thrive in the Age of Populism" reads the subtitle of one notable work.[97] It is not difficult to see how, again, the purpose seems to be defensive in nature: finding a way to protect urban progressives from the menace evoked by the conservative revolutionaries and the voters supporting them.

Social contract for a polarized society

One may find it surprising that, except for the title of this introduction, we almost never used the word "polarization" in our analysis. Descriptively, what we observe in Poland certainly satisfies the main definitions of the term found in the literature. Nolan McCarty, for instance, carefully explains how the concept highlights a specific distribution of ideological or policy preferences, either among the general public or dominant political parties. "If most voters fall toward the ideological center," points out McCarty, "we'd say there is little ideological polarization. But to the extent to which liberal and conservative ideologies become more common relative to those of the center, we'd call that polarization."[98]

Thus understood polarization—a sharp cleavage between progressive and conservative ecosystems of values, traditions, meanings, and corresponding policy objectives—is an empirical fact. At the same time, the normative presuppositions permeating the concept may still hinder the emergence of a fair progressive–conservative deal. For "polarization" creates a potential for labeling any non-centrist policy position as inherently "suspicious" from a democratic vantage. At another point, McCarty observes that, in a polarized society, "moderate views are relatively less likely and extreme liberal or conservative views are no longer rare."[99] As we highlighted at the outset of this introduction, words such as "extreme" are not normatively neutral.

Fundamentally, then, the polarization literature does not do justice to the citizens honestly supporting the conservative revolutionaries and the ardent progressives alike.[100] Overlapping with the populist strategies literature, polarization studies often think of any political position other than the centrist one as a somewhat artificial creation of political manipulators, hyper-partisan cable TV, or social media. We have already discussed how oddly these arguments fit the Polish facts.

The polarization literature tends to fall short especially when it engages in a search for modern left-leaning revolutionaries that would justify the overall normative symmetry. Except for Venezuela, that search is rather unsuccessful, although—as it is often the case in comparative law and politics—numerous close cases are being pointed to. Poland, once again, offers clarity. Our post-1989 democratic story shows clearly that the challenge to our current constitutional order comes invariably from the conservative side. In the six parliamentary elections since joining the European Union, the support for the leftist parties has never reached 20 percent, and only twice exceeded 15 percent. As we will shortly show in the next chapter, none of these parties put a constitutional challenge to our political system anywhere close to the center of their campaign platforms.

The revolutionary conservatives, by contrast, made it known that they want to fundamentally rebuild Poland—"change the political system," to quote PiS's leader Jarosław Kaczyński[101]—and routinely won over 40 percent of popular support.

Interestingly, while the general theory of polarization emphasizes the conceptual symmetry of two political "extremes," a growing streak of empirical studies within the genre undermines this very frame. Research, in particular, has shown the unique steadiness of conservative convictions and their resilience to various "depolarization" initiatives.[102] These findings are entirely in line with our call for treating conservative constitutional signals seriously.

Polish recent history is, in a sense, a powerful natural experiment in the limits of social engineering as applied to geographically clustered political differences. Joining NATO and the EU can be thought of as one big "depolarization" project: a historically generous intervention motivated partly by the dream to "modernize" Eastern Europe and anchor our societies on a moderate liberal consensus. It is deeply ironic that conservative Poles refused to be "depolarized away" and, just a year after our Westward journey was completed with EU accession, gave PiS its first chance to govern. When it came to our geographically clustered beliefs, the best that the unprecedentedly powerful incentives of Euro-Atlantic integration could accomplish was to buy a decade and a half of relative temporary timidity of our conservative compatriots after 1989. Faced with a historical opportunity, but also strict conditionality imposed by NATO and the European Union at the time of the global liberal consensus, the conservatives simply decided to, for a time, lower their voices and not fully leverage the political power that democracy handed them after nearly forty-five years of communist rule. It is clear that, now, they intend to speak up more forcefully.

At the risk of repetition: Nothing in this argument takes away from moral objections to the conservative agenda, but also from acknowledging a robust progressive mobilization in defense of liberal values. While these movements did not translate into electoral gains for the Left, they also represent part and parcel of our Polish constitutional starting point. Of particular note is the awesome power of the women's movement in defense of abortion rights, but also skilled campaigns supporting LGBT rights and opposing PiS's judicial reforms. During the 2015–23 rule of PiS, a number of manifestations of liberal opposition in Warsaw and other major cities gained hundreds of thousands of participants. While undoubtedly impressive, these numbers were similar to those achieved by large nationalist gatherings.

The effort outlined in the remainder of this volume recognizes that no "depolarizing" centrist fantasy can solve the fundamental chasm between our basic moral convictions and political aspirations. There is simply no democratic path forward other than the one which starts with acknowledging, despite all our differences, the legitimacy of our joint citizenship.

Alas, our current democratic institutions are ill-suited for effectively managing this "plural" reality of geographically clustered groups of citizens genuinely endorsing vastly different conceptions of good society and good life. Under the current constitutional system, the other political "tribe" genuinely constitutes an existential threat to what either progressives or conservatives value and hold dear. In such a winner-takes-all system, calls for "civility" or references to our "better angels" will always ring hollow. We need an institutional reform aimed at creating a system in which our differences do not threaten us so fundamentally.

The remainder of this book shows, step by step, how this can be achieved. In Chapter 1, Antoni Dudek and we editors explain why the most realistic foundation of a new social contract for Poland would be what we dub "strategic decentralization." In Chapter 2, Agnieszka Chłoń-Domińczak, Jacek Giedrojć, and Anna Wojciuk present institutional solutions protecting Poland against the potential side effects of further decentralization: widening economic inequalities between regions, or increased barriers to inter-regional mobility that both Polish progressives and conservatives would surely want to avoid. In Chapter 3, Maciej Bukowski, Mikołaj Herbst, and Tomasz Kaczor present a detailed budgetary simulation of the effects of our proposal on the revenues and expenditures of national and regional budgets. In Chapter 4, Maciej Kisilowski and Wojciech Przybylski show how the central government will function in our proposed system, and argue that decentralization can strengthen the effectiveness of the center. The last two chapters of Part I show how our proposal will ensure Poland's democratic future. Given that the very diagnosis of Poland's democratic crisis is embedded in the dispute between progressive and conservative Poland, we offer two competing chapters on the subject. In Chapter 5, Ryszard Balicki, Jarosław Gwizdak, and Fryderyk Zoll take the progressive perspective on the issue of democratic crisis, and describe how the IUS's proposed vertical separation of powers will prevent a future resurgence of the drive to establish an authoritarian state. Then, in Chapter 6, Mirosław Granat, Tomasz G. Grosse, Jacek Sokołowski, and Arkadiusz Radwan expound upon the conservative position. Starting from the premise that Polish democracy is not at risk, they argue that the benefit of the IUS proposal is to reinforce (rather than "save") Polish democracy, in particular by opening up new avenues of government accountability and public participation in regional policy-making.

Part I of this book is only a starter before the main course, however. In Part II, we show how our proposed system may work in practice. Imagine an alternative reality in which, after the 2023 parliamentary elections, a broad constitutional coalition was formed—from the Left to the liberals and the conservatives. Faced with external threats to the state, the main political forces decide that it is time to end the "Polish–Polish war" and to conclude a new social contract. The political system proposed for our country in this book becomes a reality, and the local and regional governments of the next term are already elected under the new institutions that we have proposed.

Notes

1. Cass R. Sunstein, "Incompletely Theorized Agreements," *Harvard Law Review* 108, no. 3 (1994): 1733–1772.
2. Ryszard Koziołek, "Nie róbmy tego co robimy [Let's not do what we are doing]," *Polityka*, Oct. 17, 2023.
3. Cf. Adis Merdzanovic and Kalypso Nicolaidis, "Advocacy for a Citizen-Centric Rule of Law Agenda: How Do We Bring the Rule of Law to Life?" *European Law Journal* 27, no. 1–3 (2021): 297–305.
4. Daniel Ziblatt, *Conservative Political Parties and the Birth of Modern Democracy in Europe* (Cambridge University Press, 2017); Jan-Werner Müller, "Comprehending Conservatism: A New Framework for Analysis," *Journal of Political Ideologies* 11, no. 3 (2006): 359–365; Samuel P. Huntington, "Conservatism as an Ideology," *American Political Science Review* 51, no. 2 (1957); Karl Mannheim, *Conservatism: A Contribution to the Sociology of Knowledge* (Routledge, 1986).
5. Bruce A. Ackerman, *We the People: Foundations* (Belknap Press of Harvard University Press, 1991); Bruce A. Ackerman, *We the People: The Civil Rights Revolution* (The Belknap Press of Harvard University Press, 2015).
6. Colin Crouch observes that people on the liberal left have spent much of the past two or three decades feeling that they were mainly on the losing side of a battle over economic issues, the welfare state, and workers' rights. They failed to notice that they had been on the winning side on essential moral and cultural issues since the 1960s: Colin Crouch, *Post-Democracy after the Crises* (John Wiley & Sons, 2020), 95–97.
7. Rory McVeigh, "Reflections on Studying Right-Wing Extremism in the Twenty-First Century," *Mobilization: An International Quarterly* 28, no. 4 (2024): 509–514.
8. Anna Lührmann and Staffan I. Lindberg, "A Third Wave of Autocratization Is Here: What Is New About It?" *Democratization* 26, no. 7 (2019): 1095–1113, show that we are currently in the third wave of autocratization. Unlike in previous such periods, this time the process starts in established democracies and is progressing gradually, using legal means rather than brute force. See also Grzegorz Ekiert and Noah Dasanaike, "The Return of Dictatorship," *Journal of Democracy* 35, no. 4 (2024): 177–191.
9. Adam Przeworski, "Minimalist Conception of Democracy: A Defense," in *Democracy's Value*, eds. Ian Shapiro and Casiano Hacker-Cordón (Cambridge University Press, 1999).
10. Peter H. Solomon, "Courts and Judges in Authoritarian Regimes," *World Politics* 60, no. 1 (2007): 122–145; Wojciech Sadurski, *Poland's Constitutional Breakdown* (Oxford University Press, 2019).
11. Ronald J. Deibert, "The Autocrat in Your IPhone: How Mercenary Spyware Threatens Democracy," *Foreign Affairs* 102 (2023): 72; Monika Nalepa, *After Authoritarianism* (Cambridge University Press, 2022).
12. Sheena Chestnut Greitens, *Dictators and Their Secret Police: Coercive Institutions and State Violence* (Cambridge University Press, 2016).
13. Oscar Westlund, Roy Krøvel, and Kristin Skare Orgeret, *Journalism and Safety: An Introduction to the Field* (Taylor & Francis, 2024); Christian Bjørnskov and Andreas Freytag, "An Offer You Can't Refuse: Murdering Journalists as an Enforcement Mechanism of Corrupt Deals," *Public Choice* 167 (2016): 221–243; Sallie Hughes and Yulia Vorobyeva, "Explaining the Killing of Journalists in the Contemporary Era: The Importance of Hybrid Regimes and Ssubnational Variations," *Journalism* 22, no. 8 (2021): 1873–1891.
14. Sebastian Stier, "Democracy, Autocracy and the News: The Impact of Regime Type on Media Freedom," *Democratization* 22, no. 7 (2015): 1273–1295; Sergei Guriev and Daniel Treisman, "A Theory of Informational Autocracy," *Journal of Public Economics* 186 (2020): 104–158.
15. Barbara Geddes, Joseph George Wright, and Erica Frantz, *How Dictatorships Work: Power, Personalization, and Collapse* (Cambridge University Press, 2018), 59–126.
16. Maciej Kisilowski, "The Election's Aftermath," *Verfassungsblog: On Matters Constitutional* (2023).
17. Emilie M. Hafner-Burton, Susan D. Hyde, and Ryan S. Jablonski, "Surviving Elections: Election Violence, Incumbent Victory and Post-Election Repercussions," *British Journal of Political Science* 48, no. 2 (2018): 459–488.
18. It is worth noting that during the period of PiS rule, not only the election turnout but also overall satisfaction with the democratic system increased: Larry M. Bartels, *Democracy Erodes from the Top: Leaders, Citizens, and the Challenge of Populism in Europe* (Princeton University Press, 2023), 209. A recent empirical study using Polish survey data confirms that the threat to democratic institutions posed by a political movement does not impact the support for such

movement: Marc S. Jacob, "Citizens as a Democratic Safeguard? The Sequence of Sanctioning Elite Attacks on Democracy," *American Journal of Political Science* 69, no. 2 (2024): 455–470.

19. "Embedded" and "defective" democracy were alternative influential concepts used to assess political transitions in the region. As early as 2002 Poland was considered an embedded democracy, fulfilling all sophisticated criteria defined by Wolfgang Merkel and his collaborators. See Wolfgang Merkel, "Embedded and Defective Democracies," *Democratization* 11, no. 5 (2004): 33–58.
20. Adam Przeworski, *Democracy and the Market, Political and Economic Reforms in Eastern Europe and Latin America* (Cambridge University Press, 1991), 26.
21. see Roberto Stefan Foa and Yascha Mounk, "The Signs of Deconsolidation," *Journal of Democracy* 28, no. 1 (2017): 5–15.
22. Steven Levitsky and Daniel Ziblatt, *Tyranny of the Minority: How to Reverse an Authoritarian Turn, and Forge a Democracy for All* (Random House, 2023).
23. Mancur Olson, *The Logic of Collective Action: Public Goods and the Theory of Groups* (Harvard University Press, 1965).
24. Here our argument is literally the opposite of, but (at a deeper lever) quite aligned with, Jan Zielonka, *Counter-Revolution: Liberal Europe in Retreat* (Oxford University Press, 2018); Jan Zielonka and Jacques Rupnik, "From Revolution to 'Counter-Revolution': Democracy in Central and Eastern Europe 30 Years On," *Europe-Asia Studies* 72, no. 6 (2020): 1073–1099.
25. András Sajó, "Militant Rule of Law and Not-So-Bad Law," *Hague Journal on the Rule of Law* 16 (2024): 525–549.
26. Kim Lane Scheppele, "The Treaties without a Guardian: The European Commission and the Rule of Law," *Columbia Journal of European Law* 29, no 2 (2023): 93–183; Kim Lane Scheppele, Dimitry Kochenov, and Barbara Grabowska-Moroz, "EU Values Are Law, After All: Enforcing EU Values through Systemic Infringement Actions by the European Commission and the Member States of the European Union," *Yearbook of European Law* 39 (2021): 3–121; Pech Laurent and Kim Lane Scheppele, "Illiberalism Within: Rule of Law Backsliding in the EU," *Cambridge Yearbook of European Legal Studies* 19 (2017): 3–47; Dimitry Kochenov and John Morijn, "Strengthening the Charter's Role in the Fight for the Rule of Law in the EU: The Cases of Judicial Independence and Party Financing," *European Public Law* 27, no. 4 (2021): 759–780; R Daniel Kelemen, "Is Differentiation Possible in Rule of Law?," *Comparative European Politics* 17 (2019): 246–260; Antonia Baraggia and Matteo Bonelli, "Linking Money to Values: The New Rule of Law Conditionality Regulation and Its Constitutional Challenges," *German Law Journal* 23, no. 2 (2022): 131–156.
27. Pola Cebulak, "Scholarly Activism for the Rule of Law in the EU," *The Journal of Illiberalism Studies* 4, no. 1: 45–56; Martin Krygier, "Illiberalism and the Rule of Law," in *Routledge Handbook of Illiberalism*, eds. András Sajó, Renáta Uitz, and Stephen Holmes (Routledge, 2021).
28. Rosalind Dixon and David Landau, "Transnational Constitutionalism and a Limited Doctrine of Unconstitutional Constitutional Amendment," *International Journal of Constitutional Law* 13, no. 3 (2015): 606–638; Richard Albert, "Constitutional Amendment and Dismemberment," *Yale Journal of International Law* 43, no. 1 (2018): 1–84; see generally Richard Albert, "Constitutional Handcuffs," *Arizona State Law Journal* 42 (2010): 663–715.
29. Kim Lane Scheppele, "Autocratic Legalism," *The University of Chicago Law Review* 85, no. 2 (2018): 545–584.
30. Cass R. Sunstein, *Radicals in Robes: Why Extreme Right-Wing Courts Are Wrong for America* (Basic Books, 2005).
31. Bruce A. Ackerman, *We the People: Transformations* (Belknap Press of Harvard University Press, 1998).
32. Note how the communist Polish People's Republic is conspicuously absent in the count.
33. Jessie Hellman, "Danish PM Jokes about Trump, Karl Rove at State Dinner," *The Hill*, May 14, 2015.
34. Radosław Markowski, "The Polish Election of 2023: Mobilisation in Defence of Liberal Democracy," *West European Politics* 47, no. 7 (2024): 1670–1685.
35. Timothy Snyder, *On Tyranny: Twenty Lessons from the Twentieth Century* (Crown, 2017); Madeleine Albright, *Fascism: A Warning* (Harper, 2018).
36. Tjitske Akkerman and Matthijs Rooduijn, "Pariahs or Partners? Inclusion and Exclusion of Radical Right Parties and the Effects on Their Policy Positions," *Political Studies* 63, no. 5 (2015): 1140–1157.
37. For an excellent example of an eminent constitutional lawyer endorsing the top-down political-science explanation see Wojciech Sadurski, *A Pandemic of Populists* (Cambridge University Press, 2022).

38. Ben Stanley, "A Comparison of Two Polish Party Leaders: Jarosław Kaczyński and Donald Tusk," in *Party Leaders in Eastern Europe: Personality, Behavior and Consequences*, ed. Sergiu Gherghina (Palgrave Macmillan, 2020).
39. Sarah Engler, "Corruption and Electoral Support for New Political Parties in Central and Eastern Europe," *West European Politics* 39, no. 2 (2016): 278–304. Studies showed, in particular, that voters viewed both PiS and the main liberal party of Donald Tusk as similar as far as their honesty was concerned; Kazimierz Slomczynski and Goldie Shabad, "Perceptions of Political Party Corruption and Voting Behaviour in Poland," *Party Politics* 18, no. 6 (2012): 897–917.
40. Eleanor Neff Powell and Joshua A. Tucker, "Revisiting Electoral Volatility in Post-Communist Countries: New Data, New Results and New Approaches," *British Journal of Political Science* 44, no. 1 (2014): 123–147; Hanspeter Kriesi, "The Populist Challenge," *West European Politics* 37, no. 2 (2014): 361–378.
41. Jan Zielonka, *Media and Politics in New Democracies: Europe in a Comparative Perspective* (Oxford University Press, 2015), 25–37.
42. Frank Esser, Agnieszka Stępińska, and David Nicolas Hopmann, "Populism and the Media: Cross-National Findings and Perspectives," in *Populist Political Communication in Europe*, ed. Carsten Reinemann et al. (Routledge, 2016); Agnieszka Stępińska, *Populist Political Communication across Europe* (Peter Lang GmbH, Internationaler Verlag der Wissenschaften, 2020).
43. Dorothee Bohle and Béla Greskovits, "Politicising Embedded Neoliberalism: Continuity and Change in Hungary's Development Model," *West European Politics* 42, no. 5 (2019): 1069–1093.
44. John B. Judis, *The Populist Explosion: How the Great Recession Transformed American and European Politics* (Columbia Global Reports New York, 2016).
45. Barry Eichengreen, *The Populist Temptation: Economic Grievance and Political Reaction in the Modern Era* (Oxford University Press, 2018).
46. The argument applied to East-Central Europe by Margit Tavits and Natalia Letki, "From Values to Interests? The Evolution of Party Competition in New Democracies," *The Journal of Politics* 76, no. 1 (2014): 246–258.
47. See the World Bank Data available at: https://data.worldbank.org/. See also Marcin Piątkowski, *Europe's Growth Champion: Insights from the Economic Rise of Poland* (Oxford University Press, 2018).
48. See the World Bank Data available at: https://data.worldbank.org/indicator/SI.POV.GINI?year=2015. But see Paweł Bukowski and Filip Novokmet, "Between Communism and Capitalism: Long-Term Inequality in Poland, 1892–2015," *Journal of Economic Growth* 26, no. 2 (2021): 187–239. The authors claim that official survey-based indicators regularly presented by the World Bank strongly underestimate the rise in inequality since 1989, and that capital income played a prominent role in driving the U-shaped evolution of top income shares. In their view, inequalities in Poland experienced a sharp rise with the return to capitalism in 1989.
49. In his excellent summary of the extant literature, Erik Jones, "Populism in Europe: What Scholarship Tells Us," *Survival* 61, no. 4 (2019): 7–30. explains the growing support for populist parties among the rural population in Western Europe through the EU enlargement which, in his view, deteriorated the economic situation of farmers in those countries.
50. Karolina Urbanska and Serge Guimond, "Swaying to the Extreme: Group Relative Deprivation Predicts Voting for an Extreme Right Party in the French Presidential Election," *International Review of Social Psychology* 31, no. 1 (2018): 1–11; Brian Burgoon et al., "Positional Deprivation and Support for Radical Right and Radical Left Parties," *Economic Policy* 34, no. 97 (2019: 48–93).
51. Yascha Mounk, *The Great Experiment: How to Make Diverse Democracies Work* (Bloomsbury Publishing, 2022).
52. Terry Smith, *Whitelash: Unmasking White Grievance at the Ballot Box* (Cambridge University Press, 2020).
53. Levitsky and Ziblatt, *Tyranny of the Minority: How to Reverse an Authoritarian Turn, and Forge a Democracy for All* (Penguin, 2024).
54. Hans Kundnani, *Eurowhiteness: Culture, Empire and Race in the European Project* (Oxford University Press, 2023); Michael Minkenberg and Zsuzsanna Végh, *Depleting Democracies: Radical Right Impact on Parties, Policies, and Polities in Eastern Europe* (Manchester University Press, 2023).
55. Vanessa Gera, "Polish Activists Criticize Tusk's Government for Tough Border Policies and Migrant Pushbacks," *The Associated Press*, May 13, 2024.
56. João Carvalho, "Mainstream Party Strategies towards Extreme Right Parties: The French 2007 and 2012 Presidential Elections," *Government and Opposition* 54, no. 2 (2019): 365–386; Katy Brown, Aurelien Mondon, and Aaron Winter, "The Far Right, the Mainstream and

Mainstreaming: Towards a Heuristic Framework," *Journal of Political Ideologies* 28, no. 2 (2023): 162–179 .

57. Robert Saunders, "Brexit and Empire: 'Global Britain' and the Myth of Imperial Nostalgia," *The Journal of Imperial and Commonwealth History* 48, no. 6 (2020): 1140–1174.
58. David G. Haglund, Jennie L. Schulze, and Ognen Vangelov, "Hungary's Slide Toward Autocracy: Domestic and External Impediments to Locking In Democratic Reforms," *Political Science Quarterly* 137, no. 4 (2022): 675–713.
59. Gary G DeSantis, "'We Believe in Education, Not Indoctrination': Governor Ron DeSantis, Critical Race Theory, and Anti-Intellectualism in Florida," *Policy Futures in Education* 22, no. 5 (2024): 1004–1019.
60. Matthew Karnitschnig and Wojciech Kość, "Meet Europe's Coming Military Superpower: Poland," *Politico*, Nov. 21, 2022.
61. David Clarke and Paweł Duber, "Polish Cultural Diplomacy and Historical Memory: The Case of the Museum of the Second World War in Gdańsk," *International Journal of Politics, Culture, and Society* 33, no. 1 (2020): 49–66.
62. Michał J. Wilczewski, "Review: The Pope in Poland: The Pilgrimages of John Paul II, 1979–1991, by James Ramon Felak, " *The English Historical Review* 139, no. 596: 344 (2024). Timothy A. Byrnes, "Catholic Bishops and Sexual Abuse: Power, Constraint, and Institutional Context," *Journal of Church and State* 62, no. 1 (2020): 5–25, https://doi.org/10.1093/jcs/csz086.
63. But see Jarosław Kuisz, *The New Politics of Poland: A Case of Post-Traumatic Sovereignty* (Manchester University Press, 2023), who claims that centuries of statelessness have left Poles with a deeply hiden 'post-traumatic' attitude to sovereignty.
64. Mikołaj Herbst and Anna Wojciuk, "Common Legacy, Different Paths: The Transformation of Educational Systems in the Czech Republic, Slovakia, Hungary and Poland," *Compare: A Journal of Comparative and International Education* 47, no. 1 (2017): 118–132; Maciej Jakubowski, "Poland: Polish Education Reforms and Evidence from International Assessments," in *Improving a Country's Education: PISA 2018 Results in 10 Countries*, ed. Nuno Crato (Springer, 2021).
65. Amanda Ripley, *The Smartest Kids in the World: And How They Got That Way* (Simon and Schuster, 2014).
66. Luca Manucci, "Populism and Collective Memory," in *The Palgrave Handbook of Populism*, ed. Michael Oswald (Palgrave Macmillan, 2022).
67. Milada Anna Vachudova, "Ethnopopulism and Democratic Backsliding in Central Europe," *East European Politics* 36, no. 3 (2020): 318–340; Licia Cianetti, James Dawson, and Seán Hanley, "Rethinking "Democratic Backsliding" in Central and Eastern Europe–Looking beyond Hungary and Poland," in *Rethinking 'Democratic Backsliding' in Central and Eastern Europe*, ed. Licia Cianetti, James Dawson, and Seán Hanley (Taylor & Francis, 2020).
68. Hubert Tworzecki, "Poland: A Case of Top-Down Polarization," *The Annals of the American Academy of Political and Social Science* 681, no. 1 (2019): 97–119.
69. Milan W. Svolik, "Which Democracies Will Last? Coups, Incumbent Takeovers, and the Dynamic of Democratic Consolidation," *British Journal of Political Science* 45, no. 4 (2015): 715–738.
70. R. Daniel Kelemen, "Europe's Other Democratic Deficit: National Authoritarianism in Europe's Democratic Union," *Government and Opposition* 52, no. 2 (2017): 211–238.
71. Ruth Wodak and Michał Krzyżanowski, "Right-Wing Populism in Europe & USA: Contesting Politics & Discourse beyond 'Orbanism' and 'Trumpism'" *Journal of Language and Politics* 16, no. 4 (2017): 471–484.
72. Bartels, *Democracy Erodes from the Top: Leaders, Citizens, and the Challenge of Populism in Europe* (Princeton University Press, 2023); Ezra Klein, *Why We're Polarized* (Profile Books, 2020).
73. The fact is that nothing in the following pages of this proposal prevents one from calling on our politicians to handle young Polish democracy with particular virtue, care, and responsibility. Which is perhaps why notable Polish proponents of the unfinished transition narrative are among this book's authors, e.g. Jacek Sokołowski, *Transnaród: Polacy w poszukiwaniu politycznej formy* (Ośrodek Myśli Politycznej, 2023).
74. Marina Nord et al., *Democracy Winning and Losing at the Ballot: Democracy Report 2024* (University of Gothenburg: V-Dem Institute, 2024)
75. Valerie Bunce, "Rethinking Recent Democratization: Lessons from the Postcommunist Experience," *World Politics* 55, no. 2 (2003): 167–192 .
76. See e.g. Kai Arzheimer et al., "How Local Context Affects Populist Radical Right Support: A Cross-National Investigation into Mediated and Moderated Relationships," *British Journal of Political Science* 54, no. 4 (2024): 1133–1158.

77. For a comprehensive account of engaging in a decentralization-based social contract, from a progressive perspective, see Maciej Kisilowski, "From Election to Autocracy: Can Strategic Decentralization Bring Us Back?" in *Public Administration and Expertise in Democratic Governments: Comparative Public Law in the Twenty-first Century*, ed. Susan Rose-Ackerman (Routledge, 2024).
78. Ackerman, *We the People: Foundations*, 14.
79. Id.
80. Indeed, one of us full-heartedly supported the work of Polish and international liberal legal counterrevolutionaries, both during the rule of PiS and in the wake of the second return of the liberals; see e.g. Maciej Kisilowski, "Poland's Democracy Is Crumbling," *Politico*, Dec. 24, 2015; Maciej Kisilowski, "Poland's 'Iron Broom' Shows that Democrats Can Bite Back," *Financial Times*, Jan. 15, 2024; Maciej Kisilowski, "Militant Public Administration," *Verfassungsblog: On Matters Constitutional* (Jun. 6, 2024).
81. Indeed, the said author has applied the similar logic to call for international cooperation with moderate PiS factions, while isolating the radicals, in the face of the Russian invasion of Ukraine; Anna Wojciuk, "The Battle for Democracy Can Be Won in Warsaw," *Foreign Policy*, May 3, 2022.
82. Klaus Petersen, Michele Mioni, and Herbert Obinger, "The Cold War and the Welfare State in Western Europe," in *International Impacts on Social Policy: Short Histories in Global Perspective*, ed. Frank Nullmeier, Delia González de Reufels, and Herbert Obinger (Springer, 2022).
83. Ralph Miliband, "Military Intervention and Socialist Internationalism," *Socialist Register* 17 (1980); Maud Bracke, "Which Socialism, Whose Detente?: West European Communism and the Czechoslovak Crisis of 1968" (Central European University Press, 2007).
84. Mannheim, *Conservatism: A Contribution to the Sociology of Knowledge*, 55 (Routledge, [1925] 1986).
85. Arend Lijphart, *Democracy in Plural Societies: A Comparative Exploration* (Yale University Press, 1977); A. John Simmons, *Boundaries of Authority* (Oxford University Press, 2016), 93–115; Paulina Ochoa Espejo, *On Borders: Territories, Legitimacy, and the Rights of Place* (Oxford University Press, 2020).
86. Sujit Choudhry, *Constitutional Design for Divided Societies: Integration or Accommodation?* (Oxford University Press, 2008).
87. For a recent survey of that literature see Allison McCulloch, "Introduction: Power-Sharing in Europe—From Adoptability to End-Ability," in *Power-Sharing in Europe*, ed. Soeren Keil and Allison McCulloch (Springer, 2021).
88. Wolfgang Merkel and Michael Zürn, "Conclusion: The Defects of Cosmopolitan and Communitarian Democracy," in *The Struggle over Borders: Cosmopolitanism and Communitarianism* (2019): 207–237.
89. Wolf Linder and Sean Mueller, *Swiss Democracy: Possible Solutions to Conflict in Multicultural Societies* (Springer Nature, 2021).
90. Bruce Katz and Jeremy Nowak, *The New Localism: How Cities Can Thrive in the Age of Populism* (Brookings Institution Press, 2017); Richard L. Florida, *Cities and the Creative Class* (Routledge, 2005); Benjamin R. Barber, *If Mayors Ruled the World: Dysfunctional Nations, Rising Cities* (Yale University Press, 2013).
91. The Polish case of the urban–rural electoral split was explored by, among others, Kamil Marcinkiewicz, "The Economy or an Urban–Rural Divide? Explaining Spatial Patterns of Voting Behaviour in Poland," *East European Politics and Societies* 32, no. 4 (2018): 693719.
92. Irena Grosfeld and Ekaterina Zhuravskaya, "Cultural vs. Economic Legacies of Empires: Evidence from the Partition of Poland," *Journal of Comparative Economics* 43, no. 1 (2015): 55–75.
93. Beata Halicka, *The Polish Wild West: Forced Migration and Cultural Appropriation in the Polish-German Borderlands, 1945–1948* (Routledge, 2020), 303–304.
94. Piotr Skurowski, "Dances with Westerns in Poland's Borderlands," *European Journal of American Studies* 13, no. 3 (2018): 1–16.
95. Volha Charnysh and Leonid Peisakhin, "The Role of Communities in the Transmission of Political Values: Evidence from Forced Population Transfers," *British Journal of Political Science* 52, no. 1 (2022): 235–258; Jerzy Kochanowski, Philipp Ther, and Ana Siljak, "Gathering Poles into Poland: Forced Migration from Poland's Former Eastern Territories," in *Redrawing Nations: Ethnic Cleansing in East–Central Europe, 1944–48*, ed. Philipp Ther and Ana Siljak (Rowman & Littlefield, 2001).
96. Clifford Geertz, *The Interpretation of Cultures: Selected Essays* (Basic Books, 1973).
97. Katz and Nowak, *The New Localism: How Cities Can Thrive in the Age of Populism.*

98. Nolan McCarty, *Polarization: What Everyone Needs to Know* (Oxford University Press, 2019), 10. For other similar definitions see e.g. Thomas Carothers and Andrew O'Donohue, *Democracies Divided: The Global Challenge of Political Polarization* (Brookings Institution Press, 2019); Jon C. Rogowski and Joseph L. Sutherland, "How Ideology Fuels Affective Polarization," *Political Behavior* 38 (2016); Diego Garzia, Frederico Ferreira da Silva, and Simon Maye, "Affective Polarization in Comparative and Longitudinal Perspective," *Public Opinion Quarterly* 87, no. 1 (2023): 219-23–; Murat Somer and Jennifer McCoy, *Déjà Vu? Polarization and Endangered Democracies in the 21st Century* (SAGE Publications, 2018).
99. McCarty, *Polarization: What Everyone Needs to Know*, 10.
100. Milan W. Svolik, "Polarization versus Democracy," *Journal of Democracy* 30, no. 3 (2019): 20–32.
101. Jakub Bojakowski, "Jarosław Kaczyński: W 2015 roku rozpoczęła się zmiana ustroju Polski," *WPROST.pl*, Apr. 22, 2023.
102. See e.g. Jan G. Voelkel et al., "Interventions Reducing Affective Polarization Do Not Necessarily Improve Anti-Democratic Attitudes," *Nature Human Behaviour* 7, no. 1 (2023): 55–64; David E. Broockman, Joshua L. Kalla, and Sean J. Westwood, "Does Affective Polarization Undermine Democratic Norms or Accountability? Maybe Not," *American Journal of Political Science* 67, no. 3 (2023): 808–828; Christopher A. Bail et al., "Exposure to Opposing Views on Social Media Can Increase Political Polarization," *Proceedings of the National Academy of Sciences* 115, no. 37 (2018): 9216–9221.

PART I
AGREED

1

The Republic of Our Dreams

Antoni Dudek, Maciej Kisilowski, and Anna Wojciuk

"I'll do it better"

"There is not a liberal America and a conservative America. There is the United States of America," declared a young freshman senator from Illinois at the 2004 Democratic National Convention. It would be years until Trump or Brexit, but the most talented Western politician of his generation clearly sensed that the growing chasm between what, in Poland, we call "two warring political tribes" was becoming a defining democratic challenge of the early twenty-first century. Four years later, Barack Obama made it clear what his proposed solution to the problem was. He was the solution: His unique charisma, rooted in masterful oratory, the inspirational nature of his life story, the audacity (to use Obama's favored term) of his history-defying ascent to the presidency, his world-class intellectual credentials.

Throughout the democratic world, similar liberal political entrepreneurs tried to likewise respond to the sense of crisis. Some—most notably Emmanuel Macron—followed Obama's playbook closely and employed personal charisma to transcend the traditional left–right divides. Others, such as Canada's Justin Trudeau, New Zealand's Jacinda Ardern, or Finland's Sanna Marin, believed in bringing more glamor and energy to traditional center-left platforms—not so much overcoming our political divisions as making conservative viewpoints increasingly uncool. Yet others, such as Spain's José Luis Rodríguez Zapatero, hoped to energize and mobilize the Left by casting a more unapologetically confrontational anti-conservative course. The final group, deeply rooted in what, in the Introduction, we called "the materialist argument," saw radically redistributive economic policies as key to ending "the populist crisis." Greece's Alexis Tsipras and Yanis Varoufakis or America's Bernie Sanders were prominent examples.

Poland too had its fair share of the I'll-do-it-better leaders—newcomers who believed that the main problem afflicting our democracy was that it was not them running the show. Charismatic figures, who predicted problems would go away if only they would replace the old, sleepy, complacent political elites.

Our main centrist political force, the Civic Platform, was founded precisely on this view. Formed in 2001 by three well-known liberal and conservative leaders,

Antoni Dudek, Maciej Kisilowski, and Anna Wojciuk, *The Republic of Our Dreams* In: *Let's Agree on Poland*.
Edited by: Maciej Kisilowski and Anna Wojciuk, Oxford University Press.
 DOI: 10.1093/oso/9780198979562.003.0002

including then 44-year-old Donald Tusk, it was animated by sentiments in many ways resembling those of the later Obama coalition. Above all, both movements were generational rebellions against old elites—the Clintons and Bushes of the US, and the aging founding fathers of our democracy in Poland. A belief in the possibility of a post-partisan world was another point of alignment; as its name suggests, Tusk's movement promised not a traditional party but a broader "platform" of engaged citizens.

Today, the Polish political scene looks very stable, with the Platform—a civic movement no more—still competing with the conservative PiS, also formed in the early 2000s. But that is because all subsequent efforts to "shake things up" and "do the politics better" failed quite spectacularly. This was not for lack of trying. Over the past two decades, almost all global variants of liberal democratic entrepreneurship were attempted in our country. Making progressivism cool? Polish liberals, always skeptical about our own elites, may shrug at the comparison of Ryszard Petru and his Modern party, formed in 2015, to Trudeau. Leftist Poles—especially women exasperated with the continuously male leadership of our social democratic parties—may laugh at a juxtaposition of Janusz Palikot or Robert Biedroń—the leaders of new leftist movements formed, respectively, in 2011 and 2019—with Jacinda Ardern or Sanna Marin. But the political strategy rooted in a belief that center-left ideas can be universally accepted if only they are communicated in a more agile, attractive, and understandable form was in fact remarkably alike.

Occasionally, the international inspirations of our Polish attempts to address the elusive democratic crisis were made explicit. The mid-2000s effort of Poland's post-communists to renew themselves through a radical generational change—with the 2005 election of then 30-year-old Wojciech Olejniczak as chairman, followed by the not-much-older Grzegorz Napieralski—was clearly inspired by the assertive anticlerical Spanish social-democracy of the time. The agenda of the new leadership was tellingly represented by Napieralski's nickname—"Zapateralski."[1] But ultimately the remake did not help much. By 2015, the Left's post-communist tradition was openly repudiated by the new Together Party. Like Tsipras or Sanders,[2] Together accused the traditional Left of being too timid, especially on economic issues.

The circle of history is brought to a close by Szymon Hołownia's Poland 2050—a liberal-Catholic party established in 2021. Their pitch—Poland beyond left–right divides, respectful of its tradition but dealing with big civilizational challenges—was derided by conservatives as a copycat Macronian "trick": You think you vote for a moderately conservative post-partisan Poland, but you get the same old liberal status quo.[3] But by now critics did not really need to venture to France for context: A careful observer of Polish politics would realize that Hołownia's message was in fact very much like what Donald Tusk and his associates had offered twenty years earlier when forming the Civic Platform.

The system is to blame

One reason why Polish I'll-do-it-better projects are rarely compared to similar efforts abroad is that our political entrepreneurs are *not* Obama, Macron, Trudeau, Ardern, Marin, Zapatero, or Tsipras in one fundamental sense: apart from Donald Tusk, none of them won. Virtually all the above-mentioned movements aiming to reimagine Polish politics are either formally defunct or struggle as small, marginal factions. But this, we argue, only makes the Polish case a more explicit example of a tendency seen in all the aforementioned projects. After all, the personal success of global liberal superstars, having run successive administrations, and undoubtedly exerting an impact on national and global history in numerous ways, was in no case coupled with the fulfillment of their original pledge to *truly change* things. Thirty years ago, Peter Mair offered a profound diagnosis of this disenchantment with contemporary politics and the citizens' experience of a lack of change despite the emergence of new parties and alternation in power.[4]

We hope that the conspicuous lack of even the most immediate political success of our local I'll-do-it-better aspiring saviors will make it easier for our compatriots to see that our democratic problems evade easy solutions. In that sense, the story we are outlining here mirrors the one presented in the Introduction. Just as our country proved resistant to the mainstream liberal *academic* solutions to our current democratic predicament, so too have our past two decades shown the futility of the key *practical* liberal responses to that crisis. The connection between the academic and practitioners' failure is obviously not coincidental. In their political programs and strategies, liberal political entrepreneurs incorporate elements of both the diagnosis and the prescriptions proposed by intellectuals. And since these diagnoses are invariably rooted in the notion of conservative revolutions being an "aberration" emerging in response to some discernible crisis or a policy or elite mistake, it is not surprising that the liberal movements founded on those premises have fared particularly poorly in Poland. As we demonstrated in the Introduction, there really is no crisis in Poland; the situation of most Poles has, in the past thirty years, improved as never before in our history. Like few other countries, Poland shows that our democratic problems cannot and will not be solved by one "comprehensive reform" or, even less so, by a single politician, no matter how charismatic they are. Poland's problem is not one of bad politicians or a bad public policy but rather one of the poorly designed constitutional system.

Given the number of movements and leaders over the past two decades promising Poles sweeping political change, it is quite surprising how few concrete proposals for democratic *constitutional* reforms have been put forward since the late 1990s. Only the conservative revolutionaries, starting with PiS's leader Jarosław Kaczyński, have spoken extensively about such reforms, though with an overly vague presentation of the ultimate model of the constitutional system being proposed. This shortage of detail is taken by many lawyers as proof that PiS's program essentially seeks, against the wishes of a significant portion of the party's electorate, to introduce in Poland a soft variety of authoritarianism rather than a new, compelling democratic model.[5]

In fact, the only significant leader who put an unquestionably democratic constitutional change at the center of his political platform was Paweł Kukiz—a well-known rock singer who, in 2015, surprised the nation by winning more than 20 percent of the vote in the first round of the presidential election. Kukiz's central message was to change how Poland's politics works by introducing British-style first-past-the-post elections to the lower, and more powerful, chamber of parliament, the Sejm (pron. *same*). Obviously, the fact that anyone would want to mimic Britain's political system may sound very surprising to those knowledgeable on the country's contemporary political history. The consequences of Kukiz's proposed reform can in fact be easily understood in Poland, as our Senate—which has only limited powers and which, as you will see later, we intend to fundamentally reform—is currently elected exactly through a system of single-member district, used for electing the UK's House of Commons. Consequently, following the 2023 elections, seventy-six of the one hundred Polish senators caucused either with PiS or the Civic Platform. That number would have been even higher if not for a pre-election Senate coalition that the Civic Platform formed with smaller center-left parties, running just one coalition's candidate in every district.

What is wrong with us?

Paweł Kukiz should be given credit for being the only politician to recognize the institutional aspect of the problem with Polish democracy. Yet his proposal too is, in a sense, a manifestation of the I'll-do-it-better political egocentrism. At the center of his story about the benefits of the British electoral system has always been the dream of deputies accountable to their constituents, unfettered by the party trappings that single-mandate districts would allegedly produce. Institutional change, in other words, was for Kukiz simply a waystation to the final destination: better, more noble, more responsive politicians who will change Poland.

Why is it, then, that even an audacious rock star who recognizes the shortcomings of the current constitutional system is ultimately unable to break out of the aforementioned global consensus, in which the key to repairing our democracy is politicians who will "do it better"?

The reason, we think, is that we do not have the courage to tell ourselves the truth: The problem of the Polish political system is not in the politicians. The problem lies in us! To put it another way, the weakness of the current constitutional order is not how it deals (or fails to deal) with the vices of politicians, but how it deals (or rather: does not deal) with us—the citizens.

What is wrong with us? As the motto of the Social Contract Incubator says: We are different. Poles are a very diverse people. What's more, we are diverse in a particularly insidious way, because it is invisible. One advantage of traditional "plural" societies discussed in the Introduction, including Switzerland, Canada, and Germany, is that both the political elites and ordinary voters are aware of the challenges of internal diversity. Every Swiss person knows that the future of their country depends on maintaining a balance between German-, French-, and Italian-speaking citizens and regions. Every German is aware of their country's short history of unity and, by extension, regional differences, especially between the Catholic south and the Protestant north.

In Poland, by contrast, the ethnic homogeneity shaped by the Nazi genocide and Soviet resettlement, and reinforced by half a century of communist "democratic centralism," created the myth of a homogeneous Poland. In reality, however, our country is inhabited by citizens representing distinct beliefs and visions of the good life. Geographically, Poland lies at the crossroads of cultures and traditions—of Eastern and Western cultures; of Catholic, Protestant, and Orthodox traditions; and of the influence of sometimes conflicting models of state and society.[6] This diversity was particularly evident in the years of the First Polish Republic, whose collapse in the late eighteenth century was largely a consequence of precisely the failure of the political system of the time to manage this diversity well.[7]

Our differences only deepened during the Partitions of the nineteenth century, a time that was crucial for the formation of modern national consciousness.[8] As we already mentioned in the Introduction, the postwar period added a fourth piece to these three pieces of the Polish jigsaw puzzle: our western lands, inhabited in a significant part by forcefully displaced persons from the eastern parts of the interwar Second Republic. On top of these historical divides there exist rich regional traditions, for example, the identity of the Silesians and Kashubians, or the traditions of coexistence with the Orthodox Church in some of Poland's eastern regions.[9]

Despite the multifaceted nature of all the fault lines outlined above, from the point of view of our politics it is not difficult to see a general regularity. In northwestern Poland, and in almost all large cities, progressive political currents are stronger, advocating for change in the country bringing us closer to the policies and social relations prevalent in Western Europe. In contrast, in southeastern Poland there is predominant support for more conservative policies, emphasizing the uniqueness of Polish tradition and reacting with skepticism to innovations from the West.[10]

As shown in Figure 1.1, the aforementioned differences between progressive northwestern Poland and conservative southeastern Poland are best seen in the election results. Of course, the economic situation, a leader's charisma, and political scandals that stir public interest have a significant impact on the outcome of elections. In general, however, since the 1990s the liberal and left-wing parties have never achieved a better result in the southeastern Lesser Poland than in western

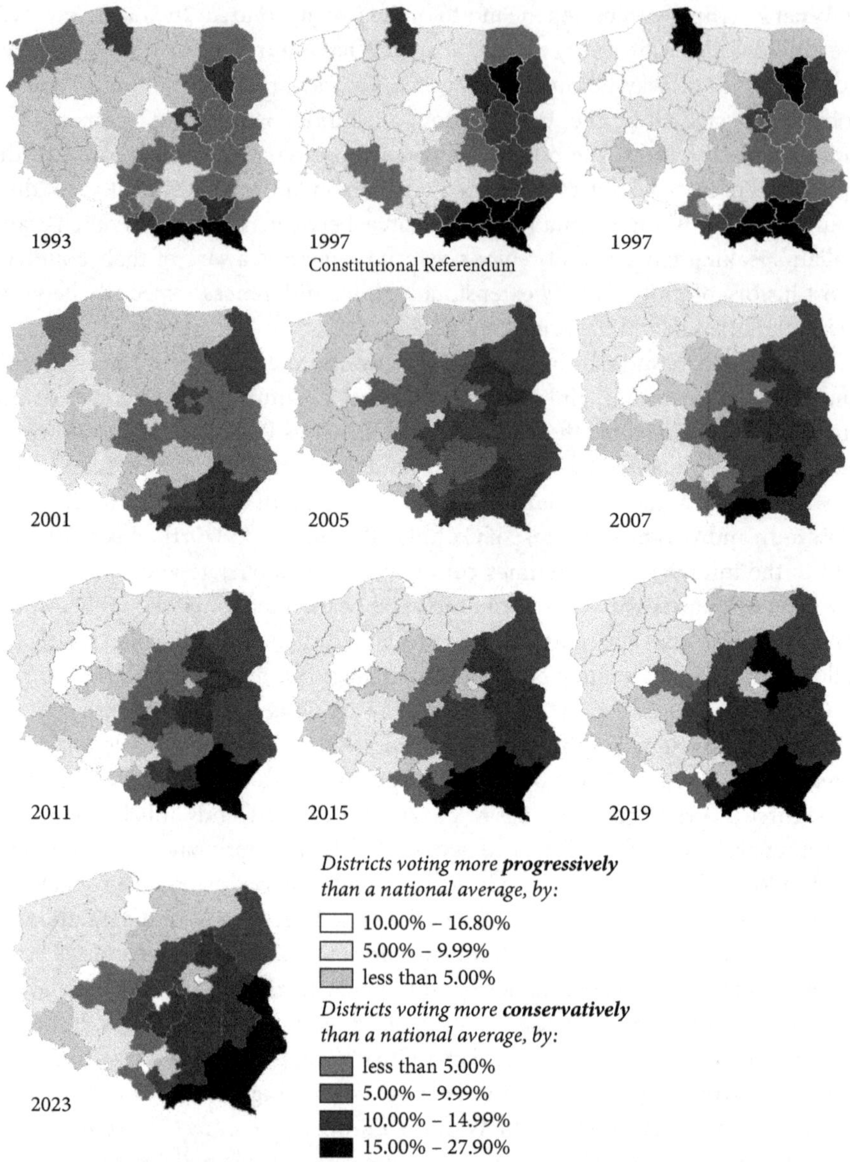

For the 1997 Referendum, the more progressive vote was to approve the new Constitution, while the conservative vote was to reject it

Figure 1.1 Territorial dimension of political polarization in Poland: results of parliamentary elections 1993–2023, and the 1997 constitutional referendum

Adapted from Maciej Kisilowski, "Constitutional Strategy for a Polarized Society: Learning from Poland's Post-revolutionary Misfortunes," in *Revolutionary Constitutionalism: Law, Legitimacy, Power*, ed. Richard Albert (Hart Publishing, 2020).

Greater Poland, and right-wing parties have never done better in West Pomerania than in eastern Podlasie.

Moreover, despite Poles' proclaimed homogeneity, the political and ideological chasms are deepening, as can also be seen in Figure 1.1. This reflects the paradoxical effect of the top-down, winner-takes-all constitutional system that was already mentioned in the Introduction: Although its premise is to distrust the idea of recognizing differences among Poles, a practical consequence of this system is the deepening of these differences and animosities.[11]

In summary: we are different

Polish politics is full of disputes, fights, and sometimes open hatred, not because our politicians are particularly bad, but because these politicians represent a very diverse electorate. This is an electorate of Poles who by and large agree in their attachment to the national sovereignty and belonging in the democratic West, who are united by our language and many elements of a common culture. The problem, however, is that these same voters disagree on many other very important issues: on matters that are certainly not existential from the point of view of the future of the nation as a whole, but are—not infrequently—of fundamental importance to many of us as individuals.[12]

Among these points of contention is the role of the Catholic Church and the moral principles of public life that it preaches.[13] This fundamental divergence is often reduced to issues concerning the rights of women[14] and non-heteronormative people, but its reach is much broader and affects policies on education (including religious instruction and the display of religious symbols in public schools), economics (keeping shops open on Sundays, the degree of state support for the Church), and health. Equally profound are differences in how we approach the key, identity-defining points in history, particularly the negotiated model of our 1989 political transition.[15] We differ, finally, in the degree to which we prioritize improving our economic growth or, instead, focusing on the protection of values and traditions important to us.

These deep axiological and ideological differences not only exacerbate political divisions, but are also behind much of the supposed weaknesses and inactions of our state. Take, for example, the controversy over the key reforms proposed during Civic Platform's first stint in power (2007–15): lowering of the school age from 7 to 6 years old, or raising of the retirement age to 67 years. Both reforms were treated by many experts as an example of the clash between "rational" public policy and the "irrationality" of reform opponents.

However, this is not a sufficiently thorough analysis. The preferences of opponents to both policies may be perfectly rational. Earlier retirement shortens the contribution period, reducing the amount of the pension or increasing taxes for those who work. A later school age also shortens the period of labor productivity and may have a negative impact on educational outcomes. Nevertheless, fully rational citizens can consciously accept these costs as worth sacrificing in favor of other values: a longer childhood, understood as time before school, or the opportunity to enjoy more years in retirement. Similarly, the PiS government's 2017 decision to abolish middle schools need not be perceived as an irrational destruction of the system, which—as international studies have shown—had been extremely effective in bridging structural differences in general education outcomes,[16] but could be seen as a rational calculation in which greater differences in education are a reasonable price to pay for the possibility of children staying for longer in the local school or, even more significantly, in traditional local social structures.

Even the supposedly "canonical" examples of our governmental inefficiency—the abysmal condition of Poland's public health system, or the lack of progress in eliminating smog from many Polish cities—conceals, in fact, a conflict of values and priorities. One of the most widely commented-on policy decisions of the post-2015 PiS government was to spend a huge amount of state funds—about 8 percent of the budget—on the so-called 500+ Program, which offered a monthly cash grant of 500 złotys (about 125 euro) for each child to every family in the country. If all these funds had been allocated to health care or other public services, we would undoubtedly have seen a significant improvement in their availability and quality. This does not mean, however, that the government's program was irrational—although it may, for many, have been unacceptable. A perfectly rational voter will prefer the certain gain of 500 złotys over the uncertain possibility of obtaining better medical care, potentially prolonging their life, when sick. Similarly, a voter may prefer the certain benefit of being able to heat their home with cheap (but dirty) fuel over the uncertain risk of getting cancer. Such preferences are particularly understandable among voters who interpret misfortune, such as serious illness, through the lens of their faith and a belief in God's direct influence on their fate.

Contract not domination

In the Introduction, we compared Poland's diversity to that of the traditionally "plural" democratic states. The upside of their linguistic, religious, or ethnic differences is that (with a few tragic exceptions) their citizens and elites have rarely been animated by a preposterous idea of "solving" these differences by having one group conquer and dominate others—by forming a state of people who are all alike. Unfortunately, this is precisely the idea that has defined the thinking of both progressive and conservative Polish politicians over the past two hundred years.

In the concluding chapter of this book we will offer a historical account of this prevalent mindset. For now, let us focus on our contemporary political culture. Imagine that one day the German-speaking Swiss consider French- or Italian-speaking compatriots an "animal element"[17] that urgently needs to be Germanized.

That is how in 2016 Jarosław Kaczyński described progressive voters. Or imagine that, just like the 2007 liberal activists who advocated "stealing your granny's ID"[18] in order to prevent her from voting for Kaczyński, a group of Protestant Germans organize a pre-election "take away a Bavarian's ID" campaign. Imagine that leading Italian politicians begin to refer to southerners as "the Sicilian Sect," to paraphrase "the Smolensk Sect"—a derisive liberal term for Poles doubting the official report on the deadly 2010 crash of the Polish presidential plane in Smolensk, Russia.[19] Or that they mock the "Calabrian berets," to echo Donald Tusk's 2005 comments regarding PiS voters.[20] Or that the head of the ruling party in Canada calls the Quebecois "a worse sort," to refer once again to the words of the PiS leader, in 2015.[21]

Returning to constitutionalism: imagine that in Switzerland, Germany, Italy, or Canada, the idea emerges to draw up a new basic law. As a result of an unfortunate coincidence, due to the peculiarities of the electoral system, representatives of the French-speaking Swiss or Canadians, the Catholic Germans, or Southern Italians do not get into parliament. Can we imagine a parliament formed following such elections deciding to push through a new constitution, without the participation of the aforementioned groups?

Unfortunately, this is precisely how the current Polish Constitution was drafted and enacted in 1997. Let us recall this story in some detail. In the early 1990s, the Sejm—which since 1989 has been elected on a proportional basis in multi-mandate constituencies—was highly fragmented. In response, an electoral threshold was introduced. Only parties that gained at least 5 percent of votes nationally, or coalitions that reached as much as 8 percent, would get any seats in the more powerful chamber of our legislature. The 1993 ballot was the first under the new system. The conservative parties did not fully grasp the consequences of the reform and ran, as before, in a number of small factions. In effect, nearly 35 percent of the popular vote, cast overwhelmingly for the Right, was "wasted" on many small parties that failed to clear the threshold.

The Solidarity labor union, by then seen as the main representation of the Polish conservatives, argued that because of this electoral accident, any work on the new Constitution should involve the conservative parties that ended up outside the Sejm. The parliamentary majority, consisting of the post-communists and liberals, rejected this view. Progressive politicians led the process of drafting the new basic law despite the vociferous opposition of Solidarity and the Catholic Church. In 1997, a few months before the next general election—which would be won by the Right—the Constitution was overwhelmingly approved by the assembly consisting of all members of the Sejm and Senate elected in the 1993 ballot. The left-wing president, Aleksander Kwaśniewski—who, in 1995, narrowly denied Solidarity's leader, Lech Wałęsa, his second term in office—supported the document with the full force of his office. Each Polish family received a copy with a presidential cover letter. Despite these efforts, in the ratifying referendum, the basic law received a weak democratic mandate: a 53 percent majority with just a 43 percent turnout. By contrast, in a 2003 vote on joining the European Union, more than 77 percent of Poles said yes; the turnout was nearly 59 percent.

In Chapter 13, we will return to what the drafting process of the 1997 Constitution tells us about our Polish political instincts. For now, suffice it to point out that the constitutional systems of the most successful and stable plural democracies are not instruments of the tribal conquest. Instead, they represent a form of contract between major groups in which citizens share power in the state. If you agree with us that the historical, ideological, and identity differences between progressive Poland and conservative Poland are as enduring and politically significant as the linguistic, ethnic, or religious differences in many other countries, then the goal of the necessary constitutional reforms is to share power in such a way that, regardless of the results of parliamentary or presidential elections, both progressive and conservative Poles feel at home in their own country.

Subnational governments: promise and limitations

Our proposed changes to Poland's constitutional system, designed in the spirit of precisely such a power-sharing agreement, envision a much deeper involvement of local and regional governments in the governing of our country. We are not, however, advocating a revolution that throws into the garbage can what Polish citizens have achieved so far. Poland's subnational governments, established by two comprehensive reforms in 1990 and 1997 (and discussed in greater detail in Chapter 13), are in fact among the country's most successful institutions. As Figure 1.2. shows, trust in local government consistently and significantly dwarfs that placed in the Sejm, the Senate, or the Cabinet.

With their strength and entrenchment fully acknowledged, the ability of the subnational governments to contribute to the management of our national diversity is constrained by three troublesome limitations. To begin with, the power of these levels of government is very unevenly distributed. Most formal competencies, and money, belong to the lowest level, comprising 2,543 municipalities. Given Poland's overall population of just shy of 37 million, the average municipality is a relatively tiny community of less than 15,000. But this level of governance also includes sixty-six large towns and cities, including Warsaw, with nearly two million inhabitants, and Cracow, with almost one million. On paper these big municipalities have only slightly greater powers than any other municipality; to be specific, they integrate the municipal competencies with those of the second level of Poland's subnational government, that is, that of a county. Counties, however, have so few independent powers that they are rarely mentioned in this book. What does make the large governments of towns and cities different is thereby not their formal status but the reality of their large budgets, accumulated social capital, and political prestige.

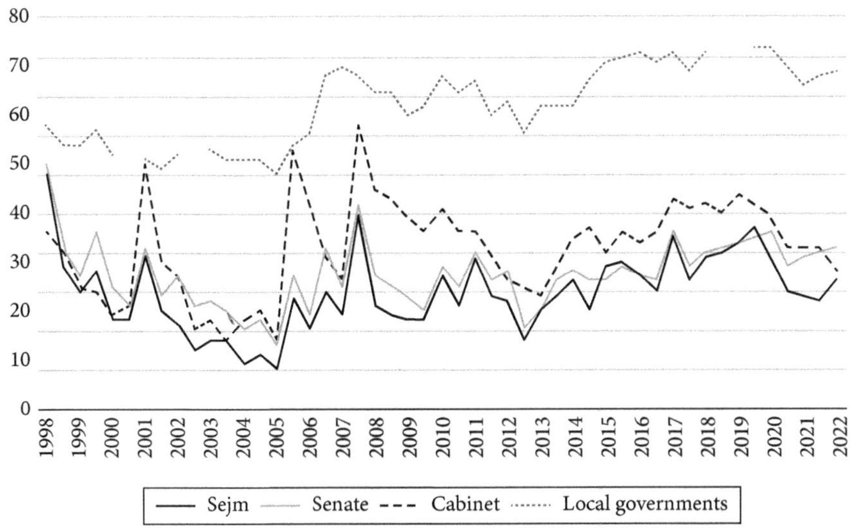

Figure 1.2 Trust in the Sejm, the Senate, the Cabinet, and local governments
Source: CBOS

The power of large municipalities can be usefully contrasted with that of our sixteen regions, known by their traditional Polish name as voivodships. Figure 1.3 illustrates the map of these provinces. Established in 1999, each voivodship has a whole set of democratically elected institutions. Its popularly elected legislature is called the sejmik (pron. *same-meek*)—"the little Sejm" in Polish. Its executive is the voivodship board, elected by the sejmik and chaired by the voivodship marshal. As we will show later, these existing representative bodies will play an essential role in our project of increasing the stability and responsiveness of Poland's constitutional system. But their promise and potential are currently seriously underused. The voivodships have very few independent competencies.

The losers under this system are mostly conservative citizens living outside the major cities. While urban Poles have strong city governments that represent their interests and particular ideological preferences, rural citizens cannot rely on an equally strong subnational government. Their municipalities are very small, while counties and voivodships are powerless.

This brings us to the second, even more serious limitation. While our subnational governments provide a lot of public services—for instance, they run public schools, many hospitals, and cultural institutions—and while they also issue a lot of important individual decisions, their legislative functions are particularly limited. In their day-to-day operations, municipalities, counties, and voivodships must generally implement detailed rules and mandates enacted by the national Sejm and Senate in Warsaw. This severely limits their ability to contribute to managing the deep ideological cleavages between Poles, to respond to

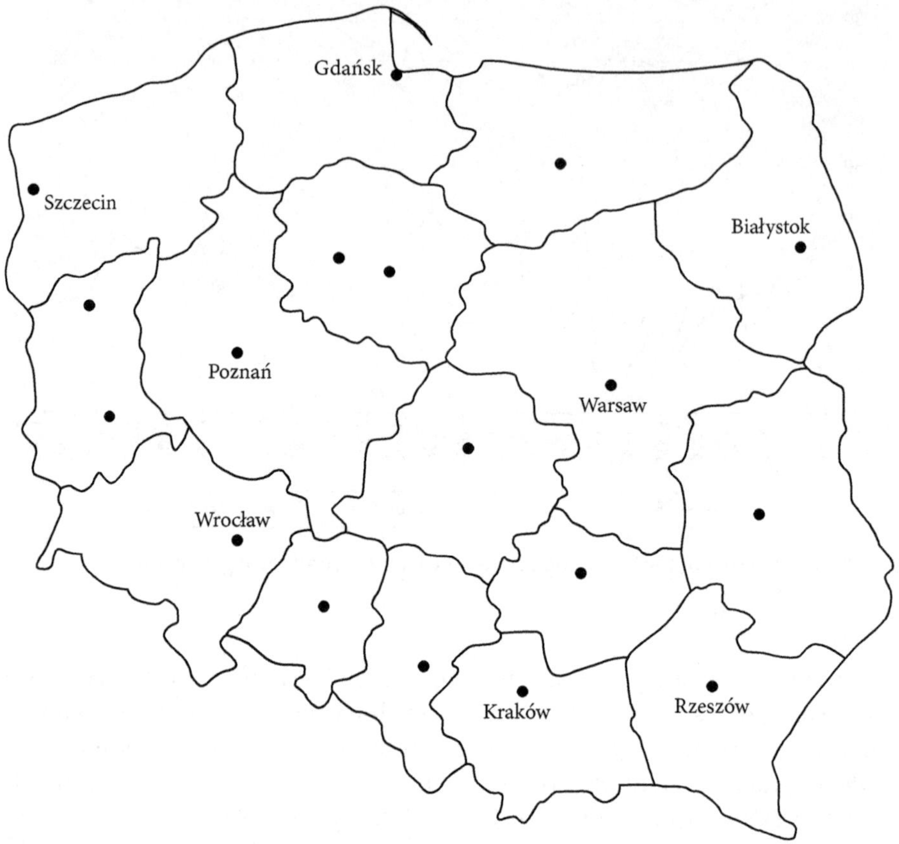

Figure 1.3 Polish Voivodships and their capitals (two regions have dual capitals)

the geographically distributed differences in our vision of the good life and good society. This wasted opportunity to use decentralized governance—and decentralized legitimacy—to diffuse national political tensions is also represented by the final weakness of the current system: the almost non-existent participation of subnational governments in the decision-making at the center.

Our proposal

Our proposal addresses all these issues, transforming the current system of subnational government into the main core of the new conservative–progressive power-sharing social contract. The "magic bullet," shown in Figure 1.4, is multilevel governance, or the establishment of powerful vertical connections between the municipal, provincial, national and European levels of governance.

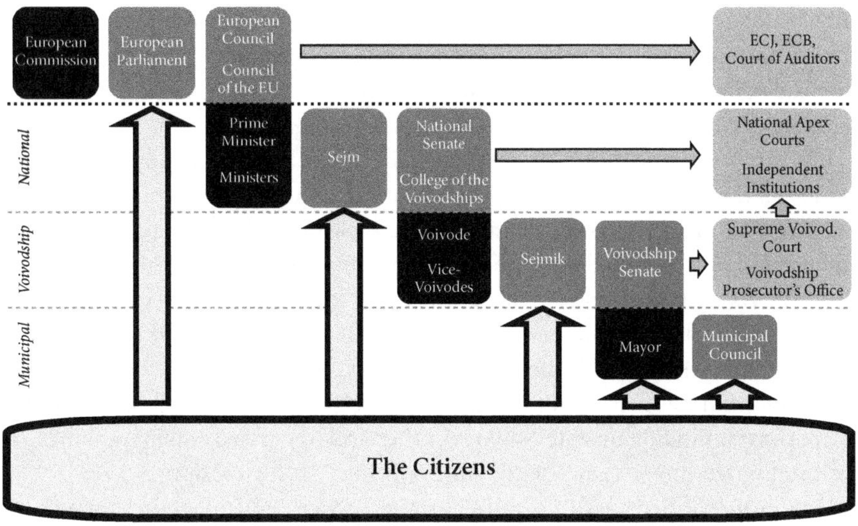

Figure 1.4 Multi-level governance from the municipality to Brussels

We propose creating a coherent and logical system of power sharing. This concept clearly takes into account the constitutional role of our membership in the European Union (unfortunately not stipulated in the current constitution). It sets out a plan for managing public affairs, from the municipality all the way up to Brussels.

This vision will be accomplished chiefly by the introduction of two innovative institutions. In Warsaw, the new national Senate will consist of voivodship chief executives—who, for reasons we will explain soon, will no longer be called "marshals" but voivodes. The Senate of the Voivodes will be approving all national legislation by a majority of citizens represented. The citizens in each region will decide, in their voivodship charter, whether they want the voivode to be directly elected or prefer the continuation of the current system of the sejmiks electing and dismissing the regional chief executives. Following the examples of Berlin, Hamburg, and Vienna, we propose that Poland's largest cities—at least Warsaw and Cracow—should be granted the status of separate urban voivodships, with their mayor-voivodes sitting in the national Senate. A somewhat similar proposal for Warsaw was considered by the PiS government.

The new and small national Senate of the popularly accountable voivodes will immediately strengthen our diverse regions by transforming their chief executives into key players in national politics. Their power will in fact be second only to the country's President, Prime Minister, and Cabinet members. We believe that this important power shift would quickly trigger a deep decentralizing stimulus in many areas of policy making. In the remainder of this book, we often suggest which of these areas could be strategically decentralized. But these are our suggestions only, which would not require being set in stone in the proposed constitutional reform. Instead, it will be the job of the new Senate to negotiate with the Sejm, unchanged in its structure and representing common national interests, how the new vertical distribution of policy-making powers will look.[22]

It is obviously essential for our voivodships to be "democratically prepared" to handle all the new powers that the Senate of the Voivodes will successfully whisk away from the grip of Warsaw centralization. A particularly serious concern is that of the new potent regional governments overrunning our already successful municipalities. As we worked on this proposal, many local government officials shared with us their worries about the current "Warsaw centralism" being replaced by the similarly heavy-handed dictates of regional governments. This problem plagues many communities in large American states. Progressive cities in Texas, or conservative communities in upstate New York, often feel oppressed and marginalized by their state governments representing the opposite ideological option.

Our proposal here uses Poland's "second mover" advantage in strategic decentralization. Unlike federal countries whose historical trajectories started with the strong middle, regional level of governance, our starting point, as mentioned earlier, is a unitary state with strong municipalities. We want to keep the benefits of this bottom-heavy decentralization and limit the potential excesses of stronger regional governments by introducing a second chamber to each provincial legislature: the Voivodship Senate. These senates will consist of the mayors of all the municipalities belonging to a given voivodship, with their vote—as in the national Senate—weighted strictly by the number of citizens represented. Such a reformed bicameral voivodship legislature, composed of the existing sejmik and the new voivodship senate, would become the main legislator for all subnational governments—municipalities, counties, and the voivodship—in a given region. Our proposal builds on existing institutions with strong popular legitimacy and, in particular, on mayors who are close to the inhabitants of each municipality. This will bring government closer to the people and open up new avenues for citizen participation to address the crisis of democratic representation.[23]

Local government under special supervision

To show why the new national Senate and the voivodship senates are so central to the fair conservative–progressive power-sharing social contract, we need to present a little more context. Today, one of the foundational ideas defining our system of subnational government is that of the "Chinese walls" between local governments and the central government, and between the local and regional governments. Under the existing system, local governments have no formal influence over central government decisions, and municipalities have no influence over voivodship government decisions (and vice versa).

This approach was understandable given that the design of Poland's local governance took shape during the final years of communist dictatorship in the 1980s (which we discuss in greater detail in Chapter 13). At the time, central authority was synonymous with oppression. Local government was supposed to be but a small respite from this oppression for the citizens—a limited space of freedom.[24]

In today's conditions, however, the downsides of the "Chinese wall" clearly outweigh the benefits. To begin with, local and regional governments have no mechanisms to temper the ideological overreach of politicians in Warsaw. The new national Senate would change that by defending local and regional governments from recentralization—the central attempts to deprive municipalities and regions of their competences or funds. Given the geographic aspect of the division between progressive and conservative Poland, the Senate of the Voivodes would truly represent Polish diversity.[25] For much of the past decade, PiS governed about half of Poland's voivodships, with the rest controlled by the center-left parties. The 2024 local elections, coming right after PiS's loss in the national elections, were tough for the Right, but still five southeastern voivodships remain under conservative rule.

But the "Chinese wall" idea has numerous other negative consequences. It entrenched in Polish constitutional thinking the stark conceptual distinction between, on the one hand, "state authorities" in the center and, on the other, the authorities of voivodships, counties, and municipalities referred to in Polish constitutional and administrative law as "the self-governments" of the inhabitants. That distinction, loosely adopted from German administrative law, fits very oddly the cherished unitary character of the Polish Republic (which we will discuss later). Its practical implication is the belief widely shared by the political elite that the Polish state is represented only through its central government. Local "self-government" provides citizens with a limited space to express themselves, but always under the watchful eye of the central overseer.

Institutionally, this thinking is represented by perhaps the most bizarre aspect of Poland's contemporary constitutional system: the dualism in our regional governance. For, apart from the earlier-mentioned board, elected by the sejmik and led by the regional marshal, each province is "co-run" by a voivode, who is today appointed centrally by the Prime Minister. The marshal and the voivode are often housed in the same building. With meager independent competencies, the voivode is literally a full-time supervisor of the local and regional government in their province.

From the vantage of the power-sharing logic of our proposed new constitutional contract, the absurdity of the role of today's voivodes becomes evident. All public officials do indeed have to be supervised—in terms of the legality of their actions by independent courts, in terms of integrity by anti-corruption agencies, and in terms of fidelity to the interests of the Polish Republic by counterintelligence services. But these remarks apply just as much to the provincial marshal or to a minister in Warsaw! And, to our knowledge, no one is proposing the appointment of a supervisor for each minister—an "über-minister" sitting in the office next door and looking over the minister's shoulders.

Given that the widespread belief in the need for special oversight of local and regional governments has become so entrenched in Polish political culture, our proposal does not advocate its elimination, but rather its rationalization through the integration of that oversight in the office of the national Presidency. Performed under the control of the administrative courts, the role of guardian of the cohesion of a decentralized but unitary Republic seems to us a good use of the strong mandate of our popularly elected president. At the regional level, however, the functions of today's marshal and voivode will be merged in the popularly accountable voivode chairing the regional board—and, as mentioned earlier, also holding a seat in the national Senate.

The most effective way to curb abuses of power is through democratic control. Hence our proposal for the voivodship senates, in which elected representatives of municipalities would share in decisions taken at the provincial level. An additional control mechanism would be that of strengthened local media, receiving funds for its activities on a competitive basis from an independent national fund. This fund's authorities would be elected for long terms by the Sejm, Senate, and President, with one-third of the incumbents changing every four years.

Voivodship legislators

Doing away with the "Chinese walls" is also essential for bringing significant legislative powers closer to the people. The 1997 Constitution already lists local laws as the sources of binding law in our country along with national statutes and international agreements. In practice, however, the ability of local and regional governments to enact those laws is exceedingly modest. This leads to a situation in which the local governments perform a significant part of public tasks—managing schools, municipal infrastructure, cultural institutions, and hospitals—but have very little influence on how these tasks are to be performed. Indeed, in carrying out their tasks, local governments must strictly adhere to the regulations passed in Warsaw.

Combined with the aforementioned "special supervision" of the voivodes, today's local government resembles a worker digging a hole surrounded by a garland of very important regulators and supervisors from Warsaw. Although the worker obviously knows best how a particular hole should be dug, he basically has no say in the matter. The Warsaw VIPs set the rules of digging, and scrupulously supervise their observance—particularly thoroughly if the digger happens to represent the opposing political faction.

This system is not only ineffective, but also squanders a huge opportunity to mitigate tensions in our diverse country. As we have already repeatedly mentioned, Polish diversity has a clear geographic aspect. Moving many decisions from the level of central laws, enacted by the current parliamentary majority in a "winner-takes-all" logic, to the level of provincial government would allow legal regulations to be better tailored to the needs and expectations of Poles with different preferences and values.

When we say "provincial government," we mainly mean the strengthened sejmiks and the new voivodship senates. Here again, rejecting the idea of "Chinese walls" between the multiple levels of our governance opens up new possibilities. At present, the voivodship government has no relationship with the municipal government. As a result, the only body empowered to pass decentralized laws on municipal matters is the Municipal Council. It is difficult to imagine transferring significant legislative powers from the Sejm to more than 2,500 Polish municipalities. In our proposal, the municipalities, through their voivodship senate, become part of the provincial decentralized administration. And it is at that provincial level, and not in Warsaw, that laws concerning the decentralized policy areas will be passed.

How many of the issues regulated in Warsaw today could be transferred to provincial legislatures? The members of our Social Contract Incubator differ in their assessment here. For example, in regard to whether shops can stay open on Sundays, whether we should have middle schools or longer eight-grade primary schools, whether the school age should be 6 or 7, how universities and cultural institutions should be structured and run, whether to support in vitro procedures, how to spend the funds from PiS's earlier-mentioned 500+ family support program (which, due to inflation, has now become the 800+ program), and what the retirement age should be, most of us agree that regulating these issues at the provincial level would help defuse existing social tensions, while simultaneously changing the very way we debate over difficult political choices. Instead of resorting to abstract arguments, new solutions and reforms could be tested in certain voivodships, so that we could all see how these ideas work in practice.

Tough and super-tough topics

The question as to whether a similar decentralization logic could be applied to the "toughest" topics dividing Poles is more contentious. In 2019, opponents of our proposals warned that we would make abortion laws a matter of voivodship regulation. For those critics, it was unacceptable that the provincial government would decide on "matters of life and death." We were also accused of wanting to "decentralize human rights."

So let's clarify: most IUS members are against the decentralization of family or abortion laws. Nevertheless, our critics could be a bit more specific in outlining their dystopian scenarios, even under the very maximalist interpretation of our proposal. In Australia, for instance, abortion has always been the domain of state law. Rather than a nationwide political scramble, over the past quarter-century individual states, starting with Western Australia in 1998, have liberalized their abortion restrictions to varying degrees. Regulations differ mainly with regard to how late in the course of pregnancy abortion can be freely performed and the conditions for exceptional abortions after that date.

For opponents of abortion, this outcome is certainly not ideal. But let us remember that, in a decentralized system, anyone can continue to fight for their causes—both in West Pomerania and Western Australia. The social contract we are proposing is about the rules that govern how the democratic game is played, not the outcome of that game.

To reiterate: one can disagree with the idea of decentralizing abortion law. But it is naïve to claim that the abortion issue represents a different caliber of responsibility for which subnational government is not ready. After all, local governments already routinely decide "matters of life and death." For example, they invest (or they don't) in road infrastructure, and there is no doubt that many of the nearly 2,000 annual fatalities on single carriageway roads, mostly local, are a consequence of such decisions. Every day, millions of Poles entrust their health and lives to the local governments, using trains, streetcars, or buses managed by them. Public transport is, by the way, extremely safe, with a few dozen fatalities caused by accidents every year. Local governments also manage other infrastructure that has a direct impact on people's lives, such as water supply systems.

As for arguments concerning the decentralization of human rights, as we mentioned in the previous chapter, the different conceptions regarding the desirable scope of modern human rights protections are indeed at the center of our political cleavages—not only in Poland. It is difficult to envision a substantive progressive–conservative agreement on those issues in the foreseeable future. Our proposal relies on the "European solution" to this dilemma. Poland is, after all, a member of the world's most extensive system of human rights protection under the European Convention on Human Rights. Regardless of whether laws are made by the Sejm and Senate in Warsaw, or the sejmik and the new provincial senate in Rzeszów or Poznań, all bodies of the Polish state are obliged to comply with the Convention.

Our proposal, described in Chapters 5 and 6, to strengthen the independence of the courts by including regional government in the process of nominating judges is aimed, among other things, at ensuring that all Polish authorities—state and local—effectively respect human rights. It is worth noting that today almost all Polish complaints going to the European Court of Human Rights, which interprets the provisions of the Convention, concern the actions of central authorities, not local governments.

How the EU accidentally revolutionized parliamentarism

Speaking about "European solutions" and inspirations embedded in our proposal, let us take another look at the central elements of our social contract, namely the new national Senate of the Voivodes and the voivodship senates. It is not hard to see that all of them are structured in the same way. These legislative chambers will comprise the chief executives from the lower level of national governance: mayors in the voivodship senates, and voivodes in the new national Senate.

Readers attached to the traditional Montesquieu principle of separation of legislative, executive, and judicial powers may find such a proposal strange. Why are we making representatives of the lower executive branch part of legislatures at the higher governance level? In a nutshell: because it turns out that such a system works exceptionally well, and particularly so in managing internally diverse polities. The arena in which the strengths of this senate composition have been particularly well tested is the European Union. When the EEC was founded in 1957, the delegating of key decisions to a Council composed of Member States' cabinet ministers stemmed from an understanding of the Community as a traditional intergovernmental international organization. The tremendous progress in European integration, and the consequent growth of EU legislation coupled with the creation of the European Parliament in the late 1970s, led to the transformation of the EU Council into a de facto European "senate"—the upper house of the EU legislature, whose approval (in addition to that of the Parliament—the de facto lower house) is needed for any directive or regulation to enter into force.[26]

Despite its rather haphazard history, this European "senate" has proven a hit for three reasons. First, sitting ministers (and, on the most important issues, presidents or prime ministers) do not argue about issues that are theoretical to them. While the goal of a professional MP is generally to be "visible" in the Sejm, a minister deciding on the EU Council's new directive thinks, first and foremost, about how they will later implement this directive. It is the practical operations of the directive—or, more broadly, the overall performance of a given area of public policy—that voters would generally consider when holding a cabinet minister accountable. The minister therefore has little incentive to engage in flowery rhetoric or to ratchet up tensions just for show. Instead, pragmatic compromises are more important.

Second, the Council does not operate on a term system, but is a continuous body. Ministers come and go, but a certain institutional memory, unwritten rules of reciprocity and professionalism, persist. Again, the effect is a greater tendency to compromise, a sense of give and take.

Third, somewhat paradoxically, the effectiveness of the EU Council is due to the limited time available to its members. For a professional MP, verbal skirmishes on the floor or in committees are the essence of their full-time job. For ministers or prime ministers, activity in the EU Council is a "second job." Less time again strengthens the motivation for pragmatism and compromises, often thrashed out during famous all-night Brussels negotiations.

All these proven strengths of our European "senate" can be replicated in our proposed new national Senate as well as the voivodship senates. Unlike in the I'll-do-it-better proposals for "fixing Poland" discussed at the outset of this chapter, our upper chambers of the nationwide and provincial legislatures will work in a spirit of pragmatism and compromise not because they will be populated by political angels but because, like ministers in Brussels, the voivodes in Warsaw and mayors in the provincial capitals will simply have strong incentives to demonstrate such pragmatism.

Let's talk about money

Let us now turn to another aspect of our proposal: the thorny issue of money. Without increasing the financial independence of local and regional governments from the politicians in Warsaw, our new social contract for Poland will be purely illusory. That's why, in Chapter 3, we offer a detailed proposal for a new tax revenue-sharing system.

In essence, we propose to fully regionalize our personal and corporate income taxes. This may sound incredibly radical. Yet the fact is that for Poland, as for other EU Member States, income taxes are not the main source of public-sector revenue, which is mainly derived from the Value Added Tax (VAT) and the social security contributions paid by all workers. While personal and corporate income taxes are the mainstay of public finances in the United States, in Poland they account for barely 15 percent of our governmental spending. This happens to be much less than what our local and regional governments spend even today. It thereby makes perfect sense for both income taxes to be fully decentralized: imposed by regional laws, collected by voivodship authorities, and spent entirely on supporting decentralized public services. Again, our colleagues will fill in a lot of details in Chapter 3. For now, let us focus on the constitutional "big picture."

Today, the lion's share of the budgets of the subnational governments comes from grants and subsidies awarded by the central government. This system incentivizes politicians in Warsaw to use funding as leverage over local governments, especially those controlled by the opposition.[27] Legislative changes were made in an attempt to remedy this problem by creating a fixed statutory formula granting municipalities a specified fraction of personal income taxes generated within the municipal territory. This solution, alas, proved equally susceptible to abuse. Politicians of all parties have grown accustomed to proposing popular income tax cuts knowing that the cost of these changes will largely be borne by the municipalities, which will receive a statutory share of the now lower tax revenues.

This situation is sick even today, let alone in the system we are proposing. Voivodes will not be able to provide an effective check on Warsaw politicians or veto divisive ideas in the new national Senate with a fiscal gun put to their heads. That is why, in our proposal, personal and corporate income taxes become fully provincial taxes, operating similarly to how municipal property taxes function today.

Moreover, the new social contract must, in our view, involve the co-management of our public assets, still significant despite the waves of post-1989 privatizations. Poles agree that the system in which state-owned companies and other public entities such as the State Forests become loot for the current party in power is not only flawed, but downright repugnant. However, the idea of pushing the privatization of the remaining state assets further is politically divisive. Again, contrary to the opinions of experts, the disagreements in this area are not a manifestation of some irrational, atavistic resistance against private property, but a rational reflection of the fundamental conflict of assessments and values sketched earlier. Distrust of Western companies taking over privatized enterprises is in line with the worldview of conservative voters, who are more wary of foreign countries, even those allied with Poland.

Our proposal here once again offers a way out of the political clinch. Instead of the impossible choice between privatization and the current system of spoils for the party in power, we propose a third way. Except for the truly strategic assets related to energy or defense, the remaining state-owned companies, as well as other entities such as the State Forests, should be transferred to voivodship governments in proportion to their population. Regional governments would be the first to receive the assets located within their territory.

Developmental impulse

Let's now put all our previous proposals together. Self-governing voivodships with a much greater degree of freedom in shaping regional laws, especially those related to public services already performed by subnational governments of all levels; income taxes regulated (within a general, national framework) and collected in the provinces; and state-owned companies, especially those already associated with a particular region, transferred to regional governments.

To the above, let us add a role the voivodships already perform, but which we have not yet mentioned. As we have already discussed, the new regional institutions were given barely any powers following the 1999 reforms. What saved our regions from total irrelevance was Poland's EU accession. Since 2004, our country has been a major recipient of EU developmental aid. The funds are often tied to strategies and operational programs drafted at the regional level. This novel but challenging task was given to the sejmiks and the marshals. Our regional democratic institutions responded excellently, developing enormous expertise in both the art of regional development strategy and the practice of successfully securing EU funds.[28]

This intellectual capital residing in our regions will complement the new regulatory and taxation powers perfectly. In effect, the political system that we are proposing may generate a powerful developmental impulse for the Polish economy. Building on existing regional competencies, we envision development driven mainly by the voivodships, or alliances of voivodships, which in our proposed system get the tools to implement ambitious strategies tailored to the regional conditions.

A foreign reader may be surprised that, in our constitutional proposal, such prominence is given to economic development issues. Is not Poland, as we ourselves pointed out, already an outlier case of economic success? Why change anything if it is working so well? In Poland, the response for nearly twenty years now has been that the "developmental fuel" powering our meteoric economic rise is about to run out. This is partly the consequence of our success: as Poland gets more prosperous, the economic model based on being a low-cost destination for production or back-office services will gradually become obsolete. That is why, since the mid-2000s, successive governments have worked on a host of ambitious plans to (re)accelerate our economic development.

Unfortunately, the history of these plans is very similar to the saga about the ideas to fix Polish politics sketched out at the beginning of this chapter. Whether leftist, liberal, or conservative, all economic grand strategies have been vivid representations of the I'll-do-it-better philosophy. A telling sign is that each became known by the surname of its key political proponent: the Hausner Plan, after social democratic Minister of Economy, Prof. Jerzy Hausner; the Boni Plan, after Donald Tusk's top advisor, Dr Michał Boni; and the Morawiecki Plan, after PiS's Finance Minister and later Prime Minister, Mateusz Morawiecki. Each of these weighty documents promised a bold new approach. But all shared a common conviction that Poland's further growth could be designed in Warsaw, based on a single blueprint to be applied in Lublin, Katowice, Warsaw, Łódź, or Szczecin.

The effect of these grand ideas, and their contribution to the country's development, has, to put it mildly, been insubstantial. The reason for this is again the stubbornly reappearing internal diversity of Poland and the Poles, consistently unacknowledged by our political elites. Poland as a nation is too large and too diverse to be an optimal strategic planning unit. Good strategy means searching for attractive niches, so-called competitive advantages.[29] It is impossible to find such advantages if we want to forcefully reduce the economy of a country of forty million people to the lowest common denominator!

This is precisely why real strategic planning is already taking place precisely within the earlier-mentioned EU Regional Operational Programs at the voivodship level—regions that can better identify their unique advantages in the global market. Our proposal accepts this fact, giving regional governments additional and useful instruments for competing on European and global markets. In the logic of shared responsibility for Poland, the economic success of each of our voivodships will be the success of us all.

Federalism, unitarism, and everything in between

Now that we've put our main cards on the table, it's time to brace for attacks on our proposal. Somewhat incomprehensibly, since we began to publicly discuss our new social contract in 2019, the main thrust of such criticism has not been about some dysfunctionality of the system we envisioned—instead, the disapproval has been purely conceptual. It revolves around the claim that what we argue for is the "federalization of Poland," which in Article 3 of the 1997 Constitution declares itself "a unitary state." Quite often, the critics are so convinced that the "f-word" constitutes a mortal blow to our proposal that no further argument is needed.

This is deeply paradoxical, on so many levels. To begin with, some of the most powerful democratic countries in the world are federations. Poles tend to particularly admire the strength of the US federalism and, often less explicitly, the effectiveness of the German political system. Even more importantly, our opponents seem to have a limited comprehension of the difference between a unitary and a federal state. In itself, this would not be a problem, since the difference is not that important in today's reality. Over the past few decades, so many large and midsized nations have experimented with various decentralization reforms that the practical distinction between a federal and a unitary constitutional system has become largely academic. But, of course, it does become a problem if we scare each other with a term that we don't understand.

So let's clarify. There is nothing wrong, or weak, about federal states. We would be perfectly happy to admit it if our proposal involved federalization. But it simply does not. A federation is not a system in which "generally everything (and especially abortion) is more decentralized" than in a unitary state. Austria, for example, is a federation, while Italy is a unitary state. Yet following numerous Italian decentralization reforms, the powers of the Italian regions are in many ways greater than those of the Austrian states. The United Kingdom is a unitary state, yet the government in London has delegated most of its powers over Scotland and Wales to the Scottish or Welsh authorities. Spain is a similarly unitary state, which does not prevent Catalonia from displaying strong separatist tendencies.

Federation is a system in which sovereignty is divided between the national and regional levels. And there is no mention of any such division in our proposal. In fact, by dismantling the "Chinese wall" introduced in 1990 between central and local governments, and by embedding local and regional governments within a multilevel system of democratic governance, our proposal strengthens rather than weakens the unitary character of the Polish Republic.

The strengthening of provincial institutions and the new Polish Senate are ideas not for dividing national sovereignty, but for a better, more balanced division of *governmental power* in Poland: creating systemic incentives for a party narrowly winning the national elections not to treat the "other" Poland as its vassal territory, but instead to cooperate constructively with the opposition on issues of priority—while also respecting independent institutions.

For politicians whose intuition tells them that "they'll do it better," who feel a calling to be the saviors of the nation, the distinction between the division of their power and the division of Poland can be difficult to grasp. However, since the Enlightenment, the principle that the power of politicians must be limited, preferably by creating mechanisms that involve mutual oversight, has been a cornerstone of the modern understanding of democracy.

The realization that power fundamentally corrupts—and that absolute power corrupts absolutely—underpinned the idea of constitutional checks and balances between legislative, executive, and judicial branches of government. However, no one argues that the idea of a separation of powers between, say, the Prime Minister, whose office is on Ujazdowskie Avenue in Warsaw, and the Supreme Court, located by the city's Krasiński Square, represents some outrageous "federalization of Poland" that divides it into "Ujazdowskie Poland" and "Krasiński Poland."

Our proposal adds to this horizontal separation of legislative, executive, and judicial branches a vertical division—a greater balance between central power in Warsaw and local and regional governments across the country. This is not, and will not be, a division of Poland. Instead, it is a way by which the system compels us all to listen to each other despite our differences in axiology, ideology, and identity.

Poland's sovereignty is one. But no politician, nor any political faction that happened to do well in the last parliamentary election, should claim the right to be the sole advocate of this sovereignty. As Article 1 of our Constitution says, "The Republic of Poland shall be the common good of all its citizens." All voivodships should symmetrically[30] share the joys and burdens of participation in the common, unitary governance. And a set of smartly designed regional and national institutions should make the whole system work smoothly for ordinary citizens. The next chapter outlines some of those institutions.

Notes

1. Cezary Łazarkiewicz, "Zapateralski," *Polityka*, May 31, 2008.
2. Paweł Strawiński, "Partia Razem. Polska Syriza?," *ONET.pl*, Oct. 21, 2015.
3. Piotr Lisiewicz, "Polski Macron, czyli najbardziej przebiegła operacja ubekistanu," *Gazeta Polska*, Dec. 2, 2020.
4. Richard S. Katz and Peter Mair, "Changing Models of Party Organization and Party Democracy: The Emergence of the Cartel Party," *Party Politics* 1, no. 1 (1995): 360–362; Peter

Mair, *Ruling the Void: The Hollowing of Western Democracy* (Verso Books, 2013); Stefano Bartolini, *Restructuring Europe: Centre Formation, System Building, and Political Structuring between the Nation State and the European Union* (Oxford University Press, 2005).

5. Wojciech Sadurski, "On the Relative Irrelevance of Constitutional Design: Lessons from Poland," *Sydney Law School Research Paper*, no. 19/34 (2019); Andrea L.P. Pirro and Ben Stanley, "Forging, Bending, and Breaking: Enacting the "Illiberal Playbook" in Hungary and Poland," *Perspectives on Politics* 20, no. 1 (2022): 86–101; Marta Bucholc, "Commemorative Lawmaking: Memory Frames of the Democratic Backsliding in Poland after 2015," *Hague Journal on the Rule of Law* 11, no. 1 (2019): 85–110; Laurent Pech and Kim Lane Scheppele, "Illiberalism Within: Rule of Law Backsliding in the EU," *Cambridge Yearbook of European Legal Studies* 19: 3–47; Anna Grzymała-Busse, "How Populists Rule: The Consequences for Democratic Governance," *Polity* 51, no. 4: 707–717. (2019); Stanley Bill and Ben Stanley, *Good Change: The Rise and Fall of Poland's Illiberal Revolution* (Stanford University Press, 2025).
6. Andrzej Chwalba and Krzysztof Zamorski, *The Polish-Lithuanian Commonwealth: History, Memory, Legacy* (Routledge, 2020).
7. Jerzy Lukowski, *The Partitions of Poland 1772, 1793, 1795* (Routledge, 2014).
8. Piotr S. Wandycz, *The Lands of Partitioned Poland, 1795–1918* (University of Washington Press, 1975), 44–150; Piotr Koryś, *Poland from Partitions to EU Accession: A Modern Economic History, 1772–2004* (Springer, 2018).
9. Nicole Dołowy-Rybińska and Maciej Mętrak, "Ideological Debates around the Script of Collateral Languages: The Case of Kashubian and Silesian in Poland," *Journal of Multilingual and Multicultural Development* (2023): 1–14; Luiza Bialasiewicz, "Upper Silesia: Rebirth of a Regional Identity in Poland," *Regional & Federal Studies* 12, no. 2 (2002).
10. Krzysztof Jasiewicz, ""The Past Is Never Dead". Identity, Class, and Voting Behavior in Contemporary Poland," *East European Politics and Societies* 23, no. 4 (2009): 491–508; Tomasz Zarycki, "The Electoral Geography of Poland: Between Stable Spatial Structures and Their Changing Interpretations," *Erdkunde* 69, no. 2 (2015): 107–124.
11. Mikołaj Cześnik and Mirosława Grabowska, "Popękane polskie społeczeństwo jako pole badawcze-dane, fakty, mity," *Przegląd Socjologiczny* 66, no. 3 (2017): 9–43; Tomasz Zarycki, "Politics in the Periphery: Political Cleavages in Poland Interpreted in Their Historical and International Context," *Europe-Asia Studies* 52, no. 5 (2000): 851–873.
12. Piotr Radkiewicz, "The Axiological Clash as a Key Determinant of Expanded and Destructive Political Conflict in Poland," *East European Politics and Societies* 31, no. 2 (2017): 382–401; Geoffrey Evans, "The Social Bases of Political Divisions in Post-Communist Eastern Europe," *Annual Review of Sociology* 32, no. 1 (2006): 245–270.
13. Kamil Marcinkiewicz and Ruth Dassonneville, "Do Religious Voters Support Populist Radical Right Parties? Opposite Effects in Western and East-Central Europe," *Party Politics* 28, no. 3 (2022): 444–456.
14. Anna Gwiazda, "Right-Wing Populism and Feminist Politics: The Case of Law and Justice in Poland," *International Political Science Review* 42, no. 5 (2021): 580–595.
15. Mirosław Kofta and Wiktor Soral, "Belief in the Round Table Conspiracy and Political Division in Poland," *Social Psychological Bulletin* 14, no. 4 (2019): 1–19 .
16. Mikołaj Herbst and Anna Wojciuk, "Common Legacy, Different Paths: The Transformation of Educational Systems in the Czech Republic, Slovakia, Hungary and Poland," *Compare: A Journal of Comparative and International Education* 47, no. 1: 118–132; Maciej Jakubowski, "Poland: Polish Education Reforms and Evidence from International Assessments," in *Improving a Country's Education: PISA 2018 Results in 10 Countries*, ed. Nuno Crato (Springer, 2021)
17. Annabelle Chapman, "Winter in Warsaw," *The Spectator*, Jul. 21, 2016.
18. Alicja Natkaniec, ""Hide Your Grandma's ID": Election Campaign Heats Up," *The Kraków Post*, Oct. 11, 2007.
19. Cédric Gouverneur, "Poland's Populist Revenge," *Le Monde Diplomatique*, March 2016.
20. Tusk, in particular, referred to elderly female PiS voters as "mohair berets": see Andrew Higgins, "Who Is Donald Tusk," *New York Times*, Dec. 12, 2023.
21. Christian Davies, "The Conspiracy Theorists Who Have Taken Over Poland," *The Guardian*, Feb. 16 2016.
22. To be specific, in order to give the Sejm and Senate the ability to work this issue out, especially when it comes to legislative powers, we would need to eliminate numerous provisions of the 1997 Constitution that restrict the regulation of numerous policy issues to national statutes. The amended basic law should accept the voivodship-level laws as a permissible source of legislation in most areas.

23. Pierre Rosanvallon, "Democratic Legitimacy: Impartiality, Reflexivity, *Proximity*" (Princeton University Press, 2011); Pierre Rosanvallon, *The Populist Century: History, Theory, Critique* (John Wiley & Sons, 2021). For the Polish context see Maciej A. Górecki and Adam Gendźwiłł, "Polity Size and Voter Turnout Revisited: Micro-Level Evidence from 14 Countries of Central and Eastern Europe," *Local Government Studies* 47, no. 1 (2021): 31–53; Maciej A. Górecki, Sławomir Bartnicki, and Maciej Alimowski, "Local Voting at Local Elections Revisited: 'Friends and Neighbors Voting' at Mayoral Elections in Rural Poland," *Political Geography* 94 (2022): 1–11.
24. Jennifer A. Yoder, "Decentralisation and Regionalisation after Communism: Administrative and Territorial Reform in Poland and the Czech Republic," *Europe-Asia Studies* 55, no. 2 (2003): 263–286.
25. Grzegorz Gorzelak, "Regional and Historic Dimensions of Local Government Performance in Poland," *Polish Sociological Review* 205, no. 1 (2019): 33–50.
26. See Uwe Puetter, *The European Council and the Council: New Intergovernmentalism and Institutional Change* (Oxford University Press, 2014).
27. Paweł Swianiewicz, "Poland: Rolling Back of the Decentralized System?" in *Handbook on Subnational Governments and Governance*, ed. Claudia N. Avellaneda and Ricardo A. Bello-Gómez (Edward Elgar Publishing, 2024).
28. See https://www.gov.pl/web/funds-regional-policy/poland-at-the-forefront-of-eu-countries-in-terms-of-investing-european-funds2.
29. Michael E. Porter, *The Competitive Advantage of Nations* (Free Press, 1990).
30. It is important to note that our proposal is based on a strictly symmetrical vertical power sharing. In fact, most IUS members are very strong opponents of asymmetrical decentralization in the form of special autonomy for individual regions or provinces. Literature acknowledges that asymmetrical decentralization "may be particularly centrifugal" John McGarry, "Asymmetry in Federations, Federacies and Unitary States," *Ethnopolitics* 6, no. 1 (2007): 105–116. We believe, however, that the risks of such arrangements are understated and not even fully understood. Selective autonomy is not only dangerous for national unity because it communicates that the region's government has a "special" responsibility for its people, one that is not shared by other regional governments, and that the state's central or federal government has less responsibility for this region's people than it has for the rest of its citizens. Id. From a game-theoretical perspective, the most important thing that the asymmetrical devolution communicates is that *ex parte* deals between a given region and the center are a distinct constitutional and political possibility. Once that principle is established, there is no escape from the cycle of escalating demands for more devolution. Since negotiating even more autonomy, without regard to the views of compatriots in other regions, has proven to be possible, local political entrepreneurs will make sure that centrifugal postulates stay on the public agenda. Central political actors will, likewise, be tempted by the always available option of trading national political support of the region's representatives for devolution of even more power. That dynamic makes asymmetrically decentralized arrangements inherently unstable and, in our view, much more fundamentally dissimilar to the strictly symmetrical decentralization than the literature on federalism and power-sharing is willing to acknowledge. See e.g. Dawn Walsh, *Territorial Self-Government as a Conflict Management Tool* (Palgrave, 2018).

2
Harmony by Choice

Agnieszka Chłoń-Domińczak, Jacek Giedrojć, and Anna Wojciuk

Strategic decentralization: the imaginary risks

Today, local and regional governments in Poland are responsible for carrying out socially significant tasks. And yet, our experience discussing the new constitutional settlement for Poland reveals a curious undercurrent of apprehension regarding granting regions significant new legislative powers. Behind this fear lies an intuitive conviction that transferring competences from the center down inherently increases the risk of drastically misguided policy outcomes. Our Polish critics love to create gut-wrenching hypotheticals. "If the provinces were allowed to regulate school curricula, what would we do if one of them abolished the teaching of mathematics?" "If Warsaw City Hall is in charge of the capital's imposing Grand Theater, what if it closes it down to make space for a gigantic fast-food restaurant?"

At the root of such arguments lies a limited understanding of the mechanisms of democratic governance. The essence of democracy is that citizens and their representatives can make even weighty political decisions. In other words, in a democracy, no one can actually "guarantee" that mathematics will not disappear from the curricula, or that a fast-food restaurant will not be opened in the Grand Theater. As far as mathematics is concerned, a minor statutory change would be needed—similar to those being made in one afternoon in our Sejm. As for a fast-food restaurant in the theater, the determination of the Minister of Culture would probably suffice.

The argument about the "risk" of decentralized legislation tacitly assumes, then, that regional democracy is, for some reason, more prone to extremes than the national government. Only, the facts do not support such a hypothesis. On the contrary: It is the logic of polarization guiding our national politics that leads to sudden and drastic political decisions. Lowering the retirement age at a time when we are living longer and longer, abolishing middle schools, allocating almost a tenth of the Polish state budget to the unconditional transfers for families under the "Family 500+" (and later 800+) program, or selling a significant part of

Agnieszka Chłoń-Domińczak, Jacek Giedrojć, and Anna Wojciuk, *Harmony by Choice* In: *Let's Agree on Poland*. Edited by: Maciej Kisilowski and Anna Wojciuk, Oxford University Press.
 DOI: 10.1093/oso/9780198979562.003.0003

a major oil company to capital linked to the Russian Federation[1] are just some examples of such decisions. Whether they support these particular policy choices or not, a careful observer of Polish politics must conclude that it would be difficult to find many examples of similarly bold, drastic policy changes initiated by our local governments in their existing areas of competence. We do not hear, for instance, of Polish cities where the local government has abolished public transportation. Neither do we hear about local governments blindly closing down publicly funded schools.

Furthermore, as our co-authors mention in Chapters 5 and 6, the proposed decentralization, especially of legislative powers, is coupled with the introduction of new tools of democratic control. The main check on regional legislation will be made by the proposed voivodship senates, each consisting of all mayors from a given province. No provincial resolution would enter into force without the approval of voivodship senators representing a majority of the population of a given region. In the previous chapter, we mentioned the proposal to strengthen local media by creating an independent nationwide fund to support it.

In addition, our proposed Model Voivodship Charter, which readers can find online at LetsAgreeonPoland.org, proposes special requirements for amending resolutions on the most important issues. Examples include the division of powers between municipalities, counties, and the voivodship governments; the municipal and county boundaries; and the rules of transparency and fairness binding subnational authorities. Changes to regional laws concerning such issues will involve a complex, four-stage process: a two-thirds majority vote of the full sejmik, the approval of voivodship senators representing two-thirds of the region's residents, the approval of the new *national* Senate of the voivodes, and the final approval of the province's residents expressed in an electronic referendum (about which more in Chapter 5). Even though the proposed procedure takes place mostly within provincial self-governing institutions, it still provides a far greater guarantee of stability than our national statutes or regulations.

Worth adding is that, according to this proposal, nothing needs to change from the citizen's point of view on "day zero." Even if the Sejm and the new Senate agree with the proposal to transfer certain legislative competence to the voivodships, the provisions of existing laws and regulations will become, by law, the initial regional laws in each of the provinces. Unlike the traumatic experience of many "comprehensive reforms" and "shock therapies" of Poland's post-1989 history, the proposed regulatory decentralization does not force any changes unless these changes are initiated by the regional communities themselves, either directly (through electronic referendum, which, as we explain in Chapter 5, we want to make a permanent fixture of Polish subnational democracy) or through their representatives in the sejmik and the voivodship senate.

Strategic decentralization: the real risks

All in all, fears about decentralization somehow decreasing legal security are unfounded. Which is not to say that our project carries no risks. Such "no-cost" reforms do not exist. In the remainder of this chapter, we will focus on three areas where problems can really occur. We will then present institutional proposals aimed at reducing these "side effects" of proposed reforms.

The first real danger is that of undue inconvenience to citizens and businesses flowing from the fact that regulations, taxes, and public services will begin to differ across the provinces. To be sure, such inconveniences should not be overstated. Millions of Poles have moved abroad in search of work, for instance. Polish children find themselves in educational systems that are completely different to that in our country, and taught in languages that are foreign to them. Any realistic differences in, say, school curricula between provinces will be incomparably less drastic than the differences experienced by our emigrants. The same is true of Polish entrepreneurs, who are already active throughout the kaleidoscope of the European Union's regulatory systems. With all that being said, the political system we are proposing still envisions strong coordination mechanisms ensuring that public policies delegated to regional governments do not unduly diverge nationally. A key role in this coordination system will be played by a new institution we propose: the College of the Voivodships. More about it in a moment.

Before that, let us spell out the second genuine risk of decentralization: that of exacerbated economic disparities between the provinces. Here, too, the perception of risk is overstated. Existing or potential cross-regional differences are, in particular, viewed almost exclusively from the perspective of productivity and income, expressed in GDP terms. Meanwhile, an important trend in development economics has been to take a broader view that incorporates various aspects of well-being.[2] As the chapters in Part II of this book make clear, the new social contract gives regional communities room to shape public policies that embody different models of the good life. The possible effects of these decisions, as measured by GDP, need not be regarded as a problem of this proposal, but rather can be seen as part of the diversity our project acknowledges. It is, incidentally, by no means obvious which of the "dream" provinces presented in Part II will develop best, even in the narrow sense of GDP. With all that being said, some types of economic disparities will be viewed unfavorably regardless of our political or ideological vantage points. Of particular importance here are public services that guarantee the broadly understood health and social security of all Poles. Here, our proposal calls for strong national solidarity mechanisms, which we will soon discuss in greater detail.

The final area we will address is the need for a robust system of monitoring the legality and effectiveness of the subnational governance. While fears that decentralization will increase the risk of irresponsible or illegal political decisions are unfounded, there is every reason to strive for appropriate checks that protect citizens from abuses of power. A better distribution of powers across different levels of government offers new tools that are not available in a centralized system. Our rejection of a federalist model of divided sovereignty gives us thebest of both worlds here: we can reap the benefits of greater decentralization without facing the risks of unchecked powers of regional governments.

What to decentralize

As we mentioned in the previous chapter, our proposal does not determine a fixed list of legislative and executive competencies to be transferred to the self-governing voivodships. The national Sejm and the new Senate of the voivodes will be well positioned to negotiate these issues in a normal political process. At this point, however, we should perhaps outline a tentative list of policy areas that many members of our Social Contract Incubator see as particularly well suited for decentralization. For, without spelling out what can and should be left for residents of a particular region to decide, a discussion of safeguards and coordination mechanisms might be rather theoretical.

Fortunately, the approximate list of issues and tasks that voivodships could easily take over flows rather naturally from the general philosophy behind the proposed new social contract. As we mentioned in the previous chapter, today, our central government is largely responsible for legislating on most tasks carried out by decentralized governments at various levels. What this proposal envisages is devolving—to the carefully prepared voivodship institutions—those legislative powers. If the local government is already in charge of running schools, why does it need a supervisor in Warsaw setting curricula? If it is local governments that provide most family support; run nurseries, kindergartens, and nursing homes; and manage municipal housing, why should social welfare legislation, or maybe even family law, come from Warsaw? Since it is the self-governing voivodships that implement regional development strategies (within the framework of EU programs), why should regulations on economic policy, agricultural policy, or labor law—which, after all, are tightly constrained by EU norms anyway—be debated in Poland's Sejm in Warsaw? Why shouldn't each province decide whether or not shops are open on Sundays?

The same goes for those areas where the competencies of the decentralized governments and the center currently overlap, leading to tension and unhealthy rivalry. The best example here is culture. The internationally publicized disputes between the Ministry of Culture and the local government of the City of Gdańsk over the European Solidarity Center[3] and the Museum of the Second World War[4] highlight the consequences of such an imprecise demarcation. On many issues of culture and history, Poles with conservative and progressive views will not find common ground. Transferring both cultural policy in the regulatory sphere and the management of specific cultural institutions to politically diverse local governments is the fairest approach to the protection of Polish cultural heritage—a heritage whose immanent feature is precisely the diversity of cultural sensitivities and outlooks on history.

Finally, decentralization should cover fields such as science and higher education, the management of state-owned enterprises (excluding those of strategic or military significance), forests, and other state assets. In those areas, the central government cannot boast an exceptional track record; political purges in state-owned enterprises have long aroused the indignation of the voters.[5] Despite numerous reforms, Polish science is still far from realizing the potential of our researchers. Furthermore, universities, research centers, and state-owned enterprises should support the aforementioned development strategies, which are designed and implemented at the regional level (within the framework of EU programs) rather than centrally. In a diverse country of forty million people, innovative development cannot be effectively managed top-down. Economic development takes place in so-called clusters—geographically concentrated areas where tight networks are formed.[6] In addition to private companies, it is precisely universities and state-owned enterprises that form the core nodes of such a network.

All in all, we believe that the introduction of the powerful Senate of the voivodes, combined with the general impetus for the conservative–progressive social contract, can conceivably lead to decentralization of significant central legislative and executive powers. Significant enough that much stronger mechanisms for coordinating the activities of our subnational governments would be needed than those that exist today. But coordination need not rely on hierarchy. Hierarchical subordination increases the risk of manipulation by politicians controlling central institutions. It encourages them to take advantage of their temporary dominant position. Under the current system, provinces and their residents can be harassed when they attempt to introduce solutions not to the liking of the central government.[7] In effect, citizens supporting the current national opposition feel as though their world is collapsing, and their vision of a good state and society is under threat. This dynamic fuels further social polarization.

The creation of effective institutions coordinating the activities of regional governments is an attempt to break free of this vicious circle. Of course, those institutions will not do away with differing hierarchies of values, dissimilar visions of a good society, or disparate interests. Likewise, it would be naïve to hope for there to be only angels in the regional authorities. That lies beyond the capacity of any political project. Our task is to construct a system that best serves the people despite these challenges.

College of cooperation

Our main proposed forum for such constructive cooperation would be an entirely new institution in Polish subnational government: the College of the Voivodships. Patterned after the Council of the European Union, the College—organized into thematic configurations—would be a meeting place for all regions' deputy voivodes responsible for a given area of public policy, such as education, infrastructure, or economic development. In each thematic configuration, the tasks of the College would be the same: first and foremost, to agree upon and enforce common standards of regulation and public services provided by voivodships, municipalities, counties, and cities with county rights across Poland.

The discerning reader will easily notice that the College of the Voivodships mirrors the structure of our proposed national Senate. Indeed, the Senate would be composed of the voivodes, while the College would be composed of deputy voivodes responsible for particular areas of public policy. In both the national Senate and the College, decisions should be taken by a majority of the represented population.

The College's thematic configurations would work out common standards that apply to all regions without being imposed by the central government. The College thus reconciles coordination with flexibility, making it possible to develop best practices in the various areas of public policy. How would the College's decisions become binding on the provinces? Three approaches, perhaps complementary to one another, may be considered. First, the laws introducing the proposed decentralization reform could establish the orders and technical standards passed by the teams of the College of the Voivodships as a new category of local law. Put differently, the College could be granted powers to issue "nationwide local laws"—standards binding on all voivodships within the policy areas previously decentralized by the national Sejm and Senate.[8]

The second option would be to create a mechanism whereby the College of the Voivodships would put forward proposals for common standards, which would then be passed by central government as statutes or regulations. Such a solution would mean a lesser degree of decentralization of legislative powers and would raise concerns that the ruling parliamentary majority in Warsaw might use its position to support proposals for standards in line with its own ideology.

Third, the soft elements should not be forgotten. In addition to formal legislation, the College of the Voivodships can effectively coordinate regional solutions through recommendations and good practices. Public policy research indicates that such instruments are sometimes as effective as "hard" legislation, especially in the context of multilevel governance.[9]

To illustrate how the College would work in practice, let us return to the example of educational policy. As mentioned before, Polish conservatives have consistently pressed for the nationwide compulsory curriculum to include more literary works that demonstrate and promote patriotic values. The progressive side, on the other hand, wants more cosmopolitan themes and those critical of national myths. There is a similar battle over the teaching of history and civic education. With great fanfare, the recent PiS government introduced the mandatory *History and the Present* course into the core curriculum for secondary schools as the basis for national and patriotic education. In contrast, the current center-left coalition replaced the course with civic education.

In the College, deputy voivodes for education from progressive Pomerania and conservative Podlasie will not necessarily agree on those thorny issues. Indeed, it will not be in their political interest to convince each other. Like the "thematic" ministers in various configurations of the Council of the European Union, the deputy voivodes will focus primarily on solving pragmatic problems of educational policy coordination. The deputy voivode of Podlasie will not want to see the regional media cover problems of Podlasie children whose parents moved to West Pomerania for work.

Similar solutions can be applied to other educational policy controversies. Middle schools or no middle schools? School age at 6 or 7? Under the new social contract, it would be enough for a national statute to guarantee twelve years of total general education (there seems to be no dispute here among Poles), and for the education policy configuration of the College to establish common criteria for high school graduation exams throughout Poland. For such an outcome to emerge, we do not need to assume that politicians sitting on the College would be angels. Coordination will be the result not of altruism, but of pragmatic calculation. The effect may sometimes be surprising to Poles accustomed to centralism and uniformity: many issues that we believe "must" be the same throughout Poland can be regulated in different ways, without tragic consequences.

Critical to the College's overall effectiveness will be the provision of adequate expert support to each thematic configuration. Respected experts can help regional policymakers identify areas where coordination is necessary—and where it is just a covert way of seeking an ideological advantage by one side of our Polish political disputants. It is common for decentralized countries to have institutions that provide regional governments with subject-matter expertise. In Germany, a good example is the Standing Conference of the Ministers of Education of the Länder (Ständigen Konferenz der Kultusminister der Länder in der Bundesrepublik Deutschland), known by its abbreviated German name "KMK."

Under the proposed new social contract, we suggest creating a strong, expert Office of the College of the Voivodships, similar to the Office of the Committee on European Integration that, two decades ago, so successfully guided Poland through the arduous process of EU accession. The College's Office will inherit a cadre of experienced civil servants from central ministries whose competencies will be transferred to voivodship governments. Since, as we mentioned earlier, the regulatory status quo will become the starting point of all regional laws on the first day after our reform, it will make sense for officials of the current ministries of education, culture, science, economy, and agriculture to become the expert base counseling the College. To be sure, we do not mean all the officials in the ministries just mentioned. Officials dealing with non-decentralized issues, especially related to cooperation within the European Union, would be integrated into the new strong and prestigious national ministries that Maciej Kisilowski and Wojciech Przybylski propose in Chapter 4.

The College's experts would support the empowered regional governments in three distinct ways. The first is strengthening and developing the institutions of the subnational governments as they deal with new responsibilities. This will include wise counsel on matters of effective administration, local and regional public finance, and professional management of new assets, including the state-owned enterprises and state forests transferred to the provinces. The second direction concerns economic development and competitiveness strategies. Here we would talk primarily about economic policy, construction and urban planning, labor, rural development, tourism, science, and higher education. And finally, the College's experts should support local and regional public services. This primarily involves managing cross-regional policy coordination in education, culture, family, sport, and support for the disabled.

Close Cooperation

Moderated by experienced experts, the College of the Voivodships would become a powerful forum for nationwide coordination of decentralized public policies. But it is not the only institution we envision to incentivize cross-regional cooperation and harmony. A willing group of voivodships with converging interests or ideological preferences will have easy ways to cooperate even more closely.

This is of particular importance in the context of the discussion regarding the map of Polish voivodships. Even before our democratic transition, a notable tension had simmered between the ambition of many territories to be recognized as separate voivodships and the opinion of experts who had long argued for large and strong provinces as anchors of robust economic development. In 1975, the communist government replaced the country's seventeen provinces with as many as forty-nine voivodships! The move was widely viewed as a somewhat desperate attempt by the increasingly unpopular authoritarians to score popularity points with inhabitants of mid-sized Polish towns which, overnight, attained the prestigious status of a regional capital. After 1989, a strong expert consensus maintained that the communist shenanigans must be reversed. The 1998 reform that introduced democratically elected self-government at the regional level (while keeping voivodes centrally appointed) also proposed a radical reduction of the number of regions, to fourteen. Numerous protests broke out; in three cases, then-President

Aleksander Kwaśniewski lent his support and threatened to veto the reforms. In a compromise, the current list of sixteen regions emerged. But proponents of the larger number of regions have never been fully silenced. In 2020, a leading daily reported that PiS was considering reintroducing forty-nine voivodships.[10]

It is clear that the main goal of the experts advocating a small number of regions was in fact achieved. As previously mentioned, our self-governing voivodships are de facto the main units for planning and implementing economic strategies. Poland's provinces are significantly larger than regions in Europe, referred to in EU classification as "NUTS-2." While voivodships have an average population exceeding 2.3 million, the average region in Europe has only 1.8 million. In 2018, Poland's largest province was even split into two developmental units for the purpose of EU classification, while staying a single administrative unit from the standpoint of domestic law.

The constitutional proposal outlined in this book introduces an additional dimension to these considerations. If the map of our regions remains unchanged, then our proposed national Senate of the Voivodes will be a very small council of sixteen members, as compared to the current chamber of 100. Proponents, among the authors of this publication, of retaining the current map of provinces will probably point out that such a slimmed-down national Senate would not be an international anomaly. Of the sixty-seven countries with a bicameral parliament today, twenty-seven of them have no more than nineteen members in their senates.[11]

Nevertheless, some of the authors of this book believe that the advantages of maintaining the current, small number of voivodships are overestimated, while the social benefits of granting certain cities provincial capital status are considerable. Given that an important goal of the new social contract is to better align public policies with the preferences of large groups of Poles, it would be particularly worthwhile to consider the creation of urban voivodships out of Poland's largest cities—such as Warsaw and Cracow. Germany has successfully implemented this approach for Berlin, Hamburg, and Bremen, and Austria has done so for Vienna. For the powerful mayors of Warsaw and Cracow,[12] such a system would also provide them a seat in the new national Senate.

The key to initiating constructive debate about the voivodship map, without jeopardizing the unquestioned developmental achievements of the current voivodships, is to separate the discussion on, respectively, political-administrative and developmental units. Our proposal for addressing this issue—and strengthening interprovincial coordination in general—is to establish the institution of Close Cooperation among willing voivodships. Close Cooperation of two or more provinces will be established to holistically and continuously manage a specific area of regional government affairs. Matters such as economic development, agriculture, science, and higher education would be obvious candidates for such cooperation.

Close Cooperation would be especially needed between cities with provincial rights (Warsaw, Cracow, and potentially others) and the surrounding provinces. But Close Cooperation could come in handy even with the current map of sixteen voivodships. For instance, if the area of fisheries and water management is transferred to the regional governments, the provinces along the Oder River—Silesia, Opole, Lower Silesia, Lubusz and West Pomerania—may decide to have these matters handled, under Close Cooperation, by a joint deputy voivode. This would make it easier to manage cross-regional crises, such as the environmental disaster in 2022 when, due to pollution and high temperatures, hundreds of tons of dead fish were removed from the river.[13]

A decision to enter into Close Cooperation would mean the integration of both legislative and executive powers across an entire policy area. On the legislative side, we recommend the introduction of a special type of local law—inter-voivodship resolutions—ranked in the proposed constitutional hierarchy between ordinary voivodship resolutions and the earlier-mentioned standards of the College of the Voivodships. Inter-voivodship resolutions would be passed at the combined sessions of the sejmiks and voivodship senates of the regions that are part of the Close Cooperation. All the civic control mechanisms described in Chapter 5 would also be available for inter-voivodship resolutions. In particular, an electronic inter-voivodship referendum could be held on important issues, with the principle of a majority being required in all provinces that are party to the Close Cooperation.

On the executive side, we propose that the policy area covered by Close Cooperation should be headed by a joint deputy voivode sitting simultaneously on the boards of all participating voivodships. This deputy voivode would have a joint office responsible for the policy area in question. They would also represent all provinces participating in the Close Cooperation in the relevant configuration of the College of the Voivodships.

Diversity and security

Just as important as the institutions of policy coordination will be mechanisms to ensure social cohesion across our country. These include a uniform social security system, including pension, disability, and health insurance. The need to maintain these existing programs is obvious due to the significant disparities in the size and age structure of the population living in each municipality, county, or province. Data from the recent census showed very clearly the growth of these disparities. A significant population loss is evident in as many as 75 percent of Polish municipalities. This is particularly true in peripheral areas, especially in eastern parts of the country. On the other hand, an increase in population is visible in the vicinity of the largest cities, which attract residents due to their attractive labor markets, among other reasons.

Fortunately, there does not seem to be much political appetite in Poland to leave regions inhabited by the elderly, people in need of care, to fend for themselves. Regardless of our political persuasion, helping the vulnerable, and especially respecting our seniors, is a universally recognized value in Polish culture. Whatever our differences may be, we are all citizens of the same country, and this common identity compels us to act in solidarity.

From an economic point of view, maintaining a nationwide social insurance system is also a very effective means of redistribution. This is because redistribution through social insurance targets those who really need help: the sick, the elderly, and those with disabilities. It is also a redistribution that benefits everyone by creating the overall national safety net.[14]

In addition to the substantive arguments, symbolism is important. Health and social insurance programs are extremely costly, accounting for almost 19 percent of Poland's GDP. Yet their importance in our civic consciousness and public discourse is disproportionately meager. We mainly hear about the social security funds when their shortcomings and deficiencies are highlighted[15]—deficiencies which, to be sure, can and should be remedied.

The key reason for the disastrous "brand" of social and health insurance programs is that, as policy issues, they stand no chance in competition with economically and socially much less important, but politically much more appetizing, topics. It is plainly more attractive to inflame public sentiment by tinkering with school curricula, erecting monuments, or taking over museums than by undertaking deep reforms of the health care system. One way of viewing the systemic reform proposed in this book is that we aim to remove these divisive (and appetizing) topics from national public debate. We take away the political toys, of sorts, or excuses for "indefinitely postponing" the key challenges facing Poland.

In Chapter 4, our co-authors outline a more comprehensive vision for building the new prestige, "brand," and ethos of strategic issues retained by Poland's central government after the proposed reforms. This prestige should, in our view, definitely cover the national social and health insurance. Our Social Insurance Institution, known by its Polish acronym ZUS, or the National Health Fund, like the National Health Service in the UK, should become components of an important societal glue, the country's national identity.[16]

In line with this overall vision, the main source of financing for the National Health Fund should remain the individual health contributions,[17] which can be supplemented by programs from the national budget financing rare and expensive treatments as well as provincial and local health programs. Local and regional governments should respond to specific needs of their population. A good example is reproductive health programs, including support for in-vitro procedures, which depend on the preferences and views of regional communities. Another example is care for the elderly, especially in those regions where the proportion of elderly people is much higher than average.[18] Financial resources naturally play a key role in the expansion of provincial health programs. This is why the transfer of personal and corporate income taxes to local governments, described in Chapter 3 by Maciej Bukowski, Mikołaj Herbst, and Tomasz Kaczor, will be so important.

Decentralization should also be used to improve the efficiency of health care delivery throughout the country. Indeed, leaving nationwide health insurance in place does not mean that all health care must be centrally managed from Warsaw. Such centralization is reasonable for a certain number of rare or expensive treatments. It does not make sense to organize highly specialized teams for, say, heart transplants separately in each voivodship. In other matters, while the health *insurance* remains national, most decisions on the organization of health care *delivery* can well be transferred to voivodships. This includes, for instance, the ways in which primary health care is organized, including the GP network, as well as the possibility for the sejmiks and the voivodship senates to tailor the basket of treatments covered by the national insurance in a given province. Those decisions must, of course, be made in the context of the previously mentioned coordination instruments. The College of Voivodships should certainly include a health policy configuration, which would work closely with the national minister responsible for the health insurance system, diffusing good practices and mutual learning among the provinces. This is particularly important because, in the health care area, even the world's most developed countries are still looking for new solutions and ways to deal with civilizational and demographic challenges. There are no easy or obvious answers to many of Poland's health care problems. It would therefore be beneficial if voivodships could, on a smaller scale, experiment with new organizational concepts and, if necessary, correct mistakes by learning from others' experiences.

Another pillar of the proposed national structure of social cohesion will be the existing social security system, embracing pensions, sickness and maternity benefits, work injury benefits, and others. Like health insurance, we strongly see the need to keep the social insurance as a national program.[19] But, like with healthcare, we see a lot of potential for using proposed multilevel governance to mitigate political battles that have surrounded our pension system.

Like many other countries, Poland has been particularly shaken by disputes over the legal pensionable age.[20] This was raised during the final years of liberal Civic Platform government, only for the reform to be reversed by PiS in 2017. Nevertheless, increasing the workforce participation of seniors was one of the milestones in the post-COVID Recovery and Resilience Facility negotiated by the Polish government with the European Commission. To break this impasse, we propose to delegate to sejmiks and voivodship senates the authority to raise the retirement age in a given region above the national minimum. This would be particularly justified in provinces where there is high demand for labor, and where the labor market structure would allow people to remain active for longer. Given that the Polish public pension system has, for a quarter century now, been organized as the so-called defined contribution scheme, a nationwide pension insurance can easily coexist with a varied provincial retirement age. The existing benefit formulas, based on fair actuarial tables, would—like today—calculate the pension amount based on the beneficiary's retirement age.[21]

Local governments can also decide on how funds currently used to pay the thirteenth and fourteenth pensions, introduced by the PiS government and financed from the national budget, are spent. This issue would be an ideal candidate for a decision made by the voivodship community in an electronic referendum. The residents themselves would be able to choose whether to continue the additional benefits for pensioners, or to support other social groups, such as large families or people with disabilities.

Democratic coopetition

We have already discussed our institutional responses to two of the three challenges posed by decentralized unitary constitutional model: the issue of coordinating decentralized policies and that of raising the profile and effectiveness of nationwide safety net programs. Likewise, a more even distribution of governmental powers between the municipal, provincial, and national levels creates new instruments and incentives to improve the effectiveness and quality of regulations and public services provided to citizens.

The key word here is "coopetition," a term gaining traction in management science, which combines the logic of cooperation and competition.[22] We demonstrated earlier how the College of the Voivodships has the potential to become an efficient mechanism for coordination and cooperation between provinces—setting standards, exchanging good practices, and diffusing knowledge. We would like to use the same institution to unleash the mechanisms of healthy competition among the deputy voivodes responsible for specific areas of public affairs, encouraging them to keep each other in check through constructive oversight.

As the law stands today, there are very few mechanisms to incentivize local and regional governments to make meaningful improvements in their performance. The 1997 Constitution, which (in Article 15(1)) stipulates that "[t]he territorial system of the Republic of Poland shall ensure the decentralization of public power," significantly limits the scope of oversight over decentralized governments' activities. Despite the pronounced unitary character of the country, Article 171(1) of the Constitution restricts oversight over subnational governments to issues of legality only. In a bizarre twist, however, ordinary laws interpret this "legal oversight" so broadly that many experts argue it is difficult to distinguish it from substantive control.

The most glaring example of a departure from the constitutional model of legal oversight is regulations on receivership. Current laws give the Prime Minister an exclusive power to appoint a governing commissioner "in the event of prolonged inefficiency in the performance of public tasks by a municipality, county or province, which displays no promise for improvement." The commissioner's powers are enormous: they take over the entirety of competencies of both the legislative and executive branches of a given subnational government. The rationale for imposing receivership clearly goes beyond the constitutional concept of legal oversight. At the same time, it is clear that in some cases administrative intervention is necessary.

In 2018, for instance, Ostrowice—a municipality with a population of 2,500—was nearly 10 million euro in debt. Prime Minister Beata Szydło appointed a commissioner. The decision did not cause much controversy. However, threats to appoint a commissioner in the major city of Łódź, with a population of nearly 700,000 residents, met with quite a different reception. That very same year, as Ostrowice was facing its crisis, Hanna Zdanowska, the highly popular Łódź mayor from the Civic Platform (then in the opposition to PiS's national government) announced her intention to run for re-election. In response, PiS threatened to bring in a commissioner, citing the mayor's criminal conviction in a private matter. "PiS threatens that a vote for Zdanowska will be wasted," the Polish edition of *Newsweek* concluded. Despite these warnings, Zdanowska won more than 70 percent of the vote, and the PiS government ultimately did not dare to use the "nuclear option."

Under our proposal, the oversight by the central government will, in accordance with the constitutional intention, be limited strictly to issues of legality. On the other hand, the objectively required substantive oversight would be located within the system of decentralized government, specifically in the College of the Voivodships. In an extreme situation, it would be the College that would decide on the appointment of a governing commissioner. In the case of voivodships, such a commissioner would not replace the entire regional government, but only the specific deputy voivode responsible for the underperforming area of public affairs. Such a solution would improve the proportionality of the already drastic decision to appoint a commissioner.

Before the College exercises the last-resort option, it will have a number of softer tools at its disposal—tools that the Prime Minister lacks today. The College's thematic configurations will be able, for instance, to organize regular peer reviews in each province. The prospect of such a review will motivate deputy voivodes not only through the specter of sanctions, but also out of concern for their reputation and standing in the College. In short: most people don't like having fingers pointed at them.

Unlike the Prime Minister, who today basically has a binary choice—either appoint a commissioner or take no action—the College will be able, if problems are identified, to introduce interim sanctions: issue recommendations to the deputy voivode, or appoint advisors to support the provincial government when actions in a particular area of public policy have been ineffective for a long time.

The system of peer oversight can, of course, raise questions. What if the College configurations develop into crony "mutual admiration societies," with no one wanting to step on another's toes? To prevent such a risk, the peer oversight system will be supplemented by widely used rankings. And as we know, every ranking has the brutal property that someone must be at the bottom. It will not be possible for failures to be swept under the rug.

Rankings

Today, rankings are ubiquitous. We encounter them when we shop—and we leave ratings and comments on products or services we use. We rate our experiences in restaurants or hotels. When using a cab, we give a rating to the driver, and they rate us. In the academic world, numerous rankings show how strong a given university or program is. So why not use this tool for public services as well?

Rankings have the advantage of grabbing attention and boosting interest in public affairs. They would prompt residents and voivodes in poorly rated regions to think about why this is so. The desire to improve one's position is motivating, as is the dread of finding oneself at the bottom. Not being the best does not mean giving up. After all, there is also competition lower down the table, between local governments with similar characteristics, facing similar problems and challenges. A snapshot picture that a rating provides can activate local civil society and fuel the development of municipal or local movements. Rankings can therefore improve the quality of our democracy.

Since we want the College of the Voivodships to be responsible for regulating the system of rankings, within clear statutory mandates, their content (what would be measured how, and how to integrate partial metrics into more comprehensive ones) would be agreed upon among equal partners rather than imposed by the central authority. Once again, it would be the regional governments that would monitor one another.

What will the local and regional government rankings be about, and what metrics will they be based on? Three groups of metrics can be distinguished: objective metrics of the effectiveness and efficiency of governmental outputs; metrics related to residents' subjective assessments; and metrics of administrative capacity and competence. Objective metrics must relate to those aspects of public services that are broadly viewed as desirable and valuable by both conservative and progressive regions. These types of ratings can therefore apply to issues such as waiting time for an appointment with a medical specialist, or the math skills of the 12-year-old, but not to issues such as access to IVF or the results of religious instruction in schools.

Metrics should be chosen to enable a fair comparison of different local government units. Fortunately, there is no need to reinvent the wheel here. The number of public housing units, the density of roads, or results of the PISA survey on the level of education could constitute such metrics.[23] Many others are used in the OECD *Government at a Glance* reports.[24] These biannual analyses contain dozens of ready-made and proven metrics based on sound methodological foundations.[25]

A broader range of policies and services can be assessed through rankings in which residents express their subjective opinions. We propose that residents would be able to rate the quality of public services and their experience with subnational administration through the new Local and Regional Government Quality Assessment System for Laws and Public Services. Specifically, people would rate their satisfaction with governmental responsiveness, courtesy, completeness and clarity of information, and openness to citizens' suggestions. Ratings, expressed in the form of stars, would be anonymous and public, while descriptive comments would be provided to the management of the authority in question.

The third type of measures and rankings pertains not to outcomes of government policies and programs, but to capabilities that all government units need. Examples include anti-corruption measures, sound human resource management, budgeting, and procurement practices.

The partial rankings will be integrated into the National Ranking of Public Services, which will be compiled annually by the earlier-mentioned non-political Office of the College of the Voivodships, and will report comprehensively on the quality of public services provided by specific local and regional governments. Each local and regional government will have to report its overall ranking position in a prominent place on its main website.

In addition to fostering healthy competition, the ranking will also have a direct impact on local and regional politicians. Since Poland introduced the direct elections of mayors (but not the voivodship marshals, who are elected by sejmiks) in 2002, there has been recurring discussion over the necessity to impose term limits on mayors. Such sentiments are often expressed by experts and activists critical of liberal mayors of Poland's biggest cities, who sometimes hold their office for decades. Once again, our proposal tries to creatively bridge the conservative and progressive perspectives. We suggest that neither the (democratically elected) voivodes nor mayors should be allowed to run for re-election if the government they lead experiences a significant drop in the National Ranking of Public Services. Where the voivodes are concerned, a fall of 4 positions would disqualify them from seeking re-election, and in the case of mayors a similar effect would result from a fall of 150 positions.

The new vision for the presidency

Last but certainly not least, we need a new vision for organizing the review of legality of our local and regional governmental actions and the constitutionality of the vastly expanded subnational enactments. Today, both executive and legislative functions of municipal, county, and voivodship governments are carefully monitored by a full-time supervisor residing in each region: the voivode appointed by and reporting to the Prime Minister. The voivode stands in a notable opposition both to the marshal of the voivodship—the chief executive of the regional self-government—and, implicitly, to powerful mayors of the largest cities.

As we already mentioned in the previous chapter, eliminating the bizarre "two-head" leadership of Polish regions, and replacing it with strong popularly accountable voivodes who also sit on the new national Senate, is a central aspect of this constitutional proposal. But, in line with our intention to keep Poland a unitary state, we do not want to do away with the involvement of the national executive in the legal oversight over the subnational governments.

We say "involvement," because it is important to understand that, even today, the Prime Minister and his appointees execute their oversight functions under strict control of the judiciary. While a voivode can temporarily stay a local or regional decision it deems illegal, the final say always belongs to Poland's administrative courts. The same goes for subnational enactments: while, in the case of national statutes, the constitutional review belongs to the Constitutional Tribunal, for acts of local law the review of their consistency with the Constitution, EU and other international law, as well as national legislation is the job of administrative courts.[26] Our proposal for transferring a significant portion of legislative authority from the Sejm and Senate to the regional sejmiks and new voivodship senates will therefore have a side effect of increasing the review powers of administrative courts and decreasing those of the Constitutional Tribunal.[27] This strikes us as fortunate: as even our conservative co-authors admit in Chapter 6 of this volume, the Constitutional Tribunal is a deeply troubled institution at the epicenter of our political and constitutional disputes.[28] The administrative courts, by contrast, have emerged relatively unscathed from the decade of the Polish–Polish battles over the rule of law.

The question of who should "inherit" the powers held by the current voivodes is thereby not about choosing an absolute monarch who single-handedly nullifies decisions of democratically elected municipalities and regions—but about a guardian of legality who would execute their functions under the supervision of impartial administrative courts. Since, currently, the voivodes report directly to the Prime Minister, who also holds a number of independent supervisory functions over subnational units, including the above-mentioned power to appoint a commissioner in case of receivership, it would perhaps be natural to concentrate the legal oversight in the Prime Minister's office. We do not support this approach, however. Instead, our proposal is to assign the responsibility for overseeing the legality of our decentralized governance to the popularly elected President of the Republic.

The story of the relatively strong Polish presidency, attached to an otherwise conventional parliamentary system, is another aspect of the never-ending drama of the Polish political wars.[29] The 1997 Constitution vaguely refers to presidential powers in areas such as defense or foreign policy, while also claiming that those fields are the responsibility of the Cabinet and the Prime Minister. In effect, between 2023 and 2025 Poland lacked several dozen ambassadors, including in some key countries, because of the lack of consensus between the center-left Cabinet of Donald Tusk and the conservative President Andrzej Duda.

Our proposal reimagines the mandate of the Polish President. Instead of competing with the Cabinet for international visibility, we want the President to focus on the solemn task of acting as the guarantor of Poland's unitary nature by taking over from the Prime Minister (and the voivodes he currently appoints) the powers of legal oversight over the decentralized governments. This proposal is very much in line with the 1997 Constitution's vision of the President as a "guarantor of the continuity of State authority" who "shall ensure observance of the Constitution" (Article 126). The President is equipped with a unique political mandate obtained by popular election. With a five-year term, and only one potential re-election, the President can and should act as an arbiter rather than a "mere" political player. The Prime Minister, by contrast, is a much less compelling neutral referee of decentralized democracy. Indeed, the Prime Minister and the Cabinet are, to some extent, "rivals" of regional government officials, especially those representing the current opposition.

We see the President's oversight powers broadly. They would be able not only to refer voivodship legislation and decisions to an administrative court; in cases flagrantly detrimental to territorial integrity or national security, they would declare a provision invalid before referring it for consideration. In the event of gross and repeated violations of the Constitution, international agreements, or statutes by a sejmik, the President would have the right to shorten its term. In a situation where the actions of a sejmik threaten state security and constitutional order, the President's decision could have immediate effect. They could also dismiss a voivode (now democratically accountable and not appointed by the Prime Minister), as well as deputy voivodes or other members of the provincial Board for flagrantly and repeatedly violating the Constitution or laws.

Why such sweeping powers? On the one hand, we are convinced that the political cost of using them will reduce the risk of excessive political intervention in the activities of regional governments. Paradoxically, due to the fact that these powers are all "nuclear options," their use will be limited by the likes of public pressure and media attention. On the other hand, the President's broad scope of legal oversight is meant to reassure Poles who still fear the consequences of decentralization, especially to regional governments. Poland, for historical reasons, does not have a separatist tradition similar to those in decentralized countries such as Spain (Catalonia) or the UK (Scotland), or in centralized countries such as Turkey (Kurdistan) or France (Corsica). The risk of sejmiks and voivodship senates contemplating blatantly illegal actions is very small. But if that is the case, then there is no harm in equipping the President with powerful measures that would nip such highly unlikely moves in the bud.

Pillars of harmony

Our intention in this chapter was to present the institutions of the new social contract that will ensure harmonious coexistence and development within a diverse state. We have presented a comprehensive institutional picture based on three pillars. At the center stands our new College of the Voivodships, which will gather deputy voivodes in thematic configurations. This will be a place to develop common standards, a forum to learn from each other and diffuse best practices, and an institution for peer oversight of effectiveness.

The second pillar will be the maintenance and strengthening of a national health and social insurance systems. These systems provide intergenerational solidarity as well as solidarity between provinces and between different social classes. Moreover, they are crucial to maintaining social cohesion. In the post-Polish–Polish-war period under our new constitutional settlement, we see them as important components of our joint Polish national identity.

The final pillar comprises instruments ensuring the effectiveness and legality of the decentralized governance. An important constitutional change here will be granting substantial powers of legal oversight over regional governments to the Polish President. These broad powers align with the logic of a decentralized unitary state, in which sovereignty is not divided between the center and the territories. But our proposal also includes "lighter" tools, such as rankings and peer pressure, that would nudge subnational governments in constructive directions.

Notes

1. Marta Wilczek, "Polish State Oil Giant Sells Assets to Saudi Aramco and Hungary's MOL ahead of Merger," *Notes from Poland*, 2022, https://notesfrompoland.com/2022/01/12/polish-state-oil-giant-sells-assets-to-saudi-aramco-and-hungarys-mol-ahead-of-merger/.
2. For a classic statement see Amartya Sen, *Development as Freedom* (Alfred A. Knopf, 1999).
3. Andrew Higgins, "Poles Tussle Over an Icon of Their Past, With an Eye on the Future," *New York Times*, Jul. 28, 2021.
4. Rachel Donadio and Joanna Berendt, "Poland's World War II Museum Is Imperiled," *New York Times*, Jan. 24, 2017.
5. "Poland's State-owned Giants Cope with Unprecedented Turnover," *The Economist*, Dec. 1, 2018.
6. Michael E. Porter, *The Competitive Advantage of Nations* (Free Press, 1990). Paul Krugman, *Geography and Trade* (MIT Press, 1992); Ren Lu et al., "A Literature Review of Cluster Theory: Are Relations among Clusters Important?" *Journal of Economic Surveys* 32, no. 4 (2018): 1201–1220; Ren Lu and Torger Reve, "Relations among Clusters," *European Planning Studies* 23, no. 4 (2015): 828–845.
7. <<<REFO:BK>>>Łukasz Wiktor Olejnik and Marcin Grygo, *Dotacje dla swoich? Analiza rządowych dotacji inwestycyjnych dla samorządów w latach 2019–2023*, Instytut Finansów Publicznych (2024)<<<REFC>>>.

8. We leave aside whether the introduction of such "nationwide local laws" can be viewed as consistent with the definition of local laws prescribed by Article 87(2) of the Polish Constitution. The latter's amendment would anyway be needed, if only for the introduction of the national Senate of the voivodes.
9. A good review of the literature, in the EU context, is provided by Miriam Hartlapp, "Soft Law Implementation in the EU Multilevel System: Legitimacy and Governance Efficiency Revisited," in *Configurations, Dynamics and Mechanisms of Multilevel Governance*, ed. Nathalie Behnke, Jörg Broschek, and Jared Sonnicksen (Cham: Springer International Publishing, 2019).
10. <<<REFO:JART>>>Michał Kolanko, "PiS szykuje gorącą jesień," *Rzeczpospolita*, Jul. 19, 2020<<<REFC>>>. The discussion about optimal number of regional units is also present in literature on federalism: see e.g. <<<REFO:JART>>>Steven G. Calabresi, "Does Institutional Design Make a Difference," *Northwestern University Law Review* 109, no. 3 (2014): 577–600 <<<REFC>>>.
11. https://www.senat.fr/senatsdumonde/forumdessenats/senats_secondeschambresmonde/english/english-synthese.html
12. Adam Gendźwiłł and Tomasz Żółtak, "How Single-member Districts Are Reinforcing Local Independents and Strengthening Mayors: On the Electoral Reform in Polish Local Government," *Local Government Studies* 43, no. 1 (2017): 101–131.
13. Jennifer Collins, "Could a Mass Fish Die-off in the Oder River Happen Again?" *Deutsche Welle*, Jun. 6, 2023.
14. Nicholas Barr, *Economics of the Welfare State* (Oxford University Press, 2020).
15. European Commission, Directorate-General for Economic and Social Affairs (2024), 2024 Ageing Report. Economic and Budgetary Projections for the EU Member States (2022–2070).
16. Richard Johnston et al., "National Identity and Support for the Welfare State," *Canadian Journal of Political Science* 43, no. 2 (2010): 349–377.
17. Lycourgos Liaropoulos and Ilias Goranitis, "Health Care Financing and the Sustainability of Health Systems," *International Journal for Equity in Health* 14 (2015): 1–4.
18. Frank Bönker, Michael Hill, and Anna Marzanati, "Towards Marketization and Centralization? The Changing Role of Local Government in Long-Term Care in England, France, Germany and Italy," in Hellmut Wollmann and Gérard Marcou *The Provision of Public Services in Europe* (Edward Elgar Publishing, 2010).
19. Peter A. Diamond, *The Economics of Social Security Reform* (National Bureau of Economic Research Cambridge, 1998).
20. Agnieszka Chłoń-Domińczak, Paweł Strzelecki, and Wojciech Łątkowski, "Pension Reforms or Consequences of the Economic Crisis? Measuring the Changes of Pension Incomes in Selected EU Countries using APC Approach," *The Journal of the Economics of Ageing* 17 (2020): 100–131; Marek Szczepański et al., "Poland: A Pension System under Constant (Re)Construction," in James Kolaczkowski, Michelle Maher, Yves Stevens, and Jakob M. Werbrouck (eds) *The Evolution of Supplementary Pensions* (Edward Elgar Publishing, 2022).
21. Agnieszka Chłoń, Marek Góra, and Michał Rutkowski, *Shaping Pension Reform in Poland: Security through Diversity* (The World Bank, 1999).
22. Jacek Giedrojć, *Competition, Coordination, Social Order: Responsible Business, Civil Society, and Government in Open Society* (Peter Lang, 2017).
23. Anna Wojciuk, *Empires of Knowledge in International Relations: Education and Science as Sources of Power for the State* (Routledge, 2018), 199–224.
24. *Government at a Glance* (OECD, 2021).
25. Anders Hoffmann et al., *Handbook on Constructing Composite Indicators: Methodology and User Guide* (OECD/Joint Research Centre of the European Commission, 2008).
26. See Article 184 of the Polish Constitution.
27. Note, however, that administrative courts will still, in case of doubt, be able to refer a constitutional question to the Tribunal.
28. See also Agnieszka Sołtys, "The Court of Justice of the European Union in the Case Law of the Polish Constitutional Court: The Current Breakdown in View of Polish Constitutional Jurisprudence Pre-2016," *Hague Journal on the Rule of Law* 15, no. 1 (2023): 19–49.
29. For an in-depth discussion of the background see Bruce A. Ackerman, *Revolutionary Constitutions: Charismatic Leadership and the Rule of Law* (The Belknap Press of Harvard University Press, 2019), Chapter 10.

3

Poland of Equal Opportunities

Maciej Bukowski, Mikołaj Herbst, and Tomasz Kaczor

Follow the money

“But he who has money has everything in his hand: His is the power, his are the laws and his are the offices,” wrote the renaissance Polish bard Jan Kochanowski (1530–84). He was right. In sketching our new social contract, we must talk about money—or, more precisely, about the distribution of funds between the central, regional, and local governments, and how it is done. The mechanism in place today guarantees that the central government retains almost total control over how much public revenue gets to the municipalities, counties, and voivodships, and what type of spending it can be used for. There is little policy choice at the regional and local levels, which in practice makes subnational governments hostage to the center.

Within the framework of the proposed new social contract it is crucial for local and regional governments to gain real instruments to effectively pursue public policies within their areas of competence. In particular, they should be able to perform their tasks regardless of whether they are politically aligned with the national majority governing in Warsaw. The point is, therefore, that all regions should operate within a framework of clear and fair rules that do not change unpredictably and uncontrollably. Only under such conditions are accountability and equal opportunities for successful development possible for local governments.

That is the reason behind our two main proposals: to convert personal and corporate income taxes into regional taxes, and to transfer a significant portion of state-owned companies, land, housing, forests, universities, and cultural institutions—currently managed by the central government despite the fact that they primarily provide services for the local or regional communities—to the voivodship governments. With such resources and tax instruments at their disposal, the leftist, progressive, liberal, Christian Democratic, and conservative provinces will be able to showcase the strengths of their ideas for good living and learn from one other.

Maciej Bukowski, Mikołaj Herbst, and Tomasz Kaczor, *Poland of Equal Opportunities* In: *Let's Agree on Poland*.
Edited by: Maciej Kisilowski and Anna Wojciuk, Oxford University Press.
© Inkubator Umowy Społecznej 2025. DOI: 10.1093/oso/9780198979562.003.0004

Three types of local revenue

To understand the implications of our proposed changes, we should first explain the state of affairs of the organization of local and regional public finances since the decentralization reform of 1999. In this system, one could distinguish three groups of revenues of the decentralized governments. The first could be called the Really Own Revenues, or RORs. The word "really" is key, because for complicated reasons that are not worth discussing here, Polish laws also use the term "own revenues" for revenues over which the local or regional governments have basically no influence.[1] We will say more about that in a moment; suffice it for now to add that they were locally "owned" only ostensibly, by virtue of the label given to them by a governing statute.

In the case of RORs, however, we *can* speak of genuine local "ownership." That is because, for duties such as property tax, tax on contractual transactions, or market fees, local governments have significant control over RORs' key parameters. The amount of property tax is determined by the Municipal Council. Central statute only determines the maximum rate of this tax—and we will come back to the sensibility of this solution. As a result, in today's system, property taxes already vary between municipalities. For example, around half of the provincial capitals apply the maximum rate. However, in several of them the rates differ quite significantly—in Zielona Góra, in Western Poland, by several percentage points, for example. Moreover, the property tax is really a "local tax" because the municipality, and not the center, is the party standing vis-à-vis the taxpayer. The tax authority is not an official of the National Tax Administration, but the mayor.

At the other extreme of the post-1999 system are transfers from the center statutorily earmarked for the performance of specific tasks by local and regional governments. In the case of these revenues, the municipal, county, or voivodship governments must carry out activities commissioned and paid for by the center. Indeed, the subnational units cannot refuse to carry out these tasks, even when the funds transferred from the center do not fully cover the actual costs incurred.

With that we arrive at the crucial third group of subnational revenues: transfers from the center that were not earmarked for specific tasks. Here, subnational governments have broad discretion in using these funds, within legal limits. A significant portion of this group is the so-called General Subsidy, composed of several elements—including educational, equalizing, and balancing parts. Although these names suggest a specific purpose for a given transfer, local governments are generally free to use these funds as they see fit.

Of particular interest for us, however, is another pillar of the third revenue group: the statutorily assigned shares of the revenue from national personal and corporate income taxes (PIT and CIT, respectively). As with the General Subsidy, the advantage of these revenues lies in the freedom of spending. At the same time, however, local governments play no role in setting the rules under which these taxes were levied and collected. As a result, every centrally introduced change in the tax rate, every credit or deduction given to or taken away from citizens or companies after 1999, has financial consequences for local governments.

Central government loves to use its power to shape income tax rules. In the past two decades, the list of such changes became truly impressive.[2] Let us recall only the major ones, and only in the area of personal income tax: 2002—deduction for home renovation appears, health deduction disappears; 2003—deduction for training students disappears, credit for qualified charitable donations appears; 2004—a number of minor deductions are eliminated, deduction for charitable donations is changed; 2005—renovation deduction disappears, internet deduction and employment activation deduction appear; 2006—employment activation deduction disappears, new technology and sports sponsorship deduction appears; 2007—sports sponsorship deduction disappears, child allowance appears; 2008—new abolition and registration deduction appears; 2009—registration tax deduction turns into housing tax deduction; 2013—internet deduction and child allowance are limited; 2014—broadening of child allowance; 2015—changes to child allowances; 2017—changes in tax-reducing and tax-free amounts; 2019—new reduced tax rate. And so on.

While each of these changes was introduced for a host of political and policy reasons, a clear general pattern emerges. In particular, central governments of all political persuasions seem often to be affected by what we can call the Good Uncle Syndrome. This syndrome is a type of moral hazard that stems from the perverse incentives inherent in the system in which central government sets the rules concerning taxes that largely fill the coffers of subnational governments. The center is tempted to give taxpayers politically popular tax reliefs knowing that their costs will largely be borne by local governments, for which both PIT and CIT revenues are crucially important.

Local governments at the center's mercy

We are happy to say that, at the time of writing, things are beginning to change. In large part because of the arguments presented in the Polish edition of this book, the government introduced a comprehensive change to the deeply flawed system described above. The most significant change links the income of local governments to the size of the local tax base rather than, as before, to the total tax collected in their territory. Local government budgets will thereby become independent of the frequent and unpredictable changes in central government policies regarding income tax rates, thresholds, and tax exemptions. In the past, such dependency has been frequently criticized by experts.[3] At the same time, however, this reform will not change the ultimate dependence of the local or regional government budget on the fiscal decisions undertaken centrally. This is because in principle, future governments can tweak the introduced formulas and change the relative fiscal position of individual voivodships.

That these changes, viewed by commentators as the first major reform of the post-2023 coalition,[4] follow the general direction proposed in this book is not just a consequence of the persuasive power of the members of our Social Contract Incubator. Instead, the reforms highlight a more fundamental reality: In the geographically divided nation of Poland, meaningful and lasting systemic changes will almost inevitably have to involve some settlement between the more conservative and the more progressive parts of Poland.

And yet, enthusiastic as we are about the recent changes, there is still a long way to go. To show the degree of dependence of local and regional governments on the center, we have conducted an in-depth analysis of all revenues and expenses of the so-called General Government sector. General Government is a standard definition used, among others, by the EU[5] and the International Monetary Fund (IMF)[6] to broadly define the entirety of public institutions.[7] In particular, we added up today's expenditures of all subnational governments and their affiliated entities and compared these with their RORs. The result of our calculations for the fiscal year 2020 is shown in Figure 3.1. In today's situation, the decentralized governments' total ROR was about 147 billion zlotys, while the cost of financing the current decentralized public tasks is 347 billion. The huge hole this leaves—199 billion—is filled with transfers from the center included in the second and third groups of subnational revenues described above.

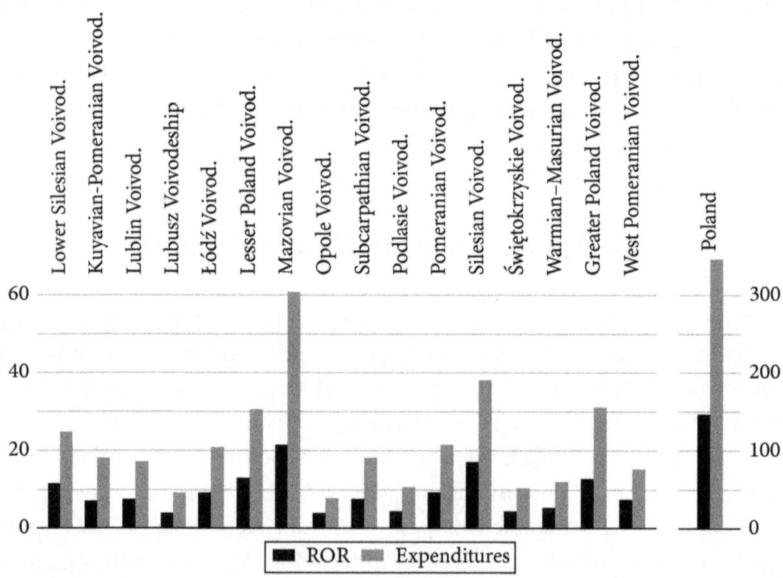

Figure 3.1 The Really Own Revenues and expenditures of subnational governments (2020, billions of zlotys).

Source: Own calculations based on 2020 data. By "subnational governments" we mean all municipalities and counties, as well as the provincial government in a given voivodship, including their subsidiaries.

Such deep financial dependence of decentralized governments on the center encourages national politicians to succumb to the aforementioned Good Uncle Syndrome, casually reducing those nationwide taxes that support decentralized governments, while increasing taxes that feed the central budget. Politicians in the center do this fully aware that the negative consequences of such populism will be borne by local and regional governments. From the vantage point of the new social contract, maintaining this dynamic would have a particularly destructive impact. As our co-authors already mentioned in Chapter 1, the strongest subnational governments are currently municipalities of Poland's largest cities. These governments have for years been dominated by mayors representing the progressive side of Poland's political chasm. As a result, when right-wing politicians come to power in the center, they have a strong incentive to financially starve the city governments, even if that happens at the expense of some conservative voters living in the major metro areas. The political appeal of this strategy is almost irresistible: progressive city halls stripped of funding (disguised, for good measure, as "own revenues") lose political credibility. When we combine this with the proliferation of special transfers distributed by central government among those municipalities and voivodships where conservatives happen to govern, we get a situation that breeds resentment in the liberal-leaning urban electorate, threatening to upset the social balance throughout the country and setting the stage for a corresponding backlash in times when liberals gain national office.

If such a dynamic emerges now, imagine what would happen in the constitutional system proposed in this volume—a system in which voivodes provide an additional vertical check on the national government and in which provinces and municipalities are free to implement policies that may not be to the liking of the current occupants of the Prime Minister's office in Warsaw. No part of this new social contract would work properly if municipalities and regions had a fiscal gun constantly pointed at them by the center. Without solving the problem of financing our local and regional governments, proposed constitutional settlement would be purely fictitious. The disputes over money would continue to be governed by the centralist "winner-takes-all" logic. That is why a key aspect of the constitutional reform we have proposed involves strengthening the financial independence of the subnational governments. To achieve this, we propose two major reforms. First, we transform PIT and CIT into regional taxes. Second, we transfer a significant portion of state assets from the center to the voivodship governments.

Regional taxes

Let's start with the first idea. In order to fulfill their role in the new social contract, the decentralized governments need new sources of revenue that are as stable as possible. Not wanting to create a revolution in the current tax system, we looked for candidates to replenish the local and regional governments' coffers within the existing revenue sources. Two of them, namely personal income tax (PIT) and corporate income tax (CIT), seem obvious candidates, first because decentralized governments already have significant shares in them today, and second because these shares have already been increased several times by decisions of the legislature. At present, these taxes already provide a significant portion of decentralized governments' revenues, are well known to them, and largely correspond to the scale of additional fiscal needs that come with transferring additional responsibilities to decentralized governments.

Our proposal is then to make PIT and CIT into a separate category of regional taxes, placed between the current nationwide and the earlier-mentioned local taxes (including the property tax).[8] Regional tax rates would, like local taxes, be set within the statutory limits by the Sejmiks and the new Voivodship Senates, and collected by provincial tax administrations formed from the transfer of relevant units of existing tax offices to voivodship jurisdiction (no need to create any offices from scratch). Also similar to today's property tax, regional PIT and CIT would become the ROR of decentralized governments, with the tax rules decided separately (though within a nationwide framework) in each region. By so doing, we would protect decentralized governments both from the Good Uncle Syndrome described above and from the risk of financial retribution from politicians at the center if they happen to disagree with the politics of a given regional government or take issue with the vigor with which the region's voivode exercises their mandate in the new national Senate. In addition, the broad room for maneuver given to the Sejmiks and Voivodship Senates with regard to tax rates and possible tax breaks could be a part of the broader economic strategy of an individual region. Competition for citizens and investors, related to the professionalism of provincial tax administrations, could prove particularly important.

At this point it is important to address possible fears that the proposed transfer of PIT and CIT to regional governments would threaten the stability of the central budget. Such fears may stem from a fairly common misunderstanding about the structure of revenues and expenditures of Poland's broader public finance sector. The actual situation in this regard is shown in Figure 3.2, demonstrating two basic facts. On the revenue side, income taxes account for only less than a fifth of total public sector revenues (17% in 2017, and 18% in 2020). Although these taxes themselves undoubtedly keep many a citizen and entrepreneur from sleeping peacefully, from the point of view of the country's finances as a whole, their role pales in comparison with two other sources of revenue: indirect taxes, mainly meaning VAT and excise duties, and social security contributions. The stronger reliance on indirect taxes and social security contributions is a feature of public finances in European Union countries. The situation is different in the US: There, any proposal to abandon the nationwide CIT and PIT would indeed bankrupt the center, and would therefore require broader reforms of the entire tax system.

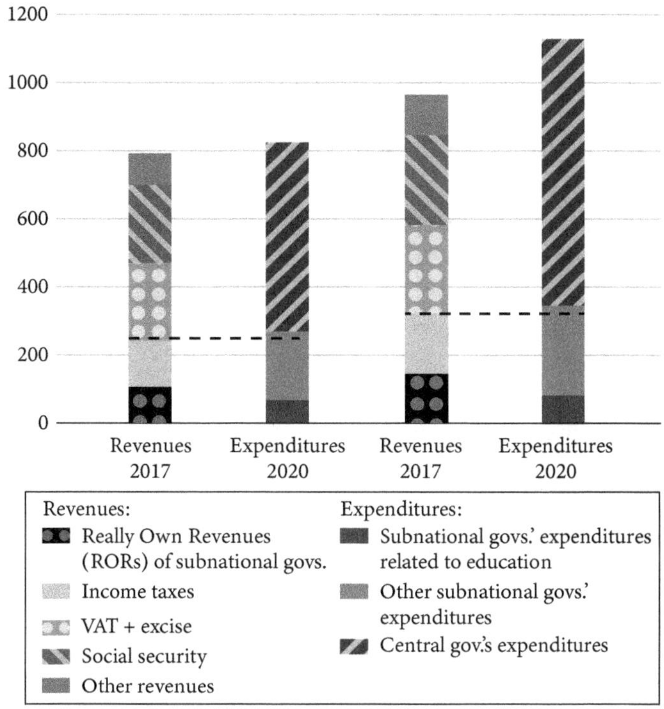

Figure 3.2 Public sector revenue and expenditure structure (2017 and 2020, billions of zlotys)

Figure 3.2 shows that there is no risk of bankruptcy of the center as a result of our proposal, especially since—after the successful decentralization reforms of 1990 and 1999—subnational governments, especially municipalities, already perform a significant portion of costly public tasks. In 2020, local government spending accounted for 30 percent of total public sector spending, including 8 percent on education-related tasks alone. For 2017, these figures were 32 percent and 9 percent. Even today, the expenditures of decentralized governments (taken together) slightly exceed the sum of revenues from existing local taxes (i.e. the RORs) and the national income taxes. This already means that the transfer of income taxes to fully regional taxes carries no risk of upsetting the fiscal position of the central budget.

To reiterate: Figure 3.2 describes the situation under the *current* division of public tasks. But our proposed constitutional change will inevitably trigger a devolution of at least some additional policy areas. If we follow the list of the most natural "candidates" for decentralization presented in the previous chapter, the total cost of newly devolved responsibilities will increase decentralized government expenditures by about a quarter, while at the same time reducing the scope of tasks that central institutions must perform.

The transfer of tasks to local and regional governments also means some increase in their RORs, primarily through the transfer of revenues of state institutions, such as agencies and special purpose funds, but also through revenues collected "incidentally" while performing tasks (such as revenue from the sale of museum tickets or fees for the issuance of certain decisions). These additional revenues amount to 43 billion zlotys, or slightly more than half of the cost of the newly devolved tasks. In effect, despite the transfer of all PIT and CIT revenues to decentralized governments, these governments will still require a subsidy from the center to fill the shortfall of nearly 70 billion zlotys between necessary expenditures and (increased) RORs. Note, however, how the scale of decentralized governments' dependence on the center will dramatically fall as compared to the status quo. While at present (cf. Figure 3.1) RORs cover only 42 percent of local government expenditures, under this proposal they will cover as much as 84 percent of a significantly larger expenditure base.

Completing this picture is Figure 3.3, which shows the consequences of the introduction of new revenue sources, primarily regional taxes, for individual provinces. In eight voivodships, accounting for two-thirds of our country's citizens,

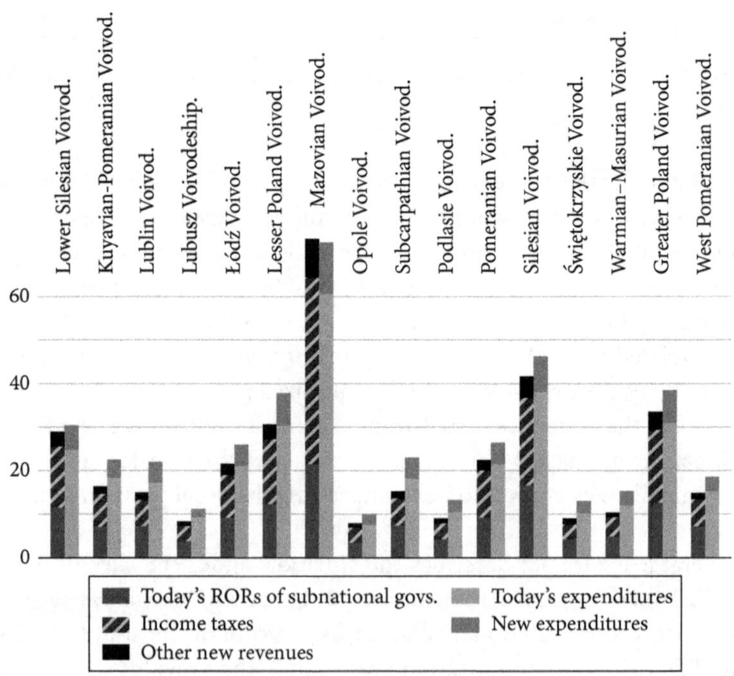

Figure 3.3 Really Own Revenues and expenditures of subnational governments: our proposal (2020, billions of zlotys)

Source: Own simulation based on 2020 data.

these changes have reduced the deficit by more than half, despite the emergence of expenses related to new tasks. In particular, in the case of Lower Silesia the deficit almost disappears, and in Mazovian there is even a small surplus, though much smaller than the special "Robin Hood" solidarity tax currently paid by this voivodship and the city of Warsaw. This province will therebyneither need subsidies from the center nor have to pay the solidarity tributes required under the current regime .

National Cohesion Fund

We hope that an analysis of the data presented in Figures 3.1–3.3 will lead the reader to the same conclusion as us: the regionalization of PIT and CIT is the only real way to significantly increase the revenues of Polish decentralized governments that are truly their own, and to increase the fiscal independence of decentralized governments from central government. No other tax is sufficiently large to distinctly improve the financial self-reliance of Polish voivodships, but also small enough that taking it away from the center will not cause problems for the state's national budget.

However, there are no ideal solutions. In the case of the five voivodships home to 21 percent of the country's population, even with the transformation of PIT and CIT into regional taxes and new sources of own revenues, a significant revenue shortfall will remain. The fundamental reason for the shortfall is the relationship of PIT, and especially CIT, to the economic activity and wealth of different parts of the country.[9]But these factors are not given once and for all. Decentralized governments largely funded by PIT and CIT revenues will have a vested interest in competing for citizens and entrepreneurs. Combined with the new regulatory powers described in other chapters, along with the new tasks—especially in the areas of science, innovation, higher education, culture, and agriculture and forestry—and the public assets transferred to the provinces from the center (more on this soon), our proposal gives provincial governments a powerful incentive for intensive economic development.

In the long term, this development should translate into tangible tax benefits for individual provinces in the form of increased CIT and PIT revenues. This, to be sure, will be a relatively slow process. For this reason, it is necessary to create an additional solidarity mechanism in which Poland's less prosperous regions would be supported from the central purse. Crucial to the new social contract would be basing such a National Cohesion Fund on a statutory formula setting the amount of support for a given province. While the earlier-mentioned reforms increase the financial independence of our subnational governments, they can at any point in the future be reversed by a simple majority in the Sejm. At the same time, however, under the proposed constitutional system, any change to the National Cohesion

Fund would require the approval of the national Senate of the voivodes. We envision a very strong multipartisan consensus of the voivodes against any changes in the system. In effect, the amount of national support for regional governments will not be the subject of blackmail by central politicians.

The amount of support to each region should be fundamentally reversely linked to the levels of its economic activity, which is a good proxy for the wealth of a given community. The National Cohesion Fund would therefore function in a manner similar to the EU Cohesion Funds, with its revenue coming from general taxes collected by central government. Since these taxes—mostly indirect—are proportional to consumption, our system would have a strong redistributive effect. Residents of wealthier voivodships, who consume more and thus pay more VAT, will contribute more to this fund than the residents of poorer provinces, while receiving proportionately less from it.

Alternative ideas can also be explored. The support from the National Cohesion Fund can be—partially or fully—tied to specific spending needs of decentralized governments (on education, culture, family support, or economic development, etc). Or it can be linked with a certain (per-resident?) level of RORs in a given region. The main reason why we opted for the "European" idea of linking the support to levels of economic activity is our persistent worry about moral hazard, or—in other words—of the Good Uncle Syndrome reappearing now in a regional incarnation.

Let us explain. If the National Cohesion Fund would base its disbursements on some measure of RORs of a given region, what would prevent the government of that region from aggressively lowering local and regional taxes only to go to the Cohesion Fund for a compensatory handout? The formula we are proposing, based on the GDP per capita of the provinces rather than a ratio of their revenues to expenditures, will prevent such a situation; the revenue shortfall emerging after a potential populist tax reduction will not be compensated from the Fund.

Avoiding a race to the bottom

While the Cohesion Fund formula prevents the most obvious instances of regional moral hazard, some readers may still have legitimate concerns. What if our voivodships feel pressured to lower their taxes even without the prospect of incoming relief from the Cohesion Fund? What if they decide to simply cut essential public services? The global discussion in tax policy circles often focuses on a "race to the bottom" scenario.[10] In our case, it could be triggered by one province, for idiosyncratic reasons, radically reducing both taxes and the scope of its public services. In the case of CIT, in particular, such a move could easily set off a domino effect. Other regions would be pressured to partake in the race, cutting taxes for fear of losing entrepreneurs who might "vote with their feet."

This risk sounds plausible, in theory. However, culture matters too. If we look at today's picture of Polish decentralized taxes, such a possibility of a tax race to the bottom seems remote. As we have already noted, in the case of property tax, the law sets a maximum rate only. A municipality may, therefore, choose to become a property tax haven, charging a 0 percent rate on real estate within its jurisdiction. A couple of years ago, the press reported that the affluent, copper-rich Polkowice Municipality had followed that path with regard to residential buildings not intended for business. *Puls Biznesu* noted that it was "most likely the only municipality" in Poland that had decided to take such a step.[11] In 2022, of the eighteen provincial capitals (including the dual capitals of the Lubusz and Kuyavian-Pomeranian voivodships), eleven applied the maximum statutory property tax rate, while two others set the tax at 99 percent of the maximum. In its 2014 report, the Association of Polish Cities, together with the Union of Polish Metropolises, called for *an increase* in the maximum statutory rate, linking it to the region's wealth.[12]

Therefore, if we look at municipalities and local taxes, the appeal of additional revenues appears to outweigh the political advantages of being a fiscal "Good Uncle." As we have already hinted at, Poland's cultural specificities, and especially the legacy of nearly half a century of communism, mean citizens are rather used to an expansive welfare state. And yet, worries may persist. PIT and CIT taxes are of far greater importance to citizens and businesses than property tax. Maybe pressure and lobbying for irresponsible tax cuts would be stronger than in the case of property taxes? How can our proposed constitutional system prevent a race to the bottom in regionalized income taxes?

The simplest solution would be to set a nationwide minimum rate for PIT and CIT. In the case of CIT, such a solution will be necessary due to the international situation. At the time of writing, 137 countries, including Poland, have agreed to introduce a minimum CIT rate of 15 percent.[13]If CIT were to become a regional tax in the Polish system, the provinces would, of course, be bound by this arrangement—just as they are by all other provisions of international law. A national law could introduce a similar minimum rate for PIT.

Indeed, an interesting legal and constitutional issue is whether the current practice of statutory limits on the *maximum* amount of local taxes is economically and democratically justified. Article 168 of the Polish Constitution says that "[t]o the extent established by statute, units of territorial self-government shall have the right to set the level of local taxes and charges," but it does not specify how this "extent" is understood. Perhaps a good solution would be to generally replace the "extent" defined by the *maximum* rate with the "extent" defined by the *minimum*.

After all, even without a law, the residents of a municipality or a voivodship have a great tool to prevent excessive taxation. And that tool is democracy! Today, the national Sejm in Warsaw could, for instance, pass a 90 percent PIT rate. It won't do so, because after such a decision those in power would be not 90 but

100 percent certain to lose the next election. Since a similar dynamic will emerge in the voivodships—especially given how much greater citizen participation we envision in regional legislative processes (more on this in Chapters 5 and 6)—the question arises as to the sensibility of additionally shackling regional government with rigid maximum tax rates. It is of course also possible to envision a law that regulates both the minimum and the maximum rate.

Another solution could be a nationwide budget rule for voivodships, under which a provincial government would not be able to make tax changes that reduce its region's total revenue without the approval of the national Senate. If a region wants to avoid having to obtain permission from its fellow voivodes in the Senate, a proposal for any change in the voivodship tax resolutions would have to be accompanied by an analysis showing that the reform "pays for itself": Additional revenue from increases in some taxes offsets the losses from reductions in others.

There are several advantages to such an arrangement. First, it gives regional governments ample room for maneuver in shaping their tax policy, linked to a broader vision for regional economic development. This is consistent with the general tenets of the proposed new social contract. Second, it eliminates the risk of provinces being so-called *freeriders* in the nationwide system of taxation and public services. Third, this approach would force every tax change proposal to be backed by thorough analyses, the quality of which could be certified, for example, by the national Ministry of Finance. Alternatively, it is worth considering the creation of an institution similar to the UK's Office for Budget Responsibility—an independent public institution that produces economic forecasts and assesses the feasibility of proposed revenue and spending changes based on them. Academics and international organizations, such as the OECD, agree that the ills of Poland's politics are caused by regulatory changes, especially tax changes that are unsupported by reliable analyses of their effects.[14]

Decentralized property

We have written much, to this point, about the concept of regional taxes, so it's time to move on to the second part of our proposal: the idea of further decentralization of public assets. We say "further" because the historic local government reform of the first Solidarity government in 1990 already transferred more than 40,000 public assets to local government units, mainly municipalities. Studies show that the management of municipal assets, while not ideal, is much more efficient than the management of central assets.[15]

More broadly, the idea of decentralizing public assets, and especially the notorious state-owned enterprises, is deeply in line with the idea of the new social contract. In the previous chapters, we have discussed at length the deep political, ideological, and civilizational divides among the Poles. One element of this divide, sometimes crisscrossing other cleavages, is the attitude toward state property. Conservative Poles in general, and democratic socialists among progressive Poles, are in favor of retaining significant public ownership in the economy. Citizens in this group are particularly distrustful of foreign capital. On the other side we have the more free-market-oriented progressive Poles, who strongly support the further privatization of state assets.

What we all agree on is that the current system, in which state-owned enterprises are political spoils of each successive party taking national power, is sick. In addition, most Poles will agree that, at least in some sectors, the renationalization of state assets started by the PiS government is beginning to lead to a monopolization that is bad for consumers. Transferring ownership of most state-owned enterprises to provincial governments is a Solomonic solution that can (at least to some extent) satisfy everyone.

We propose transferring all stakes held by the Treasury (including the so-called residuals, as it should be remembered that the Polish state has retained ownership of very small stakes in many privatized enterprises) in 23 listed companies and more than 400 privately held companies. The center would be left with forty-four companies of potential strategic importance, or those whose transfer could prove controversial. What we have in mind, in particular, are state-owned energy and defense companies, the Polish Post and Polish Public TV. The decentralized assets will be divided in such a way that each voivodship would receive an almost equal value of assets per capita: in practice, about 4,500 zlotys or about 1,000 euro according to the asset valuations we conducted in accordance with current standards.[16]

In order for decentralized assets to support regional development strategies, the largest stakes in each company will be granted, where possible, to voivodships where most of the company's economic activity is located. For example, a major stake in the KGHM copper producer will be given to the Lower Silesian province, the control of hard coal mines will be transferred to Silesia, and the shares of the successful train manufacturer from Bydgoszcz will be transferred to the Kujawsko-Pomorskie province.

What about the voivodships that are not fortunate enough to have such "crown jewels" on their territory? We propose to compensate them primarily through stakes in companies that do not have an obvious regional connection. These include the Polish lottery monopoly; the largest Polish insurer, PZU; and two large banks—PKO BP and Pekao SA. All these state-owned companies may have their headquarters in Warsaw today, but that does not have to be the case in the future. These enterprises could become the economic backbone of provinces with no state-owned manufacturing or natural resources companies.

The proposed solution can be viewed as presenting the golden mean between the support of state ownership and the free market enthusiasts. By transferring assets to provincial governments, we are demonopolizing state ownership while not prejudging whether it will be privatized or remain in public (but decentralized) hands. Classical liberals can make their case and urge the provinces to privatize newly decentralized property. And supporters of public ownership may emphasize the pro-development aspect of local government ownership. In order to completely equalize the per capita value of the property transferred to the provinces, we also propose to transfer between 40 percent and 95 percent of state-owned land (which amounts to 863,700 hectares) and 90 percent of state-owned housing (with as many as 73,670 units in total). As already mentioned, the effect of this distribution would be that all provincial governments receive assets of almost equal per capita value.

It is worth noting that in addition to the state assets distributed according to the per capita valuation outlined above, we propose to grant voivodships significant assets connected to public tasks that, in the previous chapter, we proposed be transferred to the regions. The transfer of forest management implies the transfer of the regional State Forestry Directorates to the provinces, and thus the transfer of ownership of Polish forests. The transfer of science and higher education implies the indirect transfer of valuable assets (for example, buildings used for teaching and halls of residence) belonging to public universities. The same is true for the transfer of the management of cultural institutions, although in this case local governments will of course be bound by statutory restrictions on the disposal of national heritage assets.

The process of transferring task-related assets may seem extremely complicated. However, it is worth recalling that this is exactly how assets were transferred to local governments, mainly municipalities, under the first local government reform of 1990. At that time, it was mainly about the buildings of state-run schools. That reform is widely regarded as a success, and Poles value the care that municipalities put into maintaining local schools. There is no reason to assume that the effect of the changes we are proposing would be any different.

Summary

A major objective of the presented reform proposal is to ensure that regions governed by political parties different from those in national power are not penalized financially. This follows the overarching goal to establish a new social contract that fosters financial equity among Poland's diverse regions and ensures stable local governance. The reform aims to empower decentralized governments to fulfill their role in providing services effectively, without the fiscal influence of central government policies. The new structure would level the playing field for all regions to have fair opportunities for development, irrespective of their political affiliation. The goal is to significantly increase the financial independence of regional (voivodship) and local governments in Poland. This change is necessary for local authorities to effectively pursue public policies and reduce their dependency on the central government. A major proposal involves transforming the personal and corporate income taxes (PIT and CIT) into regional taxes. Local governments would have control over these taxes, including setting tax rates within certain limits. This reform aims to establish a stable revenue source for regions, minimizing the fiscal unpredictability caused by frequent changes in national tax policies. The plan includes transferring state-owned assets, such as companies, land, forests, and universities, to regional governments. This would grant regional governments tangible resources to align economic development strategies with local priorities. Assets would be allocated to regions based on geographic and economic relevance. A specific mechanism was proposed for distributing funds between the central and decentralized governments. It helps to level the playing field, as it guarantees that provinces whose voivodes represent a different political faction than the one holding sway in the capital will be able to develop without obstruction. To ensure that less prosperous regions do not fall behind, a National Cohesion Fund is proposed. This fund would function similarly to the EU Cohesion Funds, redistributing revenue from wealthier to poorer regions based on statutory rules. The approval process for changes to this fund would require agreement from regional representatives, thereby safeguarding its integrity from political manipulation. Overall, the proposed reforms emphasize decentralization, financial independence, and equitable development, aiming to correct the imbalance of power and resources between central and local authorities. These changes are intended to foster more robust regional governance, support diverse economic strategies, and ultimately create a system where every region in Poland can thrive regardless of the prevailing political landscape.

Acknowledgments

The authors would like to thank Marcin Zielinski for his assistance in preparing the section on decentralized property.

Notes

1. Paweł Swianiewicz, "Poland: Rolling Back of the Decentralized System?," in *Handbook on Subnational Governments and Governance*, eds Claudia N. Avellaneda and Ricardo A. Bello-Gómez (Edward Elgar Publishing, 2024).
2. Marek Klimek, "Funkcjonowanie jednostek samorządu terytorialnego podczas pandemii COVID-19," *Studia Politologiczne* 64, no. 64 (2022): 89–108; Paweł Swianiewicz and Julita Łukomska, *Finanse samorządu terytorialnego w dobie pandemii*, Fundacja Batorego (2020).
3. Piotr Bury and Paweł Swianiewicz, "Grant Transfers in Financing Local Governments in Poland," in *Fiscal Decentralisation and Grant Transfers in Transition Countries: A Critical Perspective*, ed. Željko Šević (Bratislava: The Network of Institutes and Schools of Public Administration in Central and Eastern Europe, 2014).

4. Grzegorz Osiecki and Tomasz Żółciak, "Wielka reforma Domańskiego. Co się zmieni w finansach państwa?" *Money.pl*, Jul. 18, 2024.
5. EUROSTAT 2013. European System of Account. ESA 2010, Brussels: European Commission ESA 2010.
6. International Monetary Fund, *Government Finance Statistics Yearbook 2010 (Vol. 34)* (2010).
7. "General Government" is broader than the term "Public Finance Sector" used in Poland. Among the aspects of the General Government sector is the local government sector, on which we will focus; everything else is treated as the center. To avoid confusion for readers well versed in the nuances of Polish public finance, we use "Public Sector" as a synonym for General Government, to distinguish it from "Public Finance Sector."
8. Technically, regional taxes will be a subgroup of local taxes, as referred to in Article 168 of the Polish Constitution ("Local government units have the right to determine the amount of local taxes and fees to the extent specified by law").
9. Janina Kotlińska, Anna Mizak, and Anna Krawczyk-Sawicka, "Typologizacja polskich regionów w oparciu o wpływ potencjału społeczno-gospodarczego na ich kondycję finansową," *Studia Regionalne i Lokalne* 94, no. 4 (2023): 54–65.
10. Robert S. Chirinko and Daniel J. Wilson, "Tax Competition among US States: Racing to the Bottom or Riding on a Seesaw?" *Journal of Public Economics* 155 (2017): 147–163; Hanna Lierse, "A Race to the Bottom? The Politics of Tax Competition," in *Handbook on the Politics of Taxation*, eds Lukas Hakelberg and Laura Seelkopf (Edward Elgar Publishing, 2021).
11. Aleksandra Rogala, "Bogata gmina likwiduje lokalne podatki," *Puls Biznesu*, Oct. 3, 2018.
12. Paweł Rochowicz, "Podatek od nieruchomości zależny od zamożności regionu mierzonej PKB," *Rzeczpospolita*, Mar. 9, 2017.
13. Wei Cui, "Strategic Incentives for Adopting the Global Minimum Tax," *Journal of Legal Analysis* 16, no. 1 (2024): 211–234.
14. Daniel Bunn, *International Tax Competitiveness Index 2022*, Tax Foundation (2022); Marcin Zieliński and Hubert Wejman, *FOR Communication 4/2024: What's Wrong with the Polish Tax System?* Forum Obywatelskiego Rozwoju (2024).
15. Dorothée Allain-Dupré, Isabelle Chatry, and Antti Moisio, *Making Decentralization Work: A Handbook for Policy-Makers*, OECD (2019).
16. Details of our valuation analysis can be found at LetsAgreeonPoland.org.

4

Center Strong with Strategy

Maciej Kisilowski and Wojciech Przybylski

The universal appeal of strength

Almost regardless of political persuasion, Poles would agree that any constitutional settlement for our country must ensure that our state remains strong. For two centuries, Poland was devoid of independent statehood and repeatedly invaded, occupied, and brutalized by our neighbors. Moreover, despite Poles' international reputation as apologists for our own history, there are in fact few societies in whose collective memory the acute awareness of our own weaknesses is so firmly ingrained. Every Polish teenager learns that, while the voracious imperialism of our adversaries was the trigger of our historical tragedies, our own national weakness was almost always in the background, inviting attacks and encroachments. It is thereby hardly surprising that almost every Pole, whether from the left, right, or center, desires now a state that is efficient and capable of responding to contemporary challenges.

The topic of a strong state is also relevant because the twenty-first century increasingly appears to be an era of regional and global crises. Over the past fifteen years we have experienced a global collapse of financial markets of a scale not seen since the 1930s, tough moments for the single European currency, the 2015 migration crisis, Brexit, the most serious pandemic in a century, and then the largest armed conflict on the European continent since World War II. And it is also becoming clear that these challenges will pale by comparison with the looming consequences of climate and technological changes. The scale of natural disasters, global socioeconomic tensions, escalating migrations, and further pandemics that will result from global warming will be unprecedented in human history.

Is the constitutional proposal outlined in this volume doomed, then? Does our proposal, which is about devolving significant authority from the center to the regions, inherently run counter to the strong state imperative? Indeed, this is the line of criticism that is often levied against us: you offer a tempting, depolarizing vision, but for calmer, more peaceful times. In the current, rough era, we need to contend with the status quo, even at the cost of the never-ending Polish–Polish political war.

Maciej Kisilowski and Wojciech Przybylski, *Center Strong with Strategy* In: *Let's Agree on Poland*.
Edited by: Maciej Kisilowski and Anna Wojciuk, Oxford University Press.
 DOI: 10.1093/oso/9780198979562.003.0005

We find these arguments emphatically wrong. There is no tradeoff whatsoever between a strong center and the more rational multilevel assignment of powers and tasks to the European, national, regional, and local levels of our governance. Indeed, the latter is largely a prerequisite of the former. To understand why, we should begin however with a more basic question: We need a strong, or powerful, state, but what does that actually mean? Scholars in various disciplines, from public management[1] to international relations,[2] have long discussed this question. In today's world, two main competing models or visions of such a state are at serious odds.

Expansion or focus

The first, represented by authoritarian countries from China to Russia or Saudi Arabia, sees the strength of the state apparatus in its expansiveness and ability to subjugate everyone around it—from society to neighbors near and far. From the perspective of authoritarian leaders, a strong, powerful state is one that identifies more and more areas of socioeconomic life as areas of influence. State expansion can be internal—for example, when China disciplines and subjugates technology giants such as Alibaba to its party power apparatus.[3] External expansion is more dramatic, with Russia being the best example. The goal, however, is similar: a strong state is one that is constantly growing, subjugating new areas and brutally disciplining centers of dissent, opposition, or authority.

In this chapter we will present an idea for implementing, in Polish conditions, an alternative to the authoritarian model sketched out above. The key word in this other vision of the strong state is not "expansion" but "focus": a professional, strategic concentration on priorities that will enable an increase in economic and military potential and in the quality of life.[4] A "focus" that is also about backing the implementation of these priorities with adequate resources.

The resources of a focused state are primarily financial. But that's not all! Objective competencies and the motivation of public officials implementing government priorities are also crucial for a strong state. Furthermore, these resources include sufficient managerial attention and commitment from public sector leaders—which, in a democracy, usually means elected politicians. The range of tasks that a president, prime minister, or minister can personally champion is severely constrained by the practical realities of politics.

The leaders, and the state apparatus in general, must, moreover, enjoy public trust—a key resource needed for the state to carry out its tasks effectively. Both the general level of public trust and the trust of groups particularly relevant to efficient governance are important. We are talking, for example, about entrepreneurs or NGOs. At the same time, trust alone is not enough. In a democratic system, a key resource of a strong state is a social consensus around the priorities of state institutions. This consensus should be broad, embracing the largest possible number of citizens, experts, and entrepreneurs supporting the implementation of a priority as well as the smallest possible number opposing it. In a democracy, even a small, well-mobilized group of dedicated opponents has the potential to derail state action. Public consensus should also be stable, as goals that are important for the country are usually pursued over a period of years or decades.

In the system of parliamentary democracy, which Poles chose after much discussion in the 1990s, another important aspect of the strength of the state is the stability of the main political parties, both those currently in power and those in opposition. Academic research and the experiences of other countries are, unfortunately, radically different from the prevailing tone of Polish public discourse, which abounds with populist slogans about "taking away the privileges of politicians" or "making state institutions nonpartisan."[5] Of course, many specific manifestations of partisanship, such as the treatment of state-owned companies as political spoils, are outrageous. As we saw in the previous chapter, the constitutional system we propose here includes concrete suggestions for curbing such abuses. But while supporting anti-corruption solutions, we should not fall into the trap of demonizing political parties per se.

The foundation of all these resources of a strong state is a commonality of values.[6] In today's world, in which different models of the good life coexist and often compete with each other, a focus—a clear definition of the relevant areas of state action—provides the best chance of endowing the state with strong foundations of genuinely shared values. To put it differently, the more broadly we define the scope of our central government, the greater the likelihood that, for one group of citizens or another, that government will become synonymous with a threat—an instrument for imposing values alien to us.

It is largely because of how the conception of state strength as a focus fits the reality of our fundamental ideological divisions that this vision may itself be compelling to citizens with a wide variety of ideological leanings. For liberals, a streamlined yet professional state apparatus has always been an ideological aspiration. Similarly, though for different reasons, traditional Christian Democracy shares this perspective. As Łukasz Rozdeiczer and Artur Wołek mention in Chapter 11, Catholic social teaching is firmly opposed to an expansive state, which it sees as leading to totalitarianism.[7] Christian Democrats advocate the famous principle of subsidiarity, according to which central authorities should become involved in the implementation of public tasks only when smaller communities, closer to the people, are objectively unable to handle them. The vision of strengthened decentralized governments, especially at voivodship level, is a direct application of this principle to Polish conditions.

The abandonment of expansion in favor of a focused state may at first glance seem more difficult to reconcile with leftist ideas. Yet this dissonance is illusory.

All over the world the Left is pondering how, under modern conditions, to effectively manage a state that, in the leftist vision, broadly identifies the scope of goods and services provided to citizens. Nothing pleases the Left's competitors more than examples of leftist governments unable to mobilize the bureaucratic apparatus to efficiently implement extensive social programs and find sufficient resources to fund them.

In this context, our proposal gives the Left a new blueprint for turning its ideas into reality. Since we break down the performance of state tasks into four levels—well-established municipalities, newly strengthened voivodships, an efficient center, and the existing institutions of the European Union—it is easier to implement elements of an expansive welfare state at each of them. Even with the ambitious goals of the state as a whole, governance at each level is manageable. An excellent example of what such multilevel leftism could look like in practice is provided by Chapter 10 of this book, by Alicja Pacewicz, Jan Smoleński, and Michał Żabicki.

A group for whom the vision of a focused state will certainly not be appealing includes Poles inclined toward national socialist, or neofascist, ideas. The growing number of parties in Europe combining economic leftism with radical national conservatism makes it impossible to overlook this ideological preference. For them, we do not offer a good compromise: in fascism, the state economic interventionism characteristic of socialism is combined with the imperative to implement, in all manifestations of this interventionism, a unified "will of the people"—defined top-down by political leaders.

The ministerial puzzle

If you are at least tentatively persuaded by the idea that focusing on coherent, clear priorities is a condition for the strength and effectiveness not only of the state, but also of any organization, then you will easily understand why central institutions in Poland are currently not among the most effective. Based on the official catalog prescribed by law, our central government handles more than sixty areas of public affairs. Most of them—from the economy or public finance to science or tourism—are listed in the Law on Divisions of Government Administration. Some of these areas are identical to the fairly specific tasks of specialized government agencies, such as the police, the Social Security Administration, the National Health Fund, or the Environmental Protection Fund.

The sheer number and breadth of areas of central government activities raises concerns about its ability to implement them effectively. But an even more serious problem is how the governmental work in the aforementioned areas is organized. This is because Poland's reforms of the 1990s introduced a truly absurd model for organizing this work. Basically, any time a new prime minister takes office they can in principle divide these sixty tasks as they please among ministers. This fluid definition of governmental portfolios applies, furthermore, not only to ministers, but also to the ministries they head. In other words, Poland's most essential civil servants, responsible for key issues on which our collective future depends, work in an organizational environment that is—by design—unstable and resembles a constantly reshuffled ministerial jigsaw puzzle.

Who is, for instance, tending to Poland's success in the digital age? It depends on when. From 2005 to 2011—the Ministry of Internal Affairs and Administration and, partly, the Ministry of Infrastructure. From 2011 to 2015—the Ministry of Administration and Digitization. From 2015 to 2020—the Ministry of Digitization. From 2020 till 2023—the Prime Minister's Office. And, since 2023—again, the Ministry of Digitization.

The issues of economic competitiveness were, in turn, overseen by the Ministry of Economy from 1999 to 2003, by the Ministry of Labor and Social Policy from 2003 to 2005, again by the Ministry of Economy from 2005 to 2015, by the Ministry of Development from 2015 to 2020, by the Ministry of Development, Labor and Technology from 2020 to 2021, and by the Ministry of Development and Technology since 2021. The development of Poland's critical infrastructure was managed by the Ministry of Infrastructure in 2001–2005, the Ministry of Transport and Construction in 2005–2006, the Ministry of Transport in 2006–2007, the Ministry of Infrastructure in 2007–2011, the Ministry of Transport, Construction and Maritime Economy in 2011–2013, the Ministry of Infrastructure and Development in 2013–2015, the Ministry of Infrastructure and Construction in 2015–2018, the Ministry of Investment and Development between 2018 and 2023, and, since 2023, again the Ministry of Infrastructure.

Small—though significant for a mid-sized European country—fragments of various ministries made fantastical journeys, with perhaps the most memorable being the creation of the Ministry of Maritime Affairs in 2006. Despite managing only one narrow area of public affairs, it eagerly organized its own Office of the Minister, Office of the Director General, Legal Office, Office of European Affairs, Office of Defense Affairs, and Office of Internal Audit. All of these structures, created together with the establishment of the ministry itself, were dissolved just over a year later when the mini-ministry was reintegrated into the Ministry of Infrastructure.

The most interesting aspect of this maddening organizational kaleidoscope is that respected Polish specialists in public administration consider the system to have significant advantages![8] Its advocates emphasize its "flexibility" and the supposed benefits of being able to tailor the structure of ministries to the preferences and priorities of the prime minister and the government coalition.

Anyone who has worked in a successful organization or a close-knit group of people would intuitively understand the flaw in such thinking. The US Department of State—the world's most successful foreign affairs ministry—was established in

1789. Marco Rubio, the Secretary of State at the time of this writing, is the seventy-second person to hold the position. Working at the State Department has been a dream of students at top American universities for hundreds (!) of years. A key aspect of their motivation is not the salary, but the prestige associated with the opportunity to have a real impact on the fate of the world. Indeed, fresh graduates of the best American universities choose to work in the American foreign service knowing that they could earn a dozen or several dozen times more on Wall Street. Meanwhile, a young Polish diplomatic employee could, alternatively, earn only a few times more in Warsaw's financial district.

If we go beyond public sector examples, it's worth noting that one would search in vain for a logic analogous to our "ministerial puzzles" among corporations or other organizations that have proved successful. When Tim Cook took over from Steve Jobs at the helm of Apple Inc. in 2011, it didn't occur to anyone to divide or shuffle the Cupertino-based company to make it a "better fit" for the new CEO. And when Harvard University elected history professor Drew Gilpin Faust as its first female president in 2007, no one suggested that departments not matching her interests should be removed from the university's structure. Governmental ministries, just like departments in a company or faculties at a university, are not there to satisfy the goals or ambitions of their bosses.

Many faces of strength

The ministerial puzzle system ignores everything we know about strong and effective organizations. The strength of organizations like the State Department, Harvard or Apple comes from the stability of their brand. It is the brand that is critical in attracting and retaining motivated and talented employees.

We began this chapter by listing the various types of resources that a focused and strategic state is able to effectively mobilize to achieve its stated priorities. The truth, however, is that talent is one of these resources that is in a "class of its own."[9] "Personnel is policy"—the famous saying of Scot Faulkner, director of human resources in the Ronald Reagan administration—should become the motto of Polish politicians. After all, the ability to achieve political goals begins and ends with the right selection of people to achieve those goals.

The governmental center of the Polish state will be strong only if working for it is—like working at Apple, Harvard, or the State Department—the aspirational goal of thousands of the most talented professionals. The system of ministerial jigsaws is extremely effective in preventing this goal from becoming a reality. For an organization to be considered a prestigious employer, it must have a stable and recognizable brand—a brand built over decades, not over a few months, before succumbing at the next reorganization.[10]

When we talk about brand, we don't just think about a prestigious name. Even more important is a certain organizational culture, developed over a long period of time.[11] Particularly in high-stakes creative work—and the management of the country's governmental center is just such—not everything can be regulated by formal procedures. What instead matters, perhaps most, is *esprit de corps*—unwritten values, norms of reciprocity, professionalism, and trust.[12] To develop these norms and values takes time. In addition, norms and values form around a clearly defined mission—the specific role that the ministry and its officials[13] play in the state apparatus. Putting it all together, a strong brand is a prerequisite to developing a distinctive work ethos.[14]

One of the most beneficial consequences of having a clearly defined brand, mission, and ethos is the effective self-selection of candidates for employment in a given organization. This self-selection, a spontaneous process by which candidates with specific interests or predispositions apply for positions in a particular ministry, cannot be replaced by even the best of recruitment procedures. Once these fitting candidates are brought on board, mission and ethos help to keep them motivated and aligned with key strategic priorities.[15]

Knowledge is also important. And not just that in the individual's head. Organizational knowledge is crucial,[16] whether codified in the form of repositories or case studies, supported by modern information technologies,[17] or informal. In today's world, even the best-prepared official will face problems that take them by surprise. In such a situation, an intra-organizational network of connections and relationships makes it possible to quickly identify other employees who may be experts in a particular field.

Which brings us to the topic of networks. Strength in today's world is heavily dependent on the intensity of your connections to other organizations.[18] This is especially true of other ministries or agencies,[19] but also of businesses[20] or non-governmental organizations.[21] Before the September 11, 2001 attack, both the FBI and the CIA were regarded as organizations with almost mythical powers and influence. However, as later investigations have shown, a simple lack of coordination or mutual exchange of information allowed a dozen terrorists armed with box cutters to organize the bloodiest terrorist attack in US history.[22]

In Poland, too, it has long been said that the central administration suffers from "departmentalism"—that is, insufficient coordination between ministries.[23] The prescription proposed by some analysts is the creation of "super-ministries," similar to those organized in Hungary by Viktor Orbán. This is not a good direction, since mega-ministries dealing with everything will have difficulty building the aforementioned distinctive brand and ethos to attract and retain the best employees. Managing such ministries is also difficult.

Most importantly, however, even if we put all Polish officials into one department, such a super-ministry would still have to function in a network of external relations in order to operate effectively. We have already mentioned the role of (transparent) relations with businesses or NGOs. However, from the point of view of a country such as Poland, a special category of external linkages crucial to our future is that of relations within the European Union and NATO.

EU and NATO as networks

In most European countries, central government administration faces the enormous challenge of finding its way in the historically unprecedented reality of European integration. Over the past two decades, formal regulations, along with the informal arrangements and coordination within the European Union, have begun to play a leading role in almost all areas of Polish central government activity.[24]

Unfortunately, the real consequences of the EU's growing role are misunderstood on both sides of our political spectrum. Conservatives, fearing a "European superstate," often pretend that Poland can be governed as if the EU did not exist. They want to shape politics in Warsaw in isolation from policy in Brussels, and see relations with the EU as an area of "foreign affairs"—relations with an "ordinary" international organization. The result of such an attitude is often that our country has no real say in the directions of EU policies. At worst, endless disputes with EU institutions and financial penalties hit us where it hurts.

The "let's pretend the EU doesn't exist" attitude is all the more unwise given that it is Polish conservatives who are pushing for European cooperation and solidarity to be extended into further areas, such as defense, energy, or foreign affairs. These areas belong to the canon of the most traditional tasks of a central government. As a result, the realization of the conservative postulates will further reduce the mythical Polish "sovereignty," by which our politicians in Warsaw often mean just their ability to do as they please.

In our perceptions of European politics, however, representatives of the progressive side are also not without fault. After all, in their euro-enthusiasm they often assume that the Union is, or will soon become, precisely the superstate that the conservatives fear. As a result, many progressives assume that institutions in Brussels, such as the European Commission and the European Parliament, rather than national authorities, will play the most important role in the formation of EU policies.

In reality, the day-to-day operation of the European Union resembles neither a superstate nor a traditional international organization. It is best to think of the EU as a dense network of links between the member states and the institutions in Brussels. The same is true of the NATO structures, especially given how Russia's assault on Ukraine is prompting Europe to take a more active role in common defense.[25]

In the EU, the main forum that coordinates the network is the Council. On major issues, it brings together—as the European Council—the heads of state or government of the member states. On other matters, it deliberates—as the Council of the European Union—in ten thematic configurations made up of the Member State ministers responsible for a particular area of public policy. Since no EU directive or regulation can enter into force without the Council's approval, a good way to think of the Council is as a—very powerful—European senate; a second chamber of the EU legislature, alongside the European Parliament. The senate model represented by the European Council—a legislative body, but made up of representatives of the lower-level executive branch—is the inspiration for our proposed new Polish Senate of the voivodes as well as the voivodship senates, composed of mayors from all the municipalities in the respective regions. Finally, the configuration of the ministers responsible for a particular area of public affairs—the Council of the European Union—motivated the design of our College of the Voivodships discussed in Chapter 2. This institution will coordinate the legislative work of the provincial governments and be composed, analogously to the Council of the EU, of the deputy voivodes from all provinces responsible for a specific policy area.

However, the European network does not extend only to the meetings of the Council. Drafts of European regulations and directives, as well as of implementing acts clarifying regulations already passed, are agreed upon in the relevant committees and working groups. These committees are also responsible for monitoring the practical functioning of the adopted regulations, and for proposing amendments.[26]

Civil servants from Member State governmental administrations play a key role in these bodies. Or, rather, they "can play" such a role, since proactivity, familiarity with the issues, knowledge of the EU's working languages, and both formal and informal contacts with partners from Brussels and other countries are essential for making a real impact.

Polish activity in the EU institutions in Brussels, and in the structures of NATO, is a very important topic in public discussion. The main problem is that in the public assessment of this activity, the heroic aspect plays too much of a role: for example, the symbolic speeches of American presidents in Warsaw, or the exciting late-night negotiations in which the Polish Prime Minister does not yield an inch.

Such aspects are sometimes important, but they do not fully determine everyday relations in EU and transatlantic cooperation. Too much emphasis on such a model of relations with the EU and NATO is also risky. In 2016, British Prime Minister David Cameron badly miscalculated by promising to negotiate unrealistic concessions for the UK. When Cameron walked out of the Council building at 5:30 a.m. on February 19, 2016, after all-night negotiations, he could boast only modest results. A few months later, the Brits decided to leave the European Union.

Among other things, the British leader's mistake was to underestimate the power of the EU institutions. The Union is an organization managing diverse interests of its members. This diversity cannot be reduced to a nineteenth-century conversation between gentlemen who divide and rule the world behind closed doors. In modern, post-imperial Europe, the more intensively you participate in decision-making processes, the greater your benefits. Conversely, by not seeking participation in all integration processes, you lose influence. Far more important than the overnight heroism of this or that prime minister is the transformation of our central, regional, and local governments so that Polish state apparatus can function for an efficient European and NATO advocacy, present and active everywhere that important decisions for our joint future are made. Considering the current emphasis on the Eastern Flank and the Russian aggression against Ukraine, which has destabilized the European security order, Poland should seize this opportunity to expand its advocacy platform by promoting more officials to top positions within the Brussels-based bureaucracy. Unfortunately, despite more than twenty years of EU membership, Poland still has too few officials in Brussels. Poles make up about 4.5 percent of the staff of the European Commission—the EU's largest institution, with 32,000 employees—while filling just under 4 percent of management positions. Meanwhile, according to EU methodology, having our country fully represented would mean filling 8.2 percent of positions.[27]

In addition to strength in numbers, it is crucial to skillfully exchange information on European practices and policies, thereby building an understanding of decision-making processes and internal power dynamics. Another key element is the creation of an informal network facilitating the flow of information and allowing for influence over EU decision-making processes. Polish officials can only build such a network if they accumulate knowledge and contacts over the long term.

It is not only Poland that has difficulties in implementing an efficient lobbying structure. There are, however, also positive examples of "EU-effective" countries, such as Ireland and Italy, that are worthy role models in this respect. Given the role of the EU and Poland's overall relations with the West in our national interests, joining the ranks of the EU's most influential members should be viewed as a high, cross-partisan priority—especially since a "seat" among the leaders of a united Europe has essentially been "reserved" for Poland ever since Britain's withdrawal from the Union. Russia's war with Ukraine has further bolstered Poland's position as a linchpin of the Western security system in the region, pursuing the most ambitious arms program in Europe. This shift is so significant that failing to consolidate it by joining the informal club of large countries setting directions in the Union would, over the decades to come, be a missed opportunity to enhance our security and capitalize on future development potential. Poland is currently pursuing this ambition through policy coordination with France and Germany under the so-called Weimar Triangle. While this collaboration requires the participation of all partners and will depend on the future leadership in these countries, Poland's effectiveness will also be guaranteed only if it can maintain the cross-partisan cohesion regarding its role in the upgraded European defense posture.

Our proposal

Values, mission, norms, ethos, brand, organizational knowledge, and deeply embedded networks both with domestic stakeholders and partners within the EU and NATO. The current organization of Poland's central government, based on the dizzying fluidity of ministerial jigsaw puzzles completely ignores those aspects of the state apparatus strong with strategy and focus. Anybody who criticizes our constitutional reform for supposedly "weakening" the Polish state is badly missing the real sources of our central weakness and dysfunction.

Indeed, the broad constitutional system proposed in this work paves the way for sensible reforms of our governmental center. Set in the spirit of the holistic *whole-of-government approach* to reforming the state apparatus,[28] our reforms of the center would consist of three important steps: First, relieving the center of distractive and divisive tasks through decentralization; second, the creation of stable and prestigious ministries with a coherent mission, brand, and ethos; and third, a radical opening of the Polish civil service corps to Europe and the world.

Let's start with the first point. Although the government and the ministries are formally the organs of "executive" power, in practice most of their tasks are related to legislation—creating draft laws and regulations (as we mentioned above, efficient lobbying in the area of EU law must be added to this). We have already pointed out in Chapter 1 that an important aspect of our proposal is the transfer of the authority to legally regulate tasks performed today by municipalities and counties to sejmiks and new voivodship senates. We argued that since local governments are already performing numerous public tasks anyway, such as in the area of education, they should have greater competence to regulate these tasks, for instance by shaping curricula. In addition, a certain number of new tasks would be transferred to the voivodship governments, especially in areas that are important for implementing aligned and attractive economic strategies. These concern mainly culture, science, higher education, and the regulation of economic and agricultural affairs.

What impact would such regulatory decentralization have on the strategic power of the center? The transfer of these regulatory competencies would reduce the earlier-mentioned mind-boggling number of sixty priority areas of the governmental center by as much as one-third. Importantly, the areas of public affairs that we propose to devolve are often issues that arouse substantial political controversy, for example education, science, labor, family, and history and cultural heritage. As such, they tend to entangle the central state apparatus and its political leaders in

<table>
<tr><td rowspan="3">Ministry of Foreign Affairs</td><td colspan="3">Prime Minister's Office</td></tr>
<tr><td>Ministry of Homeland Security</td><td>Ministry of National Defense</td><td>Ministry of Social Security</td></tr>
<tr><td>Ministry of Justice</td><td>Ministry of Finance</td><td>Ministry of Sustainable Growth</td></tr>
</table>

Figure 4.1 Our vision of a strategic center

ongoing political disputes. Partly because of this political controversy, many of the areas we propose to devolve are the most notoriously affected by constant organizational reshuffles—the "ministerial jigsaw puzzles." Transferring these matters to the provinces will thereby clean up the mandate of central administration, and allow it to focus squarely on issues that are a priority for Poland's future. This can be seen in the proposal shown in Figure 4.1 for the new organization of our central apparatus. We propose that the center would consist of the Prime Minister's Office and seven strong, prestigious ministries with clear and distinct organizational missions.

The core of the new government administration would be ministries with an established position and tradition, and therefore already functioning close to our proposed model. Such ministries would include the Ministries of Finance, Defense, Foreign Affairs, and Justice. To these we would add three ministries responding to contemporary challenges: the Ministry of Homeland Security, the Ministry of Social Security, and the Ministry of Sustainable Development.

Thus, we would once and for all bring an end to the history of ministerial jigsaw puzzles weakening the state. The list and structure of the ministries would be enshrined in law, with an established procedure for consultation with the opposition in the event of proposed changes.

The creation of stable, prestigious ministries would help realize many of the organizational goals described earlier: the creation of attractive workplaces, a distinctive ethos for potential employees, and an opportunity for the systematic networking of knowledge and contacts, at home and abroad. An additional bonus of this system would be the possibility of a new alignment of the government administration's relationship with parliament, and especially with the opposition—for the current system of our central government does not make use of many of the tools for stabilizing (and therefore strengthening) the state in the realities of a multi-party parliamentary constitutional system. Rather than dismantling this system in favor of solutions that further reinforce polarization, such as the first-past-the-post/two-party system or a presidential system,[29] our proposal allows for better use of the potential of parliamentarism.

A stable structure of ministries is a key prerequisite here. We propose the establishment of dedicated permanent parliamentary committees for each of the ministries mentioned. The role of these ministerial committees would not be limited to parliamentary oversight and discussing bills prepared by the ministries. The committees would act as think tanks for the opposition, guaranteeing it access to information (including classified information) and analytical facilities, and thus preparing the opposition to continue priority projects after taking power.

In each of the ministerial committees, the opposition would have its own Political Cabinet, that is, policy advisors paid from the public purse as well as a group of non-political civil servants—the Office of Parliamentary Affairs—which would be established in each of the ministries. The opposition MPs would, finally, be assigned office space at the ministry building.

Such a solution would force deputy prime ministers and ministers (more about them soon) to change the logic of distrust and withholding information from the opposition into a logic that would enhance stability. Decentralization would remove many controversial issues from the political center, leaving strategic issues that are not as politically emotive. That is why the vision of transparency and cooperation in areas of national consensus need not be a pipe dream.

It is worth noting that our proposal for institutionalizing the role of the parliamentary opposition is not completely new in the Polish public debate. In 2016, Jarosław Kaczyński introduced a similar idea for improving the opposition's institutional base. "The opposition leader should have the status of a deputy prime minister," argued the PiS leader.[30] Similar solutions have been adopted, for example, in Canada, where the opposition leader is even given an official residence (Stornoway).

Focus on talent

As we have already mentioned, stable prestigious ministries will more easily attract talented staff. But our "politics is personnel" emphasis will be strengthened by a number of other reforms. We should start from the top and realize that a strong state requires strong leadership. From this vantage point, the situation in the Polish public sector is quite dramatic. This is because the same 1990s reforms that introduced the ministerial jigsaw puzzles also replaced traditional Polish deputy ministers with secretaries and undersecretaries of state, borrowed from the French tradition. Under the Constitution, secretaries of state are mainly MPs of the ruling party or coalition who also work in the executive. Undersecretaries of state, in turn, are experts affiliated with the ruling party.

In practice, filling the numerous positions of undersecretaries of state (more than fifty people) is not an easy task. These roles involve a lot of work and considerable responsibility, including criminal liability, but they are poorly paid and lack prestige. The best evidence of the crisis in this area is the regular media reports of young activists straight out of college (or even not quite) taking up positions as undersecretaries of state. Many experienced civil servants can barely contain their mirth when dealing with some of these so-called experts.

The Polish state will not be strong unless there are people with experience in top-level managerial positions in the leadership of ministries. People who have sat or could sit on the boards of large corporations or international institutions. In our opinion, the devalued "brand" of undersecretary of state cannot be saved. Therefore, we propose combining the proposed radical reduction in the number of ministries with giving (vice)-ministers a promotion.

When referring to "ministers," the Polish Constitution does not stipulate that each of them must manage a separate ministry. So why not create a system in which not one but several ministers function in each of our seven prestigious ministries? A similar system is already in place in the Office of the Prime Minister, where often a number of ministers work on separate issues. Under our proposal, each ministry would be headed by a deputy prime minister, with two or three ministers in charge of key priorities, and several secretaries and undersecretaries of state handling issues that require day-to-day administration.

Since the ministers in charge of priority areas in each ministry would, along with the deputy prime minister in charge of the ministry, be part of the Cabinet (as required by the Constitution), this body's composition would reflect the totality of the government's priorities. With the proposed number of ministers in a ministry, the Cabinet would consist of a similar number of members as at present—between twenty-five and thirty.

This streamlined leadership will positively affect all the lower ranks of the civil service. But here, too, additional reforms will be needed. In particular, a stronger governmental center requires a deep change in the way employees are appraised. Currently, the biennial periodic appraisal is entirely controlled by the official's immediate superior. It is not difficult to guess that such a system tends to promote rather cautious behaviors. It also reinforces the hierarchical, feudal model of the civil service, in which the best strategy is to scratch the boss's back.

We propose replacing this system with a model of holistic evaluation based on the "360-degree feedback" that is popular in organizations today.[31] The idea is that a civil servant's appraisal should depend not only on the boss, but on a broader group of stakeholders, including colleagues from within the ministry and from other cooperating institutions, subordinates, and also the citizens and businesses served by the official. The last of these elements would be easy to implement, as our proposal calls for the creation of a nationwide, online Local and Regional Government Quality Assessment System for Laws and Public Services (discussed in Chapter 2). In a system that would serve both national and decentralized government, citizens and businesses could easily rate every interaction with a public official. Similarly, they would be able to rate proposed draft legislation, in terms of whether it includes "understandable provisions" and "good solutions." The median of these ratings should become part of the periodic evaluation.

To make our central administration more networked, it would also be essential to introduce evaluation by stakeholders, meaning the employees of other institutions with whom the civil servant interacts. The challenge here will be to motivate stakeholders to take the time to contribute to a thorough evaluation. The law should therefore make it mandatory for employees of all government institutions to respond to a request for evaluation. Yet perhaps the most important piece of this motivational puzzle would be to include international stakeholders in the evaluation process—employees of European institutions or from other countries with which the civil servant has collaborated. After all, as we mentioned, the density of international networks is one of the key instruments for strengthening the government center.

In addition to the evaluation criteria themselves, it is also essential to determine who conducts actual evaluation, that is, assesses and weights the feedback given by various stakeholders in the 360-degree format. We propose to replace today's system of evaluation by a superior with an evaluation by a committee. In addition to the civil servant's superior, the evaluators would include representatives of other departments, experts in the field of public administration and, most importantly, at least one representative of a foreign institution—preferably with a profile similar to that of the ministry where the employee being appraised works.

Civil servants may already be despairing at the impossible financial and time costs of the solutions proposed here. Who will pay for the work of the thousands of experts evaluating our civil servants, including those from abroad? Our proposal indeed marks a significant change in the philosophy of personnel policy in our civil service corps. The quality replaces quantity. Periodic appraisal could occur less frequently and be more extensive for senior officials. But it is also crucial to understand that identifying effective and ineffective employees is one of the most important tasks facing the institutions of a strong state. Under this philosophy, the importance of periodic evaluation within the scope of a ministry's various tasks simply has to increase—even if it means slowing down or postponing other tasks.

The strategic value of English

The proposal for foreign experts to participate in the periodic evaluation of civil servants opens up another important issue: language. After all, we have to admit that the (extremely complicated) Polish language will never become a global *lingua franca*. Thus, Poland—if it wants to be a powerful country—must answer the question of where we stand in the current European and global discussion on the language of international communication.

The language issue is undergoing particularly heated debate in the European Union. For the first decades of the European Communities, the language of communication was unquestionably French. This situation slowly began to change after the accession of the United Kingdom in 1973. English began to gradually displace French from the Brussels institutions. This process was accelerated by the expansion of the Union to include Scandinavian and then Eastern European countries, whose officials and politicians generally spoke English rather than French.

Brexit has raised a question mark over the continuation of this trend. One possible scenario for the future is a renewed increase in the importance of French, and perhaps German, which is also one of the three working languages of the EU institutions.

Poland should take a clear stance in this discussion. In our view, our country's interest is clear: we should support English as the first language of European and global communication. Why? We can list at least six reasons.

First of all, it is in Poland's interest to maintain a balance between Germany and France—the two largest members of the Union after Brexit—and other EU countries.

Second, communication in English will naturally bring European and transatlantic relations closer together. Poland is, and should remain, a key European ally of the United States and one of the most active members of NATO.

Third, maintaining English as Europe's lingua franca will reap the rewards of the huge, generational investment in learning the language, both in schools and through the experience millions of Poles have gained from living and working in the UK and Ireland. For example, in the EU institutions that work in English, we are more likely to fill key official positions. The reason is simple: More highly qualified Poles are fluent in English than in French.

Fourth, an English-speaking Polish administration will better diversify trade and cultural contacts as well as foreign investment. This is discussed in Chapter 8. Poland's economy will, "by force of nature," naturally gravitate toward ties with its largest trading partner, Germany. It is therefore in Poland's interest to complement this process with a conscious policy of diversifying our economic partners.

Fifth, the use of English on a par with Polish increases the pool of people whose expertise, knowledge, and contacts can be used in the work of our administration. This could be through consultation, or though the contracting of tasks carried out in a networked manner in Poland and around the world. This will also facilitate the flow, exchange and reintegration of Polish officials between the national, EU-transatlantic (EU and NATO) and global (UN) levels.

Sixth, from the point of view of internationalization, or the opening up of the Polish administration to the world, it will be crucial to choose *one* foreign language to complement our native official language. If we are organizing a regional or global conference, it makes sense that the ministry officials in charge should be able to communicate with guests in one foreign language. And the easiest way to implement this is to invest in English.

This brings us to our proposal for the civil service corps. As the law stands today, a candidate for a civil servant must document knowledge, at an intermediate level, of one of eleven foreign languages. The required level is, in our opinion, too low. For example, to study at a foreign university, advanced language skills are generally required. In order to internationalize the Polish government center, advanced English proficiency should be a requirement for all civil servants. In the diplomatic service and in selected other units (for example, the departments of the Ministry of Justice responsible for dealing with the European courts, which operate in French), advanced knowledge of both English and a relevant second foreign language should be a requirement.

Language requirements should also apply to secretaries and undersecretaries of state. Contrary to popular opinion, the minimum level here could be lower than for rank-and-file officials. After all, those in top positions have the option of using interpreters in their work. For the same reason, there is no need for language requirements for the prime minister, deputy prime ministers, or ministers.

Government campus

It will soon be twenty years since Radosław Sikorski, while still Minister of Defense in the first PiS government, proposed the idea of building a "Polish Pentagon." The proposal was applauded by experts and ... that was the end of that. Meanwhile, the issue of infrastructure, not only of the Defense Ministry but of the center of government in general, is one of the main obstacles to the creation of stronger, more professional state institutions.

"Well, we are still a poor country," some might be tempted to reply. The problem is that the modernization of our administrative infrastructure is teeming with paradoxes. While ministries crucial to state security struggle with facilities that hark back to the days of deep communism, Poland has spent billions of zlotys in recent decades on building hundreds of relatively modern office buildings for newly created municipalities.

The authors of this book support decentralization, but even so, we think we can all agree that it is absurd for an official of the trendy Warsaw district of Wilanów to work in better conditions than his colleague at the Ministries of Defense or Finance. In recent years, the government has allocated 2 billion zlotys for the purchase of VIP aircrafts. Before this, the Polish Prime Minister or president flew in planes chartered from LOT Polish Airlines. Having a fleet with advanced security systems and secure communication is undoubtedly beneficial. However, wouldn't allocating those billions to the aforementioned "Polish Pentagon" have been a better contribution to the security and efficiency of the state?

Regardless of the mistakes of the past, not only the Defense Ministry but also all proposed strategic ministries require modern campuses—office bases that not only facilitate work but also architecturally express the ethos of the central institutions, and thus the strength and prestige of the Polish Republic. At the same time, it is important that this new government center be a clear break from the legacy of the dark days of communist dictatorship and socialist realist architecture, which influenced the form of most government buildings.

The issue of the pragmatic and symbolic aspects of our government buildings occasionally surfaces in public discourse—in recent years, in the context of the PiS's correct proposal to rebuild the Saski Palace, a major historic palace surrounding the grounds of the Tomb of the Unknown Soldier in downtown Warsaw.[32] The importance of these very tangible aspects of state power has also been recognized by our Western neighbors, who have spent billions of euros on rebuilding government centers, including the Reichstag building in Berlin, which is imbued with symbolism. The European Union is paying similar attention to these issues.

The seven ministries

We intentionally left the discussion of the catalog of proposed ministries for last. Intentionally, because this catalog is less important than our overall philosophy of strengthening the government center.

Nonetheless, the proposal for a government consisting of the Prime Minister's Office and seven ministries would clearly support the general vision of a strong center outlined above. In particular, each ministry would have the opportunity to develop a distinct mission and brand, attracting (through the aforementioned self-selection process) officials who share a genuine passion for a particular area of public affairs.

As we have already mentioned, the closest to this aspirational model is the Ministry of Finance. The careers of many senior civil servants in the Finance Ministry—some of whom are broadly known and respected—exemplify the ethos of professional civil service, which should become the rule rather than the exception. It is also worth noting that officials in this ministry are among the best-paid professionals in the entire Polish government administration.

The Justice, Defense, and Foreign Ministries may also draw on aspects of this ethos. However, the mission and organizational culture of each must undergo significant change. The Ministry of Justice should once and for all separate itself from the Prosecutor's Office and focus on its mission as an impartial defender of constitutional values. Consideration should be given to creating an Office for the Defense of the Constitution, subordinate to the ministry. The Central Anti-Corruption Bureau should be transferred to this ministry, as should the administrative departments responsible for gender equality, the rights of national minorities, religious beliefs, and public media.

The Ministry of Defense should be one of the three pillars of government administration responsible for the security of the Polish people. Ensuring security for the country's citizens in uncertain times becomes not just one of the many tasks of central government, but a fundamental responsibility. This observation stands at the heart of the constitutional proposal outlined in this book. We want to move everyday political disputes to the provinces. That leaves the center precisely with ensuring the security that constitutes a prerequisite for us to be able to continue our political debates.

The Ministry of Defense will be supported in implementing this key priority by the new Ministry of Homeland Security. Key departments from the Ministry of Internal Affairs and Administration will be transferred to this ministry, including the police, firefighting, crisis management, and migration issues. Unlike the Ministry of Internal Affairs, the new ministry will be squarely oriented toward providing internal security for citizens. Civilian intelligence (except for that under the jurisdiction of the Ministry of Justice) would also be transferred here. Ensuring cyber security in the broadest sense would also be one of the key areas of the ministry's activities.

The third pillar of the new security system for Poles would be the new Ministry of Social Security. This would encompass security in a broad sense, covering health security (including the National Health Fund), national pensions (discussed in Chapter 2), and the protection of national heritage. This ministry would naturally attract experts with a strong sense of social responsibility, interested in forms and ways of providing economic and social security to Poles.

The other economic policy issues remaining after decentralization—especially in terms of climate change, energy, infrastructure, water management, and environmental protection—would become the domain of the Ministry of Sustainable Development. As concerns the "economic think tank" of the Cabinet, organizational stability will be needed like nowhere else, since these areas have been affected in the past by the ministerial jigsaw puzzles.

In our proposed vision of internationalized, networked ministries, a profound overhaul would have to take place at the Ministry of Foreign Affairs. For several decades, a dilemma for Polish government administration specialists has been how to locate European policy in our network of ministries. From the late 1990s until 2010, there was the Office of the Committee for European Integration, which—though functioning within the structure of government administration—was separate from the Ministry of Foreign Affairs, and dealt with relations with the EU. Critics of this arrangement rightly noted that the Office effectively created an alternative diplomatic service to the MFA. However, the integration of the Office and its valued staff into the structures of the MFA did not prove sustainable. Over the past decade, the powers of conducting European policy have gradually been taken over by the Prime Minister's Office.

The problem of the relationship between the Ministry of European Affairs and the Ministry of Foreign Affairs exists in many EU member states. It is part of a broader dilemma concerning the shrinking requirement for a traditional diplomatic service, especially in Europe. In a world where every part of government maintains direct, intensive contacts with partners in other countries and international organizations, diplomats are looking for new niches. The aforementioned Council of the European Union, in which ministers from all member states meet—and without the supervision of the foreign ministers—is a good example of these changes.

A strong Polish state should not wait for this dilemma to be resolved by other nations, whose long institutional traditions are often an obstacle to bold modernization and adaptation to new challenges. It is in our national interest to be a forerunner of an effective foreign policy that is adapted to modern realities.

Our proposed model of a "Ministry of Foreign Affairs for the twenty-first century" is that of a horizontal ministry providing support to the Prime Minister's Office and other ministries, particularly the Ministry of Defense. A twenty-first-century MFA would also be at the disposal of the decentralized governments, would help coordinate foreign policy goals through a strategic foresight toolbox, and would create and coordinate inter-ministerial networks from the local government to the European level.

Power without domination

Our main goal in this chapter was to illustrate how the vision of the new social contract presented in this book, which reduces the intensity of political conflict and strengthens democratic checks and balances through the clever use of multilevel governance, can contribute to building a truly powerful state.

The detailed solutions we have proposed should be regarded as illustrations and examples. The broader proposal for a political system presented in this publication is not dependent on a specific number of ministries or the way civil servants are evaluated. It is more about a certain philosophy of governance that does not equate power with conflict and domination. It is about the strength of the state understood as the focus and effective networking of activities, all based on stability, consensus and shared values. It is about the strategic focus of attention and efforts by Polish citizens, yielding better results than an endless war at the top.

Notes

1. Donald F. Kettl, *Sharing Power: Public Governance and Private Markets* (The Brookings Institution, 1993).
2. Andrew Moravcsik, "Europe, the Second Superpower," *Current History* 109, no. 725 (2010).
3. Megha Shrivastava, "Emerging Dynamics Between the Chinese State and Big-Tech: The Case of Alibaba," *Strategic Analysis* 47, no. 1 (2023): 19–29 .

4. For a comprehensive analysis see Maciej Kisilowski and Izabela Kisilowska, *Administrategia. Jak osiągnąć sukces osobisty zarządzając w administracji publicznej* (Studio Emka, 2016).
5. Ingrid Van Biezen, "Political Parties as Public Utilities," *Party Politics* 10, no. 6 (2004): 701–722; Ingrid Van Biezen and Petr Kopecký, "On the Predominance of State Money: Reassessing Party Financing in the New Democracies of Southern and Eastern Europe," *Perspectives on European Politics and Society* 2, no. 3: 401–429; Kevin Casas-Zamora, *Paying for Democracy: Political Finance and State Funding for Parties* (ECPR Press, 2005).
6. Curtis Ventriss et al., "Democracy, Public Administration, and Public Values in an Era of Estrangement," *Perspectives on Public Management and Governance* 2, no. 4 (2019): 275–282; Eva Witesman and Lawrence Walters, "The Public Values of Political Preference," *International Journal of Public Administration* 39, no. 1 (2016): 63–73.
7. See e.g. John Paul II, Centesimus Annus (1991), for criticism of a "totalitarian state" that "tends to absorb within itself the nation, society, the family, religious groups and individuals themselves."
8. An excellent summary of the arguments for the ministerial puzzle system, and the practical consequences of this system, is presented by Marek Woźnicki, "Zmiany zakresów działania ministrów kierujących działami administracji rządowej w latach 1997–2016," *Annales Universitatis Mariae Curie-Skłodowska, sectio G–Ius* 64, no. 1 (2017): 243–263. See also Radoslaw Zubek, "A Core in Check: The Transformation of the Polish Core Executive," *Journal of European Public Policy* 8, no. 6 (2001): 911–932.
9. Foteini Kravariti and Karen Johnston, "Talent Management: A Critical Literature Review and Research Agenda for Public Sector Human Resource Management," *Public Management Review* 22, no. 1 (2020): 75–95; Paul Boselie and Marian Thunnissen, "Talent Management in the Public Sector: Managing Tensions and Dualities," in *The Oxford Handbook of Talent Management*, ed. David G. Collings, Kamel Mellahi, and Wayne F. Cascio (Oxford University Press, 2017).
10. An excellent stage of the consequences of instability in Polish public administration is presented by Stanisław Mazur, Michał Możdżeń, and Marek Oramus, "The Instrumental and Ideological Politicisation of Senior Positions in Poland's Civil Service and Its Selected Consequences," *NISPAcee Journal of Public Administration and Policy* 11, no. 1 (2018): 63–89 .
11. See, for example, Donald P. Moynihan and Sanjay K. Pandey, "The Role of Organizations in Fostering Public Service Motivation," *Public Administration Review* 67, no. 1 (2007): 40–53 .
12. See, for example, Dong Chul Shim and Sue Faerman, "Government Employees' Organizational Citizenship Behavior: The Impacts of Public Service Motivation, Organizational Identification, and Subjective OCB Norms," *International Public Management Journal* 20, no. 4 (2017): 531–559; Rachel Parker and Lisa Bradley, "Organisational Culture in the Public Sector: Evidence from Six Organisations," *International Journal of Public Sector Management* 13, no. 2 (2000): 125–141 .
13. See Przemysław Hensel and Beata Glinka, *Urzędnicy i przedsiębiorcy: kulturowe bariery współpracy* (Wydawnictwo Poltext, 2012).
14. James L. Perry and Annie Hondeghem, *Motivation in Public Management: The Call of Public Service* (Oxford University Press, 2008); Julie Rayner et al., "Public Service Ethos: Developing a Generic Measure," *Journal of Public Administration Research and Theory* 21, no. 1 (2010): 27–51.
15. Wouter Vandenabeele, Gene A. Brewer, and Adrian Ritz, "Past, Present, and Future of Public Service Motivation Research," *Public Administration* 92, no. 4 (2014): 779–789.
16. David E. McNabb, *Knowledge Management in the Public Sector: A Blueprint for Innovation in Government* (ME Sharpe, 2007).
17. Patrick Dunleavy et al., *Digital Era Governance: IT Corporations, the State, and e-Government* (Oxford University Press, 2006).
18. Erik Hans Klijn and Joop Koppenjan, *Governance Networks in the Public Sector* (Routledge, 2015); Robert Agranoff, *Managing Within Networks: Adding Value to Public Organizations* (Georgetown University Press, 2007); Stephen Goldsmith and William D. Eggers, *Governing by Network: The New Shape of the Public Sector* (Brookings Institution Press, 2005).
19. Eugene Bardach, *Getting Agencies to Work Together: The Practice and Theory of Managerial Craftsmanship* (Brookings Institution Press, 1998).
20. Urszula Kobylińska, "Trust and Cooperation Between Companies and Public Administration Institutions in Poland" (2019); Kirk Emerson and Tina Nabatchi, *Collaborative Governance Regimes* (Georgetown University Press, 2015); John D. Donahue and Richard J. Zeckhauser, *Collaborative Governance* (Princeton University Press, 2011).
21. Kathleen Hale, *How Information Matters: Networks and Public Policy Innovation* (Georgetown University Press, 2011).
22. Thomas H. Kean and Lee Hamilton, *The 9/11 Commission Report: Final Report of the National Commission on Terrorist Attacks upon the United States*, vol. 1 (Government Printing Office, 2004).

23. See e.g. Jerzy Hausner and Stanisław Mazur, eds., *Państwo i My. Osiem grzechów głównych Rzeczypospolitej* (Fundacja Gospodarki i Administracji Publicznej, 2015).
24. Peter L. Lindseth, *Power and Legitimacy: Reconciling Europe and the Nation-State* (Oxford University Press, 2010).
25. See generally Anne-Marie Slaughter, *A New World Order* (Princeton University Press, 2004); Anne-Marie Slaughter and David Zaring, "Networking Goes International: An Update," *Annual Review of Law and Social Science* 2, no. 1 (2006): 211–229.
26. Christian Joerges and Jürgen Neyer, "From Intergovernmental Bargaining to Deliberative Political Processes: The Constitutionalisation of Comitology," *European Law Journal* 3, no. 3 (1997): 273–299; Peter L. Lindseth, "'Weak' Constitutionalism? Reflections on Comitology and Transnational Governance in the European Union," *Oxford Journal of Legal Studies* 21, no. 1 (2001): 145–163.
27. Adrian Purzycki, "Polacy w instytucjach unijnych—niewykorzystany potencjał," *Fundacja Instytut Wolności*, Apr. 19, 2019; European Commission, *Report from the Commission to the European Parliament and the Council pursuant to Article 27 of the Staff Regulations of Officials and to Article 12 of the Conditions of Employment of Other Servants of the European Union (Geographical Balance)* (2018).
28. Tom Christensen and Per Lægreid, "The Whole-of-Government Approach to Public Sector Reform," *Public Administration Review* 67, no. 6 (2007): 1059–1066.
29. Juan J. Linz, "The Perils of Presidentialism," *Journal of Democracy* 1, no. 1 (1990): 51–69; Bruce Ackerman, "The New Separation of Powers," *Harvard Law Review* 113, no. 3 (2000): 633–729.
30. Zuzanna Dąbrowska and Michał Szułdrzyński, "Lider opozycji powinien mieć status jak wicepremier," *Rzeczpospolita*, Dec. 21, 2016.
31. John W. Fleenor, Sylvester Taylor, and Craig Chappelow, *Leveraging the Impact of 360-Degree Feedback* (Berrett-Koehler, 2020). This system has been introduced to public administrations in South Korea, among others: Pan S. Kim, "Utilising 360-degree Feedback in the Public Sector: A Case Study of the Korean Central Government," *Asian Journal of Political Science* 9, no. 2 (2001): 95–105.
32. "Poland Begins Work to Rebuild Historic Saxon Palace: Officials," *Polskie Radio*, Aug. 19, 2022, https://www.polskieradio.pl/395/7784/artykul/3022082,poland-begins-work-to-rebuild-historic-saxon-palace-officials. But see Monika Stobiecka, "Heritage of Empty Spaces: The Case of the Tomb of the Unknown Soldier in Warsaw," *International Journal of Heritage Studies* 31, no. 2: 1–15.

5

Return to Democracy

Ryszard Balicki, Jarosław Gwizdak, and Fryderyk Zoll

Why the new Round Table

What exactly, where Poland is concerned, does a "return to democracy" mean? Those of us who look back with horror on the period of PiS rule from 2015 to 2023, seeing it as a time of profound destruction of the democratic order, too rarely ask ourselves this question. We instinctively think of a return to democracy in terms of the elections of October 2023, which were won by a coalition of parties declaring respect for the foundations of the rule of law.

The question we would like to pose in this section, however, is: What should happen now? The June 2025 election of Karol Nawrocki—a staunch PiS ally—as president signals, at best, a continuation of the fraught 2023–2025 cohabitation period with the outgoing right-wing president, Andrzej Duda, who systematically blocked the center-left government's attempts to restore the rule of law. At worst, the coming months and years may lay the groundwork for a Trump-style return of PiS to power—whether in the general election scheduled for autumn 2027 or even earlier.

Importantly, the twists and turns of the ongoing "Polish–Polish war" between the right and the center-left hardly affect the core argument of this chapter. After all, the original Polish version of this essay was written in 2022, when PiS held undivided—and increasingly authoritarian—power. Even then, we observed many of our fellow legal scholars clinging to the hope that the next election might serve as a magic wand to resolve Poland's constitutional crisis. Our response—then and now—remains: Even if the center-left wins, what happens then? Are we to assume that the right will never again triumph at the ballot box? Such an assumption is not, and never was, a viable strategy for rebuilding the rule of law.

As things stand, any future conservative government is likely to view its central mission as aggressively dismantling current restoration efforts—and personally targeting those involved in today's institutional cleanup. The return of Donald J. Trump to the US presidency in 2025 serves as a cautionary tale. PiS leaders, along with President Duda, have already begun echoing Trump's pre-2024 rhetoric, characterizing the post-2023 efforts to restore the rule of law as the supposedly "true" cases of unconstitutionality.

Ryszard Balicki, Jarosław Gwizdak, and Fryderyk Zoll, *Return to Democracy* In: *Let's Agree on Poland*.
Edited by: Maciej Kisilowski and Anna Wojciuk, Oxford University Press.
 DOI: 10.1093/oso/9780198979562.003.0006

As our co-authors mentioned in the introduction to this volume, thirty years ago one of Poland's most outstanding contemporary political scientists, New York University professor Adam Przeworski, introduced a key thought: Democracy can be considered consolidated when its basic rules are the only game that politicians play. "All the losers want to do is to try again within the same institutions under which they have just lost," Przeworski wrote about a stable democratic system.[1]

The key year for the return of Polish democracy was therefore not 2023, when a democratic opposition came to power. That moment of truth for our democracy will come in 2027, 2031, or some other year in which—as is natural in a democracy—the majority that emerged in 2023 will lose the trust of the voters, and the Right again wins a parliamentary majority and takes the reins of government.

For centrist, leftist, or liberal voters, that year will obviously not be a particularly pleasant one. It is normal that on the day the Right takes over, many progressive voters will be concerned about the direction of economic, social or international policy. Such is the charm of democracy. What is not normal is that after a right-wing electoral victory we are concerned about the future of our constitutional system, our obligations as a member of the European Union,[2] or the independence of our judiciary.

Only when we, as a state and society, reach a point where the future of our constitutional system is certain, regardless of which of the main political forces wins the elections—only then will we be able to recognize that we have indeed returned to a stable and consolidated democracy. Poland cannot afford to constantly undermine its basic constitutional institutions or the legitimacy of the judiciary depending on partisan electoral results. There is no escape from reality. The only way to restore stable constitutional democracy in Poland is for all political forces to attempt a constitutional settlement. And, yes—no matter how our argument may raise the blood pressure of readers outraged by PiS's destruction of the rule of law—"all forces" must also include representatives of the Right.

We therefore argue that it is imperative for Poles to convene a new Round Table, focused on setting boundary conditions for respecting basic constitutional norms, and in particular the institutions of our judiciary. Let us be blunt: there is no alternative to the Round Table. Even if the center-left coalition had secured the presidency and removed the powerful veto player from its legislative path, ordinary legislative reforms aimed at restoring the rule of law would still have not been sufficient. Without a constitutional settlement, each successive government will try to reverse even the best reforms, undermining judicial independence and delegitimizing the entire system. That is why the only lasting solution here is to reach an agreement on the judiciary, so that its further instrumentalization is not possible.

Modern negotiation theory distinguishes between two basic strategies for reaching agreement between parties pursuing conflicting objectives.[3] The first is compromise—finding a mutually acceptable way to *share the pie*. The second, and much more promising, is *expanding the pie*—finding a new, attractive solution that satisfies both parties.

As individual lawyers, we naturally have many comments and opinions on the detailed proposals presented by Social Contract Incubator—the unique cross-partisan association behind the proposal outlined in this book, of which we are all members, and which we refer to by its Polish acronym "IUS" (particularly fitting this chapter's topic!). In general, we support IUS's proposal precisely because its premise is to seek a fair and fully democratic starting proposal for the essential talks with the Right regarding the political system. The proposal embodies both the logic of compromise—"sharing the pie"—and the creative expansion of that "pie."

In the first logic—the logic of compromise—one must first and foremost include the idea of reforming the judiciary, based on decentralization and taking into account the societal input expressed by subnational government bodies in the process of nominating judges. We should also restore the National Council of the Judiciary as a body independent of politicians. As we will show later in this chapter, the IUS's proposal is a viable compromise between the traditional continental model of legitimizing judges through knowledge and integrity, and the Right's stated desire to strengthen something we can broadly call the "social sensibility" of our judiciary. No one will be fully satisfied here, but—perhaps—the IUS's proposal may be sufficiently acceptable to both sides to ensure the stability of the agreement reached.

However, the proposals for the judiciary would not be so appealing, in our opinion, if they were not part of a broader vision for the state, which—while preserving the unitary nature of the Republic—provides a chance for a real leap forward. This systemic solution, from both the progressive and conservative angles, could be our way to "expand the pie."

Focus on the Citizen

The fact is that politicians across the spectrum—left, center, and right—insist that their primary goal is to increase the influence of ordinary people on how government is run. In 2015, PiS took over the reins of government by attacking elites and "castes"[4] supposedly detached from society. Yet they took over from a party that not only had "civic" in its name, but was originally formed in the early 2000s precisely as a closer-to-the-citizen version of a centrist party (our co-authors discuss this more broadly in Chapter 1). Poland's oldest existing political party, PSL (Polish People's Party), has had "people" in its name since its inception in the late nineteenth century. The Left also regularly claims to stand for the dignity of ordinary people.

The IUS's proposal is a way of saying "check" to all these political declarations and aspirations. If the wars over the judiciary and independent institutions are, as the combatants declare, a fight for the influence of "citizens," "ordinary folks," or "the people" over detached elites, then perhaps the first step toward reaching a compromise on difficult constitutional issues could be to agree on concrete initiatives to strengthen that civic influence?

This is especially so since, objectively, there is room for change here.[5] Poland fares poorly, for instance, when it comes to confidence in government institutions. In 2021, of the forty-one countries included in the OECD survey, only Slovakia and Chile had less confidence in their executive than Poland, where only 25.9 percent of the population expressed confidence.[6] Performing only slightly better than our executive is the parliament, with more than 50 percent of citizens expressing distrust and fewer than 30 percent claiming to trust it. In contrast, the army, NATO, and the European Union enjoy high levels of confidence, with a clear majority of the public expressing confidence in these institutions.[7]

In its essence, the IUS's proposal changes the logic of "I can't do anything" into thinking "I can do a lot"—because I am a citizen. In addition to the local government unit in which we live, the proposal gives Poles a "middle" homeland and a field for civic activity: the strengthened voivodship.

Scale is of great importance here. Activity at the municipal level is possible for the "common person," as evidenced by the popularity of municipal participatory budgets[8] (also known as "civic budgets"[9]), urban movements,[10] and other similar initiatives. However, with the exception of the largest cities, the municipality and even the county are too small governance units to allow for many important public policies to be truly decided at their level.

In today's system, with very weak self-governed provinces, anything that cannot be delegated to the municipalities is retained at the center. And at the center, despite the tremendous efforts of numerous NGOs[11] and the considerable resources invested, there is little real participation by citizens and their groups in lawmaking or other forms of governance. Take the World Justice Project's "open government" ranking, based on the index that measures the ease with which citizens obtain information about government actions, the tools available to citizens and the media to make government accountable, and incentives for citizens to participate in the deliberative processes. Among all EU countries, Poland ranks an inglorious third—from bottom—with only Hungary and Bulgaria performing worse.[12]

The track record of nationwide direct democracy in defusing our political conflict is also rather unsatisfactory.[13] A perfect example is the 2015 referendum on a first-past-the-post electoral system for the Sejm, drawing an embarrassing turnout of just 7.80 percent.[14] This disaster demonstrates the broader systemic problems facing direct democracy initiatives in a country of nearly 40 million people. Nationwide referenda are nightmarishly expensive—the one mentioned above cost 72 million złotys.[15] For this reason, the Constitution rightly curtails the number of entities authorized to call a referendum—they are either the Sejm or the President, with the consent of the Senat.[16]

Nevertheless, such a framework naturally limits the reliance on the referendum to the most momentous decisions,[17] such as joining the European Union,[18] or—as in 2015—to becoming a very expensive footnote in the history of our nationwide political disputes. Examples from other countries, and most notably the 2016 Brexit referendum in the United Kingdom, illustrate the challenges of direct democracy being used in a large and diverse country to resolve issues entangled in nationwide political conflict.

Institutions that increase civic participation in governance at the national level hold little potential for reducing the intensity of the Polish–Polish war.[19] Politicians continue to outdo each other in portraying themselves as true representatives of the interests of "ordinary people," "civil society," or the "will of the nation," because we lack the tools to ensure that this "will"—whether of the people, the citizens, or the nation—is effectively expressed on specific issues.

The transfer of meaningful powers to the provincial level will help change this logic. By reducing the scale, there will be a real opportunity to strengthen meaningful civic participation in governance. We have already mentioned our successful municipal participatory budgets and active urban movements. Well, the largest Polish cities—where such forms of public participation are flourishing—are, in terms of population, similar to the small Polish voivodships. However, in order to convince skeptics that more civic democracy is possible at the provincial level, let us now add perhaps the most innovative aspect of our proposal: the idea of employing ICT tools to deepen the civic nature of our decentralized democracy.

E-Democracy

Think of a physical bank branch and an online banking app, or an e-health system that makes your prescription appear in your mailbox or a text message providing a visit to your area clinic.[20] It's more convenient to place a transfer or secure a prescription using your own device, over a cup of coffee, than to spend time in line at the post office or clinic waiting room.

Recent years have seen a great expansion in the number of commercial services provided through new technologies and devices. The COVID pandemic played a catalyzing role here.[21] After the imposition of lockdowns, it immediately became necessary to modify how we worked, how we learned, and, yes, how we engaged in public activities, including political ones. Once strict restrictions were introduced, the world around us—including the world of politics—literally moved online. The experience we acquired in the process has turned out to be positive. Many reservations previously expressed regarding the use of ICT services in political activity have been proven to be unfounded. Consequently, this has led to an increase in the popularity of e-democracy.[22]

Internet communication, and more broadly all information and communication technology used, must be regarded only as a tool for the fullest and most effective functioning of democracy. It must not in any way become an element that prevents anyone from taking part in any decision-making. The digital exclusion that still exists,[23] especially as a consequence of poverty, age, or health, must therefore be taken into account. It is incumbent on public administrations to ensure that all those eligible are truly able to participate.

E-democracy can be understood broadly,[24] but literature distinguishes three types of relations that can be facilitated by ICT tools.[25] The first type of relation is about public authorities providing information to citizens and other interested parties. This relationship is characterized by one-way communication, with public administration bodies playing a dominant role. The second, consultative relation represents a form of two-way communication, and involves the use of pre-defined forms of expression of opinions by citizens (residents) on the policies pursued by those in powers.[26] The third relation embraces active participation by interested parties. It can be implemented either as a structured dialogue, or through direct decision-making by citizens.

One can think of the IUS's proposal as a way to bring these three types of e-relationships closer together, to integrate them. It is primarily a matter of lowering the active participation threshold, which limits public participation to occasional, often politically motivated political events. As we mentioned, in the current Polish system, one participatory institution burdened with such a high entry threshold is the nationwide referendum.

The electronic form of local and regional referendums, combined with their smaller scale and reduced potential for them being weaponized in the nationwide Polish–Polish war, will increase the opportunity for their more frequent use. This approach will enable the application of this form of decision-making in all matters relevant to the functioning of local and regional communities, in particular on questions of budgetary appropriations.

Smartphones, tablets, and laptops will thus become the tools for participation in municipal, county, and voivodship government. Using them, residents will decide, for example, how to allocate the civic budget[27] or the new Civic Pro-Family Budget, proposed by IUS and created with funds from the 800+ program. It might be the case that a voivodship opts for a "700+" or "365+" program but combined, say, with expansive governmental funding of IVF procedures or a program to support large families. Decisions in this regard will be in the hands of the voivodship residents. Literally.

It is crucial that citizens are not afraid of electronic voting.[28] And that is why we propose that the National Electoral Commission, an institution independent of the local, regional, and national authorities, should watch over the proper organization and conduct of all democratic decision-making processes, including elections and e-referendums.

The National Electoral Commission will be composed of eight judges nominated by the First President of the Supreme Court and the President of the Supreme Administrative Court, plus sixteen judges nominated by the general assemblies of the new, prestigious, and independent Supreme Voivodship Courts. In accordance with the unitarian rather than federal system of the country, every Supreme Voivodship Court will be part of the nationwide system of justice, with the area of its jurisdiction matching the administrative division of the country.

The judges comprising the National Electoral Commission would be appointed for a nine-year term, while the mechanism adopted for their appointment would assume that no more than three of its members would be appointed each year. This limit would not include the situations when a term of office comes to an end for reasons other than its scheduled conclusion.

In order to directly perform the function of overseeing the organization and conduct of elections and other democratic decision-making processes in individual voivodships, the National Electoral Commission should establish Supervisory Teams. Each team should consist of two judges from the national supreme courts—that is, the Supreme Court, the Supreme Administrative Court, and the Constitutional Tribunal—one of whom would be the chairperson of the team. In addition, two judges will represent the Supreme Voivodship Courts from provinces that are not located in the immediate vicinity of the supervised voivodship. One judge would represent the voivodship in question. The judicial composition of the supervisory team would be supplemented by representatives of the various political groups active in the sejmik of a given voivodship. What needs to be considered here is their status: whether they would be equal members of the team, or merely act as permanent observers of the work of the team's judicial members.

Quick wins

Apart from the e-referendum, IUS has proposed a number of other ways of engaging citizens in our local and regional decision-making. IUS envisions a comprehensive demokracja.gov.pl online service as a hub for that engagement. Apart from e-referendums, the portal will enable Civic Dialogue over voivodship legislative proposals, and the ability to submit Civic Legislative Initiatives and to fill e-petitions. It will also be used for initiating or participating in public consultations or for allowing online access to sessions of the various bodies of local and regional governments. Any resident of a province will be able to submit comments and assessments concerning a new law, and such comments will constitute an integral part of the regulatory impact assessment.

In addition to the parliamentary debate, structured Civic Dialogue will be held for the more important regional bills. In that process, citizens will be able to express their opinions, comments, and concerns about the measures proposed. If citizens feel that a new policy issue needs to be regulated at the provincial level, they will be able to force the consideration of a new bill by the sejmik and the voivodship senate by filing a Civic Legislative Initiative.

Inaction or obstructionism by provincial authorities in response to technologically enhanced public participation will be prevented by another power granted to citizens: the ability to convene Civic Sessions of the local and regional bodies, including the sejmik and the board, on their own initiative. The constitutional members of these bodies will still obviously make decisions during these sessions, but they will be forced to discuss the agenda points brought by the citizens. This would compel local authorities to be more active and take action for the benefit of the citizens.

ITC tools such as the demokracja.gov.pl portal can also be used as real mechanisms for the scrutiny, evaluation, and accountability of elected authorities. With that goal in mind, IUS envisions a possibility of e-recall of local and regional authorities. The goal is to make the citizen an equal partner, reviewer, and critic of the authorities.

All in all, granting a genuinely stronger say to citizens, especially in the context of local and regional democracy, should appeal to all major forces on our political scene. For the Civic Platform and the Polish People's Party, it means an opportunity to recognize and return to the "civic" and the "people's" cores of their political identities. For the Left it will provide an opportunity to make a broader impact on politics, since social and redistributive demands are generally popular in Poland.

The Right, too, should welcome the new opportunities that the decentralized e-democracy will provide. After all, this side of our political scene has long decried the supposed "impossibilism"[29] of incorporating conservative demands into public policy. Looking for new ways of overcoming that "impossibilism" may be especially useful for PiS, given that its assault on the judiciary has not earned it much in terms of constructive agency, at least as perceived by its own voter base. It is also worth noting that the principle of subsidiarity, which dictates that power should be delegated to the lowest possible community, is a cornerstone of the Catholic Church's social doctrine, and that both previous successful local government reforms in Poland were designed and initiated by the Right.

In conclusion, from the point of view of our hypothetical constitutional Round Table, agreeing on greater civic participation in the exercise of power could be a so-called *quick win*. Since more power will be in the hands of local and regional governments, there will be less political pressure to completely take over and dominate power at the center. And it was that "winner-takes-all" pressure that (in our view) was the main reason why PiS initiated its thorough destruction of the judiciary.

Difficult compromises

With all that being said, it is clear that electronically enhanced participatory democracy alone will not solve the festering problems afflicting our fundamental constitutional institutions, especially those related to the administration of justice. IUS also proposes using decentralization in these "weightier" topics, so as to find a sustainable cross-partisan compromise.

Take, for example, IUS's proposal on the process of appointing judges. Under PiS's rule, the central tool for dismantling the rule of law became the institution created in 2018 to replace the constitutional National Council of the Judiciary.[30] The process involved an illegal shortening of the NCJ's term. The resulting body, established in clear violation of the 1997 Constitution, may be viewed as a "pseudo-NCJ." Judges on the pseudo-NCJ were elected by the parliamentary political majority and not, as the Constitution requires, by the national judiciary. In short, a body not recognized by the Constitution was created. The pseudo-NCJ could not and cannot perform any of the functions assigned to the Council in the Constitution. The entire system is thus tainted by the flaws of this central institution.

IUS calls here for a number of changes, obvious to the authors of this chapter, though undoubtedly a difficult compromise for the right-wing camp today. In particular, we call for the restoration of the election of judges—members of the NCJ—by the judicial community. At the same time, however, recognizing that a significant group of Poles are persuaded by the right-wing narrative of the need to balance the professional aspect of the judiciary with a more direct social impact on our administration of justice, IUS proposes that the constitutional procedure for the appointment of a judge should include not only the nomination of the constitutional NCJ,[31] but also the opinion of the subnational government. Specifically, what is meant here is the opinion expressed by the assemblies of mayors—the new voivodship senate—from the region where the judge in question is to sit.

IUS stresses that—in accordance with the Constitution—the NCJ would retain the exclusive right to nominate judges, and the opinion of the provincial senate would not be entirely binding: in the event of three consecutive candidates being rejected, the NCJ could present to the President of the Republic the candidate with the greatest support (measured by the number of inhabitants represented by the provincial senators).

Although IUS's proposal undoubtedly falls within the canon of democratic solutions, it nevertheless departs from the classic continental model of judicial legitimacy based on knowledge and integrity (and not a democratic mandate). An alternative or complementary solution might therefore be a constitutional amendment (needed anyway to implement many of IUS's proposals, including the national Senate of the Voivodes), expanding the composition of the NCJ to include not only judges and politicians, but also representatives of other segments of the legal profession. The Council could, in particular, involve representatives of the bar associations, notaries, prosecutors, registrars, and distinguished legal scholars. The judicial community should not have a majority. Such a system would still allow for proper verification of merit, protecting judicial independence[32] and making it difficult for institutions intended to guard the independence of the judiciary to be transformed into structures focused solely on protecting the interests of a particular professional community.

Another way to strengthen the legitimacy of judges could be to strengthen the National School of Judiciary and Prosecution, by making it independent of the Minister of Justice.[33] The role of the NCJ in the case of the first appointment could then be limited to determining that the prerequisites of merit and integrity have been met. It is worth noting, however, that the idea of the School's stronger position has always met with strong right-wing opposition, including from the relatively moderate late President Lech Kaczyński—brother of the current PiS leader, Jarosław Kaczyński—who tragically died in a plane crash in 2010. President Kaczyński's views are a good illustration that even moderate representatives of the Polish Right find the aforementioned continental model of judicial legitimacy—rooted solely in knowledge, professionalism, and integrity—unsatisfactory.

The difficult compromises in judicial appointment procedures could perhaps become easier if we were to use decentralization to reform other pillars of our system of administration of justice. A particularly promising field here is the Public Prosecution Service. The current model of Poland's public prosecution is, on the whole, a remnant of the Soviet system. The merger of the functions of the General Prosecutor with the Minister of Justice, which was completed by PiS in 2016[34] and which gives the Minister of Justice full prosecutorial powers, is untenable in a democratic *Rechtsstaat*.[35] It also raises serious questions of constitutionality. However, the problem with our Prosecution Service is not limited to the overall leadership. One can easily imagine a model with general oversight by the Minister of Justice, but without the right to interfere in individual cases. This is the approach taken by Adam Bodnar[36]—a former ombudsman appointed as Minister of Justice in the post-2023 Tusk government and a university professor. Even with such a self-constrained leadership, a comprehensive change in the model of the current Prosecution Service is desperately needed.

The goal should be to create a Prosecution Service that simply cannot be taken over by the political majority of a period. The centralized prosecution model makes such a takeover very easy, which returns us to our opening remark about the need to develop institutions that will contribute to the consolidation of Polish democracy and thus would not depend on the goodwill and self-restraint of the government of the day.

A particularly attractive solution would be to carry out the complete decentralization of the Prosecution Service, so that it is no longer possible, or at least is exceedingly difficult, for an overbearing politician to take over the entire service. Therefore, the current Prosecution Service should be completely dissolved, and in its place Prosecutors' Offices should be established at the courts of each level, decentralized and independent. This would prevent public prosecution from being involved in current political activities.[37]

Such a solution could, in our opinion, win conservative support. Accusations of politically motivated retribution from the liberal side are, after all, widespread on the Right. Guaranteeing the apolitical nature of the decentralized prosecution offices would therefore be in the interests of all politicians—and, incidentally, all citizens.

To return or to build?

In the wide-ranging discussion of how to clean up after PiS, many commentators focus on resolving the issue of the Constitutional Tribunal as a starting point. There is much sense in this approach. It is through the Constitutional Tribunal, taken over by PiS in 2015–16,[38] that the government wielded almost complete control over the law between 2015 and 2023.[39] As if acting on political orders, PiS's "pseudo-Tribunal," still entrenched at the time of this writing despite the change of government, can declare unconstitutional acts that, by consensus within the legal community, are either constitutional or beyond the Tribunal's jurisdiction. Conversely, it can declare acts widely regarded as unconstitutional to be constitutional. In this form, the Constitutional Tribunal has proven to be an easy target for political takeover, a highly dangerous body for the legal order, and one that threatens the very foundations of democracy.

However, in the logic of the constitutional compromise described here—the new Round Table—the topic of the Constitutional Tribunal should perhaps be considered last. Why? Because, as we wrote above, the attack on the Tribunal is a symptom rather than a cause of the right-wing disease. PiS was obsessed with subjugating the Tribunal not for the sake of subjugation itself, but in order *de facto* to not be bound by the restrictions of the 1997 Constitution. To put it another way, PiS—lacking the majority required to amend the Constitution—decided to change it *de facto* with the often utterly curmudgeonly rulings of their pseudo-Tribunal.

Reaching a meaningful constitutional compromise on key issues will remove the main motivation for political assaults on the Tribunal. If the representatives of the Polish political scene, including its right wing, agree on a mutually acceptable shape of the basic constitutional institutions, the motivation to distort the meaning of these institutions at the hands of a pseudo-Tribunal will be significantly reduced.

Critics may, of course, call us naïve. What if the faction that was demolishing the state for almost a decade agrees to a "round-table" compromise, only to then—after regaining power as hypothesized at the beginning of this chapter—violently break it? Such a risk always exists. However, let us note that the balance sheet of the PiS's constitutional destruction is an obvious disaster, including for the conservative base. The pseudo-Tribunal, for instance, has no authority whatsoever, and both in Poland and within the European Union is considered a purely political body.[40]

While in power, PiS also failed to take control of the courts. Several factors, internal and external, explain the failure. The former group includes, first and foremost, the organized self-defense of judges, who proved immune to both promises made by the authorities and threats of disciplinary or criminal liability. The judges, for the most part, did not allow themselves to be intimidated, and their attitude led to a significant slowdown in the process of seizure of control by various centers of power (often in fierce competition with each other) deriving from the so-called United Right (PiS and its smaller coalition partner Sovereign Poland).

The second group of factors includes the attitude of the EU institutions, in particular the Court of Justice, which has succeeded in developing real instruments of pressure to apply to countries systematically demolishing their rule of law. From outside the EU, the jurisprudence of the European Court of Human Rights is also an important factor.[41] This institution unexpectedly began to recognize the situation in Poland as a violation of the right to a court, one of the basic human rights.

As a consequence of the lack of consolidation of democracy, between 2015 and 2023 there was a breakdown in the constitutional order, and the emergence of a hybrid regime model, combining elements of democracy and authoritarianism.[42] The Polish political system showed its weaknesses: the monopolization of control at the center easily leads today to a situation in which, by winning elections, complete power can be seized.

Such a state of affairs threatens the very foundations of the Republic. It led to the emergence of a parallel legal reality, a dramatic collapse in the authority of state institutions including the Constitutional Tribunal, and the stirring up of a powerful conflict within the judiciary. A return to the path of building and strengthening democratic institutions therefore seems essential. At the same time, one can hope that the experience gained so far will allow politicians from diverse ideological backgrounds to rise above partisan interests and take meaningful action to restore the functioning of democratic mechanisms in Poland.

It is worth emphasizing that there is no easy "return to the past." Attempting to mechanically restore the playing field from before the assault on democracy would be incomprehensible, and—more importantly—ineffective. When thinking about reactivating democratic institutions, it is necessary to rethink them: both in terms of substance—the point here being that we should not make the same mistakes—and, in keeping with the focus in this chapter, in political terms—meaning giving democracy a chance to be consolidated or, in other words, to gain lasting and stable support from all major political factions for the fundamental constitutional institutions, and especially for the independence of the judiciary.

The classic American democratic theorist, Yale University professor Robert Dahl, emphasized that democracy understood as an ideal system-model is a state that probably cannot be achieved, but which must be constantly fought for.[43]

Under the current conditions, the goal of this struggle must be to bring about a lasting constitutional consensus.

The foundations of the IUS's proposal described above—a stronger division and balance of powers through so-called multilevel governance, and the reinforcing of citizen power through the use of new technologies—are certainly a good contribution to this new Round Table, marking out both the space for compromise ("sharing the pie" within the framework of Western democratic standards) and drawing up potential new areas for expanding this "pie," appealing to all. While the details can and should be discussed, the key question mark hangs over the future attitude of the Polish Right. As the saying goes, it takes two to tango. And to dance the polonaise, too.

Notes

1. Przeworski, *Democracy and the Market, Political and Economic Reforms in Eastern Europe and Latin America*, 26.
2. Stanisław Biernat, "Trybunał Konstytucyjny wypowiada posłuszeństwo prawu Unii Europejskiej," in *Wokół kryzysu praworządności, demokracji i praw człowieka. Księga jubileuszowa Profesora Mirosława Wyrzykowskiego*, ed. Adam Bodnar and Adam Płoszka (Wolters Kluwer Polska, 2020).
3. Andrea Cordell, *Negotiation Theory and Practice* (Routledge, 2018). For a widely popular practitioner's book introducing the concept, also widely cited in the negotiations literature, see Roger Fisher, William L. Ury, and Bruce Patton, *Getting to Yes: Negotiating Agreement without Giving In* (Penguin, 2011).
4. During the 2016 Extraordinary Congress of Judges in Warsaw, judge Irena Kamińska called judges an "extraordinary caste," in the sense of their uniqueness and responsibility. The notion of caste was soon used to highlight the alienation of judges from society by pro-government media and propaganda. See Anna Wójcik, "Six Arguments PiS Uses to Justify Poland's Judicial Overhaul—and Why They Are Wrong," *Notes from Poland*, Jan. 20, 2020, https://notesfrompoland.com/2020/01/20/six-arguments-pis-uses-to-justify-polands-judicial-overhaul-and-why-they-are-wrong/.
5. For a classic comprehensive analysis of the insufficient public participation in governmental policy-making in Poland see Susan Rose-Ackerman, *From Elections to Democracy: Building Accountable Government in Hungary and Poland* (Cambridge University Press, 2005).
6. https://data.oecd.org/gga/trust-in-government.htm, accessed Dec. 22, 2022.
7. https://www.statista.com/statistics/1193389/poland-trust-in-public-institutions, accessed Dec. 22, 2022.
8. Jarosław Olejniczak and Dorota Bednarska-Olejniczak, "Participatory Budgets of Polish Major Cities during Covid-19," *European Research Studies Journal* 24, Special Issue 2 (2021): 983–996 ; Piotr Wetoszka, "Participatory Budgets in Poland and Germany: Towards a Single Model?" *Annales Universitatis Mariae Curie-Skłodowska* 56, no. 4 (2022): 207–224.
9. Małgorzata Hartwich and Robert Romanowski, "Civic Budgets in Cities of Greater Poland Region in 2018," *Zeszyty Naukowe. Organizacja i Zarządzanie/Politechnika Śląska* 152 (2021): 47–63 .
10. Dominika V. Polanska, "Neoliberal Post-Socialist Urban Transformation and the Emergence of Urban Social Movements in Poland," in *Urban Uprisings: Challenging Neoliberal Urbanism in Europe*, ed. Margit Mayer, Catharina Thörn, and Håkan Thörn (Springer, 2016); Aldo Vargas-Tetmajer, "Urban Movements in Poland: A Short Presentation," *Urban Research & Practice* 9, no. 3 (2016): 311–321 .
11. There are 103,400 active NGOs in Poland https://stat.gov.pl/obszary-tematyczne/gospodarka-spoleczna-wolontariat/gospodarka-spoleczna-trzeci-sektor/dzialalnosc-stowarzyszen-i-podobnych-organizacji-spolecznych-fundacji-spolecznych-podmiotow-wyznaniowych-oraz-samorzadu-gospodarczego-i-zawodowego-w-2022-r-wyniki-wstepne,3,10.html, accessed Nov. 12, 2024.
12. The World Justice Project Rule of Law Index, 2020, p. 24 https://worldjusticeproject.org/our-work/publications/rule-law-index-reports/wjp-rule-law-index-2020, accessed Dec. 22, 2022.

13. Marcin Rachwał, *Demokracja bezpośrednia w procesie kształtowania się społeczeństwa obywatelskiego w Polsce* (Wydawnictwo Sejmowe, 2010).
14. See https://referendum2015.pkw.gov.pl/341_Polska.html, accessed Nov. 12, 2024.
15. See information on state budget expenditure incurred for the preparation and conduct of the nationwide referendum, 6 Sep. 2015, https://referendum2015.pkw.gov.pl/aktualnosci/0/55_Informacja_z_dnia_5_lutego_2016_r_o_wydatkach_z_budzetu_panstwa_poniesionych_na_przygotowanie_i_przeprowadzenie_referendu.html, accessed Nov. 12, 2024.
16. Art. 125 sec. 2 of the Polish Constitution.
17. Under art. 125 sec. 1 of the Polish Constitution, a nationwide referendum may be held in respect of matters of particular importance to the State.
18. https://referendum2003.pkw.gov.pl/sww/kraj/indexA.html, accessed Nov. 12, 2024.
19. This is why there is a noticeable difference of approach to national and local referendums in the doctrine of Polish constitutional law. See Marcin M. Wiszowaty, "Referendum zagrożeniem dla porządku demokratycznego? Refleksje dotyczące polskiej regulacji prawnej i praktyki referendalnej na tle najnowszych opinii zagranicznej doktryny prawa konstytucyjnego i nauk politycznych," *Przegląd Prawa Konstytucyjnego,* 54 no. 2 (2020): 91–113 .
20. Maciej Błażewski and Michał Raduła, "System of e-Health Tools. The Example of Poland," *European Review of Digital Administration & Law* 4, no. 1: 243-248 (2023).
21. Mariusz Duplaga, "A Nationwide Natural Experiment of e-Health Implementation during the COVID-19 Pandemic in Poland: User Satisfaction and the Ease-of-Use of Remote Physician's Visits," *International Journal of Environmental Research and Public Health* 19, no. 14: 1–13 (2022).
22. Magdalena Frańczuk and Aldona Piotrowska, "The Impact of COVID-19 Pandemic on the E-Government Development And on The Reduction of Digital Exclusion" (paper presented at the 38th International Business Information Management Association (IBIMA), Seville, 2021), 359; Evelina Staykova, "The Digital Transformation of Local Democracy during the Pandemic," in *Participatory and Digital Democracy at the Local Level: European Discourses and Practices*, ed. Gilles Rouet and Thierry Côme (Springer, 2023); Gilles Rouet, "The COVID-19 Crisis: An Accelerator of Digital Democracy?" in *Participatory and Digital Democracy at the Local Level: European Discourses and Practices,* ed. Gilles Rouet and Thierry Côme (Springer, 2023), 370–2.
23. Gemma Wilson-Menzfeld et al., "Identifying and Understanding Digital Exclusion: A Mixed-Methods Study," *Behaviour & Information Technology,* June: 1-18 (2024).
24. Given the predominant use of communication via the Internet, a more appropriate name would probably be "i-democracy," but the term "e-democracy," derived from "electronic democracy," is more popular. In the older literature it is seen as teledemocracy, cyberdemocracy, or electronic democracy. For an overview of the discussion regarding these notions see: Magdalena Musiał-Karg, *Elektroniczne referendum w Szwajcarii. Wybrane kierunki zmian helweckiej demokracji bezpośredniej* (Wydawnictwo Naukowe WNPiD UAM, 2012), 48–58.
25. OECD, *Promise and Problems of E-Democracy* (2004). https://www.oecd.org/en/publications/promise-and-problems-of-e-democracy_9789264019492-en.html,accessed Jan. 31, 2025.
26. See the latest activity of Polish Sejm: https://www.sejm.gov.pl/sejm10.nsf/page.xsp/konsultacje_zasady, accessed Nov. 12, 2024.
27. On the positive approach of Polish residents toward the electronic form of settling matters related to the participatory budget: Mariusz Popławski, "COVID-19 and Direct Contact-Free Democracy—Experiences from Poland," *Przegląd Prawa Konstytucyjnego*, 6, no. 58 (2020): 610–611 .
28. A public opinion poll from 2019 shows that 78 percent of respondents have a generally positive attitude towards electronic voting: CBOS (2019) Ułatwienia w głosowaniu—opinie i oczekiwania, Komunikat z Badań, nr 50/2019, ISSN: 2353–5822, p. 6. In fact, the introduction of e-voting was briefly discussed before and during the pandemic: Magdalena Musiał-Karg and Izabela Kapsa, "Postal or Electronic Voting? The Analysis of the Preferred Voting Methods in the Context of Failed Electoral Reform in Poland," *Transforming Government: People, Process and Policy* 15, no. 3 (2021): 347–359; Magdalena Musiał-Karg and Izabela Kapsa, "Debate: Voting Challenges in a Pandemic—Poland," *Public Money & Management* 41, no. 1 (2021): 6–8 . The matter has resurfaced recently, as Mariusz Witczak—a Civic Platform MP and head of the Sejm's standing subcommittee for amending the electoral law, established on 25 January 2024—announced that the planned changes to the Electoral Code include the introduction of an e-voting procedure. See Artur Radwan, "Rewolucyjne zmiany w kodeksie wyborczym. Kolejne wybory już z głosowaniem w sieci," *Dziennik Gazeta Prawna*, Feb. 6, 2024 .

29. For an English-language discussion about the concept of "legal impossibilism," advanced by PiS leader Jarosław Kaczyński, see Paul Blokker, "Populist Counter-Constitutionalism, Conservatism, and Legal Fundamentalism," *European Constitutional Law Review* 15, no. 3 (2019): 519–543.
30. A peculiar form of authorization to assume control over yet another constitutional institution came in the form of a ruling by the Constitutional Tribunal, control of which had already been achieved. Cf. Ryszard Balicki, "Nie-glosa do nie-wyroku, czyli kilka uwag na marginesie sprawy K 5/17," *Iustitia* 28, no. 2 (2017): 1. See also Leah Wortham and Fryderyk Zoll, "Weaponizing Judicial Discipline: Poland," in *Disciplining Judges: Contemporary Challenges and Controversies*, ed. Richard Devlin and Sheila Wildeman (Edward Elgar Publishing, 2021), 293–294 .
31. Fryderyk Zoll, "The System of Judicial Appointment in Poland—A Question of the Legitimacy of the Judicial Power," in *The Culture of Judicial Independence* (Brill Nijhoff, 2012), 306.
32. Zoll, "The System of Judicial Appointment in Poland," 306.
33. Zoll, "The System of Judicial Appointment in Poland," 308–9.
34. See The Law on the Public Prosecutor's Office of 28 January 2016.
35. Fryderyk Zoll and Leah Wortham, "Judicial Independence and Accountability: Withstanding Political Stress in Poland," *Fordham International Law Journal* 42 (2018): 891–923. Paulina Augustyn and Karolina Bała, "Połączenie funkcji Ministra Sprawiedliwości i Prokuratora Generalnego jako zagrożenie dla praworządności," *Roczniki Administracji i Prawa* 2, no. XXI (2021); Michał Mistygacz, "Prokuratura w Polsce: między rozczarowaniem a diagnozą," in *Zasady ustrojowe i działania prokuratury w Polsce: nowe spojrzenie*, ed. Michał Mistygacz, Jarosław Onyszczuk, and Małgorzata Szeroczyńska (Elipsa, 2023), 15.
36. See Draft of 18 January 2024, Assumptions of the amendment to the Law on the Public Prosecutor's Office (separation of the functions of the Minister of Justice and the Prosecutor General) https://www.gov.pl/attachment/391aadde-837f-4d39-a702-6c68bbd57e0e, accessed Nov. 12, 2024.
37. Zoll and Wortham, "Judicial Independence and Accountability," 947.
38. Amendments to the Act of 25 June 2015 on the Constitutional Tribunal and the course of the legislative process are presented in detail in the monographs: Sadurski, "On the Relative Irrelevance of Constitutional Design: Lessons from Poland." Piotr Radziewicz and Piotr Tuleja, *Konstytucyjny spór o granice zmian organizacji i zasad działania Trybunału Konstytucyjnego: czerwiec 2015-marzec 2016* (Wolters Kluwer Polska, 2017).
39. Fryderyk Zoll, Katarzyna Południak-Gierz, and Wojciech Bańczyk, "State Liability for Damage Caused by COVID-19 Restrictions under Polish Law," in *Coronavirus and the Law in Europe*, ed. Ewoud Hondius et al. (Intersentia, 2021).
40. Fryderyk Zoll, Katarzyna Południak-Gierz, and Wojciech Bańczyk, Primacy of EU Law and Jurisprudence of Polish Constitutional Tribunal, IP/C/JURI/IC/2022-025, 23 (European Parliament, Committee on Legal Affairs, 2022).
41. Zoll, Południak-Gierz, and Bańczyk, Primacy of EU Law and Jurisprudence of Polish Constitutional Tribunal, 20.
42. Wojciech Mojski, *Kryzys konstytucyjny. Zagadnienia teorii konstytucji* (Wydawnictwo UMCS, 2023), 159.
43. Robert A. Dahl, *A Preface to Democratic Theory* (University of Chicago Press, 1956); Robert A. Dahl, *On Democracy* (Yale University Press, 2020).

6
Strengthening Democracy

Mirosław Granat, Tomasz Grzegorz Grosse, Arkadiusz Radwan, and Jacek Sokołowski

Preliminary remarks

The condition of Polish democracy lies at the center of the dispute that today divides Poles who support PiS and those who strongly oppose the changes that took place over the eight years when the right was in power between 2015 and 2023. Experts and citizens skeptical about the alarmist voices proclaiming the end of democracy in Poland emphasize, first, that media pluralism continued to exist throughout the PiS rule. The ruling party was far from having built the information monopoly that characterizes authoritarian states. Second, opposition parties had freedom to operate, in legal and institutional terms, as well as financially. Political competition was still going strong, and the outcome of the 2023 elections showed that the opposition was able to win and a seamless transition of power ensued.

Skeptics of the narrative about Polish democracy being in crisis furthermore note that the rule of PiS contributed to the political awakening of Poles, who transformed from the atomized and politically passive society they were in the 1990s into a political nation. Since 2015, voter turnout has been rising and ties between the electorate and politicians have begun to take on a programmatic character. Voters are formulating concrete expectations toward those in power, and are less ready to settle for empty promises.

Conservative commentators point out, finally, that Polish progressives seem to underestimate the fact that the Right empowered a segment of Polish society that previously identified with Polishness, but not necessarily with the Polish state, viewing the latter as indifferent and sometimes even hostile. And with good reason: the liberal approach to the economy and the state that prevailed during the transition period allowed the stronger to capitalize on the opportunities that emerged, while offering little to those less advantaged. PiS's anti-elitism opened the way to viewing the state as a structure capable of offering something, and therefore one of which individuals could also have expectations and demands. In the long run, this could strengthen the legitimacy of the state in the eyes of the citizens, provided this is not hindered by the second current of the ruling party's policies, namely anti-institutionalism.[1]

Mirosław Granat, Tomasz Grzegorz Grosse, Arkadiusz Radwan, and Jacek Sokołowski, *Strengthening Democracy* In: *Let's Agree on Poland*. Edited by: Maciej Kisilowski and Anna Wojciuk, Oxford University Press.
 DOI: 10.1093/oso/9780198979562.003.0007

At the same time, PiS was much more successful with ad hoc interventions, such as the 500+ program or the 13th and 14th pension, than with systemic measures that build stable, democratic institutions for generations. Many conservatives feel there was a deficit in institutional thinking in the 2015–23 period. And yet strong institutions have traditionally been absolutely fundamental to conservative political philosophy.

If we take a look at the substance of the proposal put forward by the Social Contract Incubator (IUS), we see in it many aspects dear to most conservatives. The principle of subsidiarity is the unquestioned foundation of Catholic social teaching. In Poland's recent history, the two successful decentralization reforms were entirely introduced by right-wing governments—and always with the opposition of post-communists, to the end faithful to the tradition of democratic centralism: Post-communists, we should add, who—despite the many promises of the rise of the New Left—are to this day the bedrock of Polish social democracy.

Moreover, the very demand to strengthen Polish democracy is, for a conservative, the right thing to do. Indeed, taking power away from various castes and corporations, and giving citizens more agency, was a key theme of the election campaigns for the 2015 successful presidential campaign of Andrzej Duda and the parliamentary campaign that, later that year, brought PiS to power.

It is gratifying to see that a significant group of liberals and leftists is beginning to recognize the necessity to regulate the democratic rules of the game in the spirit of a social contract acknowledging the fact that there exists a right-wing side to the Polish political scene. It is a pity, of course, that such reflection was absent at the time that the 1997 Constitution was drafted. For, as a notable Polish conservative commentator once wrote, the key problem with Polish democracy is liberal elites' unwillingness to recognize the right of conservatives to govern the country.[2] With those preliminary remarks made, let's look at which of the IUS proposals are particularly interesting and appealing to a democratic conservative.

A stronger Republic

A genuine aspiration for a strong state, a strong Republic, shines through in many aspects of the proposal outlined in this volume. Besides, these elements in the work of IUS have been systematically strengthened since the first versions of the proposals were presented in 2019. One could venture to say that international developments—predicted by conservatives for years—have convinced our liberal and leftist co-authors of the need to build a strong, resilient state.

As Catholic social teaching rightly observes, wise decentralization does not contradict a strong state, but rather reinforces it.[3] This is not only about more efficient democracy at the local and provincial levels, but also about the more efficient management of public affairs and, perhaps counterintuitively for some readers, the strengthening of central government. A government that does not have to deal with contentious issues, which at the same time are not strategic for the state, is able to focus on priorities and manage them more effectively. The whole system is likely to guarantee greater efficiency and stability—for conservatives, essential values of political life.

The devolution of politically exciting but nevertheless strategically collateral policy issues gives hope for greater activity and effectiveness of the central government in the "upward" direction. We talk primarily about radically increasing Poland's involvement and influence in the European Union. For conservatives, the darkest page of the eight years of PiS rule is definitely the history of hard-to-accept failures in Brussels.[4]

Putin's onslaught in Ukraine has opened the door to forging a kind of national compromise in foreign policy. The warnings and arguments presented for years by the Right are being repeated today by liberal mainstream commentators—and are even generating discussion, and long-awaited guilt, among Poland's western partners.

What undermines the chances of such a compromise, and the implementation of a policy of long-term influence on EU institutions (independent of the current majority in Poland's Sejm), is the existing differences in domestic policy. If at least some of these differences could, in the spirit of subsidiarity, be resolved by strengthening the self-governing provinces, then such an idea is at least worth discussing.

Following a period of modernization through imitation, we should cherish the ambition to take another step toward modernization through innovation.[5] History provides us with reasons to approach this task with optimism and confidence: the political system of the First Republic (fifteenth to eighteenth centuries) was unique in Europe, the May 3 Constitution (1791) was the first written basic law in Europe and the second in the world, the Union of Lublin (1569) was the prototype of a voluntary supranational organization,[6] the Union of Brest (1595) was an innovative solution to religious conflict,[7] and the Statute of Kalisz (1264) was exemplary for its time in mitigating religious tensions.[8]

Poles today have ever greater ambitions: they want their next smartphone to be better, they want to drive better cars, and they want to have household appliances performing ever more functions. Why shouldn't they have similarly rising expectations regarding the country's constitutional system, democratic institutions, and public services? Apart from the many international challenges, a major task we face and for which future generations will hold us accountable is how we deal with the internal differences that exist in our society.

Supporters of both the PiS government and the current center-left government would likely agree that the strong political polarization and resulting political dispute in Poland are highly detrimental to our country, both in foreign and domestic policy. The spillover of this internal dispute into international forums weakens the

Polish state, diminishes its influence, harms its image, and triggers significant economic costs.

The strategic goal of reform should be to reduce the social cost and externalities resulting from the ongoing political disputes. We are under no illusion that the differences underlying our modern tensions—diversity in values and in attitudes to history, the role of the Church, the model of the family, globalization, the coexistence of cultures, and many other issues—are deep and real.[9] Politicians can deftly read, exploit, and deepen these differences, but they are not their ultimate creators.[10]

However, at least from the perspective of citizens, it seems that neither side believes it can permanently and ultimately defeat the other. And since the conflict will not be resolved by either persuasion or social Darwinism; since neither side will convince the other, nor will either side die out; since compromise on fundamental values is usually either impossible or unsustainable; since all great national reconciliations have survived for no longer than the emotions that triggered them, one is left with a realistic diagnosis, which, incidentally, is the Incubator's motto: "Agreed. We are different." It is simply necessary to recognize this fact, and then to manage the diversity in such a way that the conflict it generates is the least costly to the state's institutions and Poland's strategic interests.

Our proposal is neither about one convincing the other, nor about compromise, nor about the victory of one system of values over another. The point is that, recognizing that it exists and will continue to exist, we should position this dispute in a place where its destructive effect on the institutions of the state and on social cohesion will be as small as possible.

This cost is so high today because both parties are playing the winner-takes-all game. From 2015 to 2023, the party representing a conservative approach to moral issues had the upper hand. It is therefore understandable that supporters of this fraction, then holding all the power and resources, would be inclined to defend the status quo or even push further. However, it all changed when PiS lost the elections and a center-left coalition took steps in the direction of liberal reform—and of course that applies to the entire country, including regions where the vast majority of residents strongly oppose such a shift in moral values.

The pendulum is swinging back ever more, and we know well what this means for the dynamics of change. Suffice to recall how the moral disputes were resolved in traditionally Catholic Spain and even more Catholic Ireland, where the Church also played a significant role, and where there were also alliances between the altar and the throne and scandals involving the clergy.

We now see Poland under a center-left coalition rule radically reprogramming the country's course on important moral issues. Now, the Left becomes a beneficiary of centralization, using the numerous instruments provided by the current system to push its axiological agenda. In such a scenario, the social contract proposed here can in fact be expected to be most opposed not by conservatives but by the Left, the Polish iteration of which is, for the most part, strongly statist and centrist, partly due to the communist provenance of the main part of this camp.

Rebuilding trust

The goals we are outlining can only be achieved if we rebuild cross-partisan trust in the state's core institutions. Institutions should be viewed as the referees of the political game, recognized by all parties. When rebuilding them, it will be essential to design them in such a way that they are both accountable to citizens and unsusceptible to "hacking"—through political appropriation or hollowing out.

In the discussion concerning institutions, the issue of the judiciary comes to the fore. The progressive side of Poland's political dispute considers any attempt to reform the judiciary an attack on the rule of law. Meanwhile, from the point of view of conservatives, the courts' social sensibility is also crucial. The institutional model that PiS tried to reform from 2015 was characterized by a very high level of self-governance of the judicial corporation. This included the appointment of judges (inbreeding) and the accountability of their work, which largely remained an internal affair for the judiciary. The judicial corporation controlled these key elements of the system, determining how the courts operated and how citizens experienced interaction with the judiciary.[11]

Another important problem from the point of view of the Right was the failure to hold judges accountable for how they had performed their functions between 1944 and 1989, as well as how they approached cases of former communist collaborators and victims of numerous communist crimes.[12] These were factors that, for much of the population, contributed to the low level of legitimacy of the Third Polish Republic, and PiS's program built its support on this very real socio-political development. At the same time, the claim that Polish courts needed decommunizing was essentially untrue. At the time when PiS judicial reforms were taking place, the average age of a judge was about 40.[13] The claim's carrying power, however, stemmed from the voters' strong feeling that in the process of transformation, the courts had sided with the former communists rather than with their victims.

But what was of fundamental importance was the often unsatisfactory experience of citizens in their dealings with the justice system. According to the 2017 survey, 51 percent of respondents had viewed the functioning of the justice system negatively, with 12 percent describing it as functioning very badly. Only 36 percent had a favorable opinion of the judiciary, and only 2 percent thought the system was working very well.[14] These unflattering assessments were mainly due to the protracted nature of proceedings and the experience of overly complicated procedures.[15]

Although there are no systematic surveys on a representative sample in Poland, there is much to indicate that in citizens' encounters with the courts, so-called subjective procedural justice was a challenge. This refers to situations in which citizens feel that in their dealings with the administration of justice, the outcome was not fair. Even if a citizen loses in court, as long as certain conditions are met, the likelihood of them finding the process fair increases significantly. This occurs when they have the opportunity to present their position, when the court is impartial, when the court addresses the parties with respect, and when the court's statements are understandable.[16] It is a challenge for the Polish courts to be closer to citizens, to communicate with them in a clear, understandable, and careful manner, and to ensure that when dealing with the judiciary, the citizen subjectively experiences the process as fair.

During the time of PiS government, a powerful symbol of this social detachment of the judicial corporation was conveniently provided by the judges themselves. At the 2016 conference organized to protest the PiS judicial reforms, Irena Kamińska, the president of a major association of judges, called her profession "an extraordinary caste." The conservative critics highlighted this comment as proof of the problems that they had long pointed out. In response, Judge Kamińska and her defenders argued that the expression was taken out of context.[17] However, it is difficult to see what that broader context adds to how the critics understood her message. The phrase was used at the very end of her speech, which was followed by the applause of the dozens of judges present. Here we quote the final part in its entirety:

> My whole life, I defended the judges. I believe that this is an *absolutely extraordinary caste of people*. And I think, ladies and gentlemen, that we will make it! And regardless of how many congresses and meetings we will organize—because they are very important, and this current one is truly pathbreaking—we must remember that each of us, in the courtroom, is a defender of democracy, human rights and judicial independence. Thank you very much. [emphasis added][18]

Moreover, even more liberal voices have also long drawn attention to the judiciary's problems with social embeddedness. In 2012, the then Ombudsman, Professor Irena Lipowicz, launched the public campaign for "citizen-friendly official language." Professor Ewa Łętowska, the first Polish Ombudsman and former judge of the Constitutional Court, has repeatedly highlighted the problem, noting among other things that "there is a lack of evaluation of jurisprudence; those who write well are not appreciated, those who do not apply themselves to the task are not reprimanded, and those who simply do not know how are not being taught."[19] Rulings are sometimes written schematically or copied, making it difficult for a citizen to understand how their case was resolved, and why such a ruling was reached.[20]

These negative experiences with the judiciary are real, and weigh on citizens' assessments of and trust in the courts. Conservative circles argue that the bureaucratic and formalized nature of court operations is another element of the legacy of the past system. In addition, the protracted nature of proceedings, and the inability to break free of procedural pitfalls through common sense, often leads either to judgments that are perceived as unjust, or to judgments that are practically meaningless to the parties at the time of delivery. *Justice delayed is justice denied.*

For years now, it has been impossible to reform the protractedness of proceedings, which is very troublesome for the parties involved, or to de-bureaucratize the courts. The democratically elected authority is therefore faced with the dilemma of whether, while respecting the self-governance of the judicial corporation, to admit its inability to reform the judiciary and limit its actions to incentives and negotiations with judicial communities; or to take more decisive steps to increase the accountability of the courts, but risk resistance and protests from the judicial community and political forces advocating full self-governance of the judiciary.

Conservatives view the interference of EU institutions in Poland's judiciary with concern. They not only consider it an overreach of the Union's treaty powers but also view it as a procedure intended to reduce the control of national democracy over the judiciary, including democratic influence over the selection of judges. In the post-2023 period, conservatives have been noticing glaring double standards when EU authorities not only fail to criticize, but in fact openly support, actions of the current liberal government that violate procedural legality. That is why we support the idea put forward by the IUS to increase the democratic influence of local communities over the appointment of judges, while allaying the fears of EU institutions that politicians at government level may have undue influence on the process.

Locally legitimized judges

The new social contract proposed by IUS offers a chance to break the stalemate. The project outlined in this volume aims to achieve the goals of the PiS judicial reforms: greater accountability of judges by curbing the corporatism embedded in their profession. At the same time, it is free of the flaws identified in the 2015–23 reforms, and does not pose a threat to judicial independence.

The key is to anchor judges' social accountability and sensitivity not in the parliamentary majority of the day, but in the most publicly trusted elected state institution—the municipal government. A promising means to this end, a forum focused on the social aspect of judicial appointments, will be the new voivodship senates—assemblies of mayors wielding a vote weighted by the size of the population represented.

In the IUS proposal, we retain the general structure of the judicial appointment process governed by Article 179 of the current Polish Constitution, according to which judges are appointed by the President of the Republic on the motion of the National Council of the Judiciary (NCJ). However, we add an important element: a motion can only be submitted to the President by the NCJ if the candidate has received an endorsement from the voivodship senate of the province in which they would be administering justice. Such an endorsement will require the support of mayors representing at least 60 percent of the province's population.

We hope that conservative readers who have long felt their blood boil at the "extraordinary caste" mentality in our judiciary will, like the authors of this chapter, enthusiastically envision the following symbolic scene: a candidate for a judgeship presented by the NCJ stands before a gathering of popularly elected mayors from the region where they wish to serve. They answer questions from the mayors/voivodship senators and NGO representatives during a public and transparent hearing—before the citizens on whose behalf they will administer justice.

In addition to the symbolic dimension, however, the obligatory endorsement of mayors allows us to achieve a real, substantive balance between the professional and social aspects—a balance that conservatives have been seeking for years. The NCJ (about whose proposed composition we will write more below) ensures that all candidates under consideration meet the required professional criteria. Local government officials, on the other hand, evaluate the social aspect—in short: whether, for example, a judge adjudicating in Białystok, a voivodship capital, is likely to enjoy real authority in the community of the Podlasie region.

The formula for an obligatory endorsement, especially in the context of IUS' broader proposal for multi-level governance, does not pose a risk of politicization of the judicial selection process. The regional senate, composed of mayors, will not have any realistic ability to force the nationwide NCJ to nominate this or that judge. Instead, the system itself will ensure that the legal community is compelled to nominate *judges of a certain type*: people who are genuinely recognized locally as figures of authority and who, through open discussion, are able to gain the confidence of "ordinary people."

A construct requiring the cooperation of two bodies for the appointment of a public official is not a novelty in the Polish legal system. And this is precisely why we need to be aware of the key danger of this arrangement: the specter of long-term deadlock—an inability to appoint candidates due to disagreements between the two bodies, or even deliberate obstructionism on the part of one of them. An example of such a problem is the past conflict within the PiS camp over the staffing of the Council of the Supreme Audit Office. This is because appointing a member of the Council requires the cooperation of the President of the Supreme Audit Office and the Speaker of the Sejm. At the end of the second PiS term in power, only nine of the nineteen Council's member positions were filled.

Learning from this experience, the IUS proposal incorporates an original anti-obstruction mechanism, which also happens, to our knowledge, to be one of the first examples of utilizing the insights from game theory in the Polish legal system. The starting point of the proposal is how to deal with the situation of a candidate proposed by the NCJ *not* securing the required endorsement of provincial senators representing at least 60 percent of their voivodship's population. The IUS proposal requires the NCJ to propose another candidate, and, in the event of this one also not being granted a positive opinion, a third one.

And here we come to the key moment: if three consecutively proposed candidates do not receive the required support, the NCJ has two options. It can either keep trying, that is, start the process again from the beginning, or submit to the Polish President the nomination of the one of the three candidates who received the most support among the mayors. For example, if the first candidate received the support of senators representing 32 percent of the province's population, the second received 44 percent support, and the third 27 percent, then the NCJ can submit the nomination of candidate number two.

We should note that the NCJ presents candidates to the voivodship senate *one at a time*. Consequently, the mayor-senators have no incentive to vote "strategically"—because they simply do not know whether the next candidate will, from their point of view, be "better" or "worse." They also know that once three candidates have been presented, the NCJ will be able to nominate the one with the highest number of votes.

On the other hand, the NCJ will not be able to simply ignore the social perspective represented by the mayors. If it wants to fill a particular judicial post (which, after all, is in the interest of the profession), it will have to nominate, if not a candidate who obtains the required mandate from the mayors, then at least the candidate with relatively the highest support.

Let us reiterate that our goal is not to secure the nomination of this or that judge, but to overcome a somewhat stagnant element of our judicial culture. Even if the NCJ exercises the option of selecting the candidate with relatively the highest support (though not above the 60 percent threshold), the cumulative effect of many such choices would be to gradually change the norms of behavior in our judiciary, toward greater social accountability and sensitivity.

Systemic changes

The inclusion of local governments in the process of judicial appointments may (but does not have to) be accompanied by change in the structure of the Polish judiciary and the way the NCJ is staffed, tying these structures more firmly to the rest of our proposal for the constitutional reform.

The first step proposed by the IUS would be to establish strong and prestigious Supreme Voivodship Courts by merging the current appellate courts and provincial administrative courts. As it stands today, the appellate districts do not even align with Poland's administrative divisions. There are eleven courts of appeal (hearing civil, criminal, and social insurance cases) but sixteen voivodships, each with a provincial administrative court. Strengthening both types of courts by merging them will clarify the voivodship senate's role in nominating judges who sit in a given province.

Such a solution is also desirable in the context of reviewing the constitutionality of actions performed by the authorities under the proposed new social contract. After all, it is important to recognize that the regulatory decentralization proposed by the IUS—involving the transfer of a significant share of legislative powers from the Sejm and national senate to provincial legislatures—will also impact the competencies of the judicial authorities. According to Article 184 of the Constitution, the constitutionality of subnational law is assessed not by the Constitutional Tribunal, but by the administrative courts. In other words, an expanded role for regional legislation within the legal system as a whole means reducing the Constitutional Tribunal's influence, while increasing the role of the administrative courts. In the current situation, the Tribunal has become a focal point of acute political conflict, and, according to the more vocal critics, has turned into a *zombie* institution. However, it so happens that this conflict has not affected the administrative courts, which further supports the desirability of our proposed change.[21]

The Supreme Voivodship Courts, with a separate administrative chamber constituting an administrative court of first instance, composed of judges with not only a professional mandate from the NCJ but also a social mandate expressed in the endorsement of the voivodship senate, will be well positioned—under the appellate control of the Supreme Administrative Court—to watch over the rule of law and the constitutionality of the activities of the strengthened regional government.

The concept of strong Supreme Voivodship Courts would also help find a Solomonic solution to the problem of the National Council of the Judiciary. Article 187 of the Constitution stipulates that the NCJ consists of fifteen members chosen from among judges of the Supreme Court, common courts, administrative courts, and military courts. The manner by which judges are appointed as members of the NCJ is highly controversial.

Under the IUS proposal, it is easy to imagine that most of these judges would be appointed by the General Assemblies of the prestigious and trusted Supreme Voivodship Courts which we envision. If the current structure of sixteen provinces remains, the General Assembly of each Voivodship Court could elect a member of the NCJ for every second term, thus filling eight positions. If the option to grant provincial rights to Warsaw and Cracow were realized, this would result in nine of the fifteen positions being filled.

Such a solution would, after a certain period, result in the majority of judges serving on the NCJ coming from an appointment that took into account the social factor that we consider so important, namely, the endorsement of the voivodship senates. As we wrote earlier, their profile and thinking would better balance the formal-legal and social aspects of a judge's work. This, in turn, would influence the profile of candidates presented by the NCJ to the voivodship senates.

Subsidiarity and accountability

We have described and reviewed the IUS proposal concerning the judiciary so thoroughly for two reasons. First, this topic has for years been one of the main headaches of conservatives concerned about the real (rather than imaginary) problems of Polish democracy. Second, the proposal is a kind of case study illustrating the broader philosophy of the Incubator.

Due to the role of the voivodship senates, the concept largely implies strengthening municipalities and their mayors. In keeping with the principle of subsidiarity, the voivodship in the IUS proposal is to a large extent a forum for municipalities to participate in shaping their own future. We have more than 2,400 municipalities in Poland, which form loose, voluntary associations. Mobilizing such a large number in practice, together with their leaders, is unrealistic. But the situation is different in the provinces, where—as is easy to count—each has about 150 municipalities on average. Such a number of local leaders, brought together in a formal body—the voivodship senate—with considerable powers, is capable of organizing itself into a serious force defending the interests of ordinary citizens in local Poland.

Also promising for civic-minded conservatives are the proposals for Close Cooperation between the provinces, and especially in the aspect of economic and development policy. The IUS idea here involves an easy-to-implement solution in which cooperation in a given area can be implemented by a member of the board shared by two (or more) provinces, and with the support of an inter-provincial office.

Why is this important? Because back when the current regional reforms were introduced by the right-of-center government in 1998, many conservatives were somehow torn between understanding the need to create strong and large centers of development, and the fear of dividing the country into several large and overly independent regions. The most recent iteration of this dilemma was PiS's proposal to divide the Mazovian voivodship.[22]

The IUS proposal gives room for potential compromise here. If the political units—the voivodships—do not have to correspond to the developmental units (which can include several provinces forming Close Cooperations with each other), then we no longer need to fear exclusion of the largest cities, such as Warsaw and Cracow, as cities with provincial rights, or even the division of the largest provinces, especially the huge Mazovian voivodship surrounding Warsaw. Such changes could bring the political map of Poland more in line with the realities of the strength of conservative communities, while (in the spirit of a fair social contract) granting greater independence to urban clusters of leftists and liberals.

The final aspect of the IUS proposal of interest to conservatives that we would like to mention is the package of solutions that we would generally call "anti-clique." Leading voices of the Polish Right correctly point out that our local and regional government is not some institutional "promised land." Poles should not have to choose between partisan Warsaw elites and similarly inbred and corrupt elites in the regions.

The numerous IUS proposals offer hope here. A centrally run National Ranking of Public Services, discussed by our colleagues in Chapter 2, will give citizens and community organizations the tools to press for improvements in public services, and the tools to appreciate public services where they work well. Especially since the IUS proposal links the ranking's score to another topic important to conservatives: term limits for local and regional government officials. Under the IUS proposal, a mayor or voivode will not be eligible for reelection if, during their term of office, the position of their municipality or province in the averaged National Ranking of Public Services has dropped by 4 or more positions in the case of provinces, or by 150 or more positions in the case of a municipality.

A similar role will be played by the Local and Regional Government Quality Assessment System for Laws and Public Services, also introduced in Chapter 2 of this volume. Through an online app, citizens would be able to evaluate local and regional laws, and assess the quality of public services and interactions with local and regional administration, on an ongoing basis.

There would be two aspects to the evaluation of regional laws. The first would be anonymous and expressed in the form of stars awarded by citizens in two categories: "understandable provision" and "good solution." The second would involve a non-anonymous descriptive evaluation of the regional law in question. Similarly, the evaluation of public services and interactions with the local and regional administration, expressed in the form of stars, would be anonymous and public. In contrast, a descriptive review would be communicated to the management of the regional administration office in question.

The democratization of Polish political life should also, in our view, involve greater use of popular referendums as an instrument, whether at the central, provincial, or local level. Such a solution would create an opportunity for citizens to be the ones to settle disputes, including ideological ones, where political tensions surface that are difficult to overcome among strongly divided and antagonistic party elites. Of course, such settlements cannot violate the Constitution of the Republic of Poland, unless a majority of the Polish political class agrees that issues concerning amendments to the basic law should first be subject to a nationwide referendum.

The electronic referendum proposed by IUS could also lead to a major improvement in accountability. After all, the issue of using technology in the electoral process elicits a passionate response among conservatives around the world. On the one hand, the Brexit referendum demonstrated the opportunities offered by direct democracy to conservatives. On the other, particularly in the United States, there are concerns that the liberal elites dominating the IT sector may use technology to manipulate election results.

The IUS proposal offers a particularly innovative golden mean. The idea is that in matters of lesser importance (and not involving elections for individual positions) a new type of voting could be introduced, in addition to the existing open and secret ballots. IUS calls it *the confidential ballot*. In this form of voting, a citizen casts their ballot using an online application operated by the National Electoral Commission—an institution independent of the central, regional, and local governments. However, unlike traditional electronic voting, in which the computer system makes it impossible to check an individual vote to ensure absolute secrecy, in the case of confidential voting the said National Electoral Commission would maintain a named record of the votes cast. This would give every citizen the ability to verify their vote with the said Commission, which would dispel doubts about the integrity of electronic voting.

The register of votes would be treated as classified information, with any disclosure by staff of the National Electoral Commission carrying a criminal sanction. These safeguards, combined with the institutional distance between the authorities of a given local or regional government and the National Electoral Commission, will provide sufficient protection of the privacy of citizens' political preferences. By solving the problem of trust in e-election algorithms, the IUS proposal could dramatically reduce the institutional and financial obstacles to direct democracy.

Benefits of the new settlement

From a conservative point of view, the proposal for a new social contract presented in this volume has many appealing themes. First, its entire logic is based on the principle of subsidiarity—the foundation of the social teachings of the Catholic Church, which remains a guiding light for Polish conservatives, who draw heavily on Christian moral philosophy. It is also a continuation of the reforms that the Right introduced in Poland after 1989—reforms that are at the opposite end of the logic of centralism that guided the communists.

Second, the proposal makes it possible to break the impasse on the issue of the judiciary in a way that addresses a key demand of the right: namely, the introduction of greater accountability and social sensibility of judges. By integrating this element of the legacy of PiS's 2015–23 rule, the new social contract makes it possible to break the dangerous stalemate that Poland finds itself in, stuck in domestic and international disputes over the rule of law. These disputes are weakening our state, harming its international standing, and allowing some of the country's political elite to be played by external actors. A proposal for a compromise on the judiciary that would guarantee its independence, while at the same time making it more accountable, would be an important step toward strengthening the Polish Republic both internally and internationally.

Looking at the judicial landscape of AD 2025, we face a threefold task:

- to stabilize the relationship between judges and politicians, so as to at least lay the groundwork for the construction of a functional compromise on the subject of acceptable influence on public policy by one and the other;
- to strengthen the credibility of the courts—so that the judiciary can properly legitimize the state;
- to carry out—finally!—systemic reforms to the judicial apparatus and the procedures by which it operates, so that it becomes an effective regulator of civil and commercial conflicts, as well as an effective tool for fair and abuse-free criminal policy.

And third, the new social contract increases the role of the citizen in governance, which resonates with those conservatives who share republican ideals. By creating broader opportunities for decision-making through referendums, and allowing citizens to express their opinions on the functioning of local government and the quality of public services, the proposal enables a shift away from the purely elitist approach to doing politics that was one of the ills of the post-1989 Polish Republic.

Notes

1. Tomasz Grzegorz Grosse, "Perception of Polish Democracy in a Comparative Approach in Relation to the European Integration Processes," *Rocznik Integracji Europejskiej*, no. 14 (2020): 9–23 .
2. Piotr Semka, "Polska dzielnicowa—reaktywacja," *Do Rzeczy* 2019.
3. Lisa Sowle Cahill, "Catholic Social Teaching," in *The Cambridge Companion to Christian Political Theology*, ed. Craig Hovey and Elizabeth Phillips (Cambridge University Press, 2015), 67–87.
4. Tomasz Grzegorz Grosse, *Sovereignty and the Political: A Study of European Integration* (Wydawnictwo Instytutu Wymiaru Sprawiedliwości, 2022), 177–82.
5. Tomasz Grzegorz Grosse, "The Golden Straitjacket of Poland's Membership in the EU," *Yearbook of Polish European Studies*, no. 17 (2014): 117–38.
6. Andrzej Zakrzewski, "Between the Union of Lublin and the Mutual Pledge of the Two Nations," *Zapiski Historyczne* 84, no. 4 (2019): 5–40 .
7. Przemysław Dąbrowski, "Union of Brest and its Dissolution on the Territories of the Congress Kingdom of Poland, Belarusian and Lithuanian Lands," *Journal on European History of Law* 2, no. 2 (2011): 86–90 ; Frank E. Sysyn, "Church Union: The Quandaries over Acceptance of the Union of Brest (1595–96)," *Canadian Slavonic Papers* 65, no. 3–4 (2023): 468–477 .
8. Shmuel A. Cygielman, "The Basic Privileges of the Jews of Great Poland as Reflected in Polish Historiography," *Polin: Studies in Polish Jewry*, no. 2 (1987): 117–149.
9. Tomasz Herodowicz et al., "Political Divisions and Socio-economic Disparities in Poland: A Geographical Approach," *Sustainability*, 13, no. 24 (2021): 1–15; Paweł Ruszkowski, Andrzej Przestalski, and Paweł Maranowski, *Polaryzacja światopoglądowa społeczeństwa polskiego a klasy i warstwy społeczne* (Collegium Civitas Press Warszawa, 2020); Paulina Górska, *Polaryzacja polityczna w Polsce. Jak bardzo jesteśmy podzieleni* (*Centrum Badań nad Uprzedzeniami*, 2019).
10. A view emphasizing a key role of political elites is expressed by Hubert Tworzecki, "Poland: A Case of Top-Down Polarization," *The ANNALS of the American Academy of Political and Social Science* 681, no. 1: 97-119 (2018).
11. Tomasz Grzegorz Grosse, "The Rule of Law in the European Union: A Functional Perspective," in *Faces of the Rule of Law in Europe*, ed. Michał Gierycz and Piotr Mazurkiewicz (Vandenhoeck & Ruprecht, 2024), 273–299 .

12. Adam Czarnota, "Lustration, Decommunisation and the Rule of Law," *Hague Journal on the Rule of Law* 1, no. 2 (2009): 307–336.
13. Małgorzata Gersdorf and Mateusz Pilich, "Judges and Representatives of the People: A Polish Perspective," *European Constitutional Law Review* 16, no. 3 (2020): 345–378.
14. *Evaluation of the Judiciary (31/2017)*, CBOS (Warsaw, 2017).
15. Adam Czarnota, "Rule of Law as an Outcome of Crisis: Central-Eastern European Experiences 27 Years after the Breakthrough," *Hague Journal on the Rule of Law* 8 (2016): 311–321.
16. Bogna Kociorowicz-Wiśniewska and Bartosz Pilitowski, *Ocena Polskiego Sądownictwa w Świetle Badań* Fundacja Court Watch Polska (2017), 11.
17. An even more unfortunate strategy was to suggest that the phrase was invented by the PiS government itself. See e.g. Gersdorf and Pilich, "Judges and Representatives of the People: A Polish Perspective," 367, describing "the term 'extraordinary caste'" as "a collective name for judges introduced by some of the top Law and Justice politicians".
18. See https://www.youtube.com/watch?v=qAeQtznU16Q (last visited Dec. 19, 2024).
19. Patryk Słowik, "Sądowy bełkot. Dlaczego uzasadnień wyroków nie da się zrozumieć?" *Forsal.pl*, Jun. 5, 2016.
20. Patryk Słowik, "Sędziowie nie potrafią pisać. Dlatego nie rozumiemy orzeczeń," *Dziennik Gazeta Prawna*, Jun. 6, 2016.
21. Mirosław Granat, "Constitutionality of Law without a Constitutional Court in the Polish Setting," in *Constitutionality of Law without a Constitutional Court: A View from Europe*, ed. Mirosław Granat (Routledge, 2024).
22. "Wraca dyskusja o podziale Mazowsza. 17. województwo będzie skazane na kroplówkę rządu?" *Forbes*, Jul. 24, 2020.

Comment

Reimagining the Polish Constitution by Looking to the Past

Kim Lane Scheppele

Worthwhile lessons from history

Whenever I teach American constitutional law, I always discuss Poland. Many Americans like to think that they invented the written national constitution, but of course—like most worthwhile inventions—it was not the idea of only one person (or only one group of persons) in only one place. The American Framers were in Independence Hall in Philadelphia in 1787 arguing over the constitutional future of their new nation and the Poles began their great constitutional debates in the Royal Palace in Warsaw in 1788. Each assembly knew about (and corresponded with) with other. Both multi-year negotiations produced written national constitutions. The American one came into force in 1789 while Poland's constitution, proclaimed on May 3, 1791, is often called the second written national constitution in the world and the first in Europe.

But it's not clear that America really got there first. The US Constitution may have come into effect in 1789, but the Bill of Rights did not enter into force until the very end of 1791. The Bill of Rights was added to the Philadelphia Constitution as a set of amendments forged during the ratification process. In the meantime, the Polish Constitution of May 3, 1791 already included in Article IV the proclamation of "a perfect and entire liberty to all people." If one believes that both power-limiting structures and rights are necessary elements of constitutionalism, Poland was faster at putting the two together.

In any event, the Constitution of May 3, 1791 has survived much longer in the Polish national imagination than it survived in force. It remains a point of pride in Polish politics. The revolution that gave rise to the Constitution of May 3, 1791 was complicated, as all revolutions are. But while the Constitution of May 3, 1791 no doubt was inspired by Enlightenment ideas, it too was a product of a complicated compromise. In Chapter 13, Antoni Dudek, Maciej Kisilowski, and Anna Wojciuk argue that the entire May Constitution was a product of the Enlightenment that froze out the conservatives of its day. The conservatives of that time, however,

Kim Lane Scheppele, *Comment* In: *Let's Agree on Poland*. Edited by: Maciej Kisilowski and Anna Wojciuk, Oxford University Press.
DOI: 10.1093/oso/9780198979562.003.0008

betrayed their country and have no followers today. Today's patriotic conservatives and liberals can still find in the Constitution of May 3, 1791 ideas that might be reexamined now to see if they offer useful compromises in the current debate. Not all good ideas are new.

For example, we've learned from Richard Butterwick-Pawlikowski's book *The Polish Revolution and the Catholic Church, 1788–92*,[1] how the Polish constitutional Framers managed to find an official place for the Catholic Church in the Constitution while still providing equal rights for those with different beliefs. Initially skeptical, most of the bishops of the day came around to supporting this feature of the Constitution ofMay 3, 1791. Perhaps all they had to do was look at the trajectory of the French Revolution to realize that accepting a constitutional guarantee of an official state church in exchange for public tolerance of other religions was better than the other options on offer. Perhaps today's Catholic Church will appreciate the proposal of the Social Contract Incubator, deeply rooted in the doctrine of subsidiarity so fundamental to the Catholic social teaching, that gives it pride of place without excluding Poles of different beliefs from equal citizenship and freedom. This may be a particularly attractive alternative given the prospect of a centralized, rapid progressive revolution, similar to the one that took place in Ireland after decades of conservative rule. In Chapter 6, Mirosław Granat, Tomasz G. Grosse, Arkadiusz Radwan, and Jacek Sokołowski mention the possibility of such a "pendulum swing" under the current, winner-takes-all Polish system. If the bishops of 1791 realized that the Church could be endangered by the revolutionary spirit sweeping the world and therefore agreed to a constitution that guaranteed their position without giving them a monopoly, perhaps the bishops of 2025 will recognize that in a rapidly secularizing world, the Church may be best preserved if it, too, is guaranteed a constitutional place without claiming a constitutional monopoly.

Given that the creation of the Polish First Republic honored so many different claims of a diverse Polish society and given that the Polish Revolution took such a moderate tone relative to other European revolutions, perhaps it can act today as a North Star guiding a divided nation out of disagreements over the proper shape of its current constitution. In many ways, the Constitution of May 3, 1791 performed a very delicate balancing act among competing political factions given the politics of its day. And so, too, must the Polish Constitution of today.

Twenty-five years

I first came to Poland often in the early 1990s, attending many academic conferences on many drafts of what eventually became the 1997 constitution. I saw first-hand how pitched and seemingly irreconcilable the disagreements were at that time. Although Poland was the first East-Central European nation to break free of Soviet tutelage in 1989, it was the last to ratify a new constitution, because the compromises necessary to reach an agreement were painful and hard-fought. But throughout that process, the Constitution of May 3, 1791 stood for both the fact and the aspiration that Poland is a constitutional nation. A constitutional nation is one in which state power is authorized, divided, and constrained by law, as well as one that honors both the diversity of its people and their common liberty. The Constitution of May 3, 1791 came up constantly in those many constitution-debating conferences in the 1990s.

And so here we are again, discussing another set of modifications of Poland's Constitution to strengthen a common republic at a time when politics is mired in a field of disagreements. While there are many aspects of the Constitution of May 3, 1791 that no modern democracy would want to repeat, the Constitution of May 3, 1791 still holds important wisdom that is usefully remembered at this new moment of national polarization. Of course, the world of estates and power-wielding monarchies has disappeared; the franchise has become universal and equal in any democracy worthy of the name. But now, as then, constitutional debates still rage over the role of the Church in the state and over the rights of "free towns" and "agricultural people" as against the central authorities. Then, as now, a consensus can form around the idea that "All power in civil society is derived from the will of the people" (Article V). And of course, we can all see that then, as now, brooding war in the East can concentrate all minds on the importance of reaching an agreement and standing strong together in the present.

But what strikes me most in revisiting the Constitution of May 3, 1791 is its wisdom about how political bargains, once struck, may need to be revisited. The drafters of the Constitution of May 3, 1791 wisely provided for repeated renewal of the constitutional pact:

> Willing to prevent, on one hand, violent and frequent changes in the national constitution, yet, considering on the other, the necessity of perfecting it, after experiencing its effects on public prosperity, we determine the period of every twenty-five years for an Extraordinary Constitutional Sejm, to be held purposely for the revision and such alterations of the constitution as may be found requisite. (Article VI)

In short, the drafters of the Constitution of May 3, 1791 believed that no constitution would—or should—be fixed forever.

And here we are—twenty-five years after the 1997 constitution—pondering revisions. Even without the constitutional crisis that Poland presently finds itself in, the exhortation to revisit the constitution after twenty-five years was then and surely is now a very good idea. The Social Contract Incubator (IUS) proposals contained in this volume not only align with the best aspects of the May constitution, but also with the amendment timeline it wisely envisioned.

Constitutional pluralism

This book presents proposals drafted, debated, and offered not as the victory of one side over another in the present polarized political context, but instead in the spirit of respectful compromise and open debate. The process of producing these proposals has involved well-meaning people from almost all positions on the political spectrum who have both reaffirmed their joint commitment to democratic values and listened to each other. This novel process has generated new ideas that nonetheless acknowledge history.

Two themes in the IUS's proposals are particularly relevant to honoring the historic spirit of the Constitution of May 3.

The first is the commitment to liberty. Of course, liberty has never meant "anything goes." Ordered liberty permits each individual to be the author of his or her own life, consistent with that right of authorship for all others. Right now in Polish politics, there is a battle between left and right on many questions. The liberal Left wants less public intrusion into private life and more opportunities for each individual to make personal choices of conscience and identity. The Catholic Right believes that the Church provides clear answers to many questions and those answers are binding on all. The clash comes when religious believers insist that non-believers accept those clear answers and non-believers insist that believers abandon their attempts to write their religious beliefs into state law. The liberty-respecting compromise is that each person is free to believe what their conscience or their faith demands and to have their commitments respected by others. Liberty also requires that no one is empowered to impose their beliefs on others who do not share them.

The Constitution of May 3, 1791 adopted this general view. Though it firmly established in Article I that the Catholic Church constituted the national religion, it also proclaimed that "as the same holy religion commands us to love our neighbors, we therefore owe to all people of whatever persuasion, peace in matters of faith, and the protection of government; consequently we assure, to all persuasions and religions, freedom and liberty, according to the laws of the country." In short, those who did not take the Catholic faith as a personal blueprint for their lives were nonetheless protected by the Constitution of May 3, 1791 to hold different beliefs. The Catholic Church, nonetheless, remained the established religion.

Decentralization of constitutional responsibilities in the new Polish constitutional framework is the perfect answer to the problem of the present deep differences in beliefs that are difficult to reconcile. What divides the two great political forces in Polish life is precisely the role of the Church in the state, then as now. The Constitution of May 3, 1791 opted for a liberty-respecting answer—and the proposals put forward in this book do the same, but by building that commitment into constitutional structures rather than leaving it to the whims of state officials.

The IUS's proposals would push decisions most relevant to this dividing line in Polish politics down to a local level. These decisions—for example, how to organize public schooling, how to best honor Polish cultural traditions—would be made by communities most likely to share common values on these questions. Each voivodship would be able to make these decisions for its own inhabitants—and because Poland's present diversity would mean that different regions would no doubt make different decisions, this solution minimizes the number of people who would be living under a local government that did not share their beliefs. It would also generate alternative models for how different sorts of lives might be lived, all within a proud and constitutional Poland. When local communities decide on how they will reconcile the competing pulls of church and state as well as the diversity of local beliefs, it cannot be said that either the religious or secular forms of organization would be the only one that is truly Polish. Poland would be a patchwork of different solutions because its citizens represent a patchwork of different beliefs. This is a liberty-enhancing proposal in the spirit of the Constitution of May 3, 1791.

Compromise on the judiciary, in the May spirit

The IUS's proposals also carry forward the spirit of the Constitution of May 3, 1791 in its vision for the judiciary. This is the most contentious constitutional question in contemporary Poland, in which one side insists it must purify the judiciary and make it more politically accountable and the other side insists that the judiciary must remain outside the sphere of political influence. The proposals put forward here strike a balance between political accountability and professional qualifications. Potential new judges would be screened, on this model, by professional bodies who can assess whether the candidates have the requisite knowledge and temperament to be professional judges, while local leaders who are themselves accountable to their electorates will have input about whom to select from among those with the required professional qualifications.

Here too, the Constitution of May 3, 1791 reached a similar conclusion in its day. Article VIII argued, "As judicial power is incompatible with the legislative, nor can be administered by the King, therefore tribunals and magistratures ought to be established and elected. It ought to have local existence, that every citizen should know where to seek justice, and every transgressor can discern the hand of national government."

It is important to reiterate that the drafters of the Constitution of May 3, 1791 understood full well the importance of separation of powers and the dangers of having political control over the judiciary. The judiciary needs to be independent of executive and legislative power; tyranny becomes altogether too likely if the judiciary is simply controlled by the political branches. But we have also learned from what preceded the current Polish government that independence can also go too far and make the judiciary too remote from what the public believes.

So how were Polish judges selected in the Constitution of May 3, 1791? These would have been the days before law degrees and other professional qualifications, so not surprisingly, there are no requirements of professional competency for the job. It makes sense to have those now that law is much more complicated. But to deal with separation-of-powers concerns, judges under the Constitution of May 3, 1791 were chosen by local officials in the towns, regions, and sejmiks. Minus the feudalism, this is precisely what the IUS's proposals suggest—which is to tie political accountability to the local level rather than fixing it at the center.

In the Constitution of May 3, 1791, two forms of separation of powers were imagined: the horizontal separation of powers that divided executive, legislative, and judicial power at national level and the vertical separation of powers in which local and regional governments provided a check on national government. In aiming to make the judiciary independent, the Constitution of May 3, 1791 lodged the judicial appointment power at local level precisely to emphasize its separation from the center of national power, both ensuring its ability to monitor this power and simultaneously tethering the appointments process to a democratic and political check. The IUS has wisely done the same. In fact, its proposal is uncannily similar to the solution from the Constitution of May 3, 1791.

Future, anchored in proud history

Of course, countries move on and are not just stuck in the past. Contemporary Poland is not bound by its Constitution of May 3, 1791. And there are aspects of the Constitution of May 3 that it would be terribly unwise to repeat. That said, it is important that each country's constitution is not some off-the-rack model written by those who forget who they are and what their country has experienced over its history. When it comes to national constitutions, there is no one-size-fits-all solution. The IUS has managed to recover important historic achievements of Polish constitutionalism while responding to the needs of the current times. Some ideas are too good to leave in the past.

Note

1. Richard Butterwick, *The Polish Revolution and the Catholic Church, 1788–1792: A Political History* (Oxford University Press, 2011).

Comment

Winding Road to Democracy

Wolf Linder

We are different

“We are different”—this motto has a double meaning for the authors of the Social Contract Incubator (IUS). On the one hand, it explains the reasons for the institutional shortcomings of Poland’s politics. On the other, it is key to Poland achieving more and better democracy. If the country’s politics today is characterized by deep polarization between the ruling Catholic conservatives and the liberal opposition, then the Constitution of 1997 did not take into account that society is not homogeneous but diverse. This diversity not only separates Catholic and liberal blocks today, but also reflects the multicultural elements of society shaped by history: Poland lies “at the crossroads of cultures and traditions—of Eastern and Western cultures, of Catholic, Protestant and Orthodox traditions, and of the influence of sometimes conflicting models of state and society.” Such longstanding historical, ideological, and identity differences between “progressive Poland and conservative Poland” are at the root of today’s conflicts on many issues, from abortion and homosexuality to education and the structures of the judiciary. These conflicts cannot be resolved through the domination of one group over the other, where majority rule leaves the loser with nothing. Instead, a contract between the major groups should guarantee forms of power sharing, leading to political compromises under which all Poles feel at home.

The main idea of the proposed system of power sharing lies in the institutional connections—or even ties—between municipal, provincial, and national levels of government. The new Polish Senate would consist of the voivodes, with votes weighed by the size of the populations they represent. Similarly, the new voivodship senates would consist of the mayors of their municipalities. Voivodship governments would become the primary legislators for all decentralized matters. The right to levy certain taxes should be transferred from central government to the provinces. Together with other reforms, the direct representation and participation of lower levels in the decisions of higher levels of government is expected to achieve two goals: first, it should stimulate decentralized legislation and

Wolf Linder, *Comment* In: *Let’s Agree on Poland*. Edited by: Maciej Kisilowski and Anna Wojciuk, Oxford University Press.
DOI: 10.1093/oso/9780198979562.003.0009

administration; second, as an instrument of vertical power sharing, the diverse socio-cultural preferences of the voivodships (and municipalities) would have a strong voice in central (and provincial) government. This brings the state closer to the people, fostering higher political trust and more effective democratic participation.

How could these basic ideas of the constitutional proposal developed by the IUS work out in practice? Chapter 6 illustrates this using the case of Poland's judiciary—a troublesome issue—and questions of policy evaluation and oversight. With regard to the judiciary, Poland has come under pressure from the EU. However, the authors' analysis highlights issues beyond judicial independence and points to more complex deficiencies: inadequate evaluation, citizens' dissatisfaction with the justice system, complicated procedures, and, ultimately, a lack of trust in a judiciary rooted in elitist traditions.

The IUS proposes that judicial appointments begin with the nomination of the National Council of the Judiciary (NCJ), which would be submitted to the voivodship senate of the region where the judge would ultimately serve. Only with the binding opinion of the mayors assembled in the regional senate, issued after public hearings, can candidates be presented for the final appointment by the President of the Republic. The regional opinion marks a significant departure from the status quo: a candidate proposed to the President must secure the support of mayors representing at least 60 percent of the population of the province in question. Moreover, the judges of Supreme Voivodship Courts thus appointed would then elect the majority of the NCJ members at the national level.

The objectives of this procedure are described as follows: it maintains a balance between social and professional considerations, and challenges elitist corporate attitudes by opening opportunities tor a different "type" of candidate—those who enjoy the social support of democratically elected mayors and provincial senators. This would make the judges more accountable and socially aware. As judicial nominees must be cleared by provincial senates, candidates from diverse socio-cultural backgrounds are more likely to be appointed. Further provisions ensure that the appointment process cannot be obstructed.

Focus on subsidiarity

Further measures of decentralization aim to strengthen municipalities and their mayors. The quality of public services is monitored through a National Ranking of Public Services, as well as by a Local and Regional Government Quality Assessment System for Laws and Public Services. Overall, the proposals regarding the judiciary and regional government align with the general concept of the Social Contract Incubator, following the principles of subsidiarity and decentralization. The voivodship governments reflect diverse regional preferences. If their political autonomy is guaranteed, the cultural values of conservatives and liberals in the different regions, concerning the relationship between society and the state, can coexist. These varied preferences come together at the national level, ensuring that multiple voices are heard in the national Senate. This, it is hoped, will further conflict resolution in Poland's cultural divides through power sharing, negotiation, and compromise.

Decentralization, in the IUS concept, lies mainly in the participation of lower levels of government in the decision-making process of central government. These procedural aspects of decentralization are well explained. But what about the structural elements? First: Which legislative and administrative tasks—such as those justified by the principle of subsidiarity—should be deferred to regional and local levels by constitutional regulation? And, in contrast to EU regulations, which often lead to centralization within Member States, what guarantees ensure that local and regional authorities are not overruled by decisions of the central government? Second: In practice, the success of decentralization depends largely on the autonomous powers of regional and local authorities to levy taxes for their own needs. On both points, the IUS concept leaves many questions unanswered.

A National Ranking of Public Services? With personal sanctions, such as barring voivodes or mayors from re-election in the event of lower scores? I cannot regard this as a good idea. Rankings are based on limited and questionable indicators, can be manipulated, and—if made "official"—may lead to unproductive political quarrels. More importantly, if Poles are diverse, one must accept that people in different municipalities and regions want to *live* differently; that is, they want to spend more or less on a particular good or service than citizens of other regions, and they may have different criteria of "quality."

Why not, in regard to the quality of local and regional policies, use elections as the main instrument of evaluation and control? This approach works if the responsibilities of regional and local authorities are clearly defined and coincide with their rights to levy taxes. Economists refer to this alignment as fiscal coincidence, where the geographic circle of taxpayers and users is identical. Under this condition, every citizen can evaluate the quality of "their" local government by answering a simple question: "Have the authorities in power made good use of the taxes I pay?" If the majority says yes, the government is reelected; if not, it must yield to the opposition. One might argue that fiscal coincidence can only be partially achieved, and that the "sanctions" of elections are imperfect. However, they provide an authentic form of evaluation and control, lie at the basis of democratic legitimacy, and prevent the bureaucratization of political oversight.

The authors mention the greater use of the instrument of popular referendums as a means to further democratize political life in Poland. This underlines the courageous and innovative character of the IUS concept. Referendums can be held in various forms—initiated by a group of citizens, plebiscites ordered by the authorities, legally binding or advisory, and so on. Depending on their form and the particular political culture of a country, referendums can serve very different functions and have varied consequences, which have to be clarified. In any case, it may be prudent to start exploring and comparing the potential of direct democracy instruments at the local level.

The authors are optimistic about the use of digitalization in public affairs. Based on twenty years of experience of Switzerland, I would be skeptical of the benefits of digitalization in direct democracy. In many other countries, digitalization has made political mobilization much easier, but has been of little help for transforming political issues into organized political life. Moreover, the tendency of social media to create small bubbles of the like-minded is not conducive to political dialogue in the broader public. However, Poland may prove to be an exception.

A creative response

The road to improving democracy is not a straight line. It has its ups and downs, its errors and detours, and sometimes even dead ends. If the IUS analysis is correct, neither a particular party nor specific politicians can overcome the impasses of Poland's democracy alone. Instead, it is a matter of how political and cultural differences in its society are perceived and addressed. The focus of this book on constitutional questions—seeking remedies in a consistent setting of power sharing, decentralization, and democratization—is therefore a creative and intelligent response, offering a promising path to overcoming political and cultural divides.

PART II

WE ARE DIFFERENT

7
Why Imagine the New Contract?

Maciej Kisilowski and Anna Wojciuk

The dilemma

How to talk about the new social contract? This question has captivated the authors of this book and other members of our Social Contract Incubator (IUS). If you agree with us that institutional reforms are the only sustainable solution to the powerful revolutionary signals sent by conservative voters, and the equally strong counter-revolutionary resolve shown by the progressives, then the question of how to put such reforms on the public agenda becomes critically important.

As the following chapters show, our response is to enrich the discussion about constitutional reform by relying on fictional, literary stories and narratives to spark the institutional imagination of our compatriots. This is, obviously, as classic an approach to constitutional discourse as decentralization is to managing political differences. As Martin Loughlin notes in his important work on constitutional imagination, the use of fictional narratives "to open up new ways of conceiving political reality for the purpose of motivating us to accept the authority of a particular type of constitutional order" was the defining strategy of early social contract thinkers, including Hobbes, Locke, and Rousseau.[1]

Despite these longstanding traditions, the format of this book's second part appears highly unusual for current times. More broadly, there is very little reflection on the communicative challenges that our Incubator faced, and that motivated us to dip our feet into storytelling. Scholars routinely discuss various ideas for constitutional reforms, and many have developed conspicuous profiles as public intellectuals or even as successful "content creators" in social or traditional media. But rarely do they invest time and attention in more theoretical thought concerning how best to advocate for constitutional reforms in present-day conditions. Many legal scholars are likewise keenly interested in the normative ideal of a deliberative democracy, but they seem to have less passion for understanding the practical contemporary obstacles to informed public debate over constitutional reforms. Even the growing body of work on legal, and constitutional, imagination[2] is developing—along with sociology and anthropology in general—in a highly theoretical direction; the fact that the above-mentioned important paper by

Maciej Kisilowski and Anna Wojciuk, *Why Imagine the New Contract?* In: *Let's Agree on Poland*.
Edited by: Maciej Kisilowski and Anna Wojciuk, Oxford University Press.
 DOI: 10.1093/oso/9780198979562.003.0010

Loughlin, published in the mid-2010s, relies on constitutional storytelling done in the seventeenth and eighteenth centuries aptly illustrates the point.

Advocating for constitutional reform

It is this paucity of academic advice on effective communication on constitutional reform that compelled us to develop our approach in a trial-and-error fashion. This gave us substantial experience in the pragmatic challenges of triggering constitutional change in a modern society barely aware of the institutional nature of its political woes. With the exception of Paweł Kukiz—the rock star-turned-politician who, as we mention in Chapter 1, envisioned a fundamental revival of Poland's democracy with first-past-the-post parliamentary ballot—ours is the first comprehensive proposal for reforming Poland's Constitution since its 1997 enactment.

Our advocacy has so far been concentrated around two periods. We first intervened in 2019, during the contentious general election campaign after the first of the two consecutive terms of revolutionary conservative PiS government. At that time, rather than producing a single proposal in a book or a white paper, we shared elements of our vision, as well as our more general motivations, in dozens of commentaries in major nationwide newspapers as well as interviews in print and digital media. We invited key political actors to a well-attended conference organized at the Polish Academy of Sciences. One of this chapter's co-authors, in her capacity as the IUS president, traveled to all sixteen regions, meeting with hundreds of local governmental officials, civic activists, and members of the general public.

The decision to present the proposal in a series of short press commentaries, obviously inspired by the classic approach of the Federalist Papers, was deliberate. Our bet was that the format would communicate the open-ended nature of our ideas and engage a broad cross-section of the Polish political elite in the process of co-creating a solution to the increasingly acute problems of Polish democracy. To further this aim, we encouraged all IUS members to bring our general vision to the attention of the political parties with which they were most closely associated. This resulted in various IUS members reaching out to PiS, the right-wing Kukiz '15, and all the major center-left opposition factions. Progress in these pursuits was uneven. PiS's leadership had a clear sense of confidence in its reelection. Those of us opposing the then-ruling party argued that that confidence was largely motivated by the increasingly authoritarian nature of the PiS government. With state-owned media becoming highly politicized, and all other state institutions supporting the government, the resulting ballot might have been free but, in the eyes of many of us, it certainly was not fair.[3] That view was corroborated by later disclosure of the wiretapping of key opposition leaders, including the head of the electoral campaign for the main opposition party, Civic Platform.[4] The IUS members with more right-leaning inclinations argued, by contrast, that ruling parties are generally unwilling to compromise, while the opposition may be more open to exploring new, out-of-the-box ideas.

Somewhat corroborating the conservative narrative, it was Civic Platform that reacted with the greatest interest to our proposal in 2019. The Platform leaders were interested in appealing to the non-urban electorate. As we explained in Chapter 1, it is the inhabitants of non-urban areas who would benefit from having strong representatives in the form of voivodes-senators, balancing the power that big-city mayors currently enjoy. In decentralization, the Platform leadership also saw a positive agenda that would unite diverse opposition factions, which apart from Civic Platform itself included leftist and Christian Democratic parties. What the party's leadership was not sure about was precisely the communicative challenge—how to "sell" the decentralized new social contract to voters. In response, IUS members sympathizing with the Platform drafted, in their own name and not as representatives of the cross-partisan movement, a detailed political strategy loosely based on the IUS proposal.

That was when the right-wing government decided to attack our efforts head on. The memo to the Platform leadership was leaked, under unclear circumstances, to a government-friendly media outlet. What followed was an onslaught of a grossly unfair and often *ad hominem* campaign in state-owned media, targeting the IUS and its project. Striking an antisemitic tone, PiS-friendly media declared the project "the Soros plan to split Poland." This was ironic, considering that both the George Soros-funded Open Society Foundation and the Batory Foundation in Poland, originally funded by Soros, had declined to financially support the project. In fact, it is not surprising that assertively progressive advocacy groups would struggle with the realist premise of our social contract: the somber admission that the conservative value system, just like the progressive one, has an entrenched social base that is not going to dissipate regardless of how much is spent on well-intentioned enlightenment programs. The vicious attack by the right-wing government on a proposal advocating for the recognition of the fundamental democratic legitimacy of the modern conservative movement confirmed to many of us the revolutionary—as well as authoritarian—nature of the PiS government. The IUS proposal was seen as dangerous precisely because of its potential to appeal to many PiS supporters. Like the passionate progressives, the PiS government in 2019 showed no interest in reaching a nationwide political settlement.

Remarkably, despite the government's onslaught, not a single conservative member of the IUS resigned. But the government achieved its main goal: The Civic Platform grew wary of running an election campaign that focused on decentralization-oriented constitutional reform. It would go on to lose the 2019 general election, followed by the 2020 presidential ballot, giving PiS another four years of undivided power.

One lesson from the turbulent 2019 campaign was that, unfortunately, the risks involved in having an open-ended proposal outweighed the benefits. The lack of a single, definitive source outlining our vision invited political actors to pick and choose aspects of the proposal and make them their own. Collaboration with Civic Platform was this being put into effect. But, at least in the realities of what many of us considered an increasingly authoritarian state, that open and welcoming approach carried unacceptable downsides. Without a definitive source, it was easy to grotesquely mischaracterize our proposal and confuse it with its potential adaptations prepared for or by major political actors.

In response to this rather unpleasant lesson, once the full electoral cycle had run its course and after the COVID pandemic had subsided, we began working on a book that would provide an approachable and creative outline of our constitutional vision for Poland. That is how the Polish edition of this book came about, becoming an unlikely nonfiction bestseller. As it happened, its launch coincided with the same point in the Polish political cycle as our earlier proposal—in the spring before another general election, this time in the fall of 2023.

The political conditions changed. The stunning return of Donald Tusk, former two-times Prime Minister and chair of the European Council, to the leadership of Civic Platform reinvigorated the opposition. The 2022 Russian invasion of Ukraine shocked Poles and made the country desperately dependent on US security guarantees. The Biden administration, represented by its energetic ambassador Mark Brzeziński (son of the late Zbigniew Brzeziński), made it clear that free and fair elections and a peaceful transfer of power were red lines in terms of the alliance between the two nations. Apart from the (ultimately prescient) Hungarian Prime Minister, Viktor Orbán, few political observers expected at the time that Donald Trump would ever return to the White House. PiS felt it needed to contend with the reality of a progressive US administration for the foreseeable future. In effect, for the first time since 2015, PiS looked weak and potentially on the losing side of the election.

The unexpected existential threat brought by the Russian invasion of our southeastern neighbor also led to a genuine realization that the "Polish–Polish political war," waged for almost two decades (although in truth, as we point out in Chapter 13, for a couple centuries), was significantly weakening the country and making it vulnerable. At the same time, the fierce domestic campaign for the general election highlighted genuine and deep divisions between progressive and conservative Poles—divisions that refused to go away even in the face of existential threats from the east. At a massive opposition rally on June 4, 2023, Donald Tusk raised eyebrows when he combined, somewhat cryptically, the call for an uncompromising post-PiS counter-revolution—"reckoning with evil and restitution to the victims"—with a firm promise of "reconciliation among Poles" as the opposition's ultimate goal.[5] This theme of reconciliation has been reiterated by Tusk and embraced by other politicians, both left and right.

The change in tone was also visible in the reception of *Let's Agree on Poland.* Leading intellectuals supported the project. The left-leaning Batory Foundation not only reversed its earlier criticism, but also generously supported a series of discussions and events around the book. Gone were confidential meetings and leaked memos; leading opposition politicians openly praised the work. Perhaps most remarkable was the reaction from the Right. Not only was there no repeat of the 2019 attacks, but senior right-wing figures even communicated directly to the IUS leadership that the project would "*not* be attacked." It was becoming increasingly clear that, with PiS seeing the possibility of losing national power, the Right would view our proposal more favorably. After all, in practice it would guarantee them a number of powerful regional governments as political safe havens.

From challenges to stories

Based on this experience, let us return to our opening question: what are the unique communicative challenges of a vision for major constitutional change? Like any major reform proposal, it surely suffers from the well-researched problems of economics of citizens' interest in and attention to political matters.[6] But unlike ordinary policy plans, major constitutional reforms are further impacted by the limitations of our institutional imagination. For four interrelated reasons, people—even those quite interested and engaged in politics—are not particularly adept at intuitively understanding how institutional change would affect our everyday political reality.

First and foremost, the impact that institutions have on issues that matter to us is indirect and frequently unclear. While sociologists rightly highlight the generally limited "capacity to range from the most impersonal and remote transformations to the most intimate features of the human self"[7]—or, in brief, "to grasp [the] points of the intersection of biography and history"[8]—this problem is particularly acute when it comes to institutions and institutional change. For an ordinary voter, or even a member of an educated elite, it is simply much easier to make sense of the impact of a change in the marginal rate of income tax, or of lowering the mandatory school age, than of the establishment of voivodship senates composed of mayors.

One reason for this discrepancy is that the impact of institutional change is mediated by our tacit assumptions about the potential posture of actors populating these institutions. An ordinary policy, such as a later retirement age, will have a specific effect regardless of anyone's behavioral choices. No matter what we do, we will work for many years while retirement will make up a shorter period. But the impact of subjecting all legislation to the approval of the new national Senate of the Voivodes depends on how we imagine the powers being used by the politicians populating this new body. Would the new senator-voivodes show independence from the party ruling in the center? Would those who are closer to the opposition act in an obstructionist way? How would other political actors react? In the market, such predictions are somewhat easier as it is broadly accepted—by enthusiasts and critics of capitalism alike—that market actors are generally driven by the self-interested maximization of profit. Not only economic analysts or researchers but also ordinary people generally agree with Adam Smith's dictum that "it is not from the benevolence of the butcher, the brewer, or the baker, that we expect our dinner, but from their regard to their own interest."[9] However, when thinking about politics, experts and laypersons alike are much less certain about even the simplest predictions, such as whether politicians can normally be expected to rationally react to incentives. In particular, our predictive statements about what politicians will do frequently become intertwined with normative ones about what we think they should do.

To make things more complicated, reforms aimed at addressing a major democratic crisis such as that faced by Poland and other countries must tackle a number of institutions at once in order to fundamentally alter the polarizing, winner-takes-all logic of the current system. That decreases even further people's ability to understand the cumulative nature of indirect, behavior-mediated effects of the changes advocated by a comprehensive institutional reform proposal. For instance, how will the new regional senates interact with the new popularly accountable voivodes, which in turn will be members of the national Senate?

Institutional imagination requires hard work. Unfortunately, numerous structural factors dissuade people from making that effort. By nature, institutions become embedded in the collective consciousness. A growing literature in constitutional sociology points out that, in the case of constitutions, the mechanisms through which they take root cannot be reduced to their technical, regulatory function. In addition, constitutions matter to people because of how they "reflect collective identities, create distinctive constitutional identities and reflect specific sets of cultural values and symbols."[10] While, in Poland's case, that sociological strength is much greater among progressives than conservatives, it still generates a powerful overall force to view any projects of major change to that order with suspicion.[11]

Furthermore, insofar as constitutions are still primarily constraints of human behavior,[12] their failure becomes evident when the limits they impose are breached or ignored. For defenders of an institutional status quo, that provides a readily available culprit—the rule breaker. One of the most frustrating responses to our proposal has been offered in the form of a metaphor, repeated by certain influential critics almost verbatim on numerous occasions: "The constitution is like the locks in your house. A determined thief will break in no matter how many locks you install." The fact is that the metaphor does not even work where residential property is concerned; empirical research shows that home protection does actually reduce the risk of burglary.[13] Applied to constitutional matters, however, this thinking combines naïve political idealism with institutional nihilism: the argument's logical conclusion is that the constitutional setup is by and large irrelevant, and the only thing that matters is the statesmanship of political actors.

Finally, our experience shows the importance of ego in ossifying an institutional design. Any proposals for modern reform must survive the scrutiny of political debate, shaped by divergent interests but also personal ambitions. Of particular importance is the attitude of a class of professional policy-oriented public intellectuals—academics, journalists, think-tank analysts, and activists of advocacy groups. All these actors have strong views on matters related to their policy expertise, but they also face other motivations: seeking visibility, expanding their professional status, differentiating themselves in the market of ideas, and making sure that viable competition does not arise.[14] Our experience shows that institutional reforms are viewed as a particularly prizeworthy trophy in this competitive intellectual market. A major institutional reform must, by design, capture the national attention for a significant time, sucking political air from other topics. The institutional outcome of such a process, with its promise of durability and the symbolic respect it commands,[15] is seen as a monument to its expert creators, even more so than the result of an ordinary policy intervention. Proposing institutional reform therefore means entering a particularly brutal subfield of a generally competitive arena of intellectual production. A reform proposal will immediately evoke strong, almost knee-jerk opposition from the proverbial founding fathers (and, occasionally, mothers) of the current institutional setup. For many of them, a suggestion to reform "their" institutions amounts to a personal attack. In that respect, nations with older institutions, whose founding parents are no longer around, may paradoxically be in a more advantageous position than Poland. Other players on the intellectual market, that is, those without a vested interest in the status quo, may be less fundamentally opposed, but may still be wary of a proposal that diverts attention and, potentially, funds from their projects.

These numerous challenges which we have faced in regard to constitutional communication motivated us to think creatively about how we could experiment with new—or, to be precise, new-old—ways of introducing, and discussing, constitutional reforms. The five chapters that follow are the result of this thought process. Our bet is that polarized times invite us to return to the classic strategy of awakening institutional imagination through storytelling. In the chapters that follow, five teams of IUS members partnered with Poland's leading fiction writers (and, for this international edition, a talented group of literary translators) to give us a taste of what political life could look like under our proposed constitutional settlement. Each author team shares in real life a specific ideological commitment, and they invite us to imagine what we could expect to happen, politically and socially, in a "dream" progressive, conservative, leftist, Christian Democratic, and classical liberal voivodship.

Why dreaming?

We call each story a "dream" not only for the banal reason that we are describing a reality not yet attained. Our stories share three essential functions that dreams play in our ordinary lives: provocation, aspiration, and imagination. The first of these is perhaps closest to the original intention of the only modern academic current that has both called for and actually practiced storytelling as a legitimate tool of legal scholarship. Within a decade of its inception in the early 1970s, the Law and Literature movement became such a noticeable phenomenon that one of this volume's co-authors, Kim Lane Scheppele, asked, in 1989: "Why is there such a rush to storytelling?"[16] Indeed, at the time law reviews published narratives, both fictional and autobiographical, as legitimate expressions of legal scholarship. The answer given then was precisely related to what we can call the provocative function of a dream, or more broadly a story: its ability to act as a "powerful means for destroying mindset—the bundle of presuppositions, received wisdoms and shared understandings."[17] For Law and Literature scholars the aim of this provocation was to include the perspectives of groups previously excluded from or overlooked in the legal discourse. At that time, throughout the democratic West, "the legal community, once comprised almost entirely of white men, had begun to admit women, people of color and those with life experiences far different than those of the lawyers whose ranks they joined."[18] The stories written from the vantage of these "outgroups" were aimed at challenging the entrenched "mindset by means of which members of a dominant group justify the world as it is."[19]

How we, in this volume, redefine the provocative function of our voivodship dreams very much represents the core original contribution of our enterprise. In our deeply divided era, we believe both sides—the progressives and the conservatives—deserve a chance to tell their story, to share their dream. This statement may be viewed as controversial, even offensive, by those who have long argued that the historical starting point of our public debate is far from equal. In the American context, the slogan "All Lives Matter" has been broadly viewed as nothing other than a white supremacist slur denigrating the "Black Lives Matter" movement.[20] When we talk about which stories we want to promote, the argument goes, we must take into account that certain groups have been grossly overrepresented while other groups have been systemically silenced.

Right as the critics may be, our work in the IUS has convinced us that, at least in Poland, one reason why modern conservatives are often attracted to revolutionary solutions is their strong perception of being overlooked and unheard—precisely in ways that motivated the Law and Literature movement. Those of us on the progressive side of the spectrum may puzzle—and have often done so—over how that perception can be true in a country with such a powerful conservative tradition, including the overwhelming cultural role of the Catholic Church. But we also became convinced that responding to this perception with outrage or dismissal was not going to further the goal of our democratic coexistence.

Beyond that functional argument, let us offer two telling anecdotes. When we decided to include the five stories included in Part II of this book, we reached out to a number of Polish fiction writers. On the progressive side we quickly secured the participation of particularly high-profile collaborators. But for our conservative dream—outlined in Chapter 9—we struggled. In the end we settled on an excellent literary editor, although they explicitly asked not to be featured as a co-author in the story's byline.

Throughout our public discussions, we heard no conservatives criticizing our progressive "dreams," while—repeatedly—left-leaning activists would harshly attack the said Chapter 9. "It outlines a vision of a religious state that is contrary to the 1997 Constitution," exclaimed a well-known think-tank leader during our book launch in May 2023. Of course, whether our conservative dream does or does not clash with the 1997 Constitution is largely irrelevant, as the volume describes a proposal for amending Poland's constitutional order. We leave it to you, the reader, to decide if even the most conservative of our dreams can be viewed as dangerously extreme. What we can state is that, if the basic political objectives of a sizable group of voters are viewed as fundamentally illegitimate and irreconcilable with the constitutional system, it should not be surprising if they are tempted to overthrow that system through revolution.

Which brings us to the second function of a good dream—that of outlining and crystallizing our aspirations. To dream means, at least partly, to hope. Bringing back the ability of our democratic state to deliver a cohesive vision is particularly important for our conservative compatriots. In Chapter 6 our co-authors invoke an observation of a well-known right-wing commentator about the progressives' inability to accept the reality that the Right can govern in Poland. Jarosław Kaczyński, the leader of PiS, has long complained about what he calls the "impossibilism" of the 1997 constitutional order, which in his view is set up in a way that prevents the conservatives from realizing any of their major objectives.[21]

Increasingly, however, it seems that the liberals may be joining the Right in how they perceive our political system as being "stuck" in some centrist malaise that satisfies nobody. Since the return of the liberal administration led by Donald Tusk, Polish progressives have suffered numerous policy upsets. A full year after the inauguration of Tusk's Cabinet, and at the time of this writing, neither the decriminalization of abortion nor legalization of same-sex civil unions has managed to pass in the Polish Sejm. The Christian Democratic Polish People's Party, a coalition member, opposes both bills. Human rights organizations were outraged by Tusk's hardline stance on undocumented migration from Belarus.[22] Given the importance of the women's protests and NGOs to the coalition's victory over PiS, the frustration is understandable. But it is also blind to the institutional reasons behind

Tusk's policies. As famously elaborated more than sixty years ago by Anthony Downs,[23] in a centralized "winner-takes-all" system the only rational strategy for political actors is to appeal to the "median voter." As voluminous research on such voters emphasizes, occupying the center of the political spectrum does not necessarily mean holding an internally consistent "centrist" position. Rather, those voters often hold a mix of inconsistent positions or reflect their overall limited interest in politics.[24] In the Polish conditions, this mix certainly includes strong opposition to irregular migration. It also includes a somewhat vague "respect for traditional values," which the People's Party tries to capture when opposing the abortion and civil union laws.

It is thus the very essence of our constitutional order that prevents both conservatives and progressives from "dreaming big." Our proposal addresses this frustrating deadlock by "unpacking" the winner-takes-all system and giving a number of strongly progressive and strongly conservative voivodships a chance to lead by example. Alongside these ideological frontrunners there will also be a large group of less ideologically set voivodships, which may strike their own unique balances on the progressive–conservative policy scale, in part by seeing what works in other regions. While the current winner-takes-all system forces Poles to join one of two political tribes, under our proposed new settlement there will be more than a dozen little Polands, with their unique political and cultural flavors.

The stories in the next five chapters further the dream's aspirational function by giving us a taste of how this "unstuck" political process may play out in practice. In showing the potential scope of newly attainable political aspirations—progressive, conservative, and in between—the stories align with contemporary developments in another academic movement that has increasingly engaged storytelling: the normative discussion about deliberative democracy. This field seeks to resolve the problems of our increasingly polarized politics by creating conditions for citizens to discuss and debate key political disagreements in a rational, fair, and equal manner.[25] However, the work of Iris Young[26] and others has highlighted significant blind spots in the deliberative theory. In particular, the exclusive focus on rational discourse may create a sterile model of "polite, orderly, dispassionate, gentlemanly argument."[27] This "type I deliberation"[28] was thereby contrasted with a broader "type II" concept, which deemed "rhetoric, humor, emotion, testimony or storytelling"[29] acceptable contributions to the deliberative exchange. The goal was to make the process more accessible to citizens from outside the educated, dominant elite; in that sense, the objective was very much in line with the quest for representation animating the aforementioned Law and Literature storytelling movement. But proponents of "type II" deliberative democracy also focus precisely on the aspirational function that we are discussing here. If the goal of deliberation is "preference formation"[30]—making voters understand what they want—then surely a narrative can be a part of the solution; its role in persuasion and mobilization has been explored since antiquity.[31]

What is certain is that we can only aspire to something we can imagine. And here comes the third essential function of a dream. As we discussed before, not only do institutional reforms need to overcome particularly strong status quo biases, but the discussion about them also suffers from cognitive problems that prevent us from envisioning an institutional system[32] that is very different to the status quo.

How can a good story overcome these problems? Surprisingly, the substantial literature on legal and constitutional imagination provides little guidance. This research does a great job in offering a sophisticated account of how existing constitutional orders entrench themselves not only by functional rationality but also by an elaborate net of meaningful symbols. "The modern constitutional imaginary," explains one noted author in the field, "informs the way in which constitutions are constructed by constitutional interpreters, and it functions as an 'implicit map of the constitutional space.'"[33] This literature has achieved a great deal in applying the general observation of law using "the resources of the larger culture ... in order to establish its own particular kind of cultural discourse"[34] to uncover deeply ingrained, taken-for-granted assumptions underlying constitutional order. As we have noted earlier, it effectively explains why changing constitutions is not only formally but also socially difficult. It has less to say, however, about how a committed reformer can spark our collective imagination to overcome this social "stickiness" of our constitutional status quo.

That is why in our search for understanding of the imaginative function of the dreams narrated in the chapters that follow we venture, perhaps somewhat surprisingly, well beyond the purview of constitutional law: to a strand of research in policy studies and international relations on foresight and scenario planning.[35] The idea of using detailed narratives about the alternative futures resulting from decisions on complex issues, made under uncertainty and leading to system-wide consequences, has its roots in military strategy.[36] Recently, however, the technique has seen a wider range of applications, including in public policy and business.[37] Organizations that develop sophisticated policies affecting many countries, such as the OECD and the EU, as well as governments of large and complex nations, such as the US, develop foresight and scenario-planning methodologies to anticipate changes that may occur in the future, identify opportunities for innovation and experimentation, and stress-test proposed strategies and policies.[38]

Research on scenario planning highlights precisely the imaginative function of storytelling. In particular, it points out that traditional analytical techniques have trouble predicting outcomes of interventions that simultaneously affect numerous parts of a given social, political, economic, or military system. Decisions such as the invasion of a foreign country or determining a certain level of future greenhouse gas emissions are not suitable for regression-based econometric analysis—not least because we do not have a readily available sample of invasions or climate emergencies. Indeed, because the policy in question will produce a number of diverse impacts, with frequent ripple effects and feedback loops, it is not even possible to use reasoning loosely analogical to the statistical approaches. Drawing alternative narrative futures allows scenario-planning methodologies to deal with the uncertainty and complexity of the environment more systematically. "Scenario planners advocate the telling of multiple stories that cover a variety of plausible future occurrences. This method opens an organization's eyes to a vast future landscape."[39] Precisely like in scenario planning, constitutional change is simply difficult to grasp and therefore evaluate. That is why dreaming about it may indeed help overcome cognitive limitations, and help us imagine interactions between the new and old institutions as well as policies that could be implemented in the proposed constitutional setup.

It is worth adding that, in addition to the role of stories in sparking our imagination, the scenario-planning literature also tackles what we have called the provocative function of narratives. In the intelligence community it is well known that "when analytical judgment turns out to be wrong, it is usually not because the information was wrong. It is because an analyst made one or more faulty assumptions that went unchallenged."[40] That is why scenario-planning methodologies encourage decision-makers to purposefully include among the scenarios considered some that include assumptions and conceptual frameworks contradictory to the dominant way of reasoning. The idea behind that practice is that good stories help decision makers challenge predominant mindsets, biases, and heuristics, avoid silencing of dissenting voices, and generally open up the discussion to overlooked perspectives.[41]

Alternative future

We hope that, with the aid of Law and Literature, type II deliberative democracy, and research on scenario planning, we have convinced you of the usefulness of a constitutional dream. Perhaps the final feature of a dream that is worth mentioning here is the temporal aspect. The dream can be both about a desired future and about an alternative, better present. This temporal flexibility of dreams comes in handy in our case. When the Polish edition of this book came out in May 2023, our dreams outlined in the subsequent chapters were still located in the future. In this dream, after the parliamentary elections of fall 2023, both sides of the Polish–Polish war realize that enough is enough. Faced with external threats to the Polish state triggered by resurgent Russian imperialism, progressives and conservatives, and everybody in between, decide to put the nation before their individual ideological inclinations—but not in a way that denies the visceral reality of their attachment to their favorite conception of good life and good society.

In our dream, in the waning weeks of 2023 the newly appointed Cabinet is devoting almost all its energy to catching up with decades of backlog in the areas of defense, internal security, and energy. That Cabinet is also working on establishing a foreign policy consensus—ending the disputes with the EU, and instead aggressively lobbying for a common defense and energy policy as well as for continuing support for Ukraine in its fight.

In light of these challenges, all the political forces in Poland realize that internal disputes and problems must recede into the background. Unfortunately, these problems—from education and school curricula, to other areas of public services and social issues, to matters related to the rights of women and minorities—refuse to recede at all! The millions of Ukrainian refugees have brought local governments to the brink of exhaustion. After a period of incredible grassroots public effort to help the refugees, fatigue has set in, and there are disputes over access to services, quality of education, and values. Friction at the ethnic and religious levels has added to the existing problems over women's or LGBT rights.

The government in Warsaw is unable to meet all these challenges while focusing on strategic priorities that, if shelved further, could pose an existential threat to Poland's future and sovereignty. Therefore, based on a broad consensus, just after Christmas 2023 and almost exactly thirty-four years after the historic December 1989 amendment ending the existence of the Polish People's Republic, a significant amendment to the 1997 Constitution is approved by the Sejm and Senate.

As we work on this international version of our book exactly eighteen months after those monumental, yet imaginary, events of December 2023, it is worth recounting, for a reader less up-to-date with Polish politics, how history diverged from our dreams. On October 15, 2023, the broad anti-PiS coalition scored a stunning upset by denying PiS a third consecutive term in power. Arguably, the democratic coalition led by Donald Tusk has been one of the first cases internationally of opposition forces managing to oust revolutionary conservatives governing for more than one term. What followed will be assessed in starkly different ways by the progressive and conservative co-authors of this book.

What we witnessed following the elections was unquestionably the longest process of Cabinet formation under the 1997 Constitution. The third Tusk Cabinet was sworn in by the President nearly two months after the ballot, on December 13, 2023. For the conservatives, the reason for this unique situation was mundane: for the first time since 1997, the party that accumulated the plurality of MPs, which was PiS, was unable to secure the required absolute majority in the Sejm. That created a situation in which the President, who, pursuant to the Constitution, appoints both the Prime Minister and each Cabinet member, followed the established custom of giving the first commission to the Prime Minister chosen by the largest parliamentary faction.

Now, per Elinor Ostrom's dictum quoted a few times already, in institutional design, details matter. The concept of a president or monarch nominating the Prime Minister is familiar to most parliamentary systems. But the Polish Constitution creates a distinct process: the new Prime Minister, and all the ministers, assume office immediately upon receiving their presidential mandate. They still need to secure a vote of confidence from the Sejm within two weeks of appointment, but in the meantime they actually govern. If the presidential appointees fail to secure parliamentary confidence, the Sejm can immediately elect its own nominees for Prime Minister and ministers. The President is then obliged to appoint those nominees, but they assume office only from the moment of the presidential appointment.

This second, parliamentary stage of Cabinet formation had not previously been used since 1997, as the President had always chosen a Prime Minister who actually had the support of the required absolute majority in the Sejm. This time it was obvious that Donald Tusk, leader of the Civic Platform, had such a majority coalition behind him. Nevertheless, the conservative President, Andrzej Duda, appointed the outgoing Prime Minister of PiS, Mateusz Morawiecki, as the new Prime Minister, and swore in a Cabinet that Morawiecki proposed. In effect, in November and December Poland ended up having three cabinets: the outgoing PiS Cabinet from the previous term, the president-appointed PiS Cabinet (different from the previous PiS Cabinet), and, after Morawiecki predictably failed to secure the confidence of the Sejm, Tusk's coalition Cabinet.

The conservatives mostly shrug over this political spectacle, perhaps (rightly) pointing out that the root cause of the turbulence was the dysfunctional transition-of-power architecture of the 1997 Constitution—a document that (as we indicated in Chapter 1) conservatives generally dislike. The progressives among us, however, saw Mr Duda's foot-dragging on appointing Donald Tusk—a candidate with a clear parliamentary majority—as an alarming signal that the very institution of peaceful transfer of power was at risk in our country. The conservatives would laugh these worries off, but the progressives wondered: What if, for instance, Poland had not had the influential US Ambassador, Mark Brzeziński, who publicly and repeatedly insisted on the peaceful transfer of power being essential for the future of US–Polish alliance? What if Donald Trump and his diplomats had been in power in the waning months of 2023? Without American pressure, would Andrzej Duda have appointed Tusk and his ministers after they were duly elected by the parliament? What would have happened if he had refused and left his preferred Cabinet in place?

An assessment of the steps taken by Tusk's Cabinet after the takeover would also differ sharply depending on one's ideological perspective. Right after the transition, the new administration made aggressive efforts to take over the public media and the prosecution service. For the conservatives, even those critical of the politicized nature of both institutions, Tusk's actions were grotesquely illegal and abusive. The lack of international outcry over those actions was also proof of politically motivated double standards on the issue of the rule of law.

The progressives among us viewed Tusk's actions as justified by the unprecedented nature of what they saw as a post-authoritarian cleanup. For them, both the public media and the prosecution service had been stuffed with political functionaries who were then protected, by clearly unconstitutional statutes, from being dismissed by the new government. Unfortunately, there was no standard way to challenge the evident unconstitutionality of the PiS laws cementing the key institutions. As already mentioned in Chapter 5, as far as the progressives were concerned, the institution tasked with declaring laws unconstitutional—the Constitutional Tribunal—ceased to exist as a legitimate constitutional body after the illegal court-packing initiated by PiS and President Duda in 2015. Given the lack of a functioning constitutional court, it was—for many of us—the Prime Minister's duty to act in accordance with his oath of office and stop the systemic breaches of the country's democratic system in the public media, prosecution service and other key institutions.

Neither the conservative nor the progressive view necessarily conflicts with IUS's broader point. Indeed, the very fact that some of us see Andrzej Duda's actions as unconstitutional, while others declare the same about Donald Tusk's decisions, proves that Poland has lost constitutional institutions in a sociological sense, that is, the rules of the game approved by all major players. Therefore, regardless of what we believe should be our side's short-term tactics in the current uncooperative game with no accepted rules, we all can and should commit to the more fundamental project of finding new, generally accepted rules.

From that vantage we can support the actions of the leaders of our political tribe in the Polish–Polish war but still dream of—and advocate for—an alternative present where nationwide settlement replaces polarization and infighting.

Alternative present

And thus we arrive at our editorial decision regarding this international edition of our book. Rather than updating our dreams and situating them in a hopeful future of Polish constitutional settlement, we choose to keep them as they were written in early 2023. As the reader will notice, many of the dreams seem to be located in a more hopeful version of 2025—about the time of this writing. For us they thereby represent a dream of a better, alternative present—a time where we all came together to accept both the pivotal importance of our joint Polish citizenship and the deep reality of what divides us. It is the post 2023-election reality where we all, to quote our movement's motto, "agree that we are different."

The starting point of this dream is, again, the December 2023 constitutional amendment that alters Poland's 1997 basic law in five important aspects. First, the new Article 87(2) creates a clear catalog of sources of sub-national law. The supreme sub-national act in each region becomes the Voivodship Charter, approved by regional referendum. The amended Article 169 transfers to the Voivodship Charter most of the rules concerning the functioning of subnational governments, including the rules and procedure for the election and dismissal of executive bodies of local and regional government units. From now on, our regional and local governments do not need to look and function exactly the same all over the country.

The charter must, of course, be compatible with the Polish Constitution, international law, and national statutes. Voivodship resolutions and ordinances, as well as municipal resolutions, must, in turn, remain in compliance with the charter. A novelty is the possibility for voivodships to conclude agreements with other provinces on close cooperation in specific areas (for example, on higher education or economic development strategies). With such cooperation in mind, the new December Amendment introduces inter-voivodship resolutions and ordinances into the catalog of sources of decentralized law.

Second, the new Article 152 leaves the voivode as the "representative of public authorities" in the province—except that, in keeping with the idea of tearing down the "Chinese wall" between central, regional, and local governments (discussed already in Chapter 1), this representative is no longer appointed by the Prime Minister (which, by the way, is not explicitly stated in the current constitution), but by the residents of the region in question. The Voivodship Charter regulates whether the residents' preference is the direct election of the voivode or the indirect election by the popularly elected sejmiks. Since Poland is one, the election of a voivode by the citizens in no way diminishes their role as a governmental representative. On the contrary, such a democratically elected representative has a much stronger mandate.

By giving a democratic mandate to the voivode, the separate function of the provincial marshal and the division between the voivode and marshal's offices have lost their purpose. These offices are merged, and the local administration of the voivode is headed by the regional board under the direction of the voivode.

Third, the revised Chapter 4 reforms the Polish Senate. Instead of 100 senators, the second chamber will be composed of voivodes deciding by the majority of the population represented.

Fourth, the amended Article 168 explicitly adds the regionalized personal and corporate income taxes to the list of current local taxes and fees.

Fifth, the December Amendment transfers supervisory powers over subnational government bodies from the Prime Minister to the President of the Republic. The new Article 171 clearly limits the scope of this supervision to the issue of the legality of local and regional government actions. At the same time, Article 171 introduces the institution of the College of Voivodships, composed of vice-voivodes from all regions responsible for individual departments of regional government. It is the College of Voivodships that is responsible for peer oversight of the effectiveness of the operations of decentralized government.

In parallel with the December Amendment, Sejm made changes to ordinary legislation concerning subnational governments. Instead of the previous rigid regulations in the minutest detail determining how local and regional governments work, the new statutes are based on an innovative solution. Namely, they introduce a model of the Voivodship Charter, or (as we have already mentioned) the highest decentralized law in a region. This model can be found at LetsAgreeonPoland.org.

The statute gives regional communities the right—but not the obligation—to modify certain provisions of the Voivodship Charter. If the provincial governments do not exercise this right, the model charter applies. Without seeking by force to create a rigid corset for all the voivodships, the law broadly defines the elements of the charter that can be modified. For example, the provinces are given the right to decide whether they will maintain a three-level administrative structure with counties in between municipalities and the voivodship, or whether the voivode or mayors are elected by popular vote or indirectly, by the sejmik or municipal councils. National unity does not necessarily mean uniformity.

On the other hand, the law clearly defines those aspects of the charter that remain rigid throughout the country. Among these elements are guarantees of the highest democratic standards and broad citizen participation in governance, including through e-governance tools. Innovations include the introduction of a provincial electronic referendum and the National Ranking of Public Services. Also unmodifiable is the role of the voivodship senate, composed of mayors voting by a weighted vote of the number of residents represented. All provincial resolutions must, to take effect, receive the approval of both the sejmik and the voivodship senate. This regional senate is necessary to protect the municipalities—it is a condition that Warsaw centralism not be replaced by a provincial centralism.

The final element of the reforms is the emancipation of a significant portion of public assets and the establishment of the nationwide Local Media Fund, mentioned in Chapter 1, which finances grants to media outlets pledging to devote a significant portion of their activity to monitoring the activities of local governments.

Local and regional governments operating under the new rules are elected in the ballot taking place on Sunday, May 28, 2024—almost exactly thirty-four years after the first democratic local elections. On the same day, provincial residents can also decide for the first time whether to adapt the Voivodship Charter model to regional needs. Contrary to the expectation that there would be wide divergence among the charter proposals, the default model proposal has been mostly adopted without many changes.

What happened next? The authors of the next five chapters invite us to dream with them. In Chapter 8, Helena Chmielewska-Szlajfer and Pawel Dobrowolski will outline a scenario for Gdańsk and the Pomeranian Voivodship under a socially progressive local government coalition. In Chapter 9, Jakub Drożdż and Sylwia Sysko-Romańczuk outline the future of Białystok and the Podlaskie province, governed by a conservative administration. In Chapter 10, Alicja Pacewicz, Jan Smoleński, and Michał Żabicki describe the West Pomeranian province, governed by an economically leftist provincial administration. In Chapter 11, Łukasz Rozdeiczer and Artur Wołek sketch a similar future for Rzeszów and the Subcarpathian province under a Christian Democratic regional administration.

Finally, in Chapter 12, Marek Tatała, Leszek Stypułkowski, and Marcin Zieliński describe the Greater Poland region governed by a free-market (classical liberal) local government.

Notes

1. Martin Loughlin, "The Constitutional Imagination," *The Modern Law Review* 78, no. 1 (2015): 9.
2. See e.g., Jiří Přibáň, *Constitutional Imaginaries: A Theory of European Societal Constitutionalism* (Routledge, 2022).
3. Consistent with the critical view of the fairness of the 2019 general election, and the preceding campaign, the report of the OSCE's observation mission indicated "media bias and intolerant rhetoric," "senior state officials using publicly funded events for campaign messages," and "the dominance of the ruling party in public media" that "further amplified [PiS's] advantage" Organization for Security and Co-operation in Europe, Parliamentary Elections, 13 October 2019: ODIHR Limited Election Observation Mission, Final Report, 1 (2020). See also Radoslaw Markowski, "Plurality Support for Democratic Decay: The 2019 Polish Parliamentary Election," *West European Politics* 43, no. 7 (2020): 1513–1525.
4. Vanessa Gera and Frank Bajak, "Polish Opposition Senator Hacked with Spyware," *The Associated Press*, Dec. 23, 2021.
5. Maciej Kisilowski, "The Election's Aftermath," *Verfassungsblog: On Matters Constitutional* (2023).
6. Ben Berger, *Attention Deficit Democracy: The Paradox of Civic Engagement* (Princeton University Press, 2011); James H. Kuklinski and Paul J. Quirk, "Reconsidering the Rational Public: Cognition, Heuristics, and Mass Opinion," in *Elements of Reason: Cognition, Choice, and the Bounds of Rationality,* eds. Arthur Lupia, Mathew D. McCubbins, and Samuel L. Popkin (Cambridge University Press, 2000).
7. C. Wright Mills, *The Sociological Imagination* (Oxford University Press, 1959), 7.
8. Id.
9. Adam Smith, *The Wealth of Nations: An Inquiry Into the Nature and Causes of the Wealth of Nations* (University Of Chicago Press, 1977), 30.
10. Paul Blokker, "The Imaginary Constitution of Constitutions," *Social Imaginaries* 3, no. 1 (2017): 171.
11. For other analyses of the social embeddedness of Eastern European constitutions see Martin Belov, "Constitutional Transitions and Transitional Imaginaries: Bridging Legacies of the Constitutional Past and Aspirations for the Constitutional Future," in *Constitutional Traditions and Constitutional Transitions*, ed. Martin Belov and Monika Florczak-Wątor (Edward Elgar Publishing, 2024); and Grażyna Skąpska, *From 'Civil Society' to 'Europe': A Sociological Study on Constitutionalism after Communism* (Brill, 2011).
12. For a classic statement see Douglass C. North, *Institutions, Institutional Change, and Economic Performance* (Cambridge University Press, 1990).
13. See e.g. Andromachi Tseloni et al., "The Effectiveness of Burglary Security Devices," *Security Journal* 30 (2017): 646–664.
14. For a classic sociological analysis of the motivations of public intellectuals see Pierre Bourdieu, *Homo Academicus* (Stanford University Press, 1988). For an analysis of an intersection of intellectual competition and intellectual change see Randall Collins, *The Sociology of Philosophies: A Global Theory of Intellectual Change* (Belknap Press of Harvard University Press, 1998). Both works present the broad and nuanced theories of public intellectuals' behavior with which our account broadly coincides.
15. Martin Belov, *Constitutional Semiotics: The Conceptual Foundations of a Constitutional Theory and Meta-Theory* (Hart, 2022).
16. Kim Lane Scheppele, "Foreword: Telling Stories," *Michigan Law Review* 87, no. 8 (1989): 2073–2098.
17. Id.
18. Id.
19. Richard Delgado, "Storytelling for Oppositionists and Others: A Plea for Narrative," *Michigan Law Review* 87, no. 8: 2411-2441 (1989).

20. See e.g., George Yancy and Judith Butler, "What's Wrong With 'All Lives Matter'?," *The New York Times*, Jan. 12, 2015; for an academic analysis see e.g. Nikita Carney, "All Lives Matter, but so Does Race: Black Lives Matter and the Evolving Role of Social Media," *Humanity & Society* 40, no. 2 (2016): 180–199.
21. Jacques Rupnik, "The Specter Haunting Europe: Surging Illiberalism in the East," *Journal of Democracy* 27, no. 4 (2016): 80.
22. See "Hundreds of NGOs and Public Figures Call on Tusk to Stop Migrant Pushbacks at Belarus Border," *Notes from Poland*, Jan. 11, 2024, https://notesfrompoland.com/2024/01/11/hundreds-of-ngos-and-public-figures-call-on-tusk-to-stop-migrant-pushbacks-at-belarus-border/.
23. Anthony Downs, *An Economic Theory of Democracy* (Harper, 1957).
24. See e.g. Anthony Fowler et al., "Moderates," *American Political Science Review* 117, no. 2 (2023): 643–660.
25. Bruce A. Ackerman and James S. Fishkin, *Deliberation Day* (Yale University Press, 2004).
26. Iris Marion Young, *Inclusion and Democracy* (Oxford University Press, 2002).
27. Id, 49.
28. André Bächtiger et al., "Disentangling Diversity in Deliberative Democracy: Competing Theories, Their Blind Spots and Complementarities," *The Journal of Political Philosophy* 18, no. 1 (2010): 32–63.
29. John S. Dryzek, *Deliberative Democracy and Beyond: Liberals, Critics, Contestations* (Oxford University Press, 2002), 48.
30. James Fishkin, "Defending Deliberation: A Comment on Ian Shapiro's The State of Democratic Theory," *Critical Review of International Social and Political Philosophy* 8, no. 1 (2005): 71–78.
31. Ed Sanders and Matthew Johncock, *Emotion and Persuasion in Classical Antiquity* (Franz Steiner Verlag, 2016).
32. For a thorough examination of the systemic nature of modern constitutions see Adrian Vermeule, *The System of the Constitution* (Oxford University Press, 2011).
33. Paul Blokker and Chris J. Thornhill, "Sociological Constitutionalism: An Introduction," in *Sociological Constitutionalism*, ed. Paul Blokker and Chris J. Thornhill (Cambridge University Press, 2018), 11.
34. Robert Post, "Introduction: The Relatively Autonomous Discourse of Law," in *Law and the Order of Culture*, ed. Robert Post (University of California Press, 1991), viii.
35. Angela Miller, "The Past Is Holding Us Back: Applying Foresight to Move the Disciplines of Political Science and International Relations Forward," *World Futures Review* 14, no. 1 (2022): 80–85; Randolph H. Pherson and Richards J. Heuer Jr, *Structured Analytic Techniques for Intelligence Analysis* (Cq Press, 2019).
36. Kees Van der Heijden, *Scenarios: The Art of Strategic Conversation* (John Wiley & Sons, 2005).
37. Ron Bradfield et al., "The Origins and Evolution of Scenario Techniques in Long Range Business Planning," *Futures* 37, no. 8 (2005): 795–812; Celeste Amorim Varum and Carla Melo, "Directions in Scenario Planning Literature—A Review of the Past Decades," *Futures* 42, no. 4 (2010): 355–369.
38. Laura De Vito and Gaia Taffoni, "Strategic Foresight and Policy Evaluation: Insights for an Integrated Approach," *European Journal of Risk Regulation* 14, no. 4 (2023): 800–806; Hasok Chang, "Foresight in Scientific Method," in *Foresight*, ed. Lawrence W. Sherman and David Allan Feller (Cambridge University Press, 2016), 82–100.
39. Thomas J. Chermack, Susan A. Lynham, and Wendy E.A. Ruona, "A Review of Scenario Planning Literature," *Futures Research Quarterly* 17, no. 2 (2001): 7.
40. Richards J. Heuer, *Psychology of Intelligence Analysis* (Center for the Study of Intelligence, 1999), 69.
41. Randolph H. Pherson, "Leveraging the Future with Foresight Analysis," *The International Journal of Intelligence, Security, and Public Affairs* 20, no. 2 (2018): 102–131.

8
The Dream Progressive Voivodship

Helena Chmielewska-Szlajfer and Paweł Dobrowolski
Fictionalized by Ziemowit Szczerek

Here comes everybody

"All right, so what do *you* do?" Amelia asked Greg. Amelia was Maciek's girlfriend and Greg was their neighbor. They were all sitting in a bar in Gdańsk, watching the Pride march slink down the Długa street. The Voivode was presiding at the helm of the march—her picture snapped by people from all over the world. After all, this was Gdańsk, a port city with links to everywhere else in the world. No wonder the street was bustling with so much life and color.

Amelia and Maciek first met Greg in front of their building in Słupsk, when he'd just moved in with his family—his wife, Ela, and teenagers, Iza and Florek. Greg and Ela had gotten together quite early on. She'd moved to Portsmouth to study and supported herself by washing dishes in an old pub with a ridiculous name, and Greg was one of the pub's customers. He'd been spending a lot of time in the pub back then. His wife had just left him and gone to Goa with an amply tattooed mindfulness expert from Italy, leaving their son behind with Greg. Ela helped him get over his despair pretty quickly and before he knew it, they'd had a child together, Iza.

So, they moved to Słupsk. Their new neighbor Maciek helped them unpack all their stuff. Their meeting happened sort of organically. He was coming back from meeting up with some friends, feeling a bit ill and wiping his nose with his sleeve, but still, he felt unusually energetic. He grabbed the first box out of the car, then another, then a bit later they were having a beer together in the new flat. And since then, they'd been hanging out here and there.

This gang of neighbors decided to take a trip to Tricity—the Gdańsk, Sopot, and Gdynia metro area. They'd rented a house in Sopot, but for some reason they wanted to grab a beer in Gdańsk first. They chipped in for the taxi ride, driven by a cheerful Belarussian fellow named Wala. The whole time he talked about how he was a surgeon by profession and and the taxi driver work was until he could get his diploma certified. The process was relatively efficient in Pomerania, thanks to the new regulations introduced by regional government… and *yet*. Wala kept the

Helena Chmielewska-Szlajfer and Paweł Dobrowolski, *The Dream Progressive Voivodship* In: *Let's Agree on Poland*. Edited by: Maciej Kisilowski and Anna Wojciuk, Oxford University Press.
 DOI: 10.1093/oso/9780198979562.003.0011

carful of passengers entertained with detailed accounts of organ transplants. Greg seemed to be fully in his element, but Maciek was slowly turning green.

"So, what do *you* do, Greg?" Amelia insisted. "You came to live in Pomerania? From England? Seriously?"

"What's your point?" replied Ela, Greg's wife, because she was a bit fed up with Amelia's strange comments. "It's just a regular place like any other. It's international! Why wouldn't a Brit want to come live here?"

"It's fine, Ela." Greg's voice was soothing, despite his heavy British accent. He took a sip of his beer and said, "There's this concept, conjured up by some people at the Kashubian Folk University in Wieżyca. A smart house for seniors. A *smart home*."

"A smart home?" Amelia snorted. "And I'm supposed to take you seriously?"

"Why not? You think just because it's Poland, nothing interesting happens here?"

"No, that's not what Amelia's trying to say," Maciek interrupted, trying to salvage the situation somehow, only to receive an unpleasant look from Amelia in response.

"Are you trying to mansplain to me now? You think you know better than I do what I meant to say?" Amelia sulked. "I'll have you know that what I actually wanted to say is exactly what Ela's suggesting. But yeah, maybe I'm wrong about what I meant?"

"All right, listen." Greg had learned the language, and to a pretty high level at that, but when he talked about what he did for a living, he started to sound like the type of AI bots he was working to build. "It's an innovative solution. I'm working on its implementation. The whole idea is that there's a system of sensors and intuitive devices, which use gestures and voice commands to monitor the health status of the home's residents (including the food stores in the fridge). It makes it possible to get in touch instantly with specific individuals—family, doctor, caretaker, senior companion …"

"What the—?" Maciek's eyes grew as big as saucers.

Greg laughed out loud.

"We call them SCs for short."

"Sounds like another bot."

"Not a bot, an actual human being, if you can imagine." Greg didn't get the joke and Amelia didn't even think it was a good joke, so they ignored it. "So, this SC," Greg went on, "is a mix of a talkative scout and a nurse. Anyway, the idea came from kids at the local high school and a group of people old enough to be their grandparents."

"The whole point is," Ela cut in, clearly exasperated, "these kids have a volunteer committee set up at school and seniors like having a real-life person around, not a bot. And you see, these kids, they get to know the seniors and then they end up giving them the support they need through this volunteer program."

"And the advantages are mutual," Greg replied. "Because the exchange goes both ways. First, the students are introduced to this group of seniors, and then they help them get around and go about their everyday tasks. In exchange, these seniors share their memories with the kids, as part of this regional partnership program called '(Un)Common Memories' which is supported by local research institutes and universities."

"Yeah, I can just see those kids elbowing each other to get better access to an old guy's stories." Maciek was laughing, but everybody glared at him. Amelia mumbled something about not being a jerk and having some faith in the young generation.

"Fine, fine," Maciek said at last, his tone defensive. "I was just joking anyway."

"Yeah, really funny," Amelia retorted. "Seriously, Maciek, you're hilarious."

"Listen, Maciek," Greg, always eager to set things straight, picked up again as soon as everybody had climbed out of the taxi and wished Wala the best of luck and plenty of successful transplants to come. "The idea is to keep these stories alive through interactions with another living person, to someone of the next generation, instead of relegating them to a recording locked up in an archive somewhere. Lots of people have joined the project, including new residents from other parts of Poland and other parts of the world. Because Pomerania has been trying to bring together as many people as possible from outside, to our classrooms, to our places of work—to balance out this gap between the number of old and young people living here."

"Oh, is that right?" Maciek interjected again—somewhat ironically, for lack of a better way to phrase it, but no one really noticed. He was surprised to see the two women staring at Greg like he was an idol as Greg continued talking, opening the door to the restaurant.

"Ultimately, even though it wasn't part of the initial plan, the program ended up being a pretty decent method for intercultural and intergenerational integration. For instance, the owner of a local bakery chain in Kartuzy came by to visit a woman who happened to be an old friend of his grandmother's. And when he got there, he saw her making pierogi from scratch with her 18-year-old SC. But the dough and filling were different from the traditional sort. And really tasty, too."

Ela and Amelia were listening intently, while Maciek stared at the wall in total boredom. He was getting pretty irritated by Greg, even though he couldn't really say a bad word about the guy. Was he talking nonsense? In spite of anything you might want to say, there was nothing nonsensical about what he was saying. Was it boring? Yeah, it might have been boring, but what was Maciek supposed to do? Tell him to cut it out? Then he'd get offended and there'd just be an uncomfortable silence in the air after that. That would make things even more boring.

"So does any of this have a practical application?" Amelia asked this because she really appreciated when certain things had practical applications.

"Well, certainly, seniors getting the help they need sounds like a pretty practical application to me, Amelia!" replied Ela, giggling a bit more dramatically than necessary. In the meantime, Maciek surmised that there was some sort of relatively light tension arising between the two women.

"But I know exactly what Amelia means," Greg said with a smile, which only irritated Maciek further. "This initiative led to the idea of setting up a chain of co-operative cafeterias called 'Grandmas & Grandkids,' and that's actually exactly what it is. Only, the grandmas and grandkids come from all over the country and around the world!"

"Bon appetit!" Maciek remarked, rather thoughtfully.

The Promised Pomerania

In the meantime, Greg and Ela's teenage progeny, Florek and Iza, were meandering between the Pride march and the streets of downtown Gdańsk, accompanied by friends they'd made at a recent music festival (who happened to be friends of their parents too). Julka and Ira were lesbians from St Petersburg who'd escaped persecution in Russia. At 20-something years of age, they were a bit older than Florek and Iza, but they'd promised their parents they'd take a stroll with the kids. None of them felt like sitting inside a restaurant when the sun was shining.

Back in Russia, Julka and Ira had been LGBTQ+ activists and founders of an organization known as Wychod or "Out." The police had been doing everything in its power to make their lives hell and politicians were stoking the flames of homophobia, so they had to go into hiding. When their daughter Jashka was born, they decided to flee to protect their child's future. Gdańsk felt relatively familiar to them, both culturally and geographically. Once they became legal residents of Pomerania, they were able to enter a civil union and establish themselves as Jashka's legal guardians. This was all possible under Pomerania's family laws.

It's important to note that the path to instating these reforms had been quite rocky. To avoid threatening the fragile status of the constitutional coalition, the December 2023 constitutional amendment did not tackle article 18 of the 1997 Constitution, which states that *marriage, being a union of a man and a woman, as well as the family, motherhood and parenthood, shall be placed under the protection and care of the Republic of Poland.* But a slim progressive majority in the Sejm passed a national statute that gave voivodships the right to introduce same-sex marriages, based on the argument that the protection of traditional marriage, as outlined in article 18, doesn't preclude the recognition of single-sex unions.

President Andrzej Duda chose to refer the statute to the restored Constitutional Tribunal. After recent constitutional reform, the Tribunal's justices are chosen by the new Polish Senate. Their election must be supported by senators-voivodes who represent no less than 60 percent of the citizens. As a result, the Tribunal is now made up of experienced lawyers, who nonetheless tend to lean toward a more conservative interpretive approach. Taking the linguistic and systemic interpretation of article 18, the Tribunal expressed their agreement with the president's doubts with respect to the law; however, it also accepted the constitutionality of same-sex civil unions on the basis of the decisions of the European Court of Human Rights. The Pomerania's voivode didn't hide her critical stance toward the Tribunal's decision, standing firmly behind the comprehensive notion of marriage equality. In addition to the legalization of same-sex unions, the provincial government implemented a program called "Family, No Matter What You Call It," aimed at training regional administration officials and teachers (including religious education instructors). The main goal of the program was to eliminate official discrimination and microaggressions, particularly with respect to queer families.

On this particular afternoon, Jashka was sitting with Ira's grandmother, who'd also emigrated, and the rest of the gang was roaming the city, keeping a good distance from the restaurant where Florek and Iza's parents were sitting. They walked a bit and stopped at a local square.

"In a normal country," Florek, who had just recently moved to Poland, complained, "for instance, Holland, it would be cool to light up a joint right here. But here … you can't even have a beer on a park bench because the cops will write you up." To be fair, Florek was showing off.

"No, they won't," Iza countered. "That law's been changed in Pomerania."

Florek pretended not to hear her comment, but he did scrupulously file it away in his memory, and turned to Julka and Ira with an air of drama.

"Why didn't you go live somewhere else, farther away?"

"Well," Julka began, "for us, the Baltic, it's home. We're from St Petersburg. Culturally, it's like we're the same, but it's still the West, you know."

"Besides," Ira added, "we get a huge amount of support when we're here—from both the city and the people. They've made me feel at home. I love Gdańsk, it's a beautiful city. And we got so lucky with our flat."

"How so?" Florek asked, even though it wasn't a topic he cared too much about. He was more into memes, working out, skating. Iza was the one who was interested in all that community stuff. But he didn't want to look like a complete dunce who didn't know anything about anything.

"For one, there's the Cooperative Real Estate Agency," replied Ira. She went into a detailed explanation of how it offered local residents reasonable choices for buying or renting property. Changes had been implemented to make it easier for those who didn't have a solid credit rating or a lower income, such as single mothers, homeless individuals, or immigrants. The agency acts as a mediator between the client and the property owner, also serving as a guarantor for the payment and protecting the owner's legal rights, as well as the interests and rights of renters from bad practices, such as sudden evictions and the like.

"Wow, aren't you the expert …" Florek remarked, a bit of snark creeping into his voice, although the truth was, he couldn't help feeling a little impressed.

"Obviously," Ira retorted. "I was an activist back in Russia, right? Social issues and community resources are something I'm extremely into. And let me tell you something else."

To Florek's dismay—as all he wanted to do was pull out his phone and start scrolling Instagram instead of listening—Ira began to explain how some branches of the agency had started combining affordable real estate services with matching people with job vacancies. They'd build career profiles and help people find the right position, on top of managing properties, maintaining residential and green spaces, offering training and work placement programs, and helping people get on their feet. And at the same time, they were an institution, a trusted partner in mediating between property owners and "riskier" clients who might not have a solid credit history.

"It's also important to know that the Cooperative Real Estate Agency makes sure the properties they offer are in different locations throughout a particular region, to avoid creating artificial 'ghettos' in specific areas," Julka added. Part of Julka's activism in Russia was related to issues of gentrification.

"So, Florek, how did you get settled around here? You're British, right?" Ira asked. "And you, Iza, you grew up in the UK too, didn't you?"

Florek stammered a bit and then admitted it hadn't been that bad, actually. Iza jumped in, leaving Florek to get back to scrolling.

"Right after we got here," she began, "notifications started popping up on our phones about local schools and where there were places available, plus after-school activities. We picked a school that ended up becoming pretty well known for its sex ed and mental health education curriculum, plus it's a green initiative incubator. A few days later, when we went to visit the school, we were relieved to see that it's pretty much like our school in the UK."

Florek piped up, with one eye still monitoring his phone screen, but his ear keeping up with the conversation, "The kids and teachers are a pretty big mix of cultures."

"Is that not something you expected?" Julka asked. "Everyone talks about how modern Poland is, how European ..."

"Yes, I guess I'd heard something or other," replied Iza. "But it's different reading about it and something else to see it. How diverse Pomerania has become." She started to describe how the corridors of the school were lined with the stretch of Polish—and local Hanseatic—history. Its many centuries of diverse traditions and multiculturalism told through posters and essays pinned up on bulletin boards and even interactive screens, composed and designed by the students themselves.

"Right," Florek said in agreement, because the conversation had finally veered toward a subject that he was actually interested in: history. He'd always enjoyed reading Tolkien and *Conan*, he'd even read *The Witcher* in class, and pretty soon he'd gotten drift of the fact that so many of these stories in fantasy had actually happened—granted, maybe without the hobbits, dragons, or elves. "It's a unique part of Poland because here, besides the whole aristo aspects, there was the whole history of Hansa, where everything was developing in a different way, sailors, merchants . . . A bit like the Netherlands."

"You see," Ira said, tousling his hair, "you've got Holland, just like you wanted."

Florek snorted, replying, "Yeah, but you still can't buy weed."

"Maybe you can get a doctor to prescribe you some. Medical marijuana's legal right? And our voivodship has made it more accessible. But you've got to grow up first, tiger!" Julka burst out laughing and lit up a joint she'd got from the CBD shop nearby.

"Stop it!" Iza cried out. "Marijuana must be consumed responsibly." Iza's polite schoolgirl decorum was shining through as she continued, "Like I saw in some meme: *Any dude will tell you weed's not addicting, that's why he's always smoking!*"

Everybody laughed, except Florek, who just resorted to snorting again, and Iza went back to talking about school, while Florek focused his attention elsewhere. She talked about how the school was offering supplementary education classes for kids just starting out in the Polish system—in language, culture, and history. How the themes were regional and international, to set everything in a more comprehensive global context.

"Why don't you just tell them everything you know about the Tricity Metropolitan Area—TMA!" Florek blurted out, divulging in the process how vested he was in the topic.

"Oh yes!" Ira exclaimed. "It's actually so cool!" And the three of them, Ira, Julka, and Iza, began one-upping each other to see who knew the most about Tricity history: how an association of fifty-nine municipalities, cities, and towns came together to streamline their public procurement, along with their plans for urban development, transportation, labor, social economics, and integrating new migrants.

"In fact, it was the TMA that was the first in Poland to build and implement a systemic solution for foreigners," called out Iza, nearly leaping off the bench. "The so-called Minimum Standard in Integration!"

"That's right. That's where you can get support in finding a job, legal advice, Polish lessons . . ." Julka added. "You can even find out more about safety and security, training for civil servants, and local initiatives related to migration. I heard about it from someone I was talking to a while ago: the founder of the Immigrant Support Center. She even said that after they'd introduced the Pomeranian Voivodship Charter, solutions put together by TMA were expanded throughout the voivodship as the foundation for their overall migration and integration policies!"

Julka reached into her pocket, pulled out a slightly crumpled flyer, and began to read from it.

"Foreigners are a key group with respect to the demographics and population of our region, as noted by the voivode, a Kashubian by origin. The voivodship government, within the framework of our employment policy, has highlighted the need for engaging in dialogue, the exchange of ideas and information, and starting collective initiatives to integrate immigrants. With this goal, we've established the position of Voivodship Migrant Ombudsman."

The voivode, who, as a result of the referendum on the Charter, is elected directly, had centered her entire campaign around inclusivity, represented by her campaign slogan *The Promised Pomerania*—a direct reference to Grzegorz Piątek's book *The Promised Gdynia*.

"Have you read it?" Julka asked Florek.

"Is it any good?" he retorted.

"It's history!"

"Then maybe I'll read it. But do they have it in English?"

"Your voivodship is offering you so much, so many Polish lessons, so you could finally go ahead and pick one!" Iza shot back.

"Maaaan, I know how to speak Polish," Florek grumbled back. "*Sorry* that I'm not as perfect at it as you three."

"Perfect accent on the 'sorry' though," Iza retorted.

Witamy/welcome

Ira and Julka decided to head back to where the kids' parents were waiting. They called first to make sure their daughter was fine, then they all walked through the Old Town in a roundabout way to get to the restaurant. When they got there, Greg was fully engaged in his thrilling description of SCs. They said hello and waited for the staff to bring over an extra chair so they could all fit around the table. Once they were all settled, they promptly returned to the topic at hand: what a wonderful thing it was to live in the Pomeranian Voivodship. They heard someone chuckling by the wall and everyone turned around to have a look. They couldn't believe their eyes.

There she was, the Voivode herself, sitting with a friend, relaxing in the warm bask of candlelight after walking in the Pride march.

And so it began, kissing of the hands, shaking of the hands, nonstop compliments, even a few genuflections. And only Amelia managed to discreetly slip out for a ciggie. Florek would have snuck out too, but he was still a minor.

"We were *just* talking about how our voivodship is offering the most remarkable support for newcomers, Madame Voivode," Greg declared, recognizing how important it was to know one's place and to fully inhabit that place.

"Oh, yes. The Pomeranian Voivodship is meant to be straightforward in its operations from end to end," the Voivode said with a smile, "not just for foreigners, but for all residents and tourists too, those who want to enjoy their holidays at the Polish seaside. We were thinking of everyone when we set up and updated our *Welcome to Pomerania* booklet for new residents, in four language editions: Polish,

English, Ukrainian, and Russian. It's also available as a free app." She unlocked her phone and the icon popped up on her screen.

"Look, all the forms you need to file a request are available in all four languages, including info on the new tax documents: PIT and CIT. The voivodship also offers its civil servants free foreign language classes. Employees who work with residents who exclusively speak a foreign language get a special bonus."

"I think Florek could do with a free class," Iza teased. "Because he's not exactly in a rush to learn Polish."

"I told you I can speak Polish!" Florek called out in frustration. "Stop it!" He made a show of standing up and walking out, mumbling something about needing a breath of fresh air. He walked up to Amelia, who was vaping, and leaned in.

"Give me a puff, why don't you, auntie," he whispered.

"I will not give you a puff. Your parents would have a total go at me," she replied, taking a peek at everyone inside through the window. If she could hear what they were saying, she would know that the Voivode was telling everyone that they shouldn't poke fun at Florek for not speaking Polish fluently because she'd heard him speak, and, just like Greg, he spoke very well—and how languages were an important issue since communication barriers could cause trouble for some people.

"After all, because of the complexity of Polish grammar and speech, we realize that tourists, visitors, and new residents depend on our good will and the language skills of our civil servants," she asserted. "We're just acknowledging this fact and making sure we're compensating employees who have those very useful, supplementary skills."

"Wait a second," Maciek countered. "Does that mean employees who don't know a foreign language are treated worse because there's no requirement for any of them to learn it?"

"What are they even talking about?" Amelia asked Florek, who was standing closer to the entrance.

"Your boyfriend, my dear auntie, is asking why he's getting the short end of the stick."

"Oh, Lord," Amelia said, rolling her eyes. Then she checked how much she had left. She wasn't going to keep vaping forever just to avoid heading back to the table.

In the meantime, the voivode was doing a great job managing Maciek's volleys.

"No, this isn't meant to discriminate at all against fine employees who don't happen to be polyglots. There are multiple ways of getting a bonus, for instance, if they get positive reviews from residents in the new (nationwide) system that's part of the reform known as the Local and Regional Government Quality Assessment System for Laws and Public Services. The officer in charge of administrative affairs told me this system has been a game-changer. In combination with the bonus program, it has greatly improved the way public services are delivered throughout the voivodship.

"So, this type of bonus, the one that rewards civil servants who speak a lot of languages, doesn't necessarily prioritize foreigners, is that right?" Maciek surmised.

From electromobility to religion in schools

"All right, let's talk about something a bit more interesting, shall we?" Amelia proposed as soon as she got back, smelling of cherry vape, making some of the others wrinkle their noses.

"How about cars?" Florek suggested. "How's the transportation situation in our voivodship?"

"Well, as it happens . . ." the Voivode replied, indicating to the man on her right, "Emil and I were just talking about this very topic. He's an expert in the field."

The waiters brought over another table and took some more orders before they could get back to the conversation at hand.

"Emil," the Voivode began, "is it true that we're putting a real focus on electromobility, public transport, and municipal laboratories?"

"Why, certainly," Emil confirmed with just the right measure of enthusiasm. "Taxpayers in Pomerania will be able to enjoy free public transport from 2024 onwards."

"Oh, really?" Florek perked up, since he knew of plenty of other ways he could be spending his pocket money than on taking the bus.

"You're not a taxpayer, though, parasite," Iza teased again.

"But *we* are," Greg interjected with a big grin. "And we're also your guardians."

"Right, right," Emil gulped, as if he was defending a dissertation. "For, um, those who are new to the city, we have an electronic integrated transport ticket, which includes the suburban rail, and then we have MEVO bikes thanks to their public–private partnership with the city."

"You see!" the voivode nodded. "When we think about making public space accessible to those members of society who might be considered at a disadvantage, it's always worth considering whether one individual's needs might be at odds with the needs of others."

"Right. So how often do you ask yourself that question, Florek?" Iza insisted.

"How about you, Amelia?" Maciek asked, shooting his girlfriend an inquisitive look.

"You guys could really stop with the bull—" Amelia began, cutting herself off when she noticed the Voivode peering at her.

"Public services adapted to the needs of new residents are surely just as helpful to those who have been long-term residents," the Voivode continued. "A fine city is one that is safe for everyone, local and foreign, adults and eight-year-olds too." She glanced at her watch, realizing how quickly the time had passed, and noted that she really had to run, but Emil stayed behind, eager to share some more of his progressive solutions for Pomerania. Everyone was pleased to have him stay, except perhaps Amelia.

"It's nice and all, but too bad the powers given to the voivodship are relatively narrow," Greg remarked. "Because a voivodship is only one piece of the puzzle, and the holistic policy of the whole nation has the greatest impact on what goes on around here. For instance, this obsession with religion. In the UK, we didn't have any of that and now the kids have religious instruction here, supposedly not mandatory, but when we hear what goes on during these lessons, it's enough to make your head spin."

"Oh, yes," Emil said, sounding slightly defeated that the topic of transportation had come and gone, as it was his pride and joy. "Poland is bound by the Concordat we signed with the Holy See back in 1993, which requires the state to allow religious instruction in public schools. But, using our new regional powers to regulate the curricula, we've done away with the ethics classes that used to be mandatory for those who opted out of the religious instruction. And we've also added new rigorous standards for teachers who teach these religion classes. These principles are now focused mainly on the subject of addressing child abuse."

"Well, this is a subject I can definitely speak on," Iza said, twirling her braids around like she was Wednesday Addams, "since I'm currently campaigning for student rights at school."

"Dad, can I have a beer?" Florek interrupted, hoping to get some attention.

"No, you can't, not till you're 18!" Ela grumbled. "Calm down, look at your posture, get a grip!"

"Mom, don't stress the kid out," Iza intervened, turning toward her brother. "You see, Florek. I'm also fighting for your rights."

"Hey, why don't you pour me out of a bit of yours ..." Florek whispered to his uncle Maciek.

"I can't," Maciek whispered back. "Your mother will have my head."

"In any case," Iza picked up again. "The Supreme Voivodship Court recently dismissed President Duda's objection raised against our regional educational reforms, specifically to the regional law stating that religious instruction should always take place at the end of the day, so that it doesn't create unnecessary scheduling gaps for students who don't participate. We know how to defend our rights! Plus, the voivodship government has been setting up programs to encourage churches and religious organizations to set up their own classes, or to volunteer to come to schools and teach. For the time being, the Catholic bishops have told local priests not to get involved in the program, but other churches can. It might sound like a paradox, but these steps will actually strengthen the bond among those in the community who are religious because they get to integrate, speak up, and participate actively in their congregations. You can really see a boost, especially when it comes to charity stuff."

"Oh yes," Ira remarked. "If we were religious, we'd definitely get more involved in the orthodox community around here."

"But..." Julka interjected.

"WE'RE NOT!" the two of them called out in unison.

Let's talk about sex (parental consent required)

"All right, so there's progress being made with sex ed," Iza interjected. "The subject's been introduced into the new regional education laws."

"Yes!" Ela exclaimed, straightening up. "And that's despite all the roadblocks set up by those old-fogey conservatives who only think of sex as a sin."

"That's true," Florek nodded, trying to score some brownie points, hoping that he'd get a sip of beer for his effort and maturity. "We've got plenty of issues related to growing up, puberty, gender identity, gender roles, and the harmful gender stereotypes we're expected to cram ourselves into, having to deal with people's opinions—especially those who complain about us instead of taking a look in the mirror and going to therapy!"

"Yup, we're really glad our parents treat us like partners," Iza added. "And they really do split the household chores right down the middle, but that's not always the case for a lot of families. I hope that they'll include something in these classes about relationships and how to build good ones rather than trying to force everybody into being a Stepford Wife. I mean, an updated look at the whole thing. But I guess you have to remember that these classes aren't mandatory, and your parents have to approve your attendance. Generally, kids from our high school were in favor. Those who were against it were, as expected, conservative activists who tried to claim it was sexualizing kids. But thankfully we won the support of the Deputy Voivode for Education."

"Yes, the support was incredibly helpful," Florek added, then turned around to ask, "Mom, can I have a sip of beer?"

"Don't even think about it!"

"Fine," Amelia sighed dramatically. She forced herself to accept that she just wasn't going to get to talk about the stuff that interested her the most, so she ordered a Red Bull and even took a puff of her vape at the bar.

"Was the conservative pushback really strong?"

"You bet it was!" Ela replied, a fiery look in her eyes. "They even launched a campaign, something called Save Our Kids from Sodom, but it ended up having the opposite effect because it made people who wouldn't have known about the classes finally pay attention. Parents and kids included. They started thinking about classes that would not be all about virtue and prayer. After a few weeks, the storm died down and the Sodom-marauders had to accept that the program wasn't going anywhere. Some people even said the noise they made was part of the promotional campaign."

Everybody laughed, even Amelia.

"So, basically," Ela surmised, "Making a fuss around the program actually helped spread the word and the Deputy Voivode ended up expanding cooperation with local health centers too. This also helped drive the campaign to make the morning after pill reimbursable and easily accessible via an app that connects you with a doctor and pharmacist. And what's more, the medical university and local biotech labs started up their own family planning programs, with testing services and fertility treatments. Eventually," Ela paused to take a breath, "it became clear that easily accessible and reimbursable pills made it possible to achieve a key goal that drove the policies of the conservative, anti-abortion government—the number of births has actually gone up as a result of these programs and services!"

"That sure came as a surprise to a lot of die-hard conservatives, let me tell you," Iza said with a wink, before reaching over to high-five her mom.

"Ela, are you really some kind of pro-abortion activist?" Amelia asked, once she'd swallowed the last drop of Red Bull. She began scanning the room for a waiter so she could order another.

"Listen, that's not what it's called. It's not 'pro-abortion.' It's 'pro-choice' and I am definitely a fan of making your own choices. At that, let me say that our voivodship has a plan to present a bill at the national Senate to make it possible for each provincial sejmik and senate to legalize abortion, in line with EU laws and guidelines, namely, in the first twelve weeks."

"But the thing about abortion ..." Amelia said, frowning. "I mean, I like to think of myself as progressive but if everyone went around getting an abortion ..."

"But who said everybody's supposed to go around getting an abortion?" Maciek shot back. "You don't want one, don't get one."

Florek couldn't help noticing that there was a dramatic note in his uncle's voice.

"Oh, the way our Voivode argued the case in the Senate session in Warsaw was amazing," Ela mused. "I watched the whole thing. Actually, I should have congratulated her on her performance when she was here ..." She looked lost in thought for a moment, then continued. "It went something like this, 'I understand that my colleagues, Senators-Voivodes from Lesser Poland and Subcarpathian voivodship, are against abortion. However, you're not suggesting you want to break off relations with your Czech or Slovak neighbors, even though they've had easy access to abortion for years. We're not asking you to change your stance. Just allow us—Pomeranians—to handle this issue in the way we see fit. This is our obligation and our moral responsibility.'"

"*Us, Pomeranians*, oh right," Florek echoed. "It sounds quite nice, actually."

"Besides," continued Ela, "you know, Amelia, personally—as an activist myself—I don't only deal with the issue of making abortion accessible but also with making it easier for those who want children to get the treatment they need if required.

Fertility, my dear, is not just a function of health; in other words, getting the right medical care during pregnancy. It's also about work–life balance, remote working, and parental leave for one or both parents for at least six months. All these elements have contributed to narrowing down the divide in terms of salary and career advancement, along with access to flexible childcare ... and so on."

"We're not planning any family for the moment, right, Maciek?" Amelia said, looking Maciek dead in the eye. Maciek sighed.

"Well, no ... because, well, you know ..." Maciek began to stammer. "It's hard out there. A child costs a lot of money, you've got to plan these things, sit down and be reasonable ..."

"Now, listen," Ela replied. "The Deputy Voivode for Economic Development wants to do away with all these worries." She waved her hand around like she was wafting away the idea.

"You mean he gets high?" Florek grunted and Maciek couldn't help but burst out laughing. Greg remained as stoic as ever, but perhaps he didn't understand what was so funny since his grasp of Polish, as noted earlier in their conversation, was quite formal.

"In any case," Ela resumed, "as part of the recent reform package, this Deputy Voivode, if you can imagine, built a pilot program to facilitate parental leave in forty companies that our region has now a stake in. What's more, he convinced his counterparts in the Mazovia and Subcarpathian voivodships to do the same. Subcarpathian, even—and you know who the ruling party is over there!"

Everyone took a sip of their drinks.

"All right, so, let's see. Take Orlen, the energy company," Ela said. "Pomerania, Mazovia, and the Subcarpathian jointly have a 40 percent stake in the company. And thanks to this initiative, it introduced a standard of parental leave nationwide!"

"Eeeeh, you sure about that?" Maciek asked, his eyebrow arched in a dubious expression.

"Seriously?" Iza doubled down.

"Who's in charge in the Subcarpathian?" Ira wanted to know. "Is it ..."

"Yup, it's them," Julka assured her. "Ira, wait, isn't that your phone ringing?"

"Ah, yes, it is. Let me go outside to get this." Ira grabbed her phone and got up to leave. "I'll be right back!"

"Actually, we should all get going," Maciek suggested. "Right, Amelia?"

"No way! It's just getting interesting," she replied. "Maybe if you listened more, you wouldn't be so out of the loop?"

"Out of the loop? Me?" Maciek's eyes grew as wide as possible, and Greg snorted.

"Let's not exaggerate, Maciek's not that bad," Greg said, before falling into a fit of laughter and Amelia gleefully joined in, while the rest of the group waited for them to finish. Maciek and Florek exchanged a knowing look and Iza even face-palmed herself in response.

From London to Słupsk

"So, how about I tell you all a bit more about environmental protection in our voivodship," Ela proposed with a wide grin. "I can see it's something you're passionate about, given your activism and all."

Florek took his phone back out of his pocket.

"So, listen, it's like this," Ela began. "The bill raised the base tax rate for large corporations, but offering reductions in return for transparency in reporting the effects of a company's activity on the immediate environment, placing the onus on the corporate body ..." She suddenly stopped talking, noticing Emil in the corner looking completely out of it. "Emil, I mean, are you asleep?" she asked.

He looked up, visibly startled. "No, I, um ... I'm not ... I was thinking about something," he stammered.

"Ah, so certainly you must know a great deal about these types of reports in the business sector, known as ESG, from the English name, Environmental, Social and Governance, right?"

"Oh, yes ... certainly." Emil blinked and looked toward his phone. "It's getting quite late actually, I think it's time to ..."

"Plus, there are even bigger rebates for companies whose ESG rankings are higher than the regional average," Ela resumed, not paying him any mind. "That's how the voivodship has built this sort of 'race to the top,' as the Brits like to say ... Right, Greg?"

Greg was clearly paying attention. "Of course, my dear Ela!" he exclaimed as enthusiastically as he could. "That's how they have forged the motivation to consistently raise the standards for ecological, social, and corporate practices!"

"That's fucking awesome," Maciek replied sarcastically and then frantically began trying to catch the waiter's eye.

Ela turned to her daughter. "Iza, from what I remember you telling me, you're quite skeptical about these ESG ratings."

"No, mom, I'm the one who's skeptical," Florek replied dryly. "I just don't believe that companies like Orlen will ever be straightforward about anything having to do with the environment and their intentions in their business. And I'm not the only one."

"I mean, me neither," Ela admitted. "Generally, I'm not really one to ramble on about work, but in London, I was working in this multinational auditing corporation and one of their focuses was these ESG ratings. The first time I heard about this approach to tying taxation to the environment was in the *Financial Times*."

"And?" Amelia prodded, even though she wasn't really feeling the conversation anymore. She didn't really know these friends of Maciek's too well and she had no idea that Ela had this super international job, probably better than her own job as a social media influencer, and she was really just starting out with the whole influencer thing, too.

"So, this FT reporter was emphasizing the innovation and courage invested in this Pomeranian solution. It might sound weird, but I felt really emotional about it. I guess because it was the first time Poland was cast in such a favorable light in a foreign publication. It wasn't about faulty brakes this time, but about a paragon of policy that could be used as a framework for other nations to implement as well."

"Oh yes, because everyone's always complaining about Poland," Amelia retorted.

"Exactly, and that's what I'm trying not to do," Ela replied. "So I started monitoring the new website set up by the Pomeranian Office of the Deputy Voivode for Finance, which was running the pilot project. And suddenly, a few weeks after the FT article, the Office announces they're opening up a competition for a few positions in a new department of the Pomeranian Treasury Administration, responsible for carrying out the ESG program."

"It wasn't a setup, this competition?" Maciek asked, sipping on his next beer—zero alcohol this time, but he still felt a bit rowdy.

"You mean to say everything's a setup if it's in Poland?" Amelia's voice rose to a shriek.

"I mean, even I thought it might be a setup," Ela admitted. "But I applied and what do you know... I got the job of deputy director of the department."

"Not bad at all," Maciek remarked.

"Needless to say, it meant a salary cut, by more than half for sure," Ela explained. "But I don't regret it. I'm part of a professional team, we're doing really interesting things for the country."

"I'd love to do my part somehow, for Poland, because it's my country too," Greg said, getting animated.

"Ours too," Ira and Julka called out, their faces radiating warm smiles.

"I mean, it is what it is, right?" Julka said. "But meeting the voivode when you're just out on the town, no security, to have a chat—it shows the country's not half-bad."

Florek rolled his eyes and began to hum his own rendition of "Ode to Joy." Maciek burst out laughing again.

"So, what's life like in our good old city of Słupsk?" Maciek asked, doing his best to be polite. "Isn't that where the Treasury headquarters are?"

"Well, obviously, it's not exactly London. But the standard of living and the resources available to our family get more and more attractive each year," Ela replied with a grin.

"And how does your situation line up with a job that lets you work for the good of the nation for half the income?" Amelia piped up, while also wondering what ESG had in common with making content as an influencer.

"All I can say is that, if we're talking about these preferential tax rates following the analysis of the ESG ranking, there's a transparent process set up within the Social Committee, which is in charge of analyzing the methodology behind the analysis. This committee is made up of representatives from various NGOs in the region and professionals who specialize in sustainable accounting practices."

"Aha," Amelia replied, as she wondered whether there was a link between sustainable accounting practices and making content as an influencer.

Stars of Pomerania

"Anyway," Ela resumed, "we all know how essential culture is, not just in Tricity, obviously. Our Deputy Voivode for Cultural Affairs and the Deputy Voivode for Infrastructure are headlining a series of cultural events in modest spaces throughout the region. These events are linked to the new regional transit system."

"This series, by the way," Greg interjected, waving his index finger in the air, "is meant to appeal not only to residents, but tourists as well, from Sweden, Lithuania, Germany. I'd be among them, but I'm not really a tourist, am I?"

"Oh, is that right?" Amelia teased, although she was beginning to see a link with her influencer activities.

"Well, yes," Greg replied. "For instance, we went to this festival in this little town in Kashubia..."

"Greg, how about I tell the story?" Ela grinned. "When you talk about it, it's like a chatbot."

"Oh right, mom, but when you tell it, somehow it's different, yeah?" Iza laughed out loud.

Ela ignored her and continued, "We were really surprised when we not only got served some local kaszëbskô malëna, but a lecture on the local history of feminism from an older lady. Can you believe she was handing out QR codes for an AR app? She told me I should check it out, that it was awesome, even though it might give me a headache."

"Exactly!" Florek piped up all of a sudden. "It turns out that getting around the town with a smartphone or, better yet, AR glasses, gives you a glimpse of the city as it is today and as it used to be—all at the same time. The app gives you a look at people from centuries ago, including what they're saying. It's really something else!" His newfound enthusiasm was bubbling up inside him.

"You can even see a futuristic view of what the city might be like in 100 years," Iza added. "Quite cool."

"The lady we met was really proud of the app," Greg mused. "It wasn't just the fact that it was a global innovation, that it'd been nominated for a bunch of awards... because she'd spent more than a year convincing locals to make recordings of their memories. And now these testimonials are part of the app!"

"I looked it up afterwards," added Ela. "And it turns out it was this pilot project called something like The Past of Our Future, and I think that's a great name for it, right? They made it with the University of Gdańsk, in partnership with smaller, self-governing bodies, NGOs and technology companies.

"The project has become super popular. It's like a new way of talking about history and seeing the past. Of course, there are plenty of critics," Greg added with a smirk. "The funny thing is, most of them aren't even from here. And they have the gall to say the founders of the project don't have enough 'Polish patriotism.'"

Maciek and Florek rolled their eyes and Amelia opened her mouth to say what she thought of people from abroad who had no idea about the "imponderables" of Polish patriotism, but something got caught in her throat. She was frozen in place, her hand in the air.

Greg spoke up instead. "In any case, Pomeranians are proud of their project because it brings so many people to Tricity: tourists, researchers, tech companies. We're all Pomeranians, really." He paused before adding, "Even though for some of us, the process has taken a bit more time."

"That was the festival where we met Julka and Ira. They're Pomeranians too, aren't they …" Ela smiled at the two of them, who had begun to gather up their belongings.

They said goodbye in the typical way of parents who are ready to go home but don't want to admit it.

"Goodbye, dears. See you soon!"

"Poles of Pomerania," Florek murmured, lost in thought. "I like the sound of it."

"Me too," Greg agreed.

"I guess I do too," Maciek said, adding his two cents.

"Stars of Pomerania," Amelia mumbled, but deep down what she actually meant to say was, "Me too."

9
The Dream Conservative Voivodship

Jakub Drożdż and Sylwia Sysko-Romańczuk
Edited by Marta Kwaśnicka

Welcome in Białystok

"Time to wake up, ma'am." The voice tore Magda from her semi-conscious slumber. A man in a smart conductor's uniform was smiling at her, his eyes understanding and kind. He spoke perfect Polish, although Magda picked up a slight Belarusian accent. People in Podlasie (pron. *pod-LAH-shyeh*) had a distinctive way of speaking anyway, softer than in the rest of the country, so the Belarusian accent seemed to fit well. Magda immediately felt at home. "We're just approaching Białystok," said the man with an apologetic smile.

He had nothing to apologize for—she was the one who had requested a wake-up call. She heaved a painful sigh. Her trip to Łomża, where she'd spent the past few days, had been exhausting and full of intense meetings; hence, her need to sleep on the train. It was only a brief nap, but it helped. And soon she'd be back on the road, heading to her parents' place near Suwałki to spend Christmas together.

"Thank you," she said to the conductor.

The man nodded graciously and continued down the train. Magda wrapped her scarf around her neck. In the past, she'd have driven to Łomża, but public transport had really improved in recent years and the railway was now perfectly reliable. You could even reach some places faster by train than by car. The Podlasie Commuter Railway meant it was possible to cover the route between Łomża, Białystok, and Suwałki, the three main cities in the voivodship, in under three hours. The cities were now known as "Podlasie's Tricity," in reference to the famous urban area comprising Gdańsk, Gdynia, and Sopot in the Pomeranian region.

As Magda stepped down from the train, she admired the newly refurbished Białystok station. Regional, suburban, and long-distance trains all intersected here, and there was a constant flow of passengers. Improving rail and road connections was one of the first challenges the provincial authorities had set for themselves following the constitutional reform. Prior to that, key decisions, including funding allocation choices, were made in Warsaw, but the central ministries neither understood nor prioritized the needs of Podlasie residents. Once upon a time, even the smallest new road had been declared open with a ceremony attended by ministers

Jakub Drożdż and Sylwia Sysko-Romańczuk, *The Dream Conservative Voivodship* In: *Let's Agree on Poland*. Edited by: Maciej Kisilowski and Anna Wojciuk, Oxford University Press.
 DOI: 10.1093/oso/9780198979562.003.0012

and MPs from Warsaw, along with other political VIPs. It was more about razzmatazz and PR opportunities than actual consideration of which investments were most important for the local community.

Now, in order to strengthen tourism, agriculture, and commerce, including export—which were fast-growing sectors in Podlasie—the regional authorities had invested in the development of transportation infrastructure. As a result, tourists had started to explore the more remote parts of the region, and entrepreneurs were more able to develop their businesses. Freeway S8 had become an express route connecting Podlasie with other voivodships. Thanks to mechanisms introduced by the December Amendment, the expansion of this vital route had been a coordinated effort with the Masovian, Łódź, and Lesser Poland Voivodships.

Family values

In 2024, the hottest topic of debate in the voivodship was the plan to ban the sale of alcohol on Sundays, which tied in with a wider discussion on trade-free Sundays. Exercising their new powers, some voivodships had decided to revoke the Sunday trading ban. Podlasie had gone the other way, introducing an additional ban—this idea came from neighboring Lithuania, where the sale of alcohol on the weekend had been restricted for several years.

The change was supported by the churches, especially the Catholic Church, which was still the largest and most influential in the region. Catholic Radio Podlasie, which also had listeners from outside the voivodship, broadcast regular prompts for people to sign petitions on the matter. The originators argued that not only would the ban be in line with conservative values, which were widely held in the voivodship, but it would also allow residents to take full advantage of the wide array of local cultural, religious, and gastronomic attractions on offer.

The ban's advocates also referred to the preamble of the Podlasie's Voivodship Charter, which clearly emphasized the role of community, family, and religion for those living in the voivodship. They concluded that Sunday could thereby become a special day set aside for meeting friends and family. Admittedly, many men in the community had expressed their dissatisfaction with the idea at first, but many women, Magda included, were very much in favor of the initiative. It had actually become a slight bone of contention between her and her husband. In any case, the plan had recently been accepted, having gained strong support from senior citizens in the e-referendum.

Incidentally, the history of the Charter's preamble was in itself interesting. After local government resolutions on family values (known colloquially as the "anti-LGBT resolutions"[1]) were defeated in administrative courts across Poland, Podlasie's Sejmik had dispensed with the services of the conservative lawyers from Warsaw who had advised on those controversial projects. The writing of the preamble of the new Charter was instead entrusted to a team that included the Archbishop of Białystok (who was also an eminent professor of theology), the Orthodox Bishop of Białystok-Gdańsk (another professor of theology), and a group of scholars from the University of Białystok Law Department (which, as a result of the constitutional reform, was now under the jurisdiction of the voivodship government). The result was a preamble that emphasized local values without excluding anyone. Not only had the document received the acceptance required for regional Charters from the new national Senate, but it was also upheld by the Supreme Administrative Court following a complaint filed by the national Ombudsman.

Magda's husband, Piotr, was waiting for her on the platform with a huge bouquet of flowers and two beaming little kids, who threw themselves into their mother's arms. Magda and Piotr wanted a big family. They had both grown up with lots of siblings, so they were hoping that chapter of their lives wasn't yet closed. Besides, large, multi-generational families were the norm in Podlasie.

Magda scooped up her youngest, Marysia, and hugged her tight, much to the dissatisfaction of Igor, who was just two years older. "My loves!" Magda shouted with joy.

"Don't I get a cuddle?" asked Piotr with a smile. Magda kissed him and he wrapped her in a big bear hug. "I hope they weren't too bad?" she whispered.

Magda usually worked from home, which meant she was also in charge of looking after the little scamps, but for the last few days they'd been solely in the care of their dad.

"We missed you. A lot," replied Piotr diplomatically. "How was Łomża? Do they still want to separate from Podlasie?"

Agricultural Valley 4.0

Many locals still remembered that before Russia invaded Ukraine, there were certain people in Łomża who had felt closer to Warsaw than to Białystok. Still, after the constitutional reform, that tendency—as much historical as it was economic—became marginal. In the new political conditions, residents of Łomża discovered that they were an important part of Podlasie and that they could influence local politics to a greater extent than would be the case in Masovia, which had a much larger population. Local patriots now supported the idea of being a second vital center of Podlasie, alongside Białystok.

The voivodship government had put a lot of effort into Łomża and its surrounding areas; the same was true of the third largest city in the region, Suwałki. Thanks to better transport links, residents from all over Podlasie could benefit from the public service investments introduced across the region in the areas of health, schooling, and higher education. Offices of the voivodship government were also spread around all the three main cities. Białystok had lost its capital status to some extent, but it had gained a sense of community.

Łomża itself was developing fast. This was in large part due to the work of the Deputy Voivode for Schooling and Higher Education, who came from Łomża herself and had been collaborating for years with the Research and Development Center for Food and Nutrition at the Warsaw University of Life Sciences. Right after taking up her new role in the regional government, she had started work on setting up the Academy of Industry 4.0 in her hometown. The mission of the new school was to conduct "implementation research and education in the design of integrated systems for agriculture and food processing, via the approach known as Industry 4.0." It sounded overly technical but it was just about creating systems that connected the machines used in agriculture and industry with the virtual world and big data. For example, specialists educated in Łomża had designed logistics solutions that enabled the export of fresh food from Podlasie to Europe. This was especially important for organic foods, which could be sold for much higher prices despite their shorter shelf life.

As a matter of fact, that had been the reason for Magda's trip. She worked with her dad, Grzegorz, who was planning to open a big logistics center in Łomża with a mind to developing export to the West. He was keen to hire specialists who had studied at the academy, and Magda's role was to discuss the investment conditions on his behalf.

"Łomża's changed massively . . ." she said with a sigh.

The negotiations had gone swimmingly: the city had agreed to their plans for setting up the center.

"Anyway," she continued, "I got a lot of contacts and spoke to some potential new producers. It looks like we'll get exclusive rights for our Podlasie Delicacy products!"

"That's awesome! Congratulations, babe!" said Piotr, giving Magda another squeeze.

The reformed voivodship government had decided to invest in the creation of a truly modern food production cluster called Agricultural Valley 4.0. It was run on behalf of the voivodship authorities by the Podlasie Development Fund. It was this idea that turned out to be the key to the electoral success of the Podlasie main right-wing party. The party's leadership had recently been taken over by a well-known PiS politician, who had experience in central government and in the Podlasie local government in addition to being an agriculture specialist. Interestingly, for the sake of Podlasie, he had resigned from a lucrative position in the European Parliament and launched a campaign for the voivode direct elections, which he won. As an agriculture specialist, he emphasized the role of this branch of the economy in the political development of the region. Modernity, in his view, meant not only efficiency of agriculture and food production, but also quality of products, especially in the organic food sector. The Podlasie Development Fund focused on the digitalization of production and Industry 4.0, heeding the opinions of experts who believed that the economic future of Podlasie's key industries depended on these tools.

The reformed voivodship authorities decided to allocate to Agricultural Valley the income from the sale of some of the State Treasury assets transferred to the region. "As part of the decentralization of state assets, we have received small stakes in the mining corporation KGHM and the largest Polish bank PKO BP," the new voivode had reported. "There was no point keeping them, so we sold them in order to invest in agriculture, which is of great strategic value for us." The residents of Podlasie had agreed to this transaction by way of a local e-referendum. And because the citizens were watching closely to see how the funds from the sale of these shares would be used, the voivodship administration was very motivated to demonstrate that the investment was a good idea.

In a series of tenders opened as part of this initiative, hundreds of farmers and entrepreneurs from the food sector applied for financing to implement digital production management systems. The new technologies developed at universities in the voivodship were gradually changing agriculture and food processing. Thanks to digitalization and big data, fertilizers and pesticides were now used much more sparingly, while maintaining high yields. Computers controlled water usage. Production had become more environmentally friendly, and more beneficial for consumers of Podlasie products. Food waste had also decreased significantly.

The ingenuity and determination of the new Deputy Voivode for Development, who had good contacts in Brussels, had also been key. The other voivodships in Poland had long since exceeded the EU wealth average and had struggled to compete for the larger EU funding programs. They had to rely on national resources to a greater extent. In Podlasie, the GDP per capita was still slightly lower than the EU average, so the region had real clout in EU institutions. In the 2028–34 financial perspective, Podlasie received 1.7 billion euros, one of the largest transfers in the EU regions. The bulk of these funds was to be allocated to the further modernization of the transport infrastructure and the development of Agricultural Valley 4.0.

The Podlasie revolution in agriculture also meant that the sector became less dependent on low-skilled labor. This was in keeping with the demographic trends in this part of Europe, and also corresponded to the preferences of residents, for whom hard physical work on farms—the main type of work in Podlasie for the last several generations—was no longer attractive. The fact that the voivodship was specializing in food production, especially high-margin, premium products, enabled many companies to accumulate large amounts of capital. One of the local success stories was the product brand and chain Podlasie Delicacy, which had not only conquered Poland but was also prospering in Lithuania, where it competed with German supermarket chains. The brand specialized in delicious cheeses, yogurts, cold cuts, and frozen ready meals of high-quality, traditional dishes.

Food products still made up a vital part of Polish export, and Podlasie was a key region for the export of eggs, dairy, and meat products. Thanks to their specialization in the production of these products, Podlasie's share in Polish export had gradually increased. In its export strategy, the region still relied heavily on its eastern neighbors. Its main partners were Belarus, Estonia, Lithuania, Latvia, and Ukraine. The ambitions of local exporters had grown with each success of the industry on the international markets. Podlasie Delicacy and other similar regional brands attracted customers from London, Berlin, and Chicago—and not only from the Polish diaspora.

The pull of Podlasie

The Podlasie Development Fund had also benefited Grzegorz's family business—he now had an opportunity to expand his exports to the west. He had received funding for the digitization of his logistics center in Łomża, with particular emphasis on environmentally friendly cold stores.

"Your dad will be proud," said Piotr, strapping Marysia into her car seat.

"I'm sure he will," said Magda. "He doesn't know about it yet. I'll tell him when we get there."

The prospect of a new contract gave Magda the freedom to revel in the beauty of the snowy morning. The car engine purred softly as they set off toward Heroes of Monte Cassino Street, aiming to get onto Route 19 as quickly as possible. Magda instinctively made the sign of the cross when she saw St. Roch's basilica in the distance. The streets were busy with traffic—they were in the midst of pre-Christmas shopping fever. Nevertheless, they soon made it out of the city center.

Piotr worked in IT, specializing in the digitalization of production management. He had come to Podlasie because, like many people in IT and engineering, he espoused conservative values. Ever since the fall of communism some 35 years ago, he had felt that, although many political parties claimed to be committed to upholding traditions, too often the leftist-liberal elite blocked the implementation of conservative proposals, playing on the fears of certain groups in society. In Piotr's opinion, conservatism had become an attractive option for contemporary Europe—an option that could win over many people and bring real results if only it was given a proper chance. As a republican, Piotr also believed that no values would materialize in politics unless citizens were allowed to be part of the decision-making. When he was living in West Pomerania, before he met Magda, he had convinced his IT colleagues that direct democracy tools, such as e-referendums or electronic public service quality assessment systems, were opportunities for conservatives.

When the Right won in Podlasie, Piotr had decided that was where he wanted to live. He would transfer his business activity there, pay his taxes there, so that his money would be supporting the values in which he believed—like in the US, where leftist California had lost many talented people from the tech sector to conservative states such as Texas. Piotr also thought that Podlasie had the potential to show the West what modern conservatism was all about.

Not long after moving to Podlasie, he met Magda and quickly proposed to her. Their wedding day had been less than three years ago and they were already parents to two wonderful children. Piotr liked the simple life; he valued Polish traditions. He couldn't imagine any other route for himself than traditional family life. He wasn't particularly religious, but he felt that Catholicism was a part of the Polish identity. He liked the fact that Magda was a believer and that they were raising Igor and Marysia in this vein. He didn't want to blur the lines between the societal roles of women and men; he was opposed to the campaign to equate LGBT relationships with traditional marriages. Still, he felt that the only way to convince others to follow traditional values was to practice them himself. By their fruits you shall know them, as the Bible says.

Magda sometimes joked that Piotr was the classic tech-y hardliner—one who disliked change for change's sake, and saw the Church as merely a form of entertainment for women and children. They had the occasional disagreement over it, but ultimately, all married couples argue. The main thing was that they loved each other, and she knew her husband truly supported her. She hadn't lost hope that Piotr would be converted eventually.

They were heading out of Białystok. Magda watched with interest as they passed street upon street of new, suburban houses, which had sprung up like mushrooms after the rain. In the summer, the buildings had almost disappeared behind the lush greenery of the gardens. Now, the trees were beautifully decorated with Christmas lights, like scenes from a fairy tale. Still, Magda would never wish to live in a place like this—the properties practically merged into one and there was zero privacy. They passed a sports field, squeezed by some miracle in between the houses, and Magda thought about her favorite soccer team. She had always supported Wigry Suwałki, though recently, due to family and work, she'd had to put her old hobbies on hold. Still, she was sometimes tempted by the idea of returning to the days when she and her three brothers had traveled around Poland in a bus full of fans, following their team. She and Piotr differed on this point—he, as a relatively new arrival in Podlasie, had taken to supporting Jagiellonia Białystok, the pride and joy of the whole voivodship.

The city of Białystok was expanding year after year, gradually taking on the features of a metropolis. Although the voivodship was ruled by the Right, Białystok itself was in the hands of the liberal Civic Platform, as it had been before the constitutional reform. The mayor was also the strongest member of the provincial Senate because votes were weighted according to the population each senator represented. Białystok was the driving force behind the development of the whole region, so no one wanted to fight with the liberal mayor.

The Białystok University of Technology, which was currently governed by the regional government, specialized in research on energy storage. The solutions being developed there enabled the management of the renewable energy produced in the vicinity of Suwałki. There were a number of solar farms in that area, which were operated by graduates of the Higher Vocational School of Renewable Energy in Suwałki. The electrical energy produced there was sold to neighboring Masovia, and to Belarus. The school itself had been the idea of the Deputy Voivode for Schooling and Higher Education. The modern building was designed by Krystyna Ilmurzyńska and Marek Budzyński, who were also responsible for the Podlasie Opera and Philharmonic edifice and the University of Białystok campus.

But it takes more than technology to make the world go round—the voivodship government had agreed with the authorities at the University of Białystok that, as part of the provincial academic strategy, the university was to play a key culture-forming role. They focused on the development of the humanities: Polish studies, philosophy, Belarusian philology, law, history of art, and history. Alongside academics, specialists from the Institute for National Remembrance were involved in the development of the educational programs.

Podlasie differed from the other voivodships in that only those who really wanted to study went on to higher education. There was no societal pressure here to get a university degree rather than a vocational qualification, as there was in some regions. The students with more academic profiles benefitted from smaller class sizes, and the lecturers got to work with truly motivated young people.

Creative hubbub

Although the bustling city life wasn't really her thing, Magda still liked the hubbub of Białystok and the creative medley that the political changes had prompted. The gastronomic sector was growing fast. Between Thursday and Sunday, it was hard to find a table at the restaurants in the city, regardless of the weather. Although there were many places to sample international dishes, the regional cuisine was always most in demand. Magda's brother Marcin also ran his own restaurant in Białystok—she always went there when she was in the city, alone or with the kids.

Marcin was the black sheep of the family; their parents had been worrying for years about how he'd get on in life. Fortunately, there were options in their voivodship, even for those who struggled at school. The Deputy Voivode for Schooling and Higher Education was convinced that the road to a prosperous and satisfying future needn't run via university. From her research into vocational training during study visits in Switzerland and Germany, she had come to see that this route was deemed much more prestigious in many affluent countries than it was in Poland, and graduates of these schools often went on to earn more than those with academic degrees. She believed the future of education was the development of various talents in young people—including vocational skills, which had not been seen as a desirable path during the educational boom of the post-1989 transition, but had nonetheless been in great demand in recent years. The voivodship administration agreed that it was better to be a good carpenter, nurse, electrician, or car mechanic than a political scientist who didn't end up working in their field of study. Why did they need so many political scientists in Poland anyway? So the regional government decided that instead of mindlessly following the trend for university degrees, it was better to raise the status of high-quality vocational education based on an extensive system of internships.

Marcin ended up at one of these schools. His culinary school cooperated with the food-processing industry and the best restaurants in Podlasie. Marcin had done an internship in a well-known fish restaurant in Augustów, quite far from home. The internship meant hard work, which he wasn't accustomed to—still, he was determined to make a good impression. And as often happens in stories like these, it had paid off. Augustów was very busy during the summer months, and Marcin wasn't exactly thrilled at having to work every evening. On the upside, on quieter days, the renowned head chef revealed to Marcin the secrets of his craft and Marcin, in turn, got the bug for cooking. After finishing school, he and some friends set up an eatery in Białystok. At first, it was a simple pancake place in the shopping mall, which did pretty well. Soon they had enough money for a spot in the city center. Marcin wasn't concerned that the competition would pose a threat. Gastronomy worked in the opposite way to other industries—the more cafes and restaurants, the more customers, and the more commonplace the culture of eating out.

It wasn't just Białystok's restaurants that attracted tourists to the region. More and more people were visiting Podlasie each year. Since 2021, the number of tourists had risen from around 440,000 a year to nearly 800,000. The voivodship administration had included tourism in the province's development priorities, alongside the food cluster and renewable energy. The region prided itself on its national parks and landscape parks. The Podlasie sanitariums were also undergoing a renaissance. Not only were they now being utilized by the healthcare system, but they had also become a tourist attraction and were known across Poland.

Magda's cousin and her husband had decided to take advantage of this boom and had opened an agritourism farm near Wiżajny. Agritourism is not a business that works in the same way all year round. Just as there were many tourists, and high profits, throughout the summer and during the winter break, there were also seasons when it was hard to make a living from room rentals alone. So Magda's cousin had started making pressed rennet cheese and matured cheese using milk from locally farmed cows. At one time, the production of these cheeses had been a fairly rare and specialized activity—if you wanted to buy them, you had to knock on every door around multiple villages to find out who was making them. Magda's cousin and her family were not what you'd call "go-getters." They were great at cheese production but had no idea where to start when it came to marketing.

It had always annoyed Magda that no one knew about these cheeses and that, despite all the noise around hand-made products, her cousin wasn't always able to sell them at a good price. The voivodship administration had received requests from local manufacturers to place more emphasis on promoting these products. Additionally, thanks to the certification system for premium agricultural goods, introduced and overseen by the College of the Voivodships, small manufacturers finally had the opportunity to attract many customers within Poland and they were no longer losing out in unfair competition with large companies that only created a façade that their products were hand-crafted. Her cousin's cheeses were now being used in some of the top restaurants, even beyond Suwałki and Białystok.

Riding the wave of the same tourism boom, another cousin of Magda's, Łukasz, and his wife Zoja, who came from one of the many Orthodox families in that part of the country, had set up a small stud farm near Hajnówka. They offered horseback tours of Podlasie. Łukasz and Zoja also taught in a vocational school for blacksmiths and horseshoe makers, which had become renowned in the district. There was a general shortage of horseshoe makers—stud farms had sprung up all over Poland, and the school in Hajnówka had been revived thanks to the voivodship government's drive to place more value on vocational education.

Yet another cousin was a farmer near Łapy, like his father and grandfather before him. It hadn't been easy for them straight after the transformation; still, their family had lived in the village since the seventeenth century and they had no intention of giving up easily.

Magda felt that the whole of Podlasie was her home—she had relatives dotted all over the province and wherever she went, there was always someone she could stay with nearby. Everyone was always asking after everyone else, and they all stayed in touch.

Every year, more and more family businesses were opening in the voivodship—small and medium-sized enterprises enjoyed special support of the regional authorities. New companies received temporary tax exemptions and start-up support. In order to respond to the family traditions of Podlasie, regional law established a new form of business association: the family corporation, somewhat analogous to a family foundation. The voivode was particularly keen to prevent unemployment, which was still too high. So the number of companies grew, including those run by new arrivals from other voivodships, like Piotr, and by foreigners. The voivodship was particularly open to Belarusians because in the opinion of the Podlasie people, thanks to cultural similarities and long traditions of cross-border contact, immigrants from Belarus integrated very well. Meanwhile, for many Belarusians who were tired of the authoritarian rule in their country, coming to Podlasie was an opportunity to realize their potential in a place with a culture not unlike their own.

Contrary to widespread opinion, Podlasie was extremely open to newcomers. Anyone who accepted the values and principles laid out in the preamble to the Voivodship Charter—the local attachment to the traditional family, respect of local faiths and the law—was welcomed with open arms and treated with characteristic Podlasie hospitality. The voivode was even the originator of the nationwide campaign "We Welcome You with Bread and Salt"—named after the traditional Slavic greeting ceremony—which encouraged residents of other voivodships to move to Podlasie. Piotr was a classic example of the campaign's success. In particular, Podlasie had a lot to offer families. Everyone in Poland was talking about the region's approach to income tax, which after the constitutional reform became a regional tax. The voivodship Sejmik and Senate introduced a tax credit for every child, as well as for marriages lasting more than years, with an additional sliding-scale credit for every five years of marriage that followed.

Magda noted with satisfaction that they had left the outskirts of Białystok. She watched the scene through the car window, admiring the thick forests.

"Shall we go to Janów after Christmas?" asked Piotr, as if he had read his wife's mind. "The kids would love it."

"Yay!" The kids' voices resounded in excitement from the back seat.

It was one of the kids' favorite places. The stud farm in Janów Podlaski, famed for its Arabian horses,[2] had been transferred to the voivodship government after the constitutional reform and remained a luxury export brand. Smaller stud farms and riding schools had sprung up like mushrooms after the rain. They provided a chance to promote a new regional hero—the horse-riding champ. Łukasz and Zoja's stud farm, small but charming, also benefitted from this trend. Magda's family were used to horses—they often visited her cousin's stables near Hajnówka. Little Igor rode a pony on a lunge line and Marysia, who also loved horses, couldn't wait to join her older brother. Magda and Piotr trusted her cousin and his wife completely, and they sometimes left the children in their care while they went out for a trek by themselves.

Of course, Magda was thrilled at Piotr's suggestion.

"Awesome idea! Maybe . . ." She broke off because Piotr's phone was ringing.

Coexistence rather than war

"Hello?" Piotr answered the phone. "What? Are you serious? Yes, we're on our way to Magda's folks. I'll call you later. Take care."

"Work?" asked Magda.

"No, that was Bartek. He says West Pomerania is rocking the boat."

"Is it a big deal? You looked worried."

"They've got an issue with their regional government. They have to apply for approval to operate in public schools but the voivodship doesn't want to let them in and they're drawing out the process. It's things like this that make me so glad I moved to Podlasie..."

Bartek was Magda's second brother. He had been working for some time as Deputy Head of the Institute of National Remembrance, known by its Polish acronym IPN. As part of the constitutional reform, the IPN had been transferred to the self-governed voivodships, along with other scientific and higher education institutions. This had created a challenge for the College of the Voivodships—a new institution in which the deputy voivodes responsible for each area of public policy from all regions established nationwide standards to ensure the consistency of solutions throughout the country.

Straight away, the College had to deal with the problem of managing the several nationwide scientific institutions that had been transferred to the regions, such as the IPN. Before long, a compromise was reached. The nine voivodships in the Northwest and the center of the country opted to jointly manage the Polish Academy of Sciences, while five southeastern voivodships, including Podlasie, took the responsibility for the IPN. In both cases, a loose institutional structure was chosen, with clearly separated provincial branches involved in local scientific and development policy. As part of the deal, the Polish Academy of Science divested its Białystok branch, known for its agricultural studies, and agreed for it to merge with the Białystok University of Technology.

Due to his role in the IPN, Bartek was also a member of the Council for the Education of Children and Young People, which operated under the Deputy Voivode for Schooling and Higher Education. The Council decided on the direction and evaluation of the policy of humanistic upbringing in the spirit of personalism, patriotism, and communitarianism. It comprised representatives of the Catholic and Orthodox churches, NGOs, the IPN, and regional liberal arts colleges, as well as leaders of pedagogical circles, including active school teachers. The Council's most well-known work was on the new approach to History and the Present—the patriotic education course, known by its Polish acronym HIT, first introduced by the national government of PiS in 2022. While after the constitutional reform many voivodships dropped HIT from their curricula, it stayed in Podlasie and, surprisingly became, well, a hit! The textbook written by Bartek and other Council members was so attractive that it won the *Textbook of the Year* award in a nationwide competition.

Based on Estonian models, the Council created multimedia activities that resembled the best computer games. It meant that students really wanted to learn about Polish traditions and culture. In the words of the Deputy Voivode for Schooling: "When we submitted a motion to the College of the Voivodships to allow voivodships to keep HIT grades on the national *Matura* certificate that each student receives upon completion of a secondary school, some of our colleagues looked at us as if we were cavemen. If it weren't for the decisive attitude of our voivode, who made his national Senate abstention in a vote on the decentralization of family laws dependent on the deal in the College on HIT, we would have failed miserably. Now, I get colleagues from other voivodships asking if they can visit us to learn more about how we teach HIT."

All in all, much had changed in Podlasie, and these changes also affected Magda's nearest and dearest. And now she was going to see them all: her parents, brothers, and numerous cousins. They were on their way to spend the Christmas holidays together.

Christmas Eve was Igor and Marysia's favorite day of the year. It was a joyous time for all of them, especially when several generations of the family sat down together to enjoy Christmas Eve supper. Happiest of all was the matriarch of the family—Jadwiga, Magda's grandma, who was 95 years old.

In 2019, the annual tradition of family Christmas Eve suppers had ground to a halt because the political conflict raging in Poland had also driven a wedge between Grzegorz and his brother Waldek. Waldek had much more liberal views, to the extent that sometimes he didn't even seem to fit in with the rest of the family. Grzegorz had pointed this out to him once during an argument, throwing in a few more insults for good measure. After that, Waldek and his children and grandchildren hadn't come to the family home for Christmas for several years.

This really upset Jadwiga, who wanted all her loved ones there around the table. The 2023 constitutional reform, which helped to resolve much of the conflict in Poland, had brought unexpected consequences for their family. Since Poland could now accommodate citizens with different values, and the majority in the Sejm in Warsaw could no longer impose their vision by force, there was no point in further poisoning a beautiful holiday tradition. Everyone, especially Jadwiga, was pleased that, as of 2024, the whole family could now sit together at the table once more.

"I can't wait. I think there'll be about thirty of us!" said Magda excitedly. Deep down, though, she worried there would be another political row. She wasn't sure her dad would manage to control himself if Waldek started up about abortion again, or made jokes about the Church ...

"I don't know how your parents will fit us all in. There's about twenty people with just your cousins. And then there's your siblings," said Piotr with a sigh.

"We'll manage. I'm sure Mom will have everything under control, and we can help her out."

Christmas gathering in a Church-friendly region

They arrived in good time, before noon. Magda's parents' house was on a large estate with a huge garden, a pond that was currently frozen over, and a two-story residence. It looked like a small manor house. As they pulled up the driveway, Magda saw that her parents were standing in front of the line of cars, waiting to greet them. Grzegorz was a large man with a shiny bald head. He resembled a bear—broad shoulders, strong arms, round stomach—but he had a heart of gold. Ewa,

Magda's mother, was a petite brunette with blue eyes and a warm smile. Together, they looked like Beauty and the Beast; their happy marriage had lasted more than thirty-five years and was still going strong. They'd joked recently that when they got married, toward the end of the era of the Polish People's Republic, they'd never have imagined that they'd benefit from a marriage longevity tax credit in a free Poland. They had raised four children: Magda, her two older brothers Marcin and Bartek, and the youngest, Maciej. They adored their grandchildren, Magda's children, who were now squealing and throwing themselves into their grandparents' arms. Grzegorz and Ewa were secretly hoping that Bartek and Marcin would have their own families too. Marcin, although he was the oldest, wasn't keen to settle down; he was busy getting his restaurant going. Bartek, on the other hand, was engaged; the wedding was planned for the following summer. Still, he and his fiancée spent Christmas apart—according to tradition, a couple only spent the holidays together after marriage, so for now they each celebrated with their own families. Maciej, meanwhile, was a clergyman; he was just starting his doctorate in theology.

The education system for students of theological seminaries of the Catholic and the Orthodox churches had experienced a real renaissance in Podlasie. The system had two priorities: promoting humanistic values, and educating people in the new technologies used in pastoral work in various environments. Clerical students and young priests came from other voivodships to Drohiczyn and Grabarka, which had become the Catholic and Orthodox educational centers, respectively. The regional student support system allowed the financing of seminarian studies from public funds. The classes on the use of new technologies in catechesis and other pastoral work, especially in youth ministry, were quite a novelty. This was to be the subject of Maciej's thesis. Another common practice was family crowdsourcing, involving families providing care, and material and financial assistance, to clerical students. Due to this support, some people were even able to study at the pontifical universities in Rome. Maciej was planning to sign up for this support program.

"We've been waiting for you!" said Ewa.

"Come on, let's go inside," replied Magda.

In the dining room, they were greeted by the scraping of chairs, followed by a sea of hugs and kisses from the rest of the family. Only one person stayed seated. Jadwiga, the matriarch of the family, had the place of honor at the table. From there, she could see all her loved ones, as well as oversee the preparations for the meal. She smiled warmly when she saw Magda, Piotr, and the little ones.

"Go say hello to Granny," said Piotr. The children ran to their great-grandmother for a hug.

"How lovely to see you, darlings," said Jadwiga, before turning to Magda and Piotr. "Now get over here, you two, and give Grandma a kiss."

Magda was just telling her father the great news from Łomża. For Grzegorz, this was the best Christmas gift—now he didn't have to keep wracking his brain, trying to figure out whether Łomża would agree to his investment plans. The Podlasie Delicacy contract was the cherry on the cake. Grzegorz was proud of Magda; she really was a natural when it came to business. He was secretly planning to transfer the management of his company to Magda and Marcin in the future. For now, though, Grzegorz was as fit as a fiddle. He intended to keep running the family business for as long as his health allowed.

Paradoxically, he was particularly proud of Bartek, who had never had much of a head for business. Still, Bartek had other, not insignificant talents—as a young, ambitious historian, he had completed a PhD at the University of Białystok and it was thanks to his involvement in popularizing historical knowledge that he had been nominated as Deputy Head of the IPN.

Magda, her mother, and some family friends—women from the nearby village—were making *uszka*, or "little ears," as the traditional tiny wild mushroom dumplings served only for Christmas Eve supper are called, owing to their shape. Piotr and Bartek went to chop wood for the fire. They liked this form of physical exercise, and it also gave them a chance to talk in private, without ruining the holiday vibes, about the difficulties the IPN was experiencing in West Pomerania. Although he had moved away five years ago, Piotr still had lots of contacts in the area, and he knew plenty of conservative NGOs. He promised Bartek that he would get in touch with the people who could help him influence the left-wing authorities of that voivodship to look more kindly on the IPN's activities in the region.

The next day was Christmas Eve. All the rooms in the large family home were crammed full of guests. Maciej had arrived too, and the long-awaited Waldek with his family, bringing with them a delicious sauerkraut and mushroom dish, and their unrivaled poppyseed cakes. At the last minute, as always, Marcin arrived in his car with the restaurant logo on the side, the trunk full of wonderful fish dishes—above all, the legendary pickled spiced herring, something that everyone at the gathering (perhaps excluding the kids) had been waiting for all year.

Grzegorz began the Christmas Eve supper with a reading from the Gospel about the birth of Jesus. Maciej led the Lord's Prayer, and everyone joined in, their voices merging into one. The sense of unity was poignant. Next, Maciej blessed everyone present. Ewa was moved as she watched her son, who suddenly seemed very grown-up.

"Thank you all for being here, folks," said Grzegorz. "It's wonderful to see our family all together. This special occasion shows that family is the foundation of everything in life."

Then they all exchanged wishes for the holidays.

The greatest wealth is health

The holidays were off to a great start, and would have continued that way if it hadn't been for Jadwiga's sudden deterioration. One minute she was feeling weak; the next, she blacked out, collapsed, and hit her head against the sideboard. Initially, Magda thought her grandma had just fainted from the emotion and that she'd come round quickly; but Jadwiga remained unconscious. Her grandsons lifted her onto the sofa and Maciej called an ambulance. Despite the snowstorm, the paramedics arrived from Suwałki in fifteen minutes.

Healthcare was among the priorities of the Podlasie authorities. At one point, only the University Hospital in Białystok had made it onto the ranking of the best hospitals in Poland. Now, thanks to the regional control over the use of Podlasie residents' share of the National Health Fund's budget, the voivodship authorities were able to fundamentally reform the way hospitals, clinics, and treatment centers operated in the voivodship. This meant that medical help could arrive on time—as it did for Jadwiga.

* * *

"What's wrong with her?" Magda asked the doctor, nervousness coming through in her voice.

"Don't worry," replied the doctor. "She just needs to rest. She was actually extremely lucky. She's been coming for regular prophylactic check-ups and we know about her ailments. She should be awake soon. She'll stay here a little while for observation, then we'll discharge her."

"The patient's waking up, doctor," said a nurse.

"Already? She's a strong woman," said the doctor, not disguising his surprise. He turned to Jadwiga. "Can you hear me?"

Jadwiga made a noise and nodded her head. The doctor did some quick checks.

"Pupils are fine," he said. "Do you remember what day of the week it is?"

"Saturday?" said Jadwiga, her voice croaky. "Of course, it's Christmas Eve! Where am I?"

"You're at the John Paul II Hospital," replied the doctor.

"What happened?" asked Jadwiga. "My head hurts." She touched her head, which was wrapped in a bandage.

"I'm not surprised. You passed out and had a nasty fall. But you're okay, it was nothing major."

"Thank God," said Magda.

"You were brought in by ambulance right after you fell. You were unconscious for a few hours."

The doctors were professional and kind, for which Magda was grateful. To improve the quality of services, Podlasie had teamed up with the left-wing authorities of West Pomerania, who were also keen to focus on healthcare. The two voivodships had brought in a harmonized electronic registration system, as well as a payment system for non-emergency appointments at peak times. Podlasie had also implemented its own specific feature. Across Poland, there was now an electronic Local and Regional Government Quality Assessment System for Laws and

Public Services in place, which could be used to review the work of office workers of the regional administration, but also healthcare professionals in public hospitals and clinics. For the health services, Podlasie was the only voivodship to have introduced double assessments, which were split into "professionalism" and "friendliness". Doctors in Podlasie now received special bonuses if they were rated above average in both categories—this was also a requirement for promotion.

"We were so worried," said Grzegorz when he was finally allowed into the hospital room.

"What on earth for? You heard the doctor—I'm fine! Anyway, Merry Christmas, everyone… Did you at least bring me some cake?" Jadwiga asked, matter-of-factly.

"Mom…"

"Mom what? I'm 95 years old. This isn't the time to start denying myself simple pleasures!"

"Glad to see your appetite hasn't suffered, Grandma," whispered Magda, and everyone burst out laughing.

Notes

1. See e.g. Adam Ploszka, "From Human Rights to Human Wrongs. How Local Government Can Negatively Influence the Situation of an Individual. The Case of Polish LGBT Ideology-free Zones," *The International Journal of Human Rights* 27, no. 2 (2023): 359–379.
2. For how the state-owned stud featured in Polish recent politics Zosia Wanat, "Poland's Purebred Arabian Horses Gallop into Election Race," *Politico*, Aug. 8, 2019.

10
The Dream Leftist Voivodship

Alicja Pacewicz, Jan Smoleński, and Michał Żabicki
Fictionalized by Sylwia Chutnik

The returns

The best parties happen in the kitchen. While everybody else was grooving to the playlist streaming off the speakers in the living room, Dorota, Piotr, and Seba huddled by the fridge, caught up in a heated debate. This is basically how they had met, ten years earlier, when they were all still at university. Between the shot and the chaser, they managed to argue over just about everything, sitting up until dawn, running through each talking point, explaining why everybody else was wrong. And it was no different all these years later.

Piotr loved debating. To the point that he was able to disagree about topics he didn't even know much about. He called himself a *bothsidesist*, which Dorota found exceptionally irritating. He really loved winding her up to the point where she'd get angry and let him know what a jerk she thought he was.

"You heard this one yet?" Piotr always had an unfunny joke up his sleeve. "Soy latte and vegan schnitzel meet up in a café. A feminist comes up to them and asks how they're doing. Oh, you know, they tell her, we're just arguing about the economy. A tattoo-covered guy on a bicycle passes them, shouting: 'Talking about numbers! That's *so* not leftist!' "

Before Dorota could even swallow her mouthful of chips and give him her two cents, Seba had already intervened.

"Can we just stop all this push-and-shove. First of all, it's not even funny. Granted, culture wars are a hot topic right now, but you've got to admit the whole gist of it is cold hard cash and basic math ... "

"The essence of what people believe to be a cosmopolitan lifestyle is dribbling down to suburban and rural areas, creating a market that's closely tied to the need for capital," Dorota chimed in, using her best professorial tone (honed during her many years as a university lecturer).

"Sure ..." Piotr insisted. "Marx and Engels are turning in their graves, but apparently we can't even mention them because they didn't write anything about donut economics or cancel culture. Anyway, to understand the notion of an open and equitable dream voivodship, we need to understand the perspectives of those

Alicja Pacewicz, Jan Smoleński, and Michał Żabicki, *The Dream Leftist Voivodship* In: *Let's Agree on Poland*.
Edited by: Maciej Kisilowski and Anna Wojciuk, Oxford University Press.
 DOI: 10.1093/oso/9780198979562.003.0013

living in a particular region. To embrace the idea of what is to be local, to give a voice to those who are directly impacted by certain policies and who stand to gain from what their local government can offer them. That's what I've been trying to tell you guys from the start … All these Warsaw-centric think pieces aren't helping anybody."

Dorota rolled her eyes. Piotr was always harping on about the articles she messaged him so he could finally get an understanding of the world. He just kept saying over and over again that only someone who grew up "local" could truly understand what it meant. Everybody else was just waxing nostalgic and sentimental about the "provincial life," making it sound way more glamorous than it was. Then there were the people who wanted to return to their roots, waiting it out until they had a chance to finally come out winning one day …

"What on earth are you talking about, Piotr?" Seba countered. "That's the whole point. You can make the most impact on a local level and those are the people who get it."

A typical conversation these days. As we have seen in the earlier chapters, returns to home regions have been trending since the constitutional reform of 2023. It turns out that the number of people joining the ranks of the protagonists in our stories is growing. In Szczecin, there's plenty of talk about politicians who are making their way back from Warsaw. For some reason, the cream of the West Pomeranian crop of lawmakers suddenly decided to give up their national mandates and run for the Sejmik.

"I think my colleagues from other regions haven't yet adapted their world view and career goals to this new reality …" This was the assessment a returning politician gave while speaking under the condition of anonymity to a local paper, *The Voice of Szczecin*. "In the meantime, the role of deputy voivode and regional leadership can offer so much more satisfaction than the frustration involved in the national politics in Warsaw, where you wait forever for your turn at the podium." Still, this sense of increased agency comes at a cost—there are no swanky television studios, so flashy gestures or catchy soundbites lose their allure. So, what's the draw for politicians who are heading away from Warsaw TV studios and back to the real life of their home region?

The newfound inclination toward West Pomeranian regional politics has mostly been the result of a series of lucky coincidences. As noted earlier, constitutional reform enacted in December 2023 radiated through Europe. For the first time in years, Poland was put forth as a positive example of how a country could be run—as a model of a cross-partisan, democratic social contract rooted in the capabilities of local and regional governments to make the right policy decisions for their constituents. What a boon it is to be hailed as a vanguard of political progress; who wouldn't want to sign their name under a few of the most promising regional bills of the near future? The new, exciting arena of governance is enticing a whole new team of top political players.

Even the members of the ruling coalition in the capital had decided to join the wave, announcing that Poland's new representative for the European Commission would not be a politician from the central government but rather a well-known leader of a provincial government. This decision was a positive one for Poland because the new commissioner was put in charge of regional and urban policy, a highly influential portfolio that happens to make up nearly one third of the overall EU budget. This was an astonishing change of course. Until the 2023 constitutional reform, it was a career in Warsaw (and not experience in local government) that served as a springboard to positions of "real" power.

"Right, so now even a regional politician can join the EU's top brass. Coming back to your roots seems like it's a pretty strategic move." The unwavering note of confidence in Dorota's voice was unmistakable.

A fresh start

"Fine, but why are we even talking about this?" It was Piotr's turn to be annoyed, feeling as though he had no arguments left to the contrary. After all, ever since his child was born, he'd stopped keeping track of all the political gossip. Sejm drama had begun to pale in comparison to the household drama of feedings, diaper changes and naps. Now he was starting to feel as if he didn't even know what was going on in his own neighborhood.

"Let me explain it to you, buddy. This very same local politician who made it all the way to Brussels was also a shoo-in to become the next voivode here. So, since he wasn't in the picture anymore, the whole political puzzle had to be rebuilt from scratch. Checkmate!" Dorota declared triumphantly.

"I really can't believe you're arguing about some guy you've only seen on TV," Seba groaned. "Let's have another round and whoever doesn't drink has to pour the next one."

People were scrambling at first. The year 2024 brought a whole new system of local and regional politics, but also a new window into the future. The old political guard was no longer relevant. Things had changed in a dramatic way. This has also ushered in an unexpected advantage for the leftists, who achieved a phenomenal—altogether historic—electoral victory. Of course, Piotr dismissed it as a one-off and a novelty of sorts, whereas Dorota continued trying to convince him that it was the "real good change."[1] The bulk of this success came from the hard work of a super-popular former MP who'd surrounded herself with a creative team of social media-savvy young people. She single-handedly defined the character of the 2024 voivodship campaign around what mattered most to people: the unsustainable surge in the cost of living and the unacceptable state of education and healthcare.

"So it's the economy, stupid, plus education and health. What else do you want?" Dorota grilled Piotr, feeling right in her element.

It so happened that this "fresh start" also saw the West Pomeranian Civic Platform come to be dominated by other politicians returning from the capital, specifically politicians from the party's left wing. Under their leadership, the Platform worked together with the Left and socially conscious "Pope-Francis" Catholics from the Poland 2050 party to create a governing coalition in the Sejmik. Many wondered whether this was even possible ... and it turned out that not only was it possible, but it could actually be successful, too. All thanks to the fact that Western Pomeranians opted, in their Voivodship Charter, for a parliamentary model of their provincial government, under which the voivode and the rest of the regional "cabinet" (formally known as the Voivodship Board) is elected by the Sejmik's majority, rather than directly by voters. In effect, the liberal-left coalition chose the earlier-mentioned former MP as voivode, while two Civic Platform politicians secured positions of deputy voivode: one in charge of finance, labor, and development; the second in charge of health. The coalition parties also divided up the remaining positions in the Board. And that was when the hard work began.

Pay up and calm down

The decision to raise taxes was imperative. And despite all the protests from local citizens (some of whom scrawled "Pay it yourself!" on the wall of the provincial government's main office building), there was no way around it. The financial situation of the voivodship was dramatic, while any programs meant to tackle the cost-of-living crisis for residents around the region were pricey. After a stormy debate, the Sejmik and the new regional Senate enacted the most progressive personal income tax in Poland as well as a progressive corporate income tax. Whoever earned more paid more into the pot. CEOs weren't happy, claiming it was a punishment for their success, but there really was no other way to get this Robin Hood-style endeavor off the ground.

At the same time, as part of an agreement introduced in the West Pomeranian Senate, several municipalities had ended up raising property taxes, while also introducing laws that would limit unhealthy tax competition between local governments. The new annual rates were 1 percent of the property value for real estate estimated at up to about 250,000 euros and 3 percent of the value over that benchmark. These new rates did not only apply in case of owners having their primary residence at a given property at the time when the tax increase came into force; the tax paid rose by 200 percent (to 3 percent and 9 percent, respectively) in the case of a property that has remained vacant for over a year.

"And what was the point? Voters have long memories and they won't forgive this disaster at the next election cycle," Piotr ventured, but Seba cut in right away to address his friend's misgivings.

"Dude, the point is not simply to pad the voivodship budget, but to discourage people from buying properties for the sole purpose of adding them to an investment portfolio. Enough of landlords owning five apartments with short-term leases. It also protects homeowners who actually live in their properties, who want peace and quiet, rather than a roulette of new neighbors."

Not everyone was happy about the changes at first. Politically, a bargain had to be struck. Mayors-voivodship senators conditioned their assent to the tax hike on the promise of swift enactment of the social programs promised by the ruling coalition. In other words, the new voivode must pay the political price not only for the rise in income taxes but also for the hikes of all other local and regional taxes.

"She went all out, it's true, but there really wasn't any other way," Dorota explained. She was pleased to see that Piotr really seemed to be taking an interest in what she was talking about. Alas, no matter how he tried, he really didn't have any argument to counter her points this time around.

One of the reasons why these changes were eventually accepted by the public at large was the right hire for the Deputy Voivode for Finance, Labor, and Development. The coalition opted not to give the portfolio to a detached economics professor. Instead, they chose a well-known, seasoned politician. So, while the experts in the Office of the Deputy Voivode (formed through a merger of the finance and budget departments of the former Voivodship Marshal's Office and former Voivodship Office) were crunching the numbers, the deputy voivode focused on talking with ordinary people and entrepreneurs. He started with a smart strategy: organizing open meetings where people were free to lambast the tax proposals.

"Thieves!" That was the battle cry that rang from the crowd gathering in front of the town hall.

"I was positive they were going to guillotine the guy," said Dorota, who'd participated in one of these early meetings. "But he stood there, unbothered, letting everyone express their anger. Then he began to explain what the benefits would be. He gave them practical examples that were really hard to undermine."

After all, no one wanted businesses to end up leaving the region, especially given that the next voivodship over, Wielkopolska or Greater Poland, had just been taken over by a radically free-market provincial government. Officially, they declared their neighborly intentions, but in secret, they had started to try and tempt business owners in West Pomerania to move. Keeping these businesses meant saving jobs, tax income, and regional development—business led to more business, by association, so to speak. Quite simply, when business is profitable, it attracts more entrepreneurship and more investment in the region. And this is advantageous to everyone—every single individual benefits from a healthy business climate.

"I guess that makes sense," Piotr mumbled, chewing on the logic along with a bite of cheese from the platter in front of him.

So, it was Seba's turn to poke polemical holes in the discussion. "Fine, but raising taxes on business owners isn't very encouraging. How'd they make it work?"

"Ah, so you see, it was a pretty slick move," Dorota said, her eyes bright. "Because they also *lowered* taxes at the same time, letting companies lower their income tax rate by several percentage points by demonstrating an equitable approach toward their employees. In other words, labor unions and leftist ideals galore!"

"Hold on a minute. Before you start singing the 'Internationale,' can you tell me who came up with this idea anyway?" Piotr countered, warming up again.

"The Deputy Voivode for Finance, Labor, and Development. He made it clear that this approach benefits everybody. In his own words, the idea was to attract people to West Pomerania by giving them a dignified way to live, but also to work. That's what he posted on social media, then somebody started asking if he'd give bonuses to civil servants, but other than that, it seemed pretty legit. They even built the Friendly Employer Rating System. It evaluates each business based on an average of the ratings given by the Voivodship Labor Inspection and by labor unions operating within the firm. Let's not forget, labor unions should be part and parcel of every business. And if for some reason there's no union, the new regional law requires calculating the company's rating as if a union gave zero points! And this just shows that, instead of going into the union-busting rabbit hole, it now pays to get it together and let people fight for their rights. Anyway, every business owner bidding for a local or regional government contract has to get a Friendly Employer Rating. The company must pay for the rating, although small and medium businesses can apply for a full or partial rebate. Everybody's got to do it, it's that simple."

Piotr was losing his enthusiasm for poking fun at all these leftist fantasies. But still he managed to muster up a bit more ire. "So, what are they rating? Casual Fridays and the like?"

"Obviously that's all you'd think about," Dorota huffed, before summarizing her main points. "The rating system considers a whole bunch of things, including labor conditions, salary, compliance with labor laws, procedures for dealing with bullying, sexual harassment, and/or discrimination. And cooperation with unions is also assessed. Plus," she added, "there are some pretty hefty penalties to pay if someone is found trying to bribe or otherwise influence the rating coming from the unions."

"The deputy voivode's office even set up a dedicated Department of Public Communication, staffed with savvy young people who managed the Left's electoral campaign. They came up with a pretty decent 'Pay Up and Calm Down' campaign to show people that even at a higher tax rate, the cost of living ends up falling," Dorota continued. "Nobody likes to pay taxes, that's clear, but the positive effects of a built-up regional budgetary 'chest' can be seen nearly right away, for instance, in the quality of hospitals and clinics."

Private healthcare no more

The party was heating up, but the kitchen conversation was just as intense. Anka passed through and heard that healthcare was on the agenda, so couldn't help sitting down to listen to what the group had to say. Her mother was battling cancer, and doctors, referrals, and tests had ruled her days for the past few years.

"The deputy voivode, who used to be the Minister of Health in Warsaw, said that even though, theoretically, nearly every Pole is covered by the national health insurance, in practice each of us spends on average about 1,500 złoty per year on private doctors' appointments. When my mother was really sick, that figure was ten times higher."

"He said not too long ago he's working to cut that figure down by 90 percent." Dorota turned to Anka and asked about her mother's health.

Meanwhile, Seba started to talk about his experience dealing with his child's illness. When he was at the clinic, he found out that most of the new revenue from taxes was supporting the public healthcare system. It was evident that the exam room had been recently renovated, which was greatly needed after years of disrepair. The National Health Fund had given the voivodship more flexibility in how budgets were spent on a regional level, no longer imposing their own restrictions on how each złoty was invested.

"Most importantly," Seba said, "the additional funds cut down on the waiting time not only for doctors' visits but for diagnostics and treatment, too. The deputy voivode is really on to something. It's clear that without making appointments more available, it's impossible to draw people into the public healthcare system. Who can wait a year to see a specialist … nope, no way. Besides, doctors don't have as many documents to fill out as they used to. When I see a doctor with my kid, I don't have to wait for her to type in all the info. Instead, she examines my little girl and actually has the time to talk to us. I finally feel like we're not a strain on her time and attention.

"I heard that the regional government set up a special task force to attract top specialists to the region from other voivodships and even from abroad. After all, plenty of Polish doctors are working in other countries … so why not make it the other way around? Finally, the voivodship made it possible for doctors who don't speak perfect Polish, but who can speak English, to work. The patient is informed about the doctor's primary language at the time of registration and they can always request a Polish-speaking specialist. Young people don't have an issue with seeing a doctor who happens to come from India or Moldova. At the same time, having more doctors available puts less pressure on the whole staff."

"I heard that clinics are open on Saturdays, Sundays, and even holidays, till late," Dorota said. "One of the goals is to maximize the use of ultra-expensive, state-of-the-art machines. It's one of the few exceptions to the regional shopping ban on Sundays and holidays. I think it also has a big impact on lessening the pressure on emergency services and urgent care because if people can see a regular doctor, they aren't showing up at hospital emergency rooms with minor stuff."

"The best part is the actual cross-partisan miracle happening right before our eyes," Seba added. "Our Left managed to team up with the ultraconservative Podlasie region and they jumpstarted an online system, it's called something like ... anyway, we call it RegMed. You log in and you can see all the available appointments for all the doctors with the right specialization in the whole region and you can sign up right away. When I think about all the time I used to waste calling one clinic after another trying to get an appointment, it makes my blood boil. I can't believe it took them so long to figure it all out."

Piotr finally looked up from his phone to add, "You know, that's true, I signed up to see a throat doctor and it wasn't bad. I could pick a free visit on a Tuesday at 1:30pm or pay 50 złoty and come in on the weekend. I paid the extra 50 so I didn't have to skip work."

"These extra charges were a massive point of contention for the Left during negotiations," Dorota mused. "But they have to get the money from somewhere and really every złoty goes a long way."

The first few months after RegMed's launch were a pretty big success. The voivode, along with her Deputy Voivode for Education and Social Policy, a Poland 2050 politician, decided to do something unheard of: put together an e-referendum to end the 500+—a signature social program of the 2015–23 PiS government[2] that provides each family with a monthly cash payment of about 120 euro per child. The voivode made a forceful pitch to replace the program with the regional Voucher for Education and Care, or the VEC.

500+? Let's vote!

"Did you guys vote in the referendum?" Seba asked, pouring some water into a glass, having remembered he'd be heading to his mother-in-law's the next day with his little one.

"I did," Dorota said, raising her hand. "I know the whole 500+ program was super controversial at the outset. I was one of the few anti-PiS activists who was actually in favor of it. But since then, I've realized it's better to put all these 500+ cash transfers in a pot and build a more comprehensive social welfare system."

"So, what was the result in the end?" Piotr asked, eyes wide.

At first, local journalists didn't give the coalition a fighting chance for pushing it through. "Madame Voivode has clearly chosen to commit an act of political suicide," summed up one journalist from the *Koszalin Voice*. But the Public Communication Department which had made so much progress in pushing through other bills from the regional "ministry of finance" got to work. And they offered some pretty solid reasoning: every person with a right to a 500+ grant would get the VEC, which in turn could be exchanged for a whole gamut of public services. The vouchers would entitle you to a free place in a nursery, and could cover extra charges at preschools (meals, after-hours care, extracurricular activities) or other paid services at schools. One of the most helpful ways the VEC could support a family is by paying for a member of the family to reside in a nursing home, which would normally cost up to 1,500 złoty. It's clear that the voivode's proposal was most helpful for families of small children or those caring for elderly family members. It was harder to convince families of school-age children, but the wider-scale educational reform helped in this regard.

Some of the activists from the Left thought it would be best to disqualify top earners from the program. The deputy voivode responsible for the reform would not agree to this stipulation, not just for political reasons but practical ones, too. Politically, it was obvious that every vote would count in trying to push the reform through. In a practical sense, she saw the advantages in integrating residents from different social strata. Moreover, one of the goals of the reform was to drain fuel from the elaborate private market for child and elderly care. The provincial leaders saw that market as particularly problematic, not least because it siphons off resources and scoops up the top personnel from the public system.

"And, once more, like in the case of clinics and hospitals, the point is to not have to pay for private care, but have the same quality of services available from the public sector. Public nurseries and the rest of it," explained Dorota.

A key theme in the campaign geared at investing the funds from the 500+ program into West Pomeranian public services is progressive education. As the Deputy Voivode for Education and Social Policy posted on social media: "Even before the constitutional reform, it was clear that Poland's educational system needs a radical change. When it comes to education, Poles agree on fundamental values: equal access for all kids, an innovative and relevant approach, streamlining the overloaded core curriculum and giving it a more local emphasis, increasing autonomy of individual schools, administrators and teachers, and democratizing schooling overall." The deputy voivode plainly stated at the press conference that none of these goals could be achieved unless funding was increased, including teacher salaries.

Since the very first meetings, the regional Sejmik and Senate put emphasis on expanding the flexibility of the system, while respecting national standards of good education, established by the College of Voivodships. The core regional curriculum, "Love to Learn," was built from the ground up—by experts and educators, along with teachers, administrators, and even young people or non-profits specializing in education.

One major priority was ensuring access to learning from nursery to kindergarten. The basis for this approach was gleaned from studies carried out all over the world, their reported findings making it clear that this early period is essential when working to balance social and educational opportunities and improve social mobility. Authorities in the region planned to dedicate ample funds from the 500+

program for nursery care across a range of formats: from small-scale home-based care to childcare and play clubs, both indoors and outside in the fresh air.

Referendum day

"It's obvious that in every referendum, the way you formulate a question has a big impact on how people understand it," Dorota noted. "If you're not clear about what you're asking, it can upend the whole voting process and it basically just goes straight in the trash. We had four options for spending these 500+ funds and the first was basically to uphold the status quo. The VEC proposal was presented by the Voivodship Board as the second option. Then the last two came from the West Pomeranian Sejmik and Senate. Some of the PiS Sejmik representatives and two from the Left suggested that in exchange for doing away with 500+ for the top 70 percent earners, the sum would be raised to 1000+ for the poorest 30 percent. In other words, making the grant means-tested. The voivodship Senate drew up a proposal in which the funds would be sent to the municipalities in the voivodship, and they would spend the money as they saw fit."

"Ahhh, and from what I remember," cut in Seba, "by law none of the options could add to the overall budgetary expenditures. And anyway, that whole website demokracja.gov.pl has a decent interface. You just drag and drop the options to rank them from best to worst."

The referendum campaign was especially fierce. No wonder, since it wasn't just money at stake, but the whole philosophy and character of the social policy. Until recently, the ideas of supporting families by cash transfers and of boosting the birth rate had been tightly linked with a specific political ideology represented by PiS. So, it was no wonder both sides poured in money and organizational resources from way beyond the bounds of the voivodship. The former Prime Minister from PiS, Beata Szydło, surrounded by a circle of her devoted supporters in Szczecin, yelled "Hands off our money!" and called upon the voters to keep 500+ the way it was. She pointed her finger at many years of liberal shaming of citizens dependent on public assistance, slurs such as calling "overly entitled" mothers "mad-ers," and insinuations about 500+ being a "handout" or even an instance of vote buying. "All this just to destroy the Polish family," she summed up in a TV interview.

At the same time, proponents of the other options focused on a less flashy door-to-door outreach. Particular creativity was shown by the supporters of the voivode's proposal, especially in how they put together the "Real Plus" campaign. They shared posters, stickers, and online memes touting the full gamut of public services that will be available for the proposed VECs: "+Nursery," +Full-day of School," "+Senior Care," and "+Fee-less Preschool." The campaign was based on a (somewhat) subtle critique of the PiS program, calling attention to the fact that its wider goals (the titular "+") had not been achieved.

Debates were held, some of them so well attended that it was hard to fit the crowd in the venue. The discussion continued in the public space, in cafés and on buses. It was one of the topics that really got people going, especially since the program itself is directly tied to household budgets.

With each week of the campaign, it became more and more clear that the dismal premonitions of the local media regarding the political future of the voivode would not come true. But the Board also did not have victory "in their pocket." What did happen was that the options presented for the referendum had stoked public debate. That dealt the biggest blow to supporters of the status quo. The 500+ program was no longer a political taboo. Its future was shaped in the public space as well as private spaces, including a crowded kitchen at a roaring house party.

The day of the e-referendum had finally arrived. Citizens who didn't have access to digital devices were allowed to use special computer stations at libraries and cultural centers. Some residents shared their Wi-Fi with neighbors and you could see people running through the city with their laptops in hand. When the time to report the results arrived, it revealed how deeply divided public opinion was on this matter: 34 percent wished to retain the program in its present form; however, the voivode's VEC proposal gained 32 percent of the votes. The concept of relaying the funds to municipalities won 25 percent, while less than 10 percent voted for keeping the program only for the poorest families. The advantage of the digital referendum was that it set up the single transferable vote, which meant that there was no need for a runoff. The digital system rejects the options with the least support; then, the secondary preferences of voters are added to the tally of the most popular options.

With respect to our referendum, the majority of residents voting for the funds to be allocated to the least well off, along with more than half of those whose first choice was to transfer the funds to the municipalities, ended up choosing the Board's proposal as their second choice. In effect, these votes boosted the VEC scheme to the top spot, driving it way above the status quo.

Living better . . . but how, exactly?

"For the first year and a half, we were working sixteen hours a day to make good on our promise of realistically reducing the cost of living for people residing in our voivodship," the voivode recalled. "Now we need to start thinking long-term. Especially since the party named 'Poland 2050' is part of our coalition. This brings up some important questions: what does a leftist, social approach to development mean for our voivodship over the next decade or two?" Essentially, how is "leftism" practically defined in the context of the regional welfare state that supports residents on every level?

The voivode indicated a few key areas of focus.

"And total respect to her for doing this," Dorota added. "Because her jumping-off point is social justice."

Piotr rolled his eyes. He despised all that leftist newspeak because to him it felt vacuous. He made fun of its slogans, adding that they could just as easily start up a campaign based on the wish for "peace on Earth" and the result would be exactly the same.

With as much patience as she could muster, Dorota explained that the voivode was not just talking about equal opportunity but also about dignity and quality of life for everyone, regardless of their professional success.

"All right, well, here I can agree," Piotr relented. "There's nothing I find more annoying than when neoliberals go on about success, along the lines of pulling yourself by your bootstraps and all that. Obviously, to those who have a job and job security, things seem much simpler."

"The next key priority is the environment," Dorota continued.

"Oh, yeah, Greta Thunberg would really love that," Piotr joked, but Dorota hushed him at once, noting that the effects of climate change end up being most disastrous for the poorest people. She further noted how global warming is tightly linked to the economic issue he held so dear.

"The effects of extreme weather impact municipalities and counties the most," Dorota retorted grimly. "There are changes to soil quality and vegetation—which are the effects of ongoing aridification taking place regionally—droughts are affecting farmers across the country; heat waves are a threat to everybody. That's why we have to work hard to save what we can in every possible way. I'm glad our region is joining the action. This is really no joking matter."

"All right, all right, I'll stop talking then," Piotr relented, especially since he was starting to feel tired and kept glancing at his watch. His threshold for partying wasn't the same since he'd turned 30. "Grasslands or desert, whatever it is, leave me out of it. Seba, don't pour me another, I'm heading home in a few."

"Are you taking the bus or a taxi?" Dorota asked, "Because I don't know if you heard but there's this new . . ."

"Did you just start working for the voivode's PR department or something? What's going on? You used to fight the system, now you just go on about amenities, change, solutions," Piotr sneered.

"You have to admit that to live better, you need to make moves. It takes a degree of finesse, miles beyond the simplistic neoliberal tax dumping. It takes work and I can appreciate the fact that these things take a lot of thought and consideration. For example, the issue of population. The areas around Szczecin are urbanized, but the southeastern parts of the voivodship are some of the least densely populated in the whole country. And so they clearly don't get as much to invest in infrastructure. What I'm interested in is whether kids have good transportation options for getting to school or if they have to walk along a poorly lit roadside. It's great that the S6 highway is complete but there are still so many ways people are being excluded from access to public transportation. You won't really feel the brunt of it in Szczecin or Koszalin, but try to get out of a more rural area without a car. The public bus runs 'once in a hundred years'— if it even runs at all. Imagine you were coming back home tonight, making your way through the woods and all that. Young people don't want to live in the countryside. So, the elderly are often left on their own and they need someone to help care for them. And yes, this means opening clinics, hiring caretakers, and so on. Obviously, the more metropolitan areas develop the quickest, but we can't forget about the rest of the region. That's why it's good that the voivodship allows new investment areas to open only after the existing areas are filled up. And before an investor starts working on anything, they must factor public transportation into the plan. No more 'desert island' residential communities, where everybody needs their own car to get in and out."

"Are you going to start going on about why cars are terrible now?" Piotr mumbled.

"Sorry, I'm a leftist, therefore I have leftist duties, so I don't like to see people being excluded. Piotr, you can keep laughing at my soy latte, even though that joke dried up a long time ago, but you can't tell me we don't have massive potential given we border the sea and Germany. With the right infrastructure and investment, the voivodship has a chance to become a vital logistics hub. And the chance to cooperate with Germany and Denmark? That gets us renewable energy and new jobs."

"Dorota, you know I love you and your leftist leanings too," interjected Piotr, raising his hand. "Plus, you know I'm a huge fan of nature. I know that foreigners are coming to us for hiking, mushroom picking, research ... We've got some great public universities, too. Koszalin University of Technology and West Pomeranian University of Technology in Szczecin! A factory of specialists!"

"I hope you're including women in your specialist roster," Dorota said pointedly.

"That's fine, I'm tired of arguing with you guys," Piotr said, standing up, blowing a kiss to his friends, and vanishing into the living room.

A better way to work

"Hey everybody, a little bird told me you're chatting about the voivodship and all the stuff that's been going on around here." It was Agata, coming into the kitchen to pour herself a glass of juice. "I have to say, trains and transportation are big on my agenda because my granny's sick and, in the past, I had to ask my dad to take me to see her as there was no way to get there by public transport. But now, the voivodship not only rebuilt the second track—you know, the one from before World War II that was dismantled and taken to the east by the Soviets—but also built numerous passing sidings for regional trains to go faster. Personally, my favorite is the West Pomerania Circle Line Railway because it means I can finally make my way to Drawsko all fine and dandy."

"I don't know anything about that," Dorota said, her interest piqued, although she was a bit annoyed she wasn't on top of every single thing that was happening locally.

"Like the name suggests, it's a loop. Something like the Circle line on the London Tube or Ringbahn in Berlin. It goes in a circle through a few cities. They're also planning to do something like that in Szczecin as part of the railway extension project. And that's good since it lets people in places about a half-hour away from each other get around more easily—to work obviously, but everywhere else too."

Agata took the empty seat at the table and reached for some of the snacks laid out in the middle. "Besides," she added, "I'm really excited about the wind turbines. You'll be able to see them from the train. I just love to watch them whirl around..."

"It'll happen soon enough," Dorota assured her. "First, Koszalin University of Technology has to complete its research. Supposedly they're working with Bornholm on some energy storage system. My neighbor's a part of the team. It's part of the whole plan to revamp the shipyard industry. No one believed it at first; it seemed the idea was kaput. And yet the investment in wind farms and the technological boost has given it another lease of life. They got a grant to modernize the turbines with a hybrid engine. My neighbor told me it's a hydrogen-hybrid engine. The deputy voivode's office managed to convince the Department of Marine Technology and Transportation at the technical uni in Szczecin to come up with a grant program and hire some international specialists to build ships and brainstorm all sorts of innovative engines. Rostock joined the whole project. My neighbor's always heading out there, he even brought me back a fridge magnet last time."

"Ooh, looks like someone's been getting presents. Is he handsome at all, this neighbor?" Agata teased, pressing her friend for more details on the mysterious young engineer.

In the meantime, Seba had fallen deep into a discussion with a freshly minted party guest by the name of Władek, who had recently returned from a three-year stint abroad working in the London office of a multinational company.

"There's no other way really, and our Deputy Voivode for Finance knows it," Władek was explaining, pausing to light a cigarette. "Reindustrialization is an essential part of the whole economic puzzle, as they say, even though most residents will end up being employed in the services sector. The point is that they have employment rights—and not the precarious trash contracts where you end up working for just the proverbial bowl of rice.[3]

"Things have finally started to budge. Take two sectors, for instance: tourism and shipping. There, the issue of workers' rights is at the forefront all the time. Except that any attempt to introduce some sort of employment regulations elicited screeching protests and taunts of bankruptcy or threats to move the business to another hub. Moral blackmail—all these hustlers want maximum earnings and minimal payouts, preferably under the table. But it just doesn't work that way. People are becoming more and more aware that they deserve certain rights."

Seba knew very well how easy it still was to fool people. In any case, the West Pomeranian authorities knew how to play the labor game. He'd recently read an article about how the voivodship had received a number of hotels from the national treasury as part of the constitutional reform. The AWM Rewita hotel corporation and West Pomeranian hotels of the Polish Hotel Holding Group were consolidated into the West Pomeranian Sustainable Tourism Group. The voivodship also received Polferries—the major Polish ferry company—as well as Polsteam, a cargo ships operator.

To select CEOs of these companies, the voivodship established a transparent selection process. Among the selection criteria were managerial qualifications needed to maximize the profit for the region. In addition, the voivodship required candidates to be trendsetters in the area of protecting workers' rights, demonstrate willingness to cooperate with unions, and have a plan for implementing environmentally sustainable business models. In all voivodship-owned companies, it was standard to address female employees using feminatives—the feminine forms of nouns in the gendered Polish language that are fervently opposed by conservatives.[4] The next step was to make the internal and external corporate communication inclusive to nonbinary people.

In effect, since these businesses were owned by the region itself, they served as a sort of pilot project for progressive practices to support good labor policies that upheld the rights of employees, human rights overall, and environmental standards. Above all, these voivodship-owned enterprises provided an organizational and financial foundation for the increasingly influential unions. "The impact of the pro-union politics of West Pomerania and the companies it owns is beginning to make itself evident, especially in the tourism sector, across all of Poland," a national union leader commented in a recent newspaper article. "Szczecin is demonstrating that even in the most competitive sectors you can successfully do business while collaborating with unions and respecting workers' rights."

"But I won't believe it until I see it," Seba remarked. "Still, the prospects for the job market aren't bad. Finally, we might not have to fight so hard at work for the most basic things. Anyway, let's change the subject. Władek, how are your kids? Have they come to grips with the school system yet?"

A better way to learn

"Let me tell you that it really feels like it's going better here than in England. Schools aren't the same as they used to be in our day and age. After all the reforms and consultations, they introduced so many new educational programs and community projects. The kids are always doing something different at school: science projects, exhibitions, shows. From the very start, they've had workshops on equality and antidiscrimination, then they come home and pepper us with tons of questions. They always want to talk about all the stuff they've been discovering in school. In June, we're going to our first annual town hall meeting on what's gone on in school over the academic year. I have to say, it's a good way not only to find out about what the kids have been doing, but also to have a say in what they'll be doing next year. Because schools do have some flexibility in terms of adapting their curricula and methods to the students' needs. The core curriculum offers a shared framework, but the teachers really do fill it out as they see fit. They don't just follow the textbooks, which, by the way, aren't as important anymore since you can get so many resources online. Schools are stepping away from outdated methods of splitting learning into more than a dozen or so subjects, and they're leaning toward more comprehensive learning blocks: social sciences, science (instead of four separate subjects), humanities, health and well-being … So, teachers no longer have to cut the world up into little unrelated pieces, while students have the opportunity to understand real-life processes and problems in a broader, interdisciplinary context. Typically, it's only the foreign language, Polish language and literature, and math teachers who focus on a single specialization. And there's one more cool thing: no bells between classes, so lessons last as long as they need to, ensuring that the kids feel they've grasped a specific concept or skill."

"You're kidding. Even now, when I hear a school bell ring, I break out in a cold sweat. All the time I spent up at the board or handing in a pop quiz come rushing back." Seba shuddered at the thought of all those anxiety-ridden school days.

"Some schools even integrate their preschoolers with first-years," Władek replied. "There's some talk of bringing middle schools back but most residents feel like another reform would be too costly and time-consuming. There aren't any typical tests either. You just keep testing yourself until you get it right. This makes things a lot less stressful for the kids, which is good for their well-being, especially kids who left the system for homeschooling and are now gradually coming back."

"What's the top school in the voivodship right now?" Seba asked once he'd fully returned from his trip to the past.

"Please. They don't do those kinds of rankings here," Władek said, shaking his head. "The school principals support each other, exchanging ideas, curricula, platforms, materials, experiences. The old rivalry is dead; it was never suitable for an educational setting anyway. They even do student exchanges in Meklemburg and Brandenburg, running some sort of joint projects with schools that have diverse profiles. They're finally teaching these kids to use their brains instead of just teaching them all to conform. There are no special distinctions on their school reports either. The school head at my kids' school said it's because 'each of us is good at something and we essentially all deserve a distinction.' There's almost no homework and assessment is more like a constructive feedback session and summary of how the child is doing. Apparently, very few kids get extra paid tutoring because there's no need. You can just attend extra study sessions at school. And there are special vouchers to cover their cost."

"Leaves no other option than to hit the books, eh?" Seba sighed. "If I had a school like that, I wouldn't have been such a bundle of nerves back then."

"Even so, you'd get the support you needed from a mental health specialist. Classroom teachers also get access to mentoring and advising when they need it. Seriously, there's nothing else to do but learn, like you said." Władek gave his friend a friendly shove.

"I wonder how they manage to combine governance in the voivodship with the 'grand politics' of the capital. After all, the voivode is also a senator. I heard she gave her support to the Pomeranian proposal on abortion—meaning that regions can make it legal up to the twelfth week. She's also meant to introduce a national law allowing regions to impose additional taxes on inheritance and gifts. Hold on, let me look it up online," he said, scrolling his phone. "Here it is: 'Zero percent for up to 100,000 złoty, then 15 percent over that for any property or gifts inherited by children or grandchildren. Twenty percent for everyone else.' We'll have to see about all that, just like we'll have to see about all these plans for building more affordable housing units."

Seba noted the list of plans he'd read about on Facebook, and he'd even commented "I guess we'll wait and see" under some posts. He'd been worried that the reforms would revolve around some typical Sejm nonsense and, instead of acknowledging the reality of regional specificity, they would provide an opportunity for the tired performative Warsaw ideological wars.

The party was slowly dying down. Having looked at all the existing photos of their kids, pets, and vacations, Seba and Dorota decided to share a taxi, since they were neighbors.

"Have you thought of moving someplace else?" Seba asked her as they stopped at a traffic light.

"I used to. But now I'm feeling pretty good about where we are. I'm really interested to see how it's all going to pan out. I might even run in the next election. I'm just so amped about all these new ideas."

"Oh wow, that would be amazing. You'd definitely have my vote," Seba assured his friend. "Keeping my fingers crossed!"

Notes

1. *Good change* was the 2015 slogan of PiS in its successful presidential and parliamentary campaign; see e.g. Joanna Fomina and Jacek Kucharczyk, "The Specter Haunting Europe: Populism and Protest in Poland," *Journal of Democracy* 27, no. 4 (2016): 48–68.
2. See e.g. Sławomir Wilk, "The Role of Family Policy in Solving Demographic Problems: Study of the Polish Program Family 500+," *European Journal of Sustainable Development* 9, no. 4 (2020): 84–92.

3. In 2013, in a secretly recorded private conversation, Mateusz Morawiecki—the future PiS Prime Minister—expressed, in rather vulgar terms, his opinion that in countries like Poland, people should be willing to work "for a bowl of rice." See Lukasz Pawlowski, "Polish Election Raises Questions over Prime Minister's Future," *Financial Times*, Oct. 24, 2018.
4. See e.g. Małgorzata Szajbel-Keck, "Opposition Discourse in the Public Debate on Gender-Inclusive Language in Poland," in *Public Attitudes towards Gender-Inclusive Language*, ed. Falco Pfalzgraf (Gruyter, 2024).

11
The Dream Christian Democratic Voivodship

Łukasz Rozdeiczer and Artur Wołek
Fictionalized by Karolina Lewestam

Believers and pragmatists

"What do you mean, Christian Democracy?" asked the middle-aged blonde woman at the head of the conference table. Next to her sat a large man, around fifty years old, twiddling his mustache. The man farther down the table, with concentration and determination etched across his face, was one of the best-known officials of the Subcarpathian regional government, Marshal of the Voivodship, Grzegorz Gerwal-Punicki.

Other than the three of them, the room was empty, barring Alina—Mr Gerwal-Punicki's assistant—who was busying herself with the kettle in the corner, and Mirek—a young researcher dressed in an immaculate suit—who was carefully arranging broken cookies on a plate.

Alina was not afraid of a challenge—far from it. She was the top student in her high school; she had been sent to Oxford-style debate tournaments in Warsaw; she had graduated with a first-class degree in sociology from the University of Rzeszów. After her studies, she had made the decision to return to Subcarpathia and work as an assistant to this highly respected local politician. In her view, the greatest challenge you could face was to position yourself in the place where you could do the most in the future—however trite that sounded.

"Christian Democracy, simple as that," replied Grzegorz, uncrossing his arms.

"In Subcarpathia? I don't buy it. Sorry, Grzegorz, I just don't. The Konfederacja party, perhaps, but not…"

"I'm telling you, Joanna, it's doable. Honest to God…" said Grzegorz in a determined tone, massaging his bald head, "Christian Democracy. We'll create a Christian Democrat Party from the moderate wing of PiS, from the Polish People's Party, Poland 2050, and a handful of those Catholics that Tusk dropped because they didn't want to liberalize abortion."

"But Christian Democracy…" Joanna shook her head.

Łukasz Rozdeiczer and Artur Wołek, *The Dream Christian Democratic Voivodship* In: *Let's Agree on Poland.*
Edited by: Maciej Kisilowski and Anna Wojciuk, Oxford University Press.
 DOI: 10.1093/oso/9780198979562.003.0014

"Christian Democracy or not," said the man with the mustache, "this is completely crazy. Are you screwing with us, Grzegorz? You're screwing with us, aren't you? You must be! Why would you do that, Grzegorz? Why?"

Grzegorz sighed wearily.

"No. I'm not screwing with you. You really think I'm the kind to enjoy speculation, Paweł? Far from it. I'm pragmatic to the bone, and proud of it."

"Alright, go on. I'll take your word for it. I'm just the treasurer, after all," said Paweł with a shrug of his broad shoulders.

"Paweł, settle down. Go ahead, Grzegorz," said Joanna, tugging at the bottom of her brown jacket to smooth it out. "Even if it's just something that appeared to you in a dream, it could be interesting, you never know. I think dreams can tell us a lot. About people and about the world. So ..." She made an encouraging gesture, signaling for Grzegorz to continue.

"Joanna, this wasn't ... It wasn't a dream." He sighed. "Anyway. Christian Democracy, right. The Christian Democrats are going to win power in Subcarpathia. This year, I mean. And that's really not a bad thing. It'll go some way toward reconciling our PiS base, the Church, and most of the more or less normal folks who are dabbling with the centrist parties. So ... after the upcoming elections, we, my friends, will be in power here."

"What do you mean?" asked Joanna. "But we're with PiS!"

"Well, Joanna, the reason I summoned you and Paweł here today is because we're the relatively normal ones in PiS, right? Tell me, why are you with PiS? Are you nuts about President Duda? No. A big fan of former Prime Minister Morawiecki? Also no. You're with PiS because you go to church, but the infighting in Warsaw gets your goat, and you can't stand the far-right Konfederacja party because you think they're dangerous, so you're stuck here with us. And you, Paweł—you're with PiS because there's nowhere else you could accomplish anything for Subcarpathia. Because you're a pragmatist. And you work hard, which is rare. I'm telling you: we will be in power. Together with other Catholics, even former Tusk guys. And we will actually have power to wield because, since the constitutional reform, the central government is responsible for security, and we take care of what's in our own back yard. And I like that. I'm a total idealist, after all." Grzegorz narrowed his tired eyes. "I may not have much of an imagination, but I am an idealist."

"It's a nice dream, Grzegorz," said Joanna wistfully. A long-time activist of the Subcarpathian branch of PiS, she spent her evenings complaining to her husband, a forester, about her colleagues from the party. "Just think, Paweł ... imagine if we could actually do something like that here ... Finally get away from those wingnuts ... And be able to develop some prosocial policies and programs ... It's actually a pretty good idea. And no one would have to be ashamed of their Catholic faith. Since my daughter left home to study in Warsaw, she's always telling me I'm backward. She goes on all the women's marches and that kind of thing."

"Of course, the priests themselves haven't done much to help the Church's cause," said Paweł philosophically.

"Good point," said Joanna. "If the Christian Democrats were in charge, the Church would be prosperous. It wouldn't have to curry favor with the other parties. It would be happy that we had the liberals under control, and it could get on with the actual work of the Church. Seriously, Grzegorz, it's a great story. You could get a book out of that, I reckon. Really inspirational stuff."

"It's not a story. It's not a story, darn it! I'm telling you, it's a solid plan for the new status quo! For that social contract proposed by the academics."

Alina approached the group at a confident pace. She hastily slid the plate of cookies onto the table, smoothed down her blazer, and took a seat.

"I suggest we get down to brass tacks," she said with authority. "Have a look at this." She pulled a small notebook from her blazer pocket and flicked through it until she landed on the page she was looking for.

"Here we are: you will form a Christian Democrat coalition with Poland 2050, the Polish People's Party, and the sane Catholics from Civic Platform. After the local government elections, you will draft the Subcarpathian Voivodship Charter, which will establish the new governance rules for our province, but also set the stage for various power struggles. You will decide as follows: First of all, the Sejmik will select the voivode. Why? Because a lot of politicians will return here from Warsaw and it will be necessary to distribute the power between many ambitious voices. It can't be a winner-takes-all situation. Second, as you know, the new regional Senate will be here. You will collaborate with the Senate ..."

"With the Senate?" asked Joanna in a weak voice, still shaken by the fact that Alina was speaking to them in the very way that they should be speaking to Alina; her tone was dogmatic and slightly impatient.

"That's right, with the Senate. The Voivodship Senate," said Mirek, who had joined them at the table and was helping himself to a cookie. "Comprising all the mayors from our region."

"But ... but there are 160 of them," said Paweł, joining in the protest. Suddenly, Grzegorz's idea was emerging from the realms of fairytale and Paweł had begun to think in real terms. "One hundred and sixty people with power complexes, all fighting tooth and nail for their own municipalities ... They'll block the voivode ... It will be pandemonium."

"It won't," said Alina resolutely, turning the page in her notebook. "There will be a compulsory vote-weighting mechanism in the Senate based on the population of each district. It's a good model in a region where you've got Aviation Valley on the one hand, and fragmented agriculture on the other. It's the representation of different interests, plain and simple. Territorial, economic, professional. Pluralism."

"Wait a minute," said Paweł, his voice raised slightly in objection. "Even if one city's vote is more heavily weighted, all it takes is for the smaller municipalities to create an anti-metropolitan coalition ..."

Here, Mirek cut in again.

"Which is why you would expand the composition of the Sejmik. Currently, we've got one member of the Sejmik for every 65,000 residents, so it's no wonder the representatives aren't really embedded at the local level. There are vast swaths of the voivodship that have no actual representatives in the Sejmik. The Voivodship Charter will more than double the number of Sejmik members to seventy. We will have large, multi-seat constituencies, which will allow the proportionality principle to actually work. And the Sejmik means political parties, not just individual local party members. Rzeszów will become an independent constituency with eight representatives."

Paweł tugged at his mustache in a gesture reminiscent of Lech Wałęsa, a comparison that he would not have appreciated. He decided that, in principle, he quite liked this Mirek guy. A bit wet behind the ears, but he was talking sense.

"If we have proportional elections and large constituencies," said Paweł, "then everything will be ruled by the parties again."

"And at the voivodship level, that's no bad thing!" replied Alina with a hint of the exasperated schoolteacher tone in her voice. "Plus, you will create executive agencies. Nonpartisan ones. Because, again, officials and experts might return to Subcarpathia from the Warsaw ministries en masse, but only if we can offer them something here, some kind of power, some room to maneuver. And of course, they will only return if they can expect to serve more than a single term. You'll give the green light to the Subcarpathian Infrastructure Development and Maintenance Agency, or the Environmental Protection Agency, or the Public Transport Board..."

Electoral odds

"Alright," said Joanna, "but what you're talking about is the organization of the voivodship. What about Christian Democracy? What are the odds of it actually working?"

Alina reached into her bag and pulled out a thick folder titled "Subcarpathian Christian Democracy: Analysis of Electoral Odds."

"Well, Mr Gerwal-Punicki and I commissioned some research," she said. "According to the results, if Poland 2050 and the Polish People's Party joined us, the Christian Democrats would have a chance of winning nearly half the votes and an absolute majority in the Sejmik. We would govern alone."

Her face expressing a mixture of curiosity and disbelief, Joanna took the folder from Alina.

"And the Church?" Joanna asked. By now, she had stopped wondering whether Grzegorz, Mirek, and Alina had actually recovered from the frenzy of the Local

Government Charity Ball that was held the previous Saturday. "How do we get the Church involved?"

"Many of the priests will be on your side," said Mirek helpfully, turning to face Joanna. "That's largely thanks to you, of course. You've built an image of yourself as a professional politician who supports the Church. I personally think very highly of you for that very reason. And it will come in handy, no doubt about that. But let's not forget that success will be built on three different qualities of the new faction." Here, Mirek stuck his thumb in the air. "First, Catholics. Second," he continued, the gold cross on his bracelet jangling as he raised his index finger, "true democratic Europeans; not the cynical European subsidy hunters, but the successors of Konrad Adenauer, Robert Schuman, and Alcide De Gasperi. Third, social activists, just like Adenauer and the others. No one can win in Subcarpathia without social programs."

"You may as well be describing me," said Joanna, not altogether modestly. "And you gentlemen, too, in a way," she said, addressing Paweł and Grzegorz. "Though perhaps you're religious to a different extent. Paweł, your daughter isn't confirmed yet, is she? When were you planning on doing that?"

Paweł looked confused, but Grzegorz came to his aid.

"Ultimately, then, the Christian Democrats will form the Voivodship Board," he declared, "and the liberals from Civic Platform, the remnants of PiS who are loyal to the old head office, the Left, and Konfederacja will be in opposition. So we will become the party in the middle. Tradition and modernity."

"Like in Bavaria," said Paweł with a laugh. "*Laptop und Lederhosen.*"

"That's it," Alina said graciously, as if she were a long-suffering parent whose child had finally learned to tie their own shoes. "Besides, that's how you attract tourists. But when you win, you will have to make sure that there actually is a decent laptop alongside those *Lederhosen*. You will be fighting poverty and inequality. And this time, you won't just be implementing programs written for you from the PiS head office in Warsaw; you'll be tackling it for real. That's why you'll be focusing on these five points." Alina turned the page in the folder and pushed it across the shiny table toward Joanna and Paweł.

Paweł read aloud:

Reindustrialization.
Improving transportation (public transport and roads).
Raising the quality of human capital by developing education.
Improving the quality of public services in peripheral areas.
Interregional and international cooperation.

His eyes sparkled.

"It sounds sensible," he said. "Very sensible, in fact. I always say … But wait a minute! I mean, sure, it looks good on paper, set out in bullet points. But it'll take a lot of work to flesh out a strategy like this in detail."

"Look," said Grzegorz, reaching into his briefcase. "Here are the program materials. They cover every topic."

Alina and Mirek had been working on this for the last month. They'd kept it a secret, so the Warsaw head office wouldn't find out.

"It's all here," Grzegorz continued. "What will happen, what we'll do. Here, Paweł, this is about industry. That's your area of interest. Everything else is there too. Read it, you'll see for yourselves. When you're done, give me a call. Will you join me in creating this Christian Democracy? Of course, if you decide against, we can just pretend this meeting never happened. Then everything will stay as it is."

Alina got to her feet, clutching the pile of printouts Grzegorz had passed her, and began handing them out to Joanna and Paweł.

"Here you go," she said encouragingly. "Please take a look. These materials should make things clearer. Right, Mirek?"

Mirek smiled, and Joanna found herself wishing she had a son like that. A son who not only dressed smartly and was always well groomed but who expressed himself well, too. Besides which—and this couldn't be overestimated—he was an altar boy; she had seen him with her own eyes.

If only my daughter … she thought to herself with a sigh as she reached for the materials.

Secret policy platform of the Subcarpathian Christian Democracy—developed at the office of Grzegorz Gerwal-Punicki

From Subcarpathia to outer space

In one respect, Subcarpathia does not fit the stereotype of a peripheral, poorly urbanized, agricultural region, one of the thirty poorest in the European Union: 90 percent of all production for the Polish aviation industry comes from the Subcarpathian Voivodship. In the previous decade, the region also recorded the highest increase in Poland in the percentage of people employed in industry. Currently, more than 31 percent of Subcarpathia's residents are working in the sector, the sixth highest figure among all Polish voivodships.[1] Similarly, Subcarpathia has seen the highest increase in the entire country in the share of industry in gross value added (plus 2.7 percent compared to the national figure of 1.4 percent in 2013–2016). Currently, the industry produces 38.2 percent of the voivodship's gross value added as compared to a national average of 33.4 percent.[2] Exports from the voivodship exceed imports by 37 percent.[3] Subcarpathia already in 2017 spent more than the national average on research and development (0.86 percent of GDP, compared to the Polish average of 0.67 percent).[4] While these data do not allow us to talk of a "Polish Bavaria" just yet, this slogan, which has been used for many years with no major consequences by the right-wing groups in the Subcarpathia region, has real foundations.

Reindustrialization has been fashionable across Europe for more than a decade, and this has little to do with Christian Democracy, specifically. The Subcarpathian Christian Democracy should base the voivodship's development strategy on reindustrialization for several reasons, including ideological ones. First, it would allow the construction of a new image of the region as one that combines tradition with modernity, along the lines of the Bavarian *Laptop und Lederhosen* concept, which is particularly important for Christian Democracy voters. It removes the odium of backwardness and enables people to hope for prosperity, but without giving up their current lifestyle. Thanks to the development of information technologies and flexible working, today it is no longer necessary to emigrate to a faraway center, or even regularly commute long distances, to work in industry.

Second, the Polish People's Party, without which the Christian Democrats would not have a majority in the Sejmik, will only join a coalition if they have free rein to support agriculture in the region. The party's electoral base will be stable if poor farm owners, who are only farmers because they are receiving subsidies to maintain the agricultural culture, sell their land to the real, wealthier farmers who vote for the People's Party. And they will sell their land if they find well-paid work in a sector other than agriculture. However, the tools used thus far to create new jobs in rural areas outside of agriculture—tools based solely on local resources—have highlighted a classic case of the Münchhausen trilemma. It turns out that it is crucial for peripheral communities to receive an external injection of resources. And the Subcarpathian Christian Democrats have a plan for how to obtain this vital injection.

Since Aviation Valley—the group of companies from the aviation industry—was established quite spontaneously and is operating successfully in Subcarpathia, the cluster cooperation mechanism should be expanded. This is already happening on a modest scale—more than forty companies from across the voivodship, mainly in the electromechanical sector, are operating as subcontractors for the major aviation firms. These companies need not be large or very technologically advanced, nor must they be located in the immediate vicinity of Aviation Valley. They may also operate in other industries, but remaining in the supply chain of large aviation companies gives them the stability that allows them to invest in development. The participation of public authorities in supporting this cooperation is also of great importance. The regional authorities might not only perform information and coordination roles but also take on part of the costs of creating new jobs or training employees.

However, the Subcarpathian Christian Democrats are proposing something beyond the use of active labor market tools. The *PL_UA in the Space of the Future* program envisages the allocation of funds for the post-war reconstruction of Ukraine to create a cross-border Polish–Ukrainian space industry cluster. Given that the Polish space industry is in its infancy, but is almost entirely located in Subcarpathia, it seems natural to obtain Ukrainian support in this area. In the Soviet division of labor, Ukraine played a key role in the research and development of space technologies, and many centers have managed to continue working in this field. For example, the space cluster in Ternopil was developing quite well until the outbreak of the war. When it comes to such a globalized industry, spatial peripherality is of secondary importance as long as it is compensated for by the quality of the personnel, which post-war Ukraine will be eager to retain. Nevertheless, space industry companies obviously prefer to locate expensive production infrastructure in a country that is considered more stable. The natural solution is therefore a collaborative effort between Ukrainian scientists and engineers, and local government officials from Subcarpathia, focused on attracting investors from the space industry with the support of European and American funds for the reconstruction of Ukraine.

For the Subcarpathian Christian Democrats, this project will be of key political significance. It will clearly demonstrate how the Christian Democrats differ from other right-wing parties in ideological and practical terms. The success of the Polish–Ukrainian space cluster will show the absurdity of far-right slogans such as "Stop the Ukrainization of Poland!"—which are, fortunately, currently on the margins of public debate, but which have great potential, according to many experts, to explode in the event of a crisis or a further decline in the standard of living in Poland. Put simply, within the Subcarpathian Christian Democrats' proposal, this so-called Ukrainization means tangible benefits for voters from small towns and villages, who constitute the main electorate of both the Christian Democrats and PiS. Thanks to investments from the space industry, they will be able to find well-paid jobs without having to migrate or commute long distances.

Subcarpathia on the move

The biggest infrastructural obstacle to the implementation of the Subcarpathia reindustrialization project is the low quality of the transport network in the voivodship. While good roads or rail are no guarantee of development, without the ability to efficiently move people and goods, we can hardly expect any investment. It is no coincidence that both Aviation Valley and the voivodship's undisputed growth pole—the Rzeszów Metropolitan Area—are located in the immediate vicinity of the European transport corridor (TEN-T) connecting Dresden with Kyiv. To the north and south of the A4 freeway and railway line 91, the polycentric settlement network of Subcarpathia (many medium and small towns, a dispersed rural settlement pattern) is poorly served by the existing system of roads and railway lines. Even the completion of the S19 expressway will not change the transport exclusion of a large part of the voivodship, especially in the east.

The Subcarpathian Christian Democrats recognize that the most important way to eliminate this exclusion is to reorganize public transport. Beyond the S19, quick improvement of the road infrastructure is unpredictable; therefore, public transport will allow for better use of the existing roads. Indeed, the residents of

Subcarpathia are fighting against transport exclusion on their own—more than 73 percent of households have a passenger car (the highest percentage in Poland),[5] but this coping mechanism is largely responsible for the low usage of human capital. In the Subcarpathian Voivodship, only 224 out of 1,000 people are working (compared to the Polish average of 259),[6] and the percentage of people out of work and not seeking work is one of the highest in the country. The "woman as homemaker" family model certainly has an impact on these indicators, but the prospect of having to own two cars to get to work (and take the kids to school) is no less important.

The new competences of the provincial government will allow the board dominated by the Subcarpathian Christian Democrats to quickly adopt a unified model of public transport for the voivodship. Based on an algorithm prepared by specialists from the Rzeszów University of Technology, which takes into account the number of inhabitants and previous passenger flows as well as the distance from the place of provision of public services, the Voivodship Board should set a standard frequency of coordinated journeys for all towns (routes) in the voivodship. Next, the provincial government should announce a tender for operators to participate in a unified public transport system, with a single tariff and a common timetable. There should be no major problem with selecting operators in cities and towns, or on intercity routes. The rates and scale of the project proposed by the Board should attract not only municipal transport companies but also European players, such as Arriva. However, in sparsely populated areas, there may be few or no responses to the tender. In this case, the provincial government must lower the set standard and increase the rate per kilometer.

Another key project is the Subcarpathian Regional Railway. In its previous term of office, the provincial government adopted an ambitious plan to invest in rail transport; however, with the sector in the thrall of the major rail companies, the plan failed to get off the ground. The constitutional reform of 2023, and in particular the transfer of a minority stake in the Polish State Railways company to the voivodships, have made it possible to put railway lines that are not of national significance in voivodship ownership, for the benefit of the local communities.

The Christian Democrats have two options here. In the most ambitious scenario, we take over all possible railway routes and create a regional railway network. The downside of this option is the enormous investment required and the potential unexpected costs of creating the road part of a unified public transport system. Alternatively, Subcarpathia can take over only lines 108 (from Jasło to Krościenko) and 107 (from Zagórz to Łupków), which will ensure transportation links in the south of the voivodship, where transport exclusion is at its worst (with the added prospect of servicing tourist traffic in the Bieszczady Mountains). These lines can be included in the unified public transport system and treated as a testing ground for the development of multimodal transport within the voivodship.

Schools and a regional university

In the social sphere, the greatest threat to the reindustrialization project, and a significant cause of poverty in the Subcarpathian Voivodship, is the competence gap—the mismatch between the skills of job seekers and the expectations of employers. If the Christian Democrats are serious about reindustrialization, based primarily on the aviation, space, and electromechanical industries, it is necessary to improve the quality of human capital. The 2023 constitutional reform gave the provincial government a completely new tool: the authority to act as a founding body of public universities. There are five vocational schools in the Subcarpathian Voivodship—as many as in the Greater Poland region in the Western part of the country, which is almost twice as populous and wealthy. Despite the large number of higher education facilities (18), the figure of 220 students per 10,000 residents puts Subcarpathia in twelfth place among Poland's sixteen regions (with the national average being 320 per 10,000), and the percentage of people with higher education is also significantly lower than the Polish average (21.9 percent compared to 23.1 percent).[7] If we also take into account the fact that our voivodship has the fourth highest percentage in Poland of young people who are not working or studying,[8] it becomes clear that without improving the state of education, greater wealth for the inhabitants of Subcarpathia will be hard to obtain.

An administration dominated by the Subcarpathian Christian Democrats can conduct a two-fold reform to tackle this issue. On the one hand, we will implement a multidimensional program aimed at involving parents in responsibility for schools. We will rely on the well-known convention of engaging non-public entities (parents' associations, religious associations) in the running of public schools. The Subcarpathian Christian Democrats are of the view that schooling must be based on the principle of subsidiarity and personalism, and the dignity of every human being includes the right to a good education. Having public schools run by non-public entities will also help defuse the conflict over religious education in schools. Regardless of the growing central pressure to remove religion from schools, parents who really care about this subject being taught in their children's school will be able to take over the governance of the school by way of an association, or request a religious order or parish to step in. The provincial government should support such initiatives with additional funds, in the mechanism of one złoty from the voivodship toward investments for each złoty above the subsidy invested in running the school by the governing body. On the other hand, we should create a comprehensive system of infrastructural support for non-public schools.

It is to be expected that the program will be enthusiastically received both by local governments, which are eager to no longer run expensive schools, especially in peripheral locations, and by parents in many towns, who will see their real influence on their school, plus the material benefits resulting from the support programs. In cities, meanwhile, many non-public schools, especially religious schools, might decide to switch to public status and thus waive tuition fees.

Quality-centered activities should focus primarily on pedagogical support for teachers, and on changing the image of education. Under Christian Democrat rule, education should become a common cause for parents and teachers. The reform should bring real benefits, opening up new life opportunities and making education the true pride of Subcarpathia. Educational outcomes should be measured through benchmarking, and additional support should be provided to schools that are evidently weaker.

In our quality-centered activities, we should also use the second pillar of the education system reform—the Subcarpathian Regional University, which would be created by merging public universities, and closely linked to the development goals of Subcarpathia. The Voivodship Board should invite all higher education facilities to participate in creating the Regional University. The University of Rzeszów, fearing for its autonomy, might be expected to reject this offer. The provincial authorities, which took on the role of supervisory body for the University of Rzeszów as a result of the constitutional reform, should respect any such decision, thus emphasizing their attachment to the value of university autonomy. The success of the Regional University and the additional funds allocated to its operation may, over time, lead the University of Rzeszów to change its position.

There is a greater chance that the Regional University will be joined by the Rzeszów University of Technology, and even the private University of Information Technology and Management. In this way, a multi-campus facility will be established, with the capacity to educate tens of thousands of students and to plan its teaching portfolio better than the small entities of today. Above all, however, it will cooperate closely with the provincial government in implementing the regional development strategy. This might take one or more of the following forms: joint research and application projects, especially for the needs of the aviation and space industry; dual studies; analytical and expert support for the provincial office (regional think tank); implementation of quality-centered projects supporting education.

Within the latter dimension, the Regional University, together with representatives of industry, should plan a comprehensive reform of vocational education. Subcarpathia is particularly neglected in this respect. Not only are the current vocational and technical schools offering an education in professions for which there is little demand in the labor market, but they are also providing poor preparation for these professions. The Christian Democrats should adopt ambitious goals here: to double the number of vocational school alumni who continue their education as future technicians and engineers in the aviation and space industries.

The educational reforms will not be cheap. In order to achieve these goals and attract highly qualified staff to the schools, we propose the introduction of an education tax of 1 percent on all income of companies in the voivodship, with a concurrent tax relief available for companies that employ graduates of Subcarpathia's higher education facilities. Since the subject of the additional levy might be controversial, we suggest calling an e-referendum.

One size fits no one

These ambitious, education-focused activities should become part of the broader plan of the Subcarpathian Christian Democrats to improve the quality of public services, and thus the quality of life, in our voivodship. The figures show quite dramatically that in this respect, Subcarpathia is actually two separate worlds. Let's take the simplest indicator of social development—infant mortality—with the average for Poland being 3.9 per 1,000 live births. The figure for the entire Subcarpathian Voivodship is 4.1 per mille, but for Krosno County it is as much as 12 (similar to Mexico); in Lesko County it is 10.6, in Tarnobrzeg County 9.9 (the same as in Armenia and Kazakhstan), and in Rzeszów 2.9 per mille.[9] In Poland, an average of 894 children per 1,000 preschool-age children attend kindergarten; in Subcarpathia, the average is 860, but in Brzozów County the figure is only 755 and in Nisko County 775, while in Rzeszów it is 1,006.[10] Given such differences in the quality of life and the quality of public services, attractive jobs often play only a secondary role in a person's decision to leave their place of birth. The Christian Democrats must be ready to support improvements in the quality of public services, but in the Subcarpathian context in particular, resource limitations must be taken into account. For example, it is not possible to maintain a full-size hospital in every county. This is not only a question of costs. Subcarpathia is one of the lowest ranking voivodships in Poland for the number of practicing physicians per inhabitant.[11] For this reason, making decisions from Rzeszów about the preferences of residents of the voivodship's peripheries, and about the things that really determine the quality of life in districts such as Lesko, Ustrzyki, or Sanok, not only goes against the principle of subsidiarity, which is important for the Christian Democrats, but is also ineffective.

Therefore, this part of the Christian Democrat Party's strategy must be linked to a reform of local administration, which has become possible thanks to the constitutional reform of 2023. In accordance with the newly amended constitution, the municipality must remain the basic unit of territorial local government and thus of local administration. However, the remaining organization of administration and the provision of public services is up to our voivodship to decide. Specifically, the constitutional reform gave the opportunity to forgo the county level of subnational government. The Christian Democrats should encourage the residents of Subcarpathia to consider this option, which, in any case, will have to be accepted by citizens in an e-referendum. However, the elimination of anything is not generally a catchy political slogan. Thus, instead of emphasizing a narrative of doing without the counties, the Christian Democrats should focus on showing residents alternatives to the current, forcibly unified model of territorial governance, which causes particular problems in internally diversified regions like Subcarpathia. Voters will intuitively understand that "one size fits none."

As an alternative, the Christian Democrats can propose two models. In the first, the largest municipalities will function as sub-regional centers that will provide public services to neighboring municipalities within a provincial legal framework enacted by the Sejmik and the newly created regional Senate. The second model is based on the creation of public service zones—quasi-counties of sorts—not as a separate level of administration, but as a communal association operating on the basis of a contract between municipalities.

Most importantly, the two models could coexist after the elimination of counties. Residents could decide on joining the public service zone by way of a local e-referendum. In the event that an application to join a communal association is rejected, the provincial authorities would decide to create a sub-regional center in the nearest large municipality, allocating additional funds so that the center could carry out tasks for its neighboring municipalities.

An administration organized in this way can take over the assets and competences of the particularly weak counties in our region, as well as the so-called special administrations—central agencies (such as the mighty Agency for Restructuring and Modernisation of Agriculture or National Agriculture Support Centre) with territorial structures parallel to, and independent of, the general system of subnational governments. Widely perceived as a back-door way to roll back the 1990 and 1999 decentralization reforms, most of those special administrations were folded back to the jurisdiction of the self-governed municipalities, counties, and voivodships by the 2023 constitutional reform.

The elimination of counties will not eradicate competition for the resources of medium-sized towns in Subcarpathia, but financial incentives from the Voivodship Board should enforce cooperation between centers that spontaneously gravitate toward each other, allowing for simple savings and the accumulation of public funds. The fastest-growing counties in the central part of the voivodship could create the Rzeszów Metropolitan Area, from Dębica to Łańcut, within which the municipalities would coordinate the provision of public services. We should also support the Jarosław–Przeworsk and Sanok–Lesko (+Zagórz) duopolies, which have long been postulated by experts, with the inclusion of the surrounding rural municipalities. In the remaining area of the voivodship, the public service zones or the operating areas of subregional centers are unlikely to differ significantly from the current territorial structure of the counties. The main advantage of the two proposed models is the strengthening of the municipalities, as opposed to maintaining weak counties, which is in line with the Christian Democrat principle of subsidiarity. Urban municipalities will be strengthened with funds to meet the needs of neighboring municipalities. Regional laws will protect the interests of rural municipalities, both in the contract model (subregional centers) and in the communal association model (service zones).

In all cases, the urban municipalities that have lost their socio-economic functions will have the opportunity to increase their demographic potential and obtain public funds to improve the quality of services provided to residents. The newly established administrative units will also become partners of the Voivodship Board in development policy, not only as recipients of support but also as creators of solutions that are in line with the voivodship strategy, and at the same time rooted in subregional specificity. This makes sense especially in connection with the concept of the Voivodship Senate, adopted in the 2023 constitutional reform, as a body composed of all mayors from our region.

The new organization of local administration will also facilitate cooperation with neighboring voivodships. Based on an agreement with Świętokrzyskie Voivodship, a quadricity will be established—an association of municipalities closely coordinating development and public services in the area of Tarnobrzeg, Stalowa Wola, Nisko, and Sandomierz, and their adjacent rural municipalities. This will create an area with more than 150,000 inhabitants and diverse resources: from competitive industry, through tourist-attracting heritage, to universities and recreational areas. From the perspective of both voivodships, the peripheral quadricity will benefit from the opportunity to create its own growth pole.

Window on the world

The Christian Democrats should also combine an attachment to traditional Polish values with an emphasis on European roots. In recent years, the anti-European right has created a caricatured vision of a "leftist Europe," citing examples mainly from the continent's largest metropolises. In reality, however, most European regions are decidedly conservative, both culturally and politically. The Subcarpathian Christian Democrats will therefore easily find partners to implement their vision of a Europe of Small Homelands (voivodships), involving cooperation between neighboring provinces in Poland, as well as with regions in different countries.

In particular, Subcarpathia should become the driving force behind the coalition of voivodships working to open up the eastern border. The border crossing in Medyka is the largest road crossing in the European Union; given that centralized Poland has long struggled to attend to the flow of people there, the post-war reconstruction of Ukraine and the prospect of its accession to the EU will probably only worsen the situation. The government in Warsaw has declared that cooperation with Ukraine is its priority, but in practice, investment in a more efficient (yet secure) border is relegated to the bottom of the list.

Subcarpathia should therefore enter into Close Cooperation with the Lublin Voivodship, as envisaged under the constitutional reform, in order to unblock road border crossings with Ukraine. In all likelihood, the neighboring region will also be governed by the Right. The priority should be to create a new crossing in the TEN-T corridor near the existing crossing in Krakowiec/Krakovets, but this is conditional on the improvement of the road infrastructure on the Ukrainian side.

The newly opened Subcarpathia liaison office in Kyiv should coordinate lobbying for the priority treatment of the Lviv–state border highway in the plan for the post-war reconstruction of Ukraine. In Warsaw, meanwhile, it is necessary to lobby for the modernization of the Warsaw–Hrebenne railway line (Lublin Voivodship), which is the shortest rail connection between Lviv and central Poland and could relieve the pressure of crossings in Subcarpathia.

The Subcarpathian Christian Democrats should also strive to sign a friendship and cooperation agreement between the Subcarpathian Voivodship and the Lviv Oblast. The agreement should elevate the role of entrepreneurs from Subcarpathia, who, thanks to their good knowledge of their Ukrainian neighbors and their needs, can lead the way for other voivodships, and even other EU countries. Taking advantage of the special privileges that companies from Subcarpathia can receive, enterprises from all over Europe will register their companies here as "Subcarpathian companies" in order to participate in the reconstruction of war-devastated Ukraine.

These activities of the provincial government will only be possible with greater institutionalization of the transnational cooperation of regional authorities. Of course, the 2023 constitutional reform left foreign policy in the hands of the central government, but the strengthened regional governments understand that for development funds the game is played on a European scale. Instead of knocking on the doors of the Warsaw ministries, they must invest in professional lobbying in Brussels. The regional government of Subcarpathia has had positive experiences in this area. Subcarpathia should also open liaison offices not only in Kyiv, but also in Lviv. This might draw criticism from the hardline faction of PiS that did not support the 2023 constitutional reform. We might expect them to call the assertive international cooperation policy of our voivodship yet another sign that the reforms amounted to a "George Soros-sponsored dissolution of the Polish state." It may, however, be awkward for even the most avid right-wing centralists to blame our staunchly conservative region for actively promoting the interests of its residents.

The next priority should be to sign a similar cooperation agreement with the Prešov region in northeastern Slovakia. It would be important to obtain additional funds to support road and rail infrastructure connecting the two regions (including the Subcarpathian Regional Railway) and for the development of enterprises, including joint international projects increasing investments in third countries, especially in Ukraine.

A beautiful dream

"Grzegorz," whispered Paweł into his smartphone. "Are you asleep?"

"Yes," replied Grzegorz with a wheeze.

"Joanna and I wanted to call ..." continued Paweł.

"I said I'm asleep!"

"We've been reading the materials, and we wanted to say ... we're on board. It looks pretty good. And as far as we're concerned, for the Subcarpathian Christian Democrats, well ... we should get going right away. Today, if possible. We'll start getting people together. We'll start planning."

"You're right, Paweł," said Grzegorz, fully awake now. "There's no time to waste."

"So, I'll call Jarecki from the Polish People's Party, Gost from Poland 2050, and the disillusioned Civic Platformers," suggested Paweł.

"Please do," said Grzegorz. "We'll start tomorrow. Now let me sleep."

Grzegorz hung up. As he drifted off, his mind launched into a dream of Donald Tusk and Jarosław Kaczyński shouting at each other. At first, he felt he was sitting right next to them, and that each rhetorical strike was pounding his bald head with redoubled force. But gradually, the sound of their yelling faded further and further into the distance, giving way to the gentle hum of the express train from Rzeszów to Lviv. A train built in the second term of the regional government of the Subcarpathian Christian Democrats.

Notes

1. *Przegląd regionalny. Województwo podkarpackie 2022* (Urząd Marszałkowski Województwa Podkarpackiego, 2023), 159.
2. *Raport o stanie Województwa Podkarpackiego za 2023 r.* (Zarząd Województwa Podkarpackiego, 2024), 13–14.
3. *Handel zagraniczny oraz bezpośrednie inwestycje zagraniczne w województwie podkarpackim w latach 2013–2019. Raport końcowy* (Urząd Marszałkowski Województwa Podkarpackiego, 2021), 16.
4. Elżbieta Wojnicka-Sycz, "Theory-Based Evaluation Criteria for Regional Smart Specializations and Their Application in the Podkarpackie Woivodeship in Poland," *Regional Studies* 54, no. 9: 1–14(2020).
5. Krystyna Siwiak, *Sytuacja gospodarstw domowych w 2017 r. w świetle wyników badania budżetów gospodarstw domowych* (Główny Urząd Statystyczny, 2017), 14.
6. Ziomek-Niedzielska et al., *Raport o sytuacji społeczno-gospodarczej województwa podkarpackiego 2023* (Urząd Statystyczny w Rzeszowie, 2023), 80.
7. *Strategia rozwoju województwa - Podkarpackie 2030* (Samorząd Województwa Podkarpackiego, 2020), 23.
8. Dawid Giemza, "Generacja NEET na rynku pracy w Polsce—ujęcie regionalne," in *Rynki, sektory i modele biznesowe w dobie globalizacji,* ed. Natalia Iwaszczuk and Krzysztof Posłuszny (Wydawnictwa AGH, 2021), 120.
9. The data is for 2021; retrieved from Local Data Bank hosted by Statistics Poland. Available at https://bdl.stat.gov.pl/bdl/start (last consulted Dec. 22, 2024).
10. The data is for 2022; retrieved from Local Data Bank hosted by Statistics Poland. Available at https://bdl.stat.gov.pl/bdl/start (last consulted Dec. 22, 2024).
11. *Strategia rozwoju województwa—Podkarpackie 2030* (Samorząd Województwa Podkarpackiego, 2020), 31.

12
The Dream Classical Liberal Voivodship

Leszek Stypułkowski, Marek Tatała, and Marcin Zieliński
Fictionalized by Piotr Siemion

Welcome to Poznań

She landed at Poznań Airport right on time, flying in on the 11:00am Frankfurt plane. Her name was Professor Jennifer Wu and she was a star libertarian icon as well as a faculty member at the University of Chicago, a place well known as a nexus of free-market ideas. People often referred to her as the "anti-Mazzucatista," a reference to Mariana Mazzucato, an equally famous left-wing economist from University College London. Incidentally, Mazzucato had also paid a visit to Poland, speaking in 2017 at the Congress of Central-European Innovators organized by the Polish conservative government in power at that time.[1]

This is where the analogies end, however. Professor Mazzucato appeared at a congress lavishly funded by several companies controlled by the government. After the 2023 constitutional reform, the majority of these enterprises were handed down to provincial governments. The Italian-born economist's Polish audience members were right-wing officials whose key idea was to centralize things as much as possible. By contrast, Professor Wu's appearance today was sponsored not by the Polish authorities but rather by a well-known American foundation widely recognized for supporting economic freedom. Last but certainly not least, the US academic was coming to Poznań primarily to listen to local reformers, as well as to collect materials for her new book on the increasingly interesting saga of free-market reforms in the Wielkopolska (or, in English: Greater Poland) region.

Professor Wu was welcomed by a man whose accomplishments had, by then, become the subject of many news stories in the online editions of the *Wall Street Journal* or *Barron's*—the man who, almost single-handedly, managed to turn Greater Poland into an island of liberal values in the middle of the over-regulated, statist Europe. The man in question was a politician frequenting the front pages of Polish web portals, leader of a small liberal party associated with the Civic Platform. As a former MP from Poznań, he had, of course, a first and a last name, but these days everyone preferred to call him the Voivode. In fact, that's precisely who he was at the time: the newly elected head of the regional government. People knew him as a down-to-earth, practical person, who was faithful to the traditions

Leszek Stypułkowski, Marek Tatała, and Marcin Zieliński, *The Dream Classical Liberal Voivodship* In: *Let's Agree on Poland*. Edited by: Maciej Kisilowski and Anna Wojciuk, Oxford University Press.
 DOI: 10.1093/oso/9780198979562.003.0015

of proverbially prudent Poznań residents. While typically always busy, today he was determined to give as much of his time as possible to the American celebrity professor during her brief stay. His reasons had mainly to do with seeking even more foreign investment for his region. A potential bestseller by Wu, he reasoned, would amount to a huge, free-of-charge promotional coup for Greater Poland.

"So this is your kingdom?" were Professor Wu's first words to the Voivode. His reply, partly because they were being watched by a row of cameras, was curt:

"A kingdom, Jennifer? Far from it. You've come to a democratic, self-governing land of free people! But, hey, we're no utopia out of Robert Nozick's pages. We're real. I'll show you how it all works down here. But first, let's walk out and grab some food together!"

"Walk out or fly out?" the professor queried. "Someone told me the organizers rent us a chopper. Is that true?"

The Voivode shot a startled look at his assistant, who only whispered: "The Americans insisted ..."

"I want it in all the local media that not a penny for this came from the public purse!" the Voivode murmured angrily, before immediately switching to a professional smile. "We're all pretty impressed with the working conditions of American academics," he remarked to Wu. "A helicopter! But things are not so bad in our country either!"

A helicopter view

A black van took them up to the hangar where a small helicopter with the large and rather incongruous sign "Scenic flights 1,200 złoty only" was waiting. The pilot handed out massive headphones to everyone so that his passengers could talk freely over the roar of the turbines. Even the Voivode had to admit that the view of the surroundings from the air was impressive: the A2 highway stretching up to the suburban horizon, through the land dotted with factories and warehouses. In affluent neighborhoods, thousands of photovoltaic panels mirrored the sun's glow. To their left, they could see the big city, with its endless rows of tenements in the orderly, European fashion. They were flying south, however, toward the forests.

"I can see lots of farmland all around here—it's not just industrial facilities," Wu's assistant observed, pressing his nose against the window. "But hey, does that mean you have to deal with a strong farmer lobby down here?"

"Oh, the farmers! It was our first victory!" Even over the din in the headphones, the pride in the politician's voice was unmistakable. "Picture this, here we go winning the provincial elections by a landslide, we get an absolute majority in the Sejmik. Remember, we'd promised everyone instant modernization, vast economic freedoms. Great. But once we won, everybody started bugging us for the specifics, the results! Since the next elections were to be held in five years, you'd think we'd have plenty of time, but no, we had to act immediately. 'We', meaning our coalition, Civic Platform Party together with the Nowoczesna, or 'Modern,' liberal party. But maybe we should now seek a broader, more conservative coalition, perhaps with the agrarian, pro-European, Polish People's Party? No way, because the conservatives would immediately set the brakes on the plan we had in mind. That's right, we had our special action plan ready!"

"We have heard about your plan even back across the Atlantic," Wu noted. "But isn't it a normal thing wherever you go that the people, your ordinary simple people, what they detest the most is when the government and the whole bureaucracy keeps on wasting their efforts? For this very reason the government, any government, must operate like a regular, efficient business, using transparent accounting policies, and refraining from meddling in regular folks' affairs. Then, instantly, everything becomes easy!"

"Oh, well. Our European political tradition is much different," the woman who was introduced as the deputy voivode remarked. She blushed when saying this, but continued gamely: "Over here, all things tended to be decided centrally, in the capital. And if not in the national capital, then in Brussels. Up until the recent constitutional reform, even in our local, municipal Poland, each provincial leader had a centrally appointed supervisor. But today, with the reforms finally in place, we have no more overseers from Warsaw, just our democratically elected leader, the voivode. How could we let outsiders decide our issues for us?"

"Sorry for asking, but have you ever wished you'd continued your professional career in the capital instead of coming here?"

"To be honest with you, not one bit. In Warsaw, well, I probably might have become a cabinet minister. But please remember: what brought us over here was the opportunity to accomplish our own, independent vision. In short, we wanted to make a huge splash here in Poznań. Just to show everyone in our region that a modern, liberal Poland is not a pipe dream, but reality in the making."

"And you, have you also been drawn to your backyard?" Professor Wu's assistant asked one of the Voivode's deputies, responsible for the all-important competitiveness policy, as well as for financial and economic affairs, agriculture, and science.

In her fluent English, the deputy explained that she did not hail from local politics. Instead, the reason for her appointment was her stellar achievements as a leading expert on economic freedom at a prominent Warsaw think tank.

"My deputy's decision is a great example of our region's way of thinking," the Voivode interjected. "Very pragmatic. Aldona comes from Pruszcz Gdański, a small place in the north, and she started out in Warsaw. But Greater Poland is the only place where she's finally able to tackle the really important stuff. These days she's busy removing barriers to the creativity, the drive, and the industriousness of our citizens, our entrepreneurs, farmers. And speaking of agriculture ..."

Their helicopter was hovering in a wide half-circle over a large livestock farm. The corrugated sheet metal of the feed silos gleamed in the midday sun.

"You were expecting mud hovels and horse-drawn carts, eh?" Aldona nudged Professor Wu's shoulder. "Look, here's another big farm. And that was precisely the issue. The region's farmers were freeriding on our green Poznań tram (yes, we paint our city trams green!). Quite simply, they used to pay no income taxes!"

At this point, the deputy voivode summarized briefly how, within two weeks of taking up office, in a memorable speech that was broadcast live by the local media, she announced the onset of a project that was downright revolutionary. From now on, she declared, all individuals and companies in Greater Poland, without exception, would become subject to a uniform flat tax of 15 percent. Personal, corporate—the same rate would apply to all. No progression, no higher brackets. The rate was equal to the minimum corporate tax rate mandated by the European Union.

"I'm sure they must have been grateful to you, the farmers," the legal advisor from the US foundation financing the visit remarked snidely. Until now, the man had kept rather silent.

"They were not entirely happy, that's true. But some people always have to take a loss," the Voivode replied with a smirk. "Still, our experts' opinions were very clear: here in Greater Poland, our taxes could never be both low and fair if such a vast group of local entrepreneurs remained exempt, for no good reason, from virtually any taxation. Yes, I'm talking about our farmers. Throughout Poland, farmers did not pay income tax. Instead, they pay a ridiculously small agricultural tax, less than 50 dollars, roughly speaking, per year per one hectare of their land."

"In other words, by introducing the flat tax rate for all, you managed to alienate thousands of voters? More than 100,000 people? Along with their families? A very bold move. I'd expect them to gather in front of your office with torches and pitchforks," the lawyer commented, though he managed to keep a straight face.

"The Voivodship Board's PR department was very much against our plan. In fact, they handed us a long list of reasons why it was a bad decision. They even tried to talk us into delaying our tax reform, giving up on it, practically speaking. They told us we were headed for disaster, a defeat on the scale of Stalingrad," was the Voivode's reply. "So I turned back to my team and asked them, just to make sure: are we going ahead with the plan? And my deputy here, you know what her answer was?"

"If we want to stay scared of everything, we should have kept our safe Warsaw jobs, that's what I said," the politician recalled. "In the end, we decided to hold a referendum. A digital one. Since the constitutional reform, they are conducted centrally, by the National Electoral Commission. Its portal, www.demokracja.gov.pl, enables you to vote and gives you several options, using the single transferable vote system. But we proposed just a single question: Do you want all residents and businesses in the Greater Poland, including farmers, to pay a flat, universal income tax of 15 percent?"

Lowering taxes

They were about to land. The helicopter was now hovering over the front lawn, the rotor blades snatching up the dust and twigs from the ground. They alighted in front of the manor, a sizeable building in the classical style. When the small tornado died down and the engines fell silent, the Voivode and his team led the American guests toward the entrance.

In the large living room, a round table was waiting for them, loaded with local and foreign delicacies. "Must be the work of those Americans, again," the Voivode observed silently. He was notorious for his frugality and his avoidance of glitz. In fact, he was still living in a rather mediocre apartment in one of Poznań's old apartment buildings. Some of the dishes were indeed transatlantic: bacon, fried potatoes, beans, barbecue sauce. But the platters were also shining white with *gzik* cottage cheese, blushing with Greater Polish ham, and loaded high with steamed *pampuchy* dumplings. Once the cutlery began clinking in earnest, the Voivode made the signal to start the presentation.

"First, let me give you the basic facts. Our region has a population of 3.5 million people. For Europe, that's sizable. We're very close to Berlin and generally to the West. There's a tradition here of private ownership and of good work ethic. It is indeed so deep that, in the eastern part of the country, they compare us to the Germans. In a word, we're a good place to launch the mission my team and I had in our collective mind. The devil, of course, is in the details. It is one thing to promise radical cuts in income taxes, but, as the provincial leaders, we were bound to balance revenues with expenditures. As liberal as we are, we're still constrained by general budgetary considerations. And by the national rules dictated by the laws implementing the December 2023 constitutional reform. Our local and regional tax revenues, including the income taxes, would not be sufficient to fund all of our public tasks. That is why the governments of all sixteen provinces, including ours, continue to receive additional support from the National Cohesion Fund. Now, to prevent moral hazard, national laws restrict each provincial government from cutting regional taxes and then reaching out to Warsaw for a handout. We can change our taxes. But if we wanted to shrink our overall tax revenues, relative to multi-year projections, it would need to be approved by the new Polish Senate."

"That should not be a problem, right?" Professor Wu smiled. "You shake a few hands, whisper a word to this or that Senator, and presto, got your approval to cut, cut, cut!"

"Well, not exactly!"—the Voivode smiled a little at this highly simplified vision of how the new Polish constitutional system operated—"Besides, the problem lies elsewhere. You see, in the past few years, things had been very tough for the provinces, right until the recent reforms. Locally, those were very lean times. Plus, unpopular as it may sound in this company, we had no intention of cutting the public expenditures down to the bone."

"So, in the end, you had no appetite for such bold decisions?" Professor Wu asked pointedly, perhaps mainly out of a habit of debating these kinds of issues with her college students. "But if so, what kind of libertarians are you?"

"We're classical liberals. We are not libertarians. There is a difference between the two," replied the Voivode and pushed a button on the remote control. On the screen popped up bars of data and diagrams. "If we deny all public services to the people, the voters will no longer trust us, and the investors will get scared. Obviously," he continued, "we should cut down on various absurd financial burdens. If we manage to secure approval from the Sejmik, our local assembly, we will further reduce the taxation on labor, abolish the dog-owning tax, the street vendor tax, sugar taxes, taxes on advertising, all local and tourist fees ..."

"Hold on! What are all these additional taxes?" The American lawyer looked astounded. "That's ridiculous!"

"The list is much longer, but we are talking just about taking the first step. Take a look at this slide, and the next one ..." Aldona, the deputy voivode interrupted, snatching the remote control. "First, we ran some analyses. Our motto was 'Help Us Make 2x15 Our Reality.' I enlisted a dozen or so very prominent economic experts from Poland and abroad to aid our my office. The idea was to make the tax rate reduction neutral for the provincial revenues, and, in parallel, to make the region kiss goodbye to the pathologies of the Polish tax system."

"What about your voters? What did they think of all this? Aren't you expecting a huge backlash from them, come the next elections?"

"With the voters, well, it depends. In any case, we have a few years left ahead of us until the next election," Aldona said. "Let me also add that, for me as the person in charge of the region's competitiveness, my mission was defined in very clear terms. They often portray us, economic liberals, as mindless tax cutters. Yes, we want rates to be as low as possible. But it is even more important for us that taxes are simple and transparent. They should be fair and they must not hinder economic development. It follows that all tax cuts must be followed by sensible reductions in spending. After all, we don't want to go too far into debt. Remember, this is our frugal Greater Poland. Over here, we put a premium on prudence, on thrift. We evaluate things very carefully. This is a great local tradition, which helps us persuade the people."

"Persuade the people to accept what, specifically?"

"One second," Aldona said with a new spark in her eyes. She could quote fiscal regulations with such passion as if she were reciting romantic poetry. "Suppose we're expected to prepare a balanced voivodship budget. Any new expenditures must be matched with revenues. When implementing the budget, we may encounter a deficit of no more than 3 percent, but it must be paid back with a matching surplus in in subsequent years. The only exceptions apply when the region is hit by an emergency, say, a massive flood. Then, the fiscal rules can be suspended. However, even in those exceptional cases, our new regional laws still require us to draw back the deficit over the period of a few years.

"But how can you stick to such stringent rules?" Aldona was interrupted at this point by the American scholar. "Have you access to manna from heaven?"

"No manna—rather, privatization," the Voivode replied before Aldona could answer. "We wanted to keep our taxes as low as possible, but at the same time we wanted to ensure the majority of people pay them, rather than having many of them take advantage of the byzantine system of deductions and credits provided for by the previous, national tax laws. And the result we achieved for the whole province was hundreds of millions in new revenues. Nice enough, but still not sufficient. So we add to this the privatization of all sorts of assets. The constitutional reform allotted our province state assets worth almost 4 billion US dollars. Plots of land, housing units, equity in many local enterprises, which added to the very substantial assets already in the hands of our local and regional government. Yet the question close to every liberal's heart is: Who would best manage those assets? The government? Or real owners?" The Voivode posed the question dramatically.

"The answer, to me, seems clear," Wu reflected. "In our country, private property is sacred. However, it's different when some very valuable property is handed to you for free. How can you reassure us that you won't go the Russian way, with all the state assets winding up in the hands of a few oligarchs? Then what? That these assets should be put to work; that they should not be used to support byzantine government projects of dubious social value—that's all out of the question! But, as they say, to sell something fast is to sell it cheap. Once you've disposed of your assets, you no longer have any power over them."

In the silence that ensued, all that could be heard was the hum of the slide projector.

"I'm glad that you caution us this way, Jennifer," the Voivode said, and proceeded to speak at length. "And the reason I'm so glad is that we just happen to have done our homework on this one. Let's remember that in Poland, in the 1990s, privatization took place gradually and in a very deliberate way. Unlike Russia, in Poland the process did not result in the emergence of any strong oligarchy. Now, under no condition would we engage in some wild fire sale of our property either. All profits from our privatization efforts go into the Greater Poland Wealth Fund—the first Polish sovereign wealth fund. Why is this a better solution? Unlike various special-purpose agencies, or funds that, allegedly, aid development, our local wealth fund observes the principles of fair competition among all market players. It never interferes in the markets using its political clout. Such tricks and grandiose 'development' strategies spawned in the minds of politicians usually do more harm than good to the economy, am I right?"

"You can say that again," the American nodded in agreement. "Economic freedom must be free from lobbying, from corruption ..."

It was clear that the economist was getting ready for a longer lecture. Fortunately for the Voivode, she choked on a crumb of St. Martin croissant, another local specialty, and went into a fit of coughing, patted on the back by those around her. The Voivode took advantage of the situation and moved on to the next slide.

"Our wealth fund operates like any other investment fund," he explained. "Its sole purpose is to generate profit for the owners. In this case, for the provincial budget. Aldona, my deputy in charge of economic competition, estimates that such a fund could eventually, long-term, produce an annual net return of about 4 percent, essentially adding close to 700 million dollars per year to our coffers. This money would work to additionally unburden our taxpayers. And, since you mention corruption and inefficiency, let me say this: when hiring its employees, our wealth fund holds competitions open to candidates from all around the world. Since we are strict followers of liberal values, we take much care not to staff the fund with political activists and their family members. We implement transparent recruitment policies and the whole process is supervised at all times by a board that includes important stakeholders from the region, including representatives from the local chambers of commerce. No taxation without representation, right?"

Wu continued to cough. They all moved to the manor's terrace, where steaming cups of coffee were waiting. The blond man, Wu's assistant, leaning closely into Aldona, whispered:

"It all sounds too good, but tell me, in all honesty. How did your voters react to the plan?"

"Very favorably," the deputy voivode answered curtly.

"Give me a break, will you? You enter Poznań with a bang, disrupt millions of local special interests, give the finger to all traditions, play games with the country's central authorities ... How did you manage to survive in the first place?" the American asked, genuinely fascinated by what he'd just heard.

The Poznań road to heaven

Aldona thought for a moment before she replied: "Okay, you want a straight answer, so I'll level with you. Initially, sure, we were facing a lot of negative buzz. 'A MULTINATIONAL TAX HAVEN in the making' pounded the left-wing portal OKO.press. 'Let's do it!' encouraged the Łódź-based liberal magazine *Liberté!* Deep down, though, everyone somehow felt the same way as us. The local people did believe that a radical simplification of the tax system was both possible and necessary. They supported our idea to limit the tax breaks and exemptions, which were often absurd and too muddy to interpret. One example I can give you is the huge deduction for restoring historical buildings, otherwise known as 'Palace+.' Yet, within days we were facing backlash. It's hardly surprising, of course, that our plan to tax the farmers and to privatize everything caused a small political eruption in our region. 'You are turning neighbors into enemies, you give root to family feuds!' a People's Party deputy yelled at us in the Sejmik. And remember, it was the Sejmik that, under our provincial charter, had to approve the referendum question. Even so, we, the Voivodship Board, still got strong support from the mayors who now form our new Voivodship Senate."

"So then you got the green light, I see."

"Not so fast! We were, how shall I put it, well prepared. The Voivodship Board hired the best political communication specialists for the job. With their help, we prepared and launched a large public campaign. The catchphrase was 'A Double Yes to the Flat 15%.' Before the vote took place, our campaign bus visited every town and municipality. I can't tell you how many times we had to take detours to bypass the picketing farmers! It may sound great on paper. The questions like 'Are you in favor of privatizing the bulk of the province's property, and for allocating the proceeds to a special wealth fund that will support public spending on schools, hospitals, culture, roads, and public transportation?' were fabulous but, inevitably, someone will lose out in the course of any such plan."

"But you got your way in the end, I understand?"

"We did. Why? We have managed to show that, in spite of everything, there will be relatively few actual losers. We also revealed to our voters how some people among those taking advantage of the tax breaks were, in fact, not farmers. They were just freeriding on the current, non-transparent tax system. We told you already: the Poznań people know how to count money. They may be risk-averse but they found our calculations accurate. So when we did pose the big referendum question, 'Do you want all residents and businesses in Greater Poland, including farmers, to pay a universal flat-rate income tax?', as many as 65 percent of voters answered in the affirmative. They ran their calculations and found that the new tax rates would be to their advantage."

"And your referendum question on privatization? Same results?"

"No, we fared a little worse on that one. We got 58 percent of the vote in favor. Either way, a significant majority."

"A real success story, huh?"

"Merely the beginning of a long journey," Aldona replied with conviction in her voice. "More coffee, anyone?"

"I'd be happy to, but ...", the American's assistant was peering into the visitors' agenda for the day. "They're about to take us into the city. Too bad: This estate park looks so beautiful."

"The place used to be state-owned. We sold the whole property for a good price," Aldona replied. "Not only that; we negotiated with the new owner that the park should be freely open to visitors from dawn to dusk."

The town hall meeting

The auditorium of the main office building of the voivodship government was getting ready for the official part of Professor Wu's visit, scheduled to begin momentarily. On the stage, two deep armchairs were waiting for the Voivode and his American guest. The stage was decorated with the regional government's new logo: a plump Angel of Entrepreneurship holding a slogan, clearly playing on the "tax haven" smears of the leftist press: 'WE'RE BUILDING OUR GREATER POLISH HEAVEN.' All seats were occupied by the local VIPs: deputy voivodes, mayors, and businesspeople. Amidst their loud applause, Jennifer Wu stepped confidently up to the stage and shouted into the microphone, somewhat theatrically: "Hi, everyone! *Dzhen dobry*, Poznan!"

Applause again. Professor Wu waved it away and, skipping the Polish, announced by way of introduction:

"I have heard that you're doing fantastic things over here, so ... today, I'm not going to try and teach you anything. Why? Because I came here to listen to you! That's why ...Thank you, thank you ... And that's why, it is to you, the great people of Greater Poland, that I'm now yielding my place in the limelight. I'm now going to shut up and just listen to you. With one caveat, though, because ... Whenever I feel that you are getting carried away and that you're losing touch with the great spirit of liberalism, well, then I'm going to interrupt you, no excuses. A deal?"

"Deal!" was the response from the full house.

The first speaker on the stage was again Aldona, the Deputy Voivode for Competitiveness.

"They say that we are building a 'heaven' here," she began. "And, you know what? They're right! It's time to admit it: that's precisely what we are doing!"

A storm of applause erupted that made even the angel above the stage shudder. Then Aldona ran with her theme:

"We are building it! Even so, does it mean that we're about done with the changes? Our budget is now almost balanced, yet we still can't afford any deficit to creep back in. That is why our Board has moved to introduce a green tax for all the businesses that produce a larger-scale carbon footprint. No, this is not a whim of the authorities! Even such eco-taxes have their liberal justification. Any emitter of greenhouse gases, just like any person dumping rubbish on a plot of land that is not their own, is interfering with other people's property. And if so, the emitter must bear the cost of their interference! Let me add that the tax is going to be low, it won't kill anyone at less than 20 dollars per ton of carbon dioxide. The figure is much lower than those in other countries that have also adopted such measures."

The applause was quieter this time.

"I want you to see that it is precisely due to our privatization initiatives that the first phase of our flat tax reform was such a success. The same applies to the emergence of the Greater Poland Wealth Fund. Local residents gave us the mandate to privatize all kinds of assets, but, at all times, we still have one duty. The duty of good stewardship. So, we must strive to get the best price for the property we sell. Remember, every act of privatization is supposed to support our regional economy. Need examples? We offered to sell the land held by the local government, first and foremost, to the tenant farmers. Why? To ensure that existing tenants continue to use that land. Any remaining unsold plots have been transferred to funds that will ultimately be offered publicly. From the perspective of the farmers who were leasing the plots, nothing changes at all, except the bank account number to which they transfer their rent fees.

"Next slide, please! Here, in turn, we see how we created a similar program concerning all the apartments held by the regional government. The right of first refusal on their sale was given to the tenants, and the remaining unsold properties were likewise taken over by the funds, known as the "REITs"—short for Real Estate Investment Trusts. REITS have been a long time in coming to Poland, even though abroad they have been a popular form of property ownership for a while. Due to a great response from small investors, our Greater Polish REITs have quickly expanded by acquiring properties in other provinces of Poland. Our REITs' earnings support hundreds of thousands of Polish retail investors, who want to beef up their future retirement savings. And that's not all. Consider the stakes in the state-owned companies that our province had received as a result of the constitutional reform. We've auctioned those off as well. In making privatization decisions, we follow best practices of the International Monetary Fund. The first step is always a thorough audit and assessment of whether there is a legitimate policy reason for a given entity to continue under state ownership."

"You try to make sure that any such enterprise works efficiently rather than being just a burden, right?" Professor Wu quizzed, as if she were probing a student in one of her seminars.

"That's right! For example, as the Greater Poland liberals, we see no reason to continue state ownership in the food sector. There are some big industrial plants in our region that were formerly part of the National Sugar Company. It was a state holding, later transformed by PiS into the National Food Group as part of its plan to build a number of 'national champions.' The Sugar Company has been on the verge of going private at least since 2004. And yet, it was only now that we have put an end to this overlong saga. We sold a portion of the Sugar Company, namely the stake in the Kluczewo sugar plant, to local farmers and plant employees. The remaining shares we offered to the public through an IPO. As for our other food plants, we're amalgamating them into the Greater Polish Food Group. Again, some of the group's shares will be sold to the employees, while some will be offered to institutional and retail investors by way of an initial public offering. We've already had good experience with these kinds of processes when we privatized local horse stud farms, setting up the Greater Polish Stud Group."

"Perfect! Why should some state-owned monstrosity keep any horses!" Professor Wu smiled and nudged the attorney from the foundation. "I genuinely like your attitude," she added. "Proactively dumping bureaucracy from the saddle!"

"It's not just about horses," said Aldona, somewhat irritated by Wu's jokes. "As for all the smaller companies, we've either sold them to their employees, or to strategic investors. The construction companies we inherited from the Polish Development Fund—yet another state assets agency—we sold to private developers who lost no time in launching new residential projects. The hotels previously consolidated by PiS into the Polish Hotel Holding we sold to an international hospitality chain. And so on. We're progressing smoothly. Our provincial government has already gotten rid of small stakes in the PZU insurance company, and in the Greater Poland Animal Breeding and Reproduction Center. We disposed of the PZU shares through the stock exchange. As for the Animal Center, the majority owner wanted to buy us out right away.

"Now, my final slide. What was still left over from the assets we received in the course of the constitutional reform were some minority stakes in the Polish State Railway company, Polish State Railway Lines infrastructure company, Polish Aviation Group, and in Polregio train operator. In those cases, we are talking about critical infrastructure. Obviously, the central government and other provinces also hold their stakes, so it is not our exclusive decision what to do with them. Locally, we decided not to divest the railway infrastructure stock in the short-term. As for the three other companies, we're negotiating their sale with some other provinces, since no regular investor will give us decent money for our small fractional equity. All of this: the fine-tuning of the new tax system, the construction of a new provincial administration, and the privatization efforts, will, of course, take many years."

"Exactly!" Professor Wu rose from her seat again. "But how much time do you have in the first place? Aren't you worried that all these initiatives will alienate your electoral base? Come the next election, the people could challenge everything you've been doing. Politics is a fickle beast, wouldn't you agree?"

"Let me use your own words, Jennifer: courage is key. We do what we do, without second thoughts. Besides, not all of our decisions are unpopular. Wanda here, our Voivodship Board Member for Talent Management, can now tell you about some decisions the voters actually liked. Wanda, come and join us! Tell us about our friendly tax administration and all the rest!"

Three times one-third

Wanda got straight to the point:

"I could go on forever on local tax and health services," she said, "But please remember that, before the reforms that we all enjoy today, every detail of how local government institutions work was regulated centrally, from Warsaw. By contrast, these days we decide most things independently, following the laws passed by our Sejmik and the regional Senate. We lost no time learning how to best use these powers. For starters, instead of hiring numerous HR managers to serve in the newly created provincial 'ministries,' the Voivodship Board appointed me—in an open competition—to coordinate the talent policies across our administration. Before my appointment, I worked as an HR director for a large IT company in Poznań. Later, I joined a governmental agency in the capital. Particularly in that latter position, when I got close to the center and its politics, I saw firsthand the reality of Warsaw's 'ministerial puzzles.' I'm talking about a government chopped into separate principalities, warring siloes. And I want to say it loud and clear: we have no intention of duplicating these pathologies here in Poznań!"

When the applause subsided, Wanda added:

"However, we in Poznań are practical people. Where do I start, then, as the province's 'chief HR officer'? How do cut through the bureaucratic fog? The first priority was to set well-defined goals for the administrators we 'inherited' after a variety of institutions: the former offices of the regional marshal and the centrally appointed voivode, former bureau of the Warsaw-sent education superintendent, and the regional branch of the National Revenue Administration. What you need is to send a clear message. As all of you know, our message was: 'Three Times One-Third.' We planned that, within two years, we would reduce our expenditures on the regional administration, per inhabitant, to a level one-third lower than the average of the five largest, industrialized Polish provinces that we use as a benchmark. Also, within two years, we would raise our civil servants' salaries to a level one-third higher than the average among the five benchmarked provinces. And finally, we would make at least one-third of the civil servants' increased salaries contingent on the results of their work, particularly as measured by the ratings received from our citizens and from our businesses, using the Local and Regional Government Quality Assessment System for Laws and Public Services.

"The opening motto, 'Three Times One-Third,' was meant to explain what kind of the managerial culture we wanted to create." Here, Wanda paused briefly. "But, if we were to cut our expenses and raise salaries at the same time, we needed to radically reduce the number of civil servants, while increasing the services' efficiency. Yes, we're raising salaries, but, at the same time, we are drastically reducing available office space. These days, most of our civil clerks operate under a hybrid system, working from their homes part-time. What's so strange about that? If I am entrusted with hard-earned złoty of our taxpayers, I'd really rather spend them on hiring top-notch professionals than on heating empty offices."

Here, Wanda paused again.

"All these, I'd say, are small changes compared to the benefits we're about to get from digitizing the administration processes. Now, but especially in the long term. I'm talking about the full digitization of all local and regional government administrative functions, at all levels. Plus, we aim to develop digital competencies among personnel. The result is that the citizens of Greater Poland no longer need to stand in any office lines! Instead, they can use a smartphone application to learn exactly where, on what day, and at what time they will be expected in our offices. Or they deal with the whole thing online. In Europe, you should know, Poland is a star example of how to digitalize the society. Our American friends who are with us today have long believed that the best sort of government is the smallest government possible. Thanks to new technologies, we are minimizing physical contact between the citizens and our administration."

"Does everyone like it?" Wanda continued. "Certainly not. Some civil servants do not appreciate the extra effort involved. For this reason, we have introduced, in our Provincial Revenue Office, the principle of full professional liability. It works like this: a variable part of each official's salary is taken away for a period of six months in the event that said official's tax-related decision is reversed either by the Supreme Voivodship Court, or the Supreme Administrative Court. People may grumble that we are stripping them of their bonuses, but believe me, nothing else will make them unlearn taking dirty shortcuts in tax collection. The only exceptions are made for the decisions that were made in the public interest with the approval of the Voivodship Board. We are already seeing that the threat of financial penalties reduce the rampant practice of issuing tax decisions that are unfavorable to taxpayers, in the hope that the affected citizen or a business does not have the energy to sue. At first, other provinces, more statist in their ways, were all too happy to learn about our plan, wishing Greater Poland luck in recruiting civil servants on such terms. As it happens, however, our Revenue Office has no shortage of excellent candidates. Thanks to our tax simplification measures and to the principle that doubtful cases should be resolved in favor of the taxpayer, our officials here have a much easier and less stressful job!"

Jennifer Wu reached for the microphone. Simultaneous translation allowed her to capture the highlights, but it was high time for her to comment.

"These are fantastic solutions," she exclaimed. "One can indeed learn things from you. Is there more?"

"There is. After we prevailed in the referendum," Wanda moved on, "It dawned on us that we had to change the entire, heavy-handed policy mindset among the province's officials. Our first successes were not accidental. Why? Because, especially given the rising costs of living, the tax cuts have made us really popular with citizens—and I'm not talking just about personal income taxes. After the cuts in corporate tax rates, we are already witnessing one of the largest waves of wage increases in the whole country. Let me repeat, we are not indulging in the proverbial race to the bottom, we're not cutting taxes to zero. For us, low taxes are only a means to an end. Our brand of liberalism is first and foremost a way to stir up the energy, the initiative, the creativity of people from Greater Poland! Here, let me pass the microphone to another member of the Board, to tell her part of the story. Stacey, our star, please join us on the stage!"

The Augean stable in public services

Stacey Novack, in her forties, had dazzling white teeth and liked making firm gestures when speaking, but exuded human warmth. Despite her foreign name, she spoke in beautiful and precise Polish.

"Maybe a few words of introduction from me first," the Voivode suddenly came to life. "Some time ago I was lucky to bring this very bright person to Poznań. Until recently, Ms Novack held a high managerial position in the mega-foundation set up by one of the famous American billionaires. She's probably the only Polish woman to have climbed so high. We were fortunate that our Stacey agreed to leave her lucrative job to take up her current position in Greater Poland as the Deputy Voivode for Public Services. It sounds easy, but what was your transition really like, Stacey?"

"Well, immediately upon my arrival I found, to a bit of horror, that the organization of local public services resembles Augean stables." Deputy Voivode Novack began. "Am I a Hercules, I asked myself. Let me give you an example. Businesses in Poland operate using very similar forms as in the US: corporations, limited liability companies, partnerships. A familiar structure. In the social services sector, on the other hand, the previous centralized Polish system was truly something else. In America, virtually all nonprofit institutions, from churches all the way up to your University of Chicago"—here Stacey turned to Professor Wu—"or the opera houses, or famous museums, are all organized as nonprofit corporations. Using this structure, it is possible, on the one hand, to maintain corporate governance standards common in the entire social sector. And on the other hand, the nonprofit corporate form gives each institution its autonomy in deciding how best to structure its activities."

"Are you with me?" The deputy voivode made sure. "Great! So now let's compare this with the Polish system I encountered. Here, the activities of all schools, universities, museums, theaters, or even nursing homes were micromanaged by hundreds upon hundreds of pages of detailed regulations imposed by the central government. Would you believe it? The regulations stipulated, for example, that the term of a university senate must be four years—no more, no less—and the term must begin exactly 'on the first of September.' I'm quoting from Article 30(1) of the past national law we recently repealed.[2] The committee conducting a competition for the principal of a public elementary school must include two, and no more than two, representatives from the education superintendent bureau (Article 63, paragraph 14, clause 2, letter a), as well as exactly the same number of representatives from the parents' council (letter b).[3] The director of any 'artistic institution' may only be appointed for a 'period of three to five artistic seasons' (Article 15(2) sentence 1), and the director of a 'cultural institution', by contrast, is to be appointed for a period of three to seven years (Article 15(2) sentence 2).[4] I could go on."

The increasingly absurd examples Stacey was reciting amused the audience, especially given that she was speaking Polish with the unlikely energy and speed of an Olympic sprinter. Professor Wu was smiling broadly. Clearly, the deputy voivode knew American-style public speaking.

"The university senate," Stacey continued, "must appoint its representatives to the 'university board' numbering 'six or eight persons' (Article 19(1)(1)). The board must also include 'the chairman of the student government' (Article 19(1)(2)).[5] At every cultural institution nationwide, employees must be entitled to a 'long-service allowance,' such benefit to be equal to precisely 'five percent of the monthly basic salary' (Article 31(2)).[6] A special amendment to the relevant law outlined an exact procedure required for inviting Boy Scout representatives to school council's meetings. If I'm sensing your incurable curiosity, here's the procedure: the invitation must be issued by the council's chairperson 'with the consent or upon request of the council' (Article 69, paragraph 3a).[7] Students' personal files must be kept in 'folders' (Article 74(2)(2)).[8] At the school council meetings, a 'nurse or school hygienist' is to report on 'issues in the field of health education and health promotion among the students,' but only 'upon the request of the school principal' (Article 69, paragraph 8)."[9]

The audience members were lapping it all up. The best proof of their rapture was the sudden lack of professorial quips or tricky queries from Professor Wu.

"Did such absurdly tight regulations serve any point? Far from it. They were just a form of usurping power. Could they be amended? Before the 2023 constitutional reform—hardly. To alter anything in the realm of public services, you needed a parliamentary act. No wonder the otherwise great idea to create integrated social service centers in smaller municipalities finally yielded, in 2019, a statute numbering eighty-one articles and almost thirty pages long.[10] Sixteen of those pages merely listed the necessary amendments to earlier laws. You have to admit it's frankly mind-boggling. For decades, the MPs in Warsaw have been passing such laws without a shred of thought that a municipality—or any other owner, manager, or donor supporting a school, a university, or a theater—could have a better idea of how to run his or her own place. Obviously, we should be the ones deciding on the proper shape of our institutions!"

"I'm with you, girl!" Jennifer Wu responded excitedly. "To me, the whole thing sounds like some Orwellian nightmare. Who's behind such idiocies, and why is no one trying to change it? How can you people function like this? Throw that stuff in the trash!"

"Exactly!" Stacey nodded in agreement. "We touch the root of our movement for the constitutional reform of 2023. The reforms were our light at the end of the tunnel. These days, in Greater Poland, public services are provided not under some centralized statute, but following regional laws made by our Sejmik and Senate. Of course, when the reforms were coming into effect, to avoid the chaos typical of many previous Polish reforms, the existing statutory regulations affecting schools, universities, and cultural institutions were grandfathered in. Every voivodship might establish its own respective laws, but only gradually so. On 'day zero' everything remained as before."

"Might establish, okay, but have they really passed their own laws?" Professor Wu chimed in.

"I don't know about other regions, but, here, yes, we are changing all such regulations. I am personally very involved in the process of cleaning up the legal shambles of thirty years left by Polish centralized lawmaking. I'm not flying solo, of course. Our vehicle of change is the Greater Poland Center for Research and Development. First off, we launched a competition for individual grants, asking each applicant to develop a legal formula for the operation of public services. The project was won by an international committee of lawyers, who in no time drafted new regulations for us, creating a new type of legal entity: the public interest corporation. In such a corporation, shareholders may not receive dividends and may only sell shares at a nominal (inflation-indexed) price. However, aside from these mechanisms reflecting their non-commercial aspect, in all other regards the public interest corporation is subject to the same corporate governance rules and standards as any business. I mean, there are two boards—the supervisory one and the management board—as is typical in continental Europe."

"Fascinating!" the lawyer for the foundation interjected, perhaps a little jealous of Stacey Novack's charisma. "Am I right to guess that the next step was to transform all your bizarre institutions into public interest corporations?"

"You are very right to guess that," she replied, somewhat condescendingly. "To be precise, if an institution can make a profit, then we'll convert it to a standard business entity. But the entities that must always be supported from our budget will become exactly public interest corporations and will be run by professionals under the supervision of our regional government. Among our first entities of this kind, I can list our public schools, theaters, museums, and even city parks. Not to mention the local universities that were handed over to us in the course of the 2023 constitutional reform. Something similar was already attempted in the 1990s following the advice of Professor Jeffrey Sachs. Many ex-communist state-owned enterprises were transformed into corporations. 'Commercialized,' we used to call it back then."

"It must have been way before Jeffrey became a declared leftist," Professor Wu remarked, to everyone's amusement.

"In any case, just as the 'commercialization' of the 1990s led to fast economic development," the deputy voivode continued, "so too will the transformation of our public service providers into nonprofit corporations give us a similar developmental impulse. The goal is for service users to know immediately whether they are being served by a for-profit, or a nonprofit corporation. We are busy organizing a new educational campaign because not all of our residents can grasp the distinction right away. Are our goals too ambitious? I am even urging some churches and religious associations to incorporate. Gently urging, because the Concordat with the Holy See does not leave any room for coercive acts in this area. But why couldn't a parish have a board of directors? Such issues are, of course, delicate. For the time being, the Polish Bishops' Conference has explicitly forbidden priests to transform their parishes into corporate entities. Our Protestant churches, on the other hand, have already embarked on such reforms.

True autonomy for education

"It's great to see that all the recent changes I just mentioned have empowered ordinary citizens to choose freely from among the most suitable business models," Novack moved on. "Before coming here, I'd been following the debates among the left-leaning circles concerning school autonomy. Still, on my return to Poland, I discovered that it was all just empty talk. You can now contrast all that with the kind of school autonomy, hyper-autonomy actually, that we have instituted here, in one brisk move. Two moves, to be precise. First, we transformed all local schools into municipal public interest corporations. Then, we invited the parents and some representatives of local NGOs to serve on the schools' supervisory boards. Turns out that what was initially considered merely a pipe dream could easily become reality. In the city of Konin, for example, we split the local school companies into two groups. One group is comprised of the operators of educational infrastructure. They own and maintain school buildings. The other group are the schools themselves. The result was that several smaller schools, each implementing a different educational model tailored to the preferences of different groups of residents, may now all operate in the same building.[11] On top of this, the municipality no longer has to be the sole owner of these incorporated schools."

"Our system of financing local education," the deputy voivode went on, "is likewise undergoing vast transformations. Under our new Voivodship Charter, we no longer call our education services 'free' or 'financed by the voivodship.' Either we indicate the specific source for the school funds—say, the privatization proceeds, or a grant from the EU—or, we plainly state that the school service is 'financed, or co-financed, by the Greater Polish taxpayers.' At the urging of local municipalities that carry the burden of running underfunded nurseries, kindergartens, and public schools, we are currently preparing another revolution. Namely, we've decided to split the entire budget allocated for educational services into individual vouchers. Each parent of a child attending a nursery, kindergarten, or school receives an education voucher to cover the expense. Students are no longer confined to a school district."

"In our country, there've been decades of debates about school vouchers," someone from the American team observed. "How does the system work in practice here in Poland?"

"Let me explain," Stacey said. "The value of the governmental subsidy attributed to a school voucher held by the parents depends on the school's tuition policies. If the facility charges significant fees (over 500 złoty per month), the voucher's value is X. If the facility charges fees lower than 500 złoty per month, the voucher's value is 1.25 of X. Finally, if the facility does not require any fees, the voucher will reflect a subsidy equal to 1.5 of X. This is our way of ensuring adequate support for children from poorer families, who choose schools which are completely tuition-free. In addition, the system incentivizes private entities to enter the field of tuition-free education."

"We apply similar principles when it comes to college education. A handy example is the recent transformation of our public universities, which were transferred to our regional government during the 2023 constitutional reform. We were keenly aware that private universities tend to perform better, as proved by the excellent Poznań-Warsaw SWPS University. Incidentally, that place, too, has decided to become a public interest corporation. In response, our province has adopted a two-pronged strategy. All the smaller, local community colleges transformed into ordinary corporations and then sold, one by one, to strategic investors from the for-profit education industry. By contrast, each of the region's key, large public universities—the Adam Mickiewicz University, the Poznań University of Economics and Business, the Poznań University of Technology, and the Poznań University of Medical Sciences—have become public interest corporations."

"Is it wise, though, to overstretch your budget by financing such behemoths?"

"Well, the regional government has no intention of remaining their sole shareholder. The Voivodship Board and the universities' respective boards have jointly commenced a wide-ranging fundraising campaign. Together, we are out to convince high net worth individuals, both from our region and from beyond it, to take equity stakes in the largest universities. In return, the donors would provide the universities with funds to finally start creating proper endowments that Polish universities lack. This fundraising effort is led by our Deputy Voivode for Competitiveness. After all, local businesspeople have treated her as a rock star since her tax cuts program was implemented."

Stacey's last words were met with instant applause from those gathered in the hall. Aldona, the said rock star, stood up and simply bowed with a smile, letting her colleague wrap up her part of the presentation.

"So, after long weeks of negotiations," Stacey went on, "as a lot of people in our audience surely know, we received the tremendous news: a well-known billionaire family from our province agreed to take a 30 percent equity stake in the Adam Mickiewicz University corporation, pledging a donation of 250 million dollars. I'm talking about the largest private donation for a specific educational purpose in the entirety of Polish history. The media reported that a key argument to convince the donors was the possibility of co-determining the direction of the university by nominating a third of the university's board members. I'm not revealing any secrets when I say this. Our *Voice of Greater Poland* daily featured a detailed report on the deal. In parallel, a group of alumni and other entrepreneurs has offered a large donation in exchange for a stake in the Poznań University of Economics and Business. The Greater Poland Chamber of Commerce took a collective stake in the Poznań University of Technology. As we speak, the Greater Poland Chamber of Agriculture is negotiating its investment in the Poznań University of Life Sciences. And it's not just about raising additional funds! On top of their donations, private donors, as well as some non-commercial shareholders, are expected to bring their know-how, impose new organizational culture, and—last but not least—push the universities to innovate.

"The Adam Mickiewicz University is a prime example. After the transformation into a public interest corporation, we resolved to nominate one-third of the university's supervisory and management boards with candidates selected from the faculty. However, the professors demanded more involvement in the university's business, so we designed an option program for them. The faculty will gain greater management influence if they contribute to increasing the university's impact on the economic and social development of the province. In this instance, we decided to introduce a parametric evaluation score system. We want to measure the university's overall socioeconomic impact, as well as the incremental value of the GDP produced by the industrial cluster centered around the university."

"And, let me add," the Voivode stood up, taking over the presentation, "all these solutions we've adopted may seem very technical, yet they are the deciding factor in boosting our local economy. We keep asking the same question over and over: how do we make our spending of public money more effective? I will now utter three magic words: transparent public procurement.

"Wherever possible, our Board strives to make the public money follow the citizen. The education voucher was already mentioned. However, in many cases, such as urban public transport, culture, social care, and infrastructure, it remains up to the local and regional governments to purchase the required goods and services. We must act in the same way as all efficient entrepreneurs and keep the procurement system agile and transparent. How do we want to achieve these goals? By breaking the monopoly municipal companies hold on delivering such services. The idea is not to create a vicious circle, with funds circulating from the local governments to their own municipal companies, and back. What's required is a deeper change in this philosophy. What do I mean by this? We decided to separate the units overseeing the municipal companies from the units in charge of allocating our funds to them. From now on, the governance and the finances, respectively, shall stay separate. If we turn a blind eye to their usual collusion, funds will likely be misallocated, or worse."

After the Voivode's final words, thunderous applause broke out in the hall.

New prospects

"Maybe it's time for our guests to comment on our presentation in a few words?" the Voivode asked at this point, obviously happy with the course of events.

Jennifer Wu walked to the stage, brushed aside her bangs, looked around the large meeting room, and said, "Let me share with you one thing I observed here. What I like the most about you is your daring. You steer clear of any platitudes. Instead, you explain in detail, openly, your whole way of thinking. Better still, you debate it! This is very American of you. In the nineteenth century, there was a Frenchman, Monsieur de Tocqueville, who traveled all over the young United States and later described our political system. One particular thing that struck him was how people were debating key issues together. Every nation has a constitution, but its high principles must be translated into a set of best practices. And those must be local ones, your very own. Democracy through participation, which is to say, a liberal democracy! It is thrilling to see that this is the road you've taken. You slash and burn the shrubs of the past to free up new space for initiative. You're doing a great job. Good luck to all of you! May your Greater Poland be ... even greater!"

Professor Wu's assistant was checking the agenda again. Amazingly, there had been no delay so far. The local folks knew how to stay organized. Now it was time for a light supper and drinks at the Arcadia building on Poznań's Liberty Square, the place made famous as the headquarters of the Malta Artistic Festival. Then they were to hop back on the plane. The next day at dawn Professor Wu was scheduled to arrive at Davos. But, for now, they were in Poznań.

At the Arcadia event, Jennifer Wu was treated to another lecture on the benefits of transforming cultural institutions into corporations.

"Even before the big reform, some well-managed private theaters, for example My Theater or the Apollo, were breaking out of the state monopoly mold," a young local government officer was explaining to her. "So, naturally, we decided to transform the Musical Theater and the Animation Theater into commercial companies. The Polish Theater became a public interest corporation. We've gone the same way with the Stanisław Moniuszko Opera Theater, the Poznań Philharmonic, and the National Museum in Poznań. All of these were handed down to us in the course of the constitutional reform, and all of them are now not-for-profit corporations."

"Sure. I've heard that, in Europe, governments finance all cultural activities," Professor Wu recalled. "We find it very odd. In America, the vast majority of cultural institutions are private."

"We consider it to be the right direction to take," the people from the local department of culture all agreed. "As with the universities, we are earmarking for-profit companies in the cultural sector for privatization, and engaging wealthy donors and sponsors to co-manage non-commercial entities. In Poland, there's no precedent to this practice. The inflow of private funds into the Greater Poland cultural domain should give the regional budget more room for expanding our cultural offer. As the first step, we, the provincial government, joined forces with the Mayor of Poznań and a group of private donors/shareholders, to launch the New Prospects, a museum of modern art. In addition to acquiring new exhibits, the museum has attracted some private collectors from abroad, all of them Polish by origin. Until now, they would exhibit their art in other countries only. You've got to see the place, it's so grand."

"If we find the time, most certainly," the American scholar quipped. Everyone was starting to feel tired after the trip and the long day in Poznań. Only the indefatigable Jennifer Wu was still shaking hands with a succession of local celebrities, cracking jokes and patting them on the back. Finally, she too slipped away from the room to get some rest on the mansion's classicist terrace. From her high vantage point, she could see the crowds milling in the cafes below. There was loud music down there—everyone was enjoying their evening in the big city.

After a while, Professor Wu was joined by the Voivode himself.

"So, how do you like it here?" he asked, by no means perfunctorily. "Just look at these crowds, it's like a carnival. We have this slogan, not exactly serious, but cool. It goes: POZNAŃ MIASTO DOZNAŃ. Something along the lines of 'A City to Feel.' It rings especially true tonight, doesn't it?"

"Seriously, I really, really like what you guys are doing. And do you know what I appreciate the most?" The American was still watching the crowds in the square below them. "I think that you've found real freedom. After all, you lived under communism for half a century. But now? You've deregulated most of your economy. You cut the tax rates. There's competition in all public services. So, honestly, what else do you have in store for this city? I'm asking you as one liberal to another. I think you understand what I'm driving at?"

The Voivode thought for a moment before answering.

"To my mind, liberalism is not just about the economy. By necessity, when you change the government system, you also affect other things, say, the local traditions, the customs, you touch many social sensitivities. For example, during the first session of the Sejmik and the provincial Senate, we lifted the formerly national law which prohibited stores from being open on Sundays and holidays unless staffed by the owner. Economically speaking, the move was more than justified, but you can't imagine the uproar we caused. Few will remember how many barriers for our entrepreneurs we lifted. The regional chamber of commerce identified for us 137 provisions we 'inherited' from the former national laws that were hampering business. We agreed with ninety-two of the chamber's recommendations. The remaining provisions are being scrutinized by a joint committee."

"The first step to get out of a hole is to stop digging," Jennifer Wu observed teasingly.

"Very true," the Voivode nodded in agreement. "We need to create a system free from all the absurd regulations that today hold back our business. We are preparing a package of best regulatory practices, to be voted on in the Sejmik and the Senate. For that, we need to assess the impact of the new rules and consult the public about them to make sure they won't create new financial burdens. And time is of the essence here. We still have a mass of old laws, long outdated, but remaining in force. That's why we want to impose an automatic sunset clause in our provincial law."

"Sounds to me like you need an army of lawyers for all this, huh?" Professor Wu reflected. "Please be very careful working with them ..."

"I need a political philosopher even more," the Voivode replied. "A liberal philosopher, preferably. We really could use some sound advice as to how to balance everyone's interests and their values, when solving economic issues. As it is, every single decision we take is going to harm someone. There will be always someone who loses out because of what we do. Just look, we abolished some strict regulations on e-cigarettes, heated tobacco, those things. And right away we entered into angry discussions with tobacco manufacturers. We also lifted the hour-based ban on liquor sales; we created city zones where liquor consumption in public places is legal. Like down here, in the square. And again, there was backlash; people accused us of turning the city into a den of drunks. But there's another thing ..."

"What's that?"

Better than America

"All right, let me tell you a little story," the Voivode mused. "When we won that election and finally got down to business, I suddenly understood that if liberalism expands the zone of freedom, then you cannot stop at matters of the economy or property. It is a question of basic individual liberty... And if so ..."

"Please, go on," encouraged Wu.

"If so, we have to take it much further. Much, much further. You know, under the reformed system, I serve, in parallel to this position, as one of Poland's senators, at the national level. Our current model is probably better than yours." Here the Voivode couldn't hold back a smile. "You see, in Poland, we avoided cases like that of California. The state has 40 million people, and yet it is entitled to the same number of votes in the US Senate as the state of Wyoming, which has less than 600,000. Now I, over here, hold precisely as many votes in the Polish Senate as I have residents of my region.

"And the media have already snickered that I am the architect of this high-profile law that was supposed to give all the provinces the opportunity to introduce full marriage equality. Just recently, the Constitutional Tribunal decided to give regions a right to legalize civil unions only. Greater Poland has become, of course, a region where such unions are not only tolerated, they are actively supported by the local authorities. These are basic individual rights. We can't pretend liberalism is only about the economy, or taxes. Agreed?"

"If you want my position, I'm in full agreement with you," Wu responded. "But, as you know, American free-marketers are divided on this issue. Is there more?"

"There sure is. As I said, we set things in motion, at last. We want a legal system that gives as much freedom as possible to our citizens. What's the harm in legalizing marijuana to grow and consume? Under reasonable regulations, for sure. We're not going crazy on this one, but still. We expect the Polish Senate to pass a new bill that would transfer all decisions concerning marijuana production, and general access to marijuana, to regional lawmakers. Just as they've already transferred the regulation of economic issues. Our Voivodship Board will announce any day now that, in our region, the production and consumption of marijuana is legal. It's happening as soon as the national law becomes effective. Another token of liberalism, won't you say?"

"But, but ... You're not afraid at all? Of taking all these bold decisions?" Wu asked.

"Let's trust the people," the Voivode responded. "Instead of keeping them in a cage of imposed views and regulations, let them choose what they believe, what they practice. As long as it does not harm others."

They were interrupted by Wu's assistant, who rushed over to them saying that it was high time to get going. The Voivode escorted Professor Wu to the car. On the landing of the hall's marble staircase, Wu stopped momentarily and faced the politician from Greater Poland.

"There's something I want to tell you," she began. "I admire all that you do, you and your little team. I envy you your energy, and so on. But let me give you a piece of advice that may surprise you, coming from the lips of a liberal economist. Please remember: in politics, grand ideas are very important. However, it is even more important not to lose touch with the people. So far, so good. You have convinced everyone that your land is on the right track and you have my great admiration for it. But always look for additional supporters. Always, everywhere. Keep finding ever-new groups of voters and making them see things your way. It's no good being a sheriff with no deputies."

"I appreciate your words of wisdom," the Voivode replied, trying not to laugh. Academics from all over the world, he thought, all share a similar sense of their self-importance, the result being that they often resort to horrible clichés.

Still, our region can only profit from all the publicity we receive when we get praised in her new book, the Voivode silently concluded. In any case, tonight he had one more meeting scheduled: he'd promised to drop by, if only for a few minutes, and talk to the board of the Greater Poland Chamber of Agriculture.

He did not expect that meeting to run smoothly. On the contrary. The prices for agricultural tools and materials were going up sharply and the agricultural market had become unpredictable. Large farms would always survive, one way or another, but what about mid-sized ones, let alone those who had invested their EU subsidies in expanding their farms? The Voivode wanted to support the region's entrepreneurs, but without interfering with the free market. The vital thing was to provide all businesspeople with access to reliable, full market information. Accordingly, even before the evening meeting, the Voivode had prepared a proposal for an R&D grant program, through which local farmers would be able to use the services of the University of Life Sciences. The agricultureprofessors did a good job—perhaps even better than the professor from America—since they produced convincing forecasts of market development, with detailed risks and possible strategies to take.

"All in all, a fascinating day." The Voivode smiled to himself. "We start in the morning debating big liberal ideas and wind up the day with new types of seeds and fertilizers. Here's the constitutional reform in a nutshell: our Greater Poland voivodship is big enough to serve as an example to the world at large, yet it is small enough for all to see right away the impact our work is having on the lives of ordinary people."

Over here it became obvious very quickly who was contributing how much to the common "household." It was for this reason that the Voivode was somehow not at all sorry to forego his mythical career in Warsaw, the one he had sacrificed for the Greater Polish heaven. At least here, everything was real.

Notes

1. "Morawiecki i Mazzucato o nowym podejściu do innowacji," *Polska Agencja Prasowa,* Mar. 28, 2017, https://www.pap.pl/aktualnosci/news%2C878028%2Cmorawiecki-i-mazzucato-o-nowym-podejsciu-do-innowacji.html.
2. Ustawa z dnia 20 lipca 2018 r. Prawo o szkolnictwie wyższym i nauce, Dz. U. 2018 Item 1668 (2018).
3. Ustawa z dnia 14 grudnia 2016 r. Prawo oświatowe, Dz. U. 2017 Item 59 (2016).
4. Ustawa z dnia 25 października 1991 r. o organizowaniu i prowadzeniu działalności kulturalnej, Dz. U. 2017 Nr 114 Item 493 (1991).
5. *Ustawa z dnia 20 lipca 2018 r. Prawo o szkolnictwie wyższym i nauce.*
6. *Ustawa z dnia 25 października 1991 r. o organizowaniu i prowadzeniu działalności kulturalnej.*
7. *Ustawa z dnia 14 grudnia 2016 r. Prawo oświatowe.*
8. Id.
9. Id.
10. Ustawa z dnia 19 lipca 2019 r. o realizowaniu usług społecznych przez centrum usług społecznych, Dz.U. 2019 Item 1818 (2019).
11. Compare David Osborne and Ted Gaebler, *Reinventing Government: How the Entrepreneurial Spirit is Transforming the Public Sector* (Plume, 1993), 5–8.

Comment

A European Dream about Polish Dreams

Kalypso Nicolaidis

I have a dream about dreams. In this dream, I walk. I walk around the world in search of places where humans have found better ways to live together. Oh no, not in harmony. Simply in peace, social peace, in peace and in joy. Places where people might have a sparkle in their eye because when they look at each other, when they run into their neighbor, they know that they share some kind of common purpose. Sure, they disagree on many things, like whether the state should do more or less, whether schools should teach religion, or whether women should have a choice about having children. But they have this sparkle in their eyes. And in this sparkle, their social contract has come alive.

In my dream, I walk. I walk inside the dream of others and make these dreams my own. Have you ever tried to penetrate the dreams of others, dear reader? It takes curiosity, abandonment, madness. It takes courage too. You can lose yourself in a utopia of their making, and surreptitiously, the utopia creeps from under your eyelids, and it is there, right in front of you; it feels so real, a realist utopia extracted from a dream, from a web of dream you have made your own.

And in this moment of awareness, it is no longer a utopia. It has happened. It is happening. In the dream I walk inside the new post-2024 Poland conjured up by Anna, Maciej, and their friends, twenty-eight conjurers of realist utopia, weaving together dream of new voivodships—"ships of dream," in my clumsy translation. I walk through the beautiful Polish landscape, from lowland plains to snowy mountains, from the Baltic Sea coast to the southern forest belt, through lakes, beaches, and rivers, through hills, swamps, and islands. I walk.

And yes, surreptitiously, their web of dreams starts to paint a political landscape for me as I walk.

The landscape harks back to old medieval times, as it seems that voivodships have always existed in this part of the world. But in the dreams, they have come alive in this moment, in our twenty-first century, filled with digital streams and virtual enhancements. They are no longer the boundaries of some semi-irrelevant administrative jurisdictions in a country where all is decided at the center, a center where the two sides battle over the supposed soul of the country.

Kalypso Nicolaidis, *Comment* In: *Let's Agree on Poland*. Edited by: Maciej Kisilowski and Anna Wojciuk,
Oxford University Press.
DOI: 10.1093/oso/9780198979562.003.0016

Instead, each voivodship has become its own exciting experiment, each with its own variations on a common dream: a new Poland of togetherness.

And so, I walk through them all: progressive Pomerania Voivodship, Christian Democrat Subcarpathian Voivodship, leftist West Pomerania Voivodship, conservative Podlasie Voivodship, classical liberal Greater Poland Voivodship. Each more fascinating than the other.

Of course, the dreamed voivodships have different shapes and colors. Their main protagonists are dreaming up different clever strategies, different star projects, different daring policies. The open and equality-based dream leftist voivodship has a different look and feel from the liberal voivodship's "democratic, self-governing land of free people."

But in all of these dreamlands, something is brewing. In all of these dreamlands, I can see a sparkle in the eyes of the people whose paths I cross, old residents from the region who now know their leaders, or the new returnees, from Warsaw or from farther afield, and even those who have come and were never there before.

Have you entered my dream about their dreams, reader? I am not Polish, but French, Greek, and British. But in this Poland, I feel at home abroad, which after all is what we mean by being European. Ah, I hear you; this has already become *your* dream. You don't need any injunction to dream, from a foreigner like me or from anyone, for that matter. You have already met them. In fact, you are a bit of them too. All of them or some of them. Ela, Maciek, Greg, Amelia, Florian, Iza, Yulka, and Ira in progressive Pomerania; Dorota of the Christian Democrat Subcarpathia; Piotr and Seba in the leftist voivodship; Magdalena and Pawel from the conservative voivodship; Aldona in the liberal voivodship. Local heroes and local patriots, whatever you all prefer to call yourselves.

In this dream of ours you have already approved a constitutional coalition covering all political preferences as long as they remain inclusive, from the Left and progressive camp, through classical liberals, to Christian Democrats and hard conservative Right. You have already voted with your feet to choose your preferred political space across the whole of this new multicolored, multiethnic, multi-ideas Poland.

You have, in short, embraced "strategic decentralization," even if this is quite a mouthful!

Coexistence, mutual recognition, transformation

This idea, this ideal, can mean many things, to you and to everyone else. It can simply mean: Let's agree! Yes. But let's agree to disagree. Peaceful co-existence. We shall each explore our social, economic, and political innovation in our own ways. Write our own provincial charters, with preambles that truly emphasize local values without excluding anyone. Pomeranians won't do taxation fairness in the same way as Podlasians, with their family credits, or Greater Poland's residents, with their single flat tax. And when it comes to spending these złotys, some will address the cost of living or housing emergency first, while others will focus on competitiveness. But they are all willing to kill their sacred cows, such as business constraints on the Left or quick privatization on the Right ... some even imagine replacing the 500+ program! And they all care about the race to the top, even if that top does not quite look the same for all.

But co-existence does not mean fragmentation. Note! There are lots of new train tracks in this decentralized Poland that can connect all these circles of autonomy. Here we have it: a densely interconnected polycentric Poland.

For strategic decentralization is also about mutuality. Beyond political coexistence, it offers the promise of mutual recognition: I see your difference, I understand where it is coming from, and so when I return to my own, I have been changed by this knowledge and yet remain myself. In this story, seeing you, next door or in the province, I accept even our disagreement about how to deal with our difference ... including on how much Warsaw should help us deal with these differences. So mutual recognition needs to reach to the most sensitive corner of our social fabric: our collective memory. Isn't it a good start when our conservative voivodship explains that "the nine voivodeships in the Northwest and the center of the country opted to jointly manage the Polish Academy of Sciences, while five southeastern voivodships, including Podlasie, took the responsibility for the Institute for National Remembrance." Division of labor, yes, but we talk!

For the voivodships will not resist the temptation of learning and borrowing from each other: employer-friendly rating system, pilot pro-worker and green standards, non-trading Sundays, electronic systems for evaluating the quality of public services, fair sovereign wealth fund—aren't these tradeable goods?

So, in spite of all these differences, in spite of all the diversity that the new voivodship Poland is able to celebrate, the dream is about a collective project of diversity in unity. And beyond mutual recognition, this is a story of shared joyful transformation. Even our conservative voivodship is busily inventing Industry 4.0 and Agricultural Valley 4.0 to connect real and virtual worlds to serve renewal. Sure, change may have different beacons on different lands. But doesn't Poznań's liberal leader speaks for all when he proclaims, "if we want to stay scared of everything, we should have kept our safe Warsaw jobs"?

We need, of course, institutional glue. In the interconnected dreams, a cohesion fund connects our voivodships who, in a common College, ensure some basic consistency across the country. And the voivodship senates take decentralization down to the municipalities to ensure that a new provincial centrism does not replace the old Warsaw centrism.

But even beyond local municipalism, isn't the ultimate thread linking these dreams a story of decentralization *all the way down?* They all say the same in different keys: decentralization in the end is about the citizens, Polish nationals and non-nationals alike, who ground this project with their collective intelligence and their collective aspirations. "Strategic" decentralization indeed. A strategy about ownership of the project by all; a strategy otherwise known as democracy! Here, people power and localism go hand in hand since the dream we are dreaming together means "giving voice to the people directly concerned, who benefit from what the local government can offer them"—from workers in the firms, to teachers in their classrooms, to doctors in the wards. Giving power to everybody in the body politic, who across our voivodships come to vote in physical or electronic referenda, including on health care, schools, taxes. This new social contract is fluid, full of political conflict and pushback, with no end, to be constantly reinvented. Paradoxically, perhaps, social acceptance for change rests on effervescence of democracy.

Are these logics of coexistence, mutual recognition, and transformation to be intertwined in the new Poland? Or will they be steps on a long and winding road? It is up to you to decide.

Do it for you and do it for us

I have a dream about your dreams. I am not Polish, but I allowed myself to make your dream my own. Why? Because what you dare or dread to call the Polish–Polish war cannot go on. Not when war is raging in Ukraine, not when we will need to rebuild Ukraine, not when we are all Ukrainians now. Split Poland hurts the Poles and it hurts all Europeans. Poland can stay whole by embracing its diversity. It can be the avant-garde of citizen participation in governance while respecting its traditions. Do it for you and do it for us. This positive model of yours, a cross-party, democratic social contract based on regional self-governance, is brilliantly valid beyond your borders. In addition to your regional government officials, you will send your ideas and your blueprints to Brussels, and in the process, through contagion and sheer envy, you will change the whole of Europe and its mosaic of voivodships.

Let us share widely and broadly this Polish dream nurtured in a Social Contract Incubator and born in this simple book weaved together by a wonderful group of committed academic-activists.

Imagine yourself, some time after this constitutional big bang. Whether you joined Jadwiga's Christmas dinner table reading the Gospel in Suwałki or Piotr and Dorota's party drinking beer till the morning in Szczecin, or landed at the "Grandmas & Grandkids" cafeteria cooperative just outside Gdańsk, I believe we can all agree with Władek of West Pomerania: "It's going better here than in England." Or, for that matter, than anywhere else in the world!

Comment

For a Strong Poland, United in Its Diversity

Peter L. Lindseth

Winner-take-all dynamics are the enemy, not fellow Poles

This is a hopeful volume. Its contributors are Poles from across the political spectrum, some elaborating on and others responding to the constitutional proposals of the Social Contract Incubator (IUS). The authors here are sending their compatriots two messages loud and clear, regardless of their political orientation:

'*We are all Poles*': despite political differences, Poles share a deep identity of common struggle, aspiration, and solidarity, constitutionally embodied in a unitary Polish state.

'*Poland's diversity is in fact its strength*': even as Poles share that deep identity, they are politically diverse, which is unsurprising in a country of 40 million people across different regions and outlooks. Poland needs a political system that can harness that diversity as a positive force rather than exploiting winner-take-all dynamics that only turn Poles against each other, undermining Poland's strength.

The balance between unity and diversity is no doubt difficult to strike. But the aim of any polity must be to achieve *e pluribus, unum*, 'out of many, one'. It is always out of a pluralism of forces that a coherent polity capable of self-government emerges. Only then can the country properly care for its people at home and defend its interests abroad. This is no less true of Poland, both as a sovereign state and a proud member of the European Union and NATO.

How to strike that balance between unity and diversity is, of course, the hard part. I am sure many Poles may find certain details in the IUS proposals to be debatable (even as sympathetic outsider, I do not agree with all of them). But the essential insight of IUS—the one that guides the main thrust of their proposals—is hard to deny:

Peter L. Lindseth, *Comment* In: *Let's Agree on Poland*. Edited by: Maciej Kisilowski and Anna Wojciuk, Oxford University Press. © Inkubator Umowy Społecznej 2025.
DOI: 10.1093/oso/9780198979562.003.0017

Over the past three decades, governments of all stripes have exploited the current system to excessively concentrate power, exacerbate political fractures, and thus undermine Poland's interests rather than advancing them.

Poland deserves better. It deserves a system that will reinforce Poland's emerging leadership in the EU. It deserves a system that consolidates its role as a front-line partner in NATO. It deserves a system that diffuses political tensions while allowing the full range of political forces to address common challenges. It deserves, in other words, a system that effectively meets the needs of the Polish people, united in their diversity.

From dream to reality

The great potential of the IUS approach is well reflected in Chapters 7–12, which the editors have specifically asked me to comment on here. These chapters reaffirm a basic insight of the IUS project: That self-government can and should operate at multiple levels, thus increasing political buy-in and a flourishing of policy experimentation, from which a strengthened legitimacy of the Polish state will emerge.

The sovereignty of the Polish people is indivisible, as this book makes clear. But the political system established to express that sovereignty need not and should not allow momentary winners of electoral battles at the national level to call all the shots in terms of policy. That has only proven to lead to constant and fruitless battles, not to mention centralized policy choices that often poorly fit Poland's rich diversity.

In advocating a partial ('strategic') decentralization of power, the IUS approach seeks to mitigate the worst aspects of the winner-take-all dynamics that currently afflict Poland. The center will be able to refocus on essential national tasks while opening the way for a diversity of political options to realize a range of programs in the voivodships and below. Subsidiarity should prevail whenever possible.

These chapters do a wonderful job describing what the transition from dream to reality might look like in various different voivodships. The result is, in one sense, a study in contrasts, at least with regard to actual policy in now-decentralized domains. But these chapters are also united in their celebration of political empowerment, responsiveness to local conditions, and the fostering of new leadership and political coalitions that can only redound to Poland's benefit nationally. They demonstrate how diversity can indeed be a source of strength.

In this way, these chapters are an optimistic conclusion to a book built on optimism about what Poles can achieve if given a chance. And yet the picture is also deeply pragmatic, very much in touch with the range of policy options currently on offer to the Polish people. Through the kind of strategic decentralization advocated by IUS, these chapters show that Poland can turn the voivodships into a laboratory for a reinvigorated, multilevel Polish democracy.

Poland's better angels

The ultimate aim of this strategic decentralization is to temper what has been called the 'Polish–Polish War'. Allowing these various political visions to flourish across the voivodships is clearly a very promising way of achieving that goal. The ambition behind the IUS proposals brings to mind the famous words of Abraham Lincoln to his fellow Americans at a moment of turmoil and conflict: "We are not enemies, but friends. We must not be enemies. Though passion may have strained, it must not break our bonds of affection. The mystic chords of memory will swell when again touched, as surely they will be, by the better angels of our nature."

The contributors to this volume, from all across the political spectrum, are reaching out to Poland in precisely that same spirit. My hope is that Poles of all political stripes, as members of a great nation whose best years are yet to come, will find the way to heed this call. Europe and the world need a strong Poland, united in its diversity.

13
Let's Do It Differently

Antoni Dudek, Maciej Kisilowski, and Anna Wojciuk

Two constitutional mindsets

How much of your country have you seen reflected in the story of the Polish–Polish war, and in our dream of conservative–progressive coexistence that we have outlined over the past few hundred pages? As we pointed out in the Introduction, the problem outlined in this volume poses a challenge to many democracies worldwide. In numerous nations, the conservative and progressive visions of good life and good society seem both deeply, culturally rooted and yet more starkly distinct than they have been for decades.

Is our proposed solution as universal as the problem it addresses? Again, if you accept our argument that the problem we face is the fundamental irreconcilability of conservative and progressive ecosystems of values, norms, and meanings then you immediately face the problem of non-fungibility of what each side of our ideological battle truly wants. If we are right, then the split-the-difference ideological compromise that Western democracies adopted in response to the previous great ideological conflict—the twentieth-century Cold War with Marxism—may not be readily available today. In the past, it was possible, especially in Western Europe, to create, in a sense, a very mild version of communism in the form of the democratic welfare state. Today, it may be difficult to institute a "soft" version of a conservative cultural program without alienating millions of citizens who remain deeply committed to the so-called Open Society, famously defined by Karl Popper as a society without religious and nationalist dogmas or traditional racial, ethnic, and gender hierarchies.[1] Indeed, we are not the first to predict that cultural conflicts will become dominant in the twenty-first century,[2] and in many ways our solution of decentralization is not only unoriginal in its general direction (although, we hope, quite innovative in important institutional details), but in numerous respects classic as a response to cultural divides.

With all that being said, we readily accept that our institutional imagination may not be broad enough. Perhaps the fundamental and salient differences between today's conservatives and progressives can be resolved in ways other than through territorial decentralization. When discussing the project in Poland, we have always emphasized that our proposal is first and foremost an invitation to

Antoni Dudek, Maciej Kisilowski, and Anna Wojciuk, *Let's Do It Differently* In: *Let's Agree on Poland*.
Edited by: Maciej Kisilowski and Anna Wojciuk, Oxford University Press.
 DOI: 10.1093/oso/9780198979562.003.0018

a different way of thinking about constitutional design. We want to talk with our fellow compatriots about how we—conservatives, we—progressives, we—liberals, we—Christian Democrats, and we—leftists will live together in a single country. How our constitutional order can better accommodate our diversity, our wealth of values.

Law students are often vaguely taught that contractarian political theory was a major inspiration for modern constitutional law. Unquestionably, in some classical texts in constitutional theory—most notably the Federalist Papers—the challenges of coexistence of numerous groups of people representing distinct visions of the good life are prominently discussed. In its modern form, the contractarian tradition is notably represented in the theory of Constitutional Moment (already mentioned in the introduction to this volume), which views democratic deliberation and voters' consent as sufficient for legitimizing even informal constitutional amendments.

And yet, Poland's rich constitutional history provides ample examples of how constitutions can be conceived and used for a different purpose. Rather than being viewed as a common set of rules under which diverse peoples share power within a common nation, constitutions can be viewed as opportunities to entrench one's preferred policy proposals. As one of this chapter's co-authors wrote in an earlier paper, rather than through inclusive "moments," basic laws are frequently made and amended through exclusionary Constitutional Opportunities.[3] In a polarized society, these opportunities can be thought of as sets of circumstances favorable to one side of a major political struggle. For various idiosyncratic reasons, the winning side gains a time-limited chance (the "opportunity") to enact or amend the basic law. They then use that opportunity to cement, through difficult-to-change constitutional provisions, their policy or institutional advantages over the losers.

Polish tradition of constitutional opportunism

Since our nation's first written constitution, enacted merely two years after the American one—on May 3, 1791—most of Poland's basic laws have arguably followed the opportunistic, rather than contractarian, model. This conclusion obviously applies to the vast periods when Polish lands were formally or de facto occupied by our neighbors. In the nineteenth century, some monarchs of the three powers that partitioned and occupied Poland—Russia, Prussia, and Austria—tried to offer concessions to Poles' national aspirations. Notably, in 1815, a very limited form of self-government was granted for a small part of the Russian partition surrounding Warsaw, in a constitution approved, and later modified and disregarded, by the Tsar. The original working draft of the constitution, stolen from Polish archives by Russians after the Nazi–Soviet joint invasion of September 1939, includes handwritten annotations made by the Russian monarch.[4] Likewise, the

1952 constitution for the People's Republic of Poland—a satellite state of the Soviet Union—contained corrections personally made by Joseph Stalin.[5] Both documents provided for high levels of centralization, and obviously no separation of powers. The communist constitution all but eliminated any form of self-governed localities and voivodships, endorsing the doctrine of "democratic centralism." Instead of local and regional governments, the 1952 constitution introduced the so-called national councils based on the Soviet model.[6] For much of the communist era, the executive bodies of these councils acted directly as organs of central government. When "field organs of unified state power" were introduced in 1950,[7] the chairman of the Presidium of the Voivodship National Council replaced the voivode as a representative of the central government.

Unfortunately, the contractarian approach to constitution-making likewise did not prevail during the approximately six decades of Poland's sovereign existence since the late eighteenth century. It is poignant that, in a nation which for much of the past two centuries endured value imposition by various occupiers, the patterns of domestic constitution-making, and political conflict more broadly, have so rarely reflected a genuine attempt to make all Polish citizens feel at home. Instead, constitutions were most often used as ammunition in internal political disputes.

This last conclusion highlights another interesting fact: at least in our country, the characterization of political polarization as a new and unprecedented phenomenon—perhaps triggered by social media and other technological changes—is deeply unconvincing. Throughout its modern history, both as an independent country and as occupied territory, Poland has been home to people with profoundly different conceptions of the good life. Before World War II, we were a multi-ethnic, multi-cultural state with deep religious and linguistic differences. For example, we resembled today's Switzerland much more than modern-day Poland. However, overlapping with these objective differences were ideological divides, at times strikingly similar to those we face today.

These differences are particularly well documented in the period of the so-called Great Sejm—the parliament that, in 1791, enacted the so-called May 3rd Constitution, one of the first written basic laws in the world. Although, as Kim Scheppele rightly points out in her comment in this volume, today we all celebrate that document regardless of political sympathies, from the point of view of the political division at the time it was clearly an expression of the victory of the progressive camp.

As aptly reported in English by the noted Polish historian Zofia Libiszowska,[8] Polish constitution drafters of the time took great interest in developments across the Atlantic. Poland's King Stanislaus Augustus, a Freemason and enthusiast of Enlightenment ideas, was an astute reader of the Federalist Papers.[9] He and other proponents of the Polish constitution were eager to emphasize the ambition of promoting liberty that they shared with the nascent American republic. However, they were quick to point out that the institutions that, in their view, would achieve that objective were radically different from the American model.[10] In particular, the May 3rd Constitution sought to transform Poland—which for centuries had adhered to a unique system with a monarch elected for life by a broad representation of male gentry—into a more conventional hereditary monarchy.[11] While the document explicitly excluded Stanislas's descendants and gave the throne to the Saxon House of Wettin after his reign, the immediate effect of a much stronger monarchy would have been to offer powerful tools to the progressive camp surrounding the king, to lead the country in their way.[12]

Critics of the emerging constitution were quick to point out how odd it was for its proponents to claim an intellectual connection with the American republican experiment while, institutionally, moving the country toward a traditional monarchy. Hugo Kołłątaj, one of the leaders of the monarchical camp, strived to distinguish the Polish case from the American model. In a passionate response to Seweryn Rzewuski—a powerful aristocrat who defended Poland's traditional governance model—Kołłątaj explained that

> From every side, the Confederated Republic of America is surrounded by safety. We, by contrast, face the risen sword of despotism everywhere. There—Ocean or savage nations; here—the most powerful empires surrounding the enfeebled nation … How does [Rzewuski] want to govern our Republic without a king?[13]

Rzewuski was not convinced. After the constitution was passed, he called upon Catherine the Great to help defeat the new basic law. When, after obliging, the empress also took huge chunks of Polish territory, Rzewuski became the iconic traitor figure. His treason has in fact become a cultural meme, with PiS politicians accusing liberals of being Rzewuski's modern incarnation (with "Brussels" playing the role of Catherine). Progressives, meanwhile, entertain a more direct analogy, portraying PiS—like Rzewuski—as the force that is pushing our country eastward, now into the grip of Vladimir Putin.

Regardless of which analogy you prefer, Kołłątaj's dilemma remains strikingly relevant. Was there an institutional compromise that could have satisfied ideological opponents such as Rzewuski while preserving the nation?[14] Is there one today? This short essay will obviously not do justice to the question, as it relates to Poland's waning years at the end of the eighteenth century. What is noteworthy, however, is how intuition concerning the response to this dilemma has remained entrenched throughout our modern independent existence. While the American founding fathers saw the way forward for their new nation in an ugly compromise with the Southern enslavers, the Polish progressives just marched ahead, disregarding the other side. The May 3rd Constitution was passed during an unannounced session of the Sejm,[15] with the majority of members absent and the troops commanded by a king's nephew overseeing the proceedings. Most importantly, the stated objective of this forceful imposition—strengthening the nation in the face of voracious despotic neighbors—demonstrably did not come to pass.

Partly as a result of Rzewuski's efforts to mobilize the Russian-backed traditionalist aristocracy against the basic law, the king was forced to repudiate the constitution merely a year after its passing. Three years later, the country ceased to exist.

Historians would surely point out that many factors influenced the downfall of the so-called First Polish Republic. But here we look at the patterns of constitutional thinking. From that vantage, it is nothing short of remarkable how, 150 years later, the elites of the reborn Poland use very similar methods and narratives to defend the nation from new external threats.

Only a few years after Poland almost miraculously regained independence, Marshal Józef Piłsudski, a social-democratic politician and a brilliant military strategist largely responsible for saving Poland from the Soviet invasion of the early 1920s, dismantled the young democracy in a 1926 coup d'etat. One of the many victims of the authoritarian turn was Article 3 of the country's first twentieth-century basic law, hastily enacted amidst the Soviet–Polish War and an Entente plebiscite that would determine the claim to the key industrial province of Silesia. The article stated that the Republic "based its system on the principle of broad territorial self-government" and "will delegate to the representatives of self-government the proper scope of legislation especially in the fields of administration, culture and farming."

Piłsudski's regime was particularly hostile to decentralized governance, worried in particular that it might empower the national aspirations of Poland's then numerous ethnic minorities. In 1933, the so-called Integration Act was adopted under the slogan of unifying the rules of operation of local governments inherited from the former Russian, Prussian, and Austrian occupation zones.[16] In reality, the law led to a further reduction of subnational governments and an increase in centralization. This was symbolized by the central government's approval being required for all persons elected as mayors.

Piłsudski's consolidation of power was strongly opposed by an odd mix of right-wing nationalist parties, the centrist agrarian People's Party (which still exists today), and social democrats disillusioned with the marshal's militaristic turn. As the 1930s drew closer, Poland's geopolitical situation deteriorated. Piłsudski's instinctive response was remarkably similar to that of the drafters of the May 3rd Constitution a century and a half earlier. Rather than seeking to unite the country in the face of external threats, the governing camp escalated repression. Key opposition figures were interned, sometimes under brutal conditions.[17] In 1935, the government pushed through the so-called April Constitution, which formally cemented an authoritarian form of government, rejecting the separation of powers and making the country's president answerable only "before God and history." As with the May 1791 Constitution, its passage was procedurally flawed: the government lacked the required two-thirds majority, but the Speaker just announced that a simple majority would suffice.[18] Unsurprisingly, the April Constitution also formalized restrictions on regional and local governments, introducing a formal "supervision... exercised by the [central] government."[19]

The April Constitution is thus another example in Polish history of one group of citizens imposing its vision of the state with complete disregard for the aspirations and values of those in opposition. The ruling camp, by then with a nearly decade-long record of competing with the opposition on an increasingly unequal footing, saw the constitution as a way to cement its advantage. Once again, the centralization of power and exclusion of opposing perspectives was viewed as a way to strengthen the country. Walery Sławek—Piłsudski's three-time Prime Minister and, like King Stanislas, a Freemason[20]—argued that Polish society "desires order and justice. With its common sense, it knows that Poland must have a strong government, founded on the authority of the head of state."[21] Yet again, these hopes backfired tragically. Piłsudski himself died of cancer the year his constitution was enacted. His followers, while frequently presenting Poland as one of Europe's superpowers, failed to protect the country from the combined Nazi–Soviet imperialism.[22] Sławek committed suicide a few months before the outbreak of World War II. And, in an almost comical finale to the history of Poland's constitutional opportunism, the all-powerful President—hand-picked by Piłsudski and granted nearly monarchical status by the April Constitution—escaped the still-fighting nation on September 17, 1939, retreating to a quiet life in Switzerland.

As we explained in Chapter 1, the Constitution of 1997 is yet another example of the logic of constitutional opportunism. The analogy obviously goes only so far. The post-communist government of the mid-1990s, which presided over the constitution-drafting process, did not detain political opponents, and armed troops did not harass MPs during the April 2, 1997 session of the joint Sejm and Senate. The right-wing parties committed a self-inflicted strategic blunder before the 1993 general election: They failed to unify in response to the newly introduced electoral threshold, which denied any MPs to parties that failed to reach 5 percent of the vote nationally, and to coalitions that did not attract at least 8 percent. This left nearly 35 percent of Poles without parliamentary representation—in a cycle that was already challenging for conservatives. Procedurally, the enactment of the 1997 Basic Law was mostly legitimate—although Bruce Ackerman has argued that the Supreme Court, clearly sympathetic to the progressive side, did not take "the principle of popular sovereignty ... seriously" enough when validating the ratifying referendum, as it saw a remarkably low turnout of less than 43 percent.[23]

And yet, we see the instincts of the framers of the 1997 Constitution as remarkably similar to those of the drafters of the earlier efforts discussed here. Indeed, as Kim Scheppele rightly observes in her comment in this volume, the drafters of the May 3, 1791 constitution at least managed to secure the general support of the Catholic Church (if not of the traditionalist aristocracy). The Constitution of 1997 failed even in that: Before the 1997 referendum, the Polish bishops argued, in an official statement, that the new basic law "raises serious moral doubts."[24]

An anecdote involving Professor Ackerman himself may illustrate our point. Early in the work of the Social Contract Incubator, we invited the famous Yale constitutionalist to a seminar in Poland to comment on our proposal. As part of our outreach, we invited a few non-members to the generally closed event. They included an eminent Polish professor of constitutional law, personally involved in the drafting process of our basic law in the 1990s. The meeting was polite until Ackerman repeated the above-mentioned claim about the turnout problem with the 1997 Polish constitutional referendum. Suddenly, all the courtesy was gone. In a dramatically raised voice, our Polish colleague all but shouted at Ackerman. Referring to the prospect of invalidating the referendum, and starting the constitutional effort from scratch, he exclaimed: "If we had done what you suggest, we would have NEVER passed a constitution!" As the meeting drew to an uncomfortable close, the Polish professor took one of this chapter's authors to the side. "This guy is a Lepper of constitutionalism," he sneered.

No, not the English "leper"—but very close. Andrzej Lepper was the leader of an agrarian populist party who gave PiS its first chance to govern in 2005. He paid a heavy price for this alliance. In an attempt to consolidate power, PiS's Justice Minister used security services to fish for evidence of Lepper's corruption. Accusations were made—later disproved, but they destroyed Lepper's career. Like Walery Sławek, Piłsudski's Prime Minister, Lepper took his own life in 2011. For a liberal intellectual, calling someone a "Lepper" is therefore the greatest insult. Jarosław Kaczyński may be an unquestioned leader of the revolutionary conservative camp, but he is also a Warsaw lawyer with a PhD. Mr Lepper, by contrast, was both a populist and a peasant. That is how low Professor Ackerman sank in the eyes of an influential Polish law professor for questioning the legitimacy of the 1997 constitution.

That angry protestation, and the classist snub, encapsulates much of the last two centuries of institutional thought, shared equally by Polish progressives and conservatives: the way to push the country forward is not by finding ways to smoothly co-habit our joint nation with the other side of our seemingly eternal ideological conflicts; it is the *other side* that is the problem, and the only solution is defeat and domination; every opportunity granted by history, our own ruthlessness, or sheer luck should be used to stack the deck against the other Poles; compromise or accord is a recipe for never-ending malaise. And this approach continues to be the first intuition among the political elites of both sides, despite powerful historical evidence that, to the extent that the goal is to strengthen Poland, the dominant method often backfires catastrophically.

Polish tradition of constitutional accord

If one wants to look at Polish history in search of a different constitutional tradition—one founded on the pursuit of broad institutional accord and creative power-sharing—an international reader might intuitively think of the Round Table talks. In 1989, Poland made global news when communists and the Solidarity opposition peacefully agreed on partly free elections that would bring about the first non-communist government in the Soviet bloc.[25] And yet, as we conclude this unusual volume, we must remain mindful of different Polish perspectives. For Polish progressives, the 1989 Round Table talks are indeed an unquestioned democratic triumph: a remarkable, bloodless dismantling of a forty-five-year-old communist dictatorship. No wonder, then, that our liberal colleagues in Chapter 5 use the "Round Table" as a metaphor for what our Incubator is calling for: a new constitutional settlement for Poland.

Polish conservatives, however, do not regard the Round Table as a high point in Poland's recent history.[26] Some view the talks with communists, who were losing power anyway because of the collapse of the Soviet bloc, as a mistake that left many unfortunate legacies.[27] Others see them as a tactical necessity in early 1989, but not as a moral foundation for a free nation.[28]

As it happens, one of the authors of this conclusion has devoted significant research to providing a cool-headed and fair assessment of Poland's negotiated transition from communism.[29] But for the purposes of this chapter, we shall refrain from using that important episode as our aspirational model for constitutional design. This choice is convenient, given the diversity of the movement we represent here; but we also have what we hope is a convincing substantive reason: The political environment in which the Round Table took place was, in some ways, more benign than what we face today. If the reader is inclined to laugh our argument off by pointing to the Soviet troops stationed in Poland in 1989, let us explain. After being soundly defeated in the partly free elections of June 4, 1989 that stemmed from the Round Table deal, the communists accepted the end of their ideological model and the new dominance of liberal democracy.[30] As two of us have explained elsewhere,[31] that transition was a "cooperative" one. Currently, in Poland, we are facing two political camps that refuse to accept each other's claim to ideological dominance. In 2015, the progressive side refused to recognize the legitimacy of PiS's conservative revolution. Since 2023, the conservatives have rejected the liberal counter-revolution. The situation is demonstrably "non-cooperative." In our search for a constitutional accord, we need to look for solutions and inspirations that accommodate a diversity that, unlike the communists in 1989, refuses to recede or relent.

That inspiration still comes from the historic Solidarity democratic movement of the 1980s—but from an element of that movement rarely mentioned in English-language historical analyses. From its very beginning, Solidarity strongly advocated for introducing more decentralization into Poland's constitutional system. Helpful for these efforts, though perhaps slightly confusing for an international reader, was a quirky linguistic convention that—for the sake of clarity—we have mostly avoided in this volume. As we briefly mentioned in Chapter 1, in Polish constitutional and administrative theory, as well as in popular language, subnational governments are considered a species of a broader category known as "self-governments." Other "self-governments" include neo-corporatist organizations such as chambers of commerce, professional associations, and, crucially for our history, labor unions.[32] In fact, such organizations are often referred to as "commercial," "professional," or "employees'" self-government (Polish: *samorząd gospodarczy, zawodowy, pracowniczy*).

Thus, in the wake of the historic 1980 strikes, when the communists yielded to the demand to allow a labor union beyond Party control, it logically opened the discussion about "self-governance" in the broader Polish sense. The full name of the new labor organization became "Independent Self-Governed Labor Union 'Solidarity'," commonly referred to as NSZZ "Solidarność," the abbreviation of its full Polish name. In October 1981, Solidarity's first national congress introduced its official policy platform, titled "The Self-Governed Republic" [Polish: *Samorządna Rzeczpospolita*]. "The hitherto system of managing the country, based on all-powerful central party-state institutions, led the country to ruin," read a stark diagnosis of the situation.[33] "The centralist system of social policy proved to be incoherent and ineffective," the document continued.[34] In response to these findings, Solidarity demanded institutional reforms that, in many aspects, were strikingly similar to what we are arguing for in this book. "Legally, organizationally and financially autonomous territorial self-government should become the true representation of local communities," read postulate number 21. "Self-governed organizations and bodies should obtain representation at the level of central state authorities," stated the next. These and other proposed changes were summarized in the program's very first "thesis": the demand to "introduce a democratic self-government at all levels of management, and the new socio-economic deal that links the plan, the self-government and the market."[35]

The reference to communist central planning reflected the broader reality of Solidarity not counting on the complete collapse of the communist system.[36] As we mentioned in Chapter 1, the focus on self-governance and decentralization stemmed not only from a linguistic convention but also from a deeper strategic choice: to push for a certain sphere of civic freedom, organized along territorial or functional lines, without explicitly challenging the core foundations of the communist state. This attempt at moderation failed to convince the communists, who two months after the publication of *Self-Governed Republic* declared martial law, disbanded Solidarity, and arrested its leaders. That violent escalation effectively ended the broader idea of using decentralization to create a compromise hybrid communist–democratic system. However, the banner of self-governance—and the term's importance in the collective identity of the Solidarity movement—would later be taken up by a group of scholars interested in subnational governance. This group was led by urban planning expert Jerzy Regulski. As Regulski himself recalls, the historic Solidarity platform did not actually influence much of his team's research, which predated the union's document.[37] But when, in the fall of 1989, Solidarity was allowed to form the first non-communist cabinet behind the Iron Curtain, the importance of the then almost decade-old postulate of self-governance to the movement's organizational identity compelled the new Prime Minister, Tadeusz Mazowiecki, to appoint Regulski as a special governmental plenipotentiary tasked with preparing local government reform.

Building on many years of academic research, Regulski's team was able to hit the ground running. In just a few months, it designed and implemented a comprehensive system of democratic municipalities. The package of laws introducing the reform was passed as early as March 1990, and included several entirely new statutes as well as amendments to more than a hundred other laws. On May 27, 1990, local elections were held as the first fully democratic ballot in postwar Poland (in the June 1989 Round Table elections, 65% of the Sejm's seats had still been controlled by the communists and their allies). This was truly a remarkable feat: the brisk and efficient election of more than 50,000 local councilors with a direct democratic mandate, and the granting of statutory powers to them to act for their local communities, was arguably the greatest success of the Solidarity government in domestic politics. In a single sweep, a vast swath of the state apparatus was rebuilt with transparency, effectively protecting citizens from the centralist tendencies of the authorities in Warsaw as practiced by the communists, and earlier—with all the differences—by the authoritarian rule of Józef Piłsudski.

As Regulski recalls in his memoirs, nothing was easy about the breakneck process leading to this reform. "We encountered serious resistance," he wrote, mostly because "the reconstruction of local government was about taking away a significant part of the competencies of the central government."[38] While, in 1981, it was universally attractive for the Solidarity leadership to decentralize power away from the Communist Party, now, in 1989, it was Solidarity that controlled the center. A powerful opponent of Regulski immediately emerged in Jacek Ambroziak, the Prime Minister's chief of staff, who viewed Regulski's ideas as radical, academic, and unrealistic.[39] One "compromise" counterproposal circulated in early 1990 was to allow appeals from each mayoral decision to a centrally appointed voivode. Regulski's team was unwavering. In the words of one of his aides, if the appeal procedure were established, "the self-government would come to nothing."[40]

Regulski emphasized that, in some cases, overcoming the resistance of newly appointed Solidarity ministers would have been impossible without the Prime Minister's personal support. For Mazowiecki—a liberal Catholic intellectual[41]—the principle of subsidiarity, a cornerstone of Catholic social teaching,[42] was intuitively appealing. Even Regulski's permanent invitation to Cabinet meetings was reportedly secured only after Mazowiecki's personal intervention. This proved to be a valuable opportunity for establishing direct contacts with individual ministers and, as Regulski himself admitted, resulted in "greater ease in dealing with various matters that had previously been very difficult."[43]

Regulski was also aware that another obvious pocket of resistance would be the extensive network of territorial branches of central government inherited from the communist times. To counter this, he pushed—against Ambroziak's objections—for the creation of a network of forty-nine regional delegates of the Government's Plenipotentiary for Local Government. Regulski skillfully lobbied for his delegates to use the infrastructure of central government's voivodship offices, while remaining formally independent of the voivodes. This proved crucial, since the voivodes, as Regulski later recalled, "were mostly old and opposed to the Solidarity government. My delegates, on the other hand, formed the first network of the already 'new' administration ... They constituted an independent network and an important channel of information, which had previously belonged exclusively to the voivodes. The voivodes therefore led the fight against them."[44] While the voivodes' opposition did not succeed in derailing the reform, the new reform ended up being limited to the municipal level. The status of voivodships, still fully controlled by the center, was to be determined later.

Nobody, however, expected it to take nearly a decade. In the 1993 general elections that we have already discussed, the post-communists staged a stunning comeback, capitalizing on social fatigue with the economic "shock therapy" pursued by the Solidarity government in parallel with the local government reform. The new administration was not interested in further decentralization. Only the subsequent center-right government elected a few months after the constitutional referendum introduced, in 1998, the present system of dual administration in sixteen voivodships, with the still centrally appointed voivode and the marshal as a head of the regionally elected Voivodship Board. The fact that the reform took place only after the passing of the constitution meant that the status of the self-governed bodies at the regional and county levels (also introduced in 1998) was regulated solely by ordinary legislation. Only the municipalities are explicitly mentioned in the 1997 basic law, although the scope of their independence and powers is also largely determined by statutory provisions.

Technically, much of the local and regional governance introduced in the 1990s is thereby not even part of Poland's *constitutional* law. And yet our decentralized governance has proven to be among the strongest and most stable institutions of the state. That reality became evident in 2015, when the revolutionary conservatives took power. Numerous institutions explicitly established and elaborately protected under the 1997 basic law proved remarkably weak in withstanding the revolutionary moment. In 2015 PiS won a razor-thin Sejm majority, far short of what was required for a formal constitutional amendment, but it still managed, just a year into its rule, to completely dominate the Constitutional Tribunal. The detailed provisions of articles 188–197 of the Constitution proved insufficient to protect the institution in the form designed in 1997.[45] Soon after, the government dismissed the entire National Council of the Judiciary—a key body tasked with nominating judges—and elected its new members in a procedure that most lawyers saw as violating the fairly specific language of article 187 of the Constitution.[46] While many citizens protested against these changes, widely viewed by lawyers as breaking explicit constitutional norms, the resistance was far from massive or decisive.

By contrast, the fate of local and regional governments after the PiS takeover reveals a striking difference. Unlike with the Constitutional Tribunal or the Judiciary Council, PiS did not need to use legal tricks or tortuous interpretative techniques to entirely dismantle Poland's decentralized governance. The self-governed voivodships and counties could have been abolished with a simple statutory amendment—the kind that PiS often pushed through the Sejm that they controlled literally within an afternoon during their time in power. With no explicit constitutional provisions addressing voivodships and counties, opponents of such a move would have struggled to offer any constitutional argument. Even with regard to municipalities, much of their powers and independence could have been taken away through clean and constitutionally uncontroversial statutory change. And yet, the local and regional governments survived through the eight years of PiS rule.

This discrepancy becomes even more glaring when we take the international context into account. Judicial bodies attacked by PiS enjoyed powerful support from the West. The Court of Justice of the European Union and the European Court of Human Rights both declared that the Constitutional Tribunal[47] and the Judiciary Council[48]—packed with PiS allies—failed to satisfy the rule-of-law standards to which Poland was obliged to adhere as a Member State of the EU and the Council of Europe. The European Commission formally declared the country in breach of the EU's fundamental values outlined in Article 2 of the EU Treaty.[49] The European Network of Councils for the Judiciary expelled the Polish body from its ranks.[50] Countless other international juridical organizations, respected lawyers, and law professors denounced PiS's actions as completely incompatible with democratic rule-of-law standards. As our colleagues acknowledge in Chapter 6, this wave of Western criticism of PiS's judicial reforms was a significant factor in undermining the legitimacy of the right-wing government. We agree, and would add that the worries about the row with the European Union potentially escalating to a "Polexit" were part of the reason why PiS lost the 2023 general election.[51]

Incidentally, that importance of the Western opposition to PiS's judicial reforms in itself highlights another unwritten element of Poland's constitutional framework. Our 1997 basic law is silent about our membership in such Euro-Atlantic organizations as the EU, NATO, and the Council of Europe. And yet, the political problems encountered by PiS showed that our place in the liberal West is, like local governance, a much stronger component of our constitutional order than many written provisions of our basic law. While many voters may be indifferent to the fate of the Constitutional Tribunal or the Judiciary Council, they do care about

Poland remaining part of democratic Europe. But that conclusion further highlights the glaring difference between the *domestic* strength of key judicial institutions set up in the 1997 constitution, and our local and regional governments. For, clearly, much of the legitimacy that our judicial bodies enjoyed during the confrontation with the revolutionary conservatives was, in a sense, "borrowed" from the West.

A thought experiment may clarify our point. Imagine an alternative history in which PiS's judicial reforms outraged domestic lawyers but did not provoke *international* condemnation. The European Commission did not see any breaches to rule of law. The EU's Court of Justice and the European Court of Human Rights both declared new judges as duly appointed and sufficiently independent. The broader global legal community failed to see a sufficient case for radical action. Even if Polish lawyers had remained deeply convinced about the unconstitutionality of PiS actions, their opposition would quickly have become an academic point.

Now consider the political calculus of Jarosław Kaczyński, PiS's leader, as he looked at Poland's decentralized governance during his 2015–23 rule. Those of us who find him guilty of authoritarian tendencies might have expected the independent political power of subnational governments, and especially of large progressive municipalities, surely to have bothered him. And if he ever contemplated doing away with Poland's subnational governance, he would have known that the potential international opposition to such a move would be incomparably weaker than the reaction to his attacks on the courts. As we have already noted, the formal constitutional arguments of opponents to even the most sweeping centralization efforts would have been much less convincing. But beyond this, there is simply no international constituency for decentralized governance whose strength and organization can be compared to the global "lobby" that protects judicial power and independence. When it comes to EU development funds, for instance, the Commission already accepts much more centralized models of those funds' disbursement than that introduced in Poland after our EU accession, and not significantly modified throughout the PiS rule. Indeed, at the time of writing, the Commission itself is considering a sweeping reform that would centralize development funding in all member states[52]—a prospect that, in our view, would be a disastrous manifestation of liberal self-destructive instincts.

To conclude, while key judicial institutions on which the 1997 Constitution was built collapsed, even with the benefit of tremendous international support, decentralized governance—with its flimsy formal protections and no powerful Western backers—endured. The stories that we have presented on the preceding pages are an attempt to convince you that this stark difference stems from the different logic behind the creation of these respective institutions: the logic of exclusionary constitutional opportunism in the case of the 1997 Constitution, and that of the inclusive constitutional accord in the case of our local government reforms.

Process and product in constitutional design

But what, exactly, do we mean by "a different logic"? In social contract theory, there is a famous discussion on the historical versus ahistorical nature of the contract—are we talking about an actual "deal" made by representatives of various social groups, or an institutional architecture designed *as if* it were conceived in such a deal?[53] Another way to conceptualize essentially the same distinction is to distinguish between a process (or input) and output legitimacy.[54] Once again, the question is what makes an institutional order stable and socially supported: the fairness and inclusiveness of the process of its creation, or the beneficial nature of the end product?

Influenced by theories of deliberative democracy,[55] contemporary constitutional thought has largely been dominated by the process legitimacy camp. However, the remarkable success of Poland's decentralization reforms amidst the broader constitutional upheaval encourages us to rethink this process-oriented intellectual trend. As we described above, our municipalities were designed by a relatively insular group of scholars who succeeded in persuading an intellectual Prime Minister to adopt their ideas. The institutions they created have proved remarkably resilient—not because, in the whirlwind winter of 1990, every voice was duly heard; rather, their staying power stems from the fact that they worked for a broad array of Poles and their communities. The reason why PiS did not shut down our local governance was that doing so would have provoked the wrath of not only urban progressives, but also deeply conservative communities who had grown used to their municipalities, not to mention the entire conservative apparatus manning the structures of our right-leaning municipalities, counties, and voivodships.

This is not to say that procedural legitimacy is totally unimportant. The glaring lack of inclusion of conservatives in the drafting process of the 1997 Constitution undoubtedly entered the collective consciousness of our Right, and fueled its assault on the constitution's key institutions. However, giving process legitimacy absolute preeminence—or asserting, as some deliberative democrats do, that our core democratic ambition should be to create deliberation that transcends self-interest[56]—strikes us as a kind of magical thinking. Why would ordinary citizens accept institutions that fundamentally work to their disadvantage, just because some civic panel talked a lot about them? Why would the descendants of those citizens care about the openness or fairness of a process that happened decades or centuries earlier? By contrast, when local citizens, and—perhaps more importantly—local elites, assertively defend the autonomy of their municipalities in Poland, it is because these municipalities serve their needs, further their interests, and help them achieve their vision of the good life. The proposal outlined in this book seeks to harness this real, and not magical, legitimizing mechanism.

One way in which the magical fixation on process affects our work on the Polish constitutional settlement is through critics dismissing our proposal as overly academic. At its core, this criticism is a process argument: after all, what the critics are implying is that robust constitutional institutions can only be designed by active politicians, who possess a unique understanding of voters' sentiments, and are supported today by an extensive apparatus of professional pollsters, communication experts, and social-media big data analysts. Our response is: just look at Poland's constitutional history. The previous local government reforms were also designed and implemented by dreamer-academics. The practical record of these reforms is, as we have also seen, viewed positively by Poles. The local government institutions designed in professors' offices have proved more durable in practice than the institutions of the 1997 Constitution, the 1935 April Constitution, and the 1791 May Constitution—all shaped by consummate political insiders of their respective times.

The story we have presented illustrates why academics can make an impact in constitutional reforms. The essence of democratic governance in a divided society is to establish a fair and credible power-sharing structure. In the specific context of decentralization, the goal is a more balanced distribution of power between the center and local or regional governments. Unfortunately, there is no logical possibility for such change to take place without there being political losers. A central politician designing decentralization reforms is therefore, in effect, a judge in their own case. As we saw in Poland in the early 1990s, the most ardent opponents of decentralization were officials in Warsaw and in territorial branches of the central government administration.

More broadly, the design of a complex institutional system that would work for decades, and simultaneously for numerous groups in our increasingly divided societies, cannot emerge in a process responsive to every critical opinion or every vested interest. Discussion and acceptance of a democratic system of government must, of course, be broad and inclusive. But the proposals put forward must, in order for them to make sense, have an internal logic and coherence. As Alec Issigonis, designer of the legendary Mini Cooper, noted, "a camel is a horse designed by committee."

Our work in the Social Contract Incubator shows, however, that there is a role for the process perspective in constitutional design. A fair process should, in particular, catalyze our instincts so that we seek institutional outcomes that honestly follow the logic of constitutional accord. While such social contract would always be "as if"—there is no option to literally construct a detailed institutional agreement among the 36 million Poles—a good process should first and foremost disabuse us of the false hope that the other side of our ideological battles could somehow be ignored or molded into our image.

Social Contract Incubator's work, spanning more than seven years, has convinced us that citizens of different ideological backgrounds can cooperate, listen to one another, and recognize each other's perspectives as legitimate views that have a place in our society—all while maintaining their own values, and without trying to impose their beliefs on others. This was possible not because we were somehow exceptional, but precisely because we created a process that ensured the representation of a diversity of views. We strived to achieve a conservative–progressive balance in both the Incubator's leadership and our work teams. We also consistently checked whether our original commitment to ideological pluralism was being maintained at the various stages of the project's preparation. Rather than searching for opportunities to exclude people with different values, we sought ideological diversity as something desirable, without which our endeavors would not make sense. At the same time, outside of our work, many of us engaged and spoke publicly on political issues, often proclaiming radically different views.

The composition of this book's authors also reflects this inclusive approach. In particular, the authors and contributors to the five stories in Part II are genuine advocates of the ideas with which they identify, and for the support of which they are known in Poland. It may be pointed out that this agreement was easy for us; after all, an "incubator," by definition, provides favorable conditions. True as that may be, in the recent years of political polarization—when it has been growing increasingly difficult for us to agree even on basic facts—our movement has been a unique endeavor. Our work demonstrates that agreeing on a set of stable democratic ground rules is within the reach of all of us—in Poland and elsewhere.

We began this book with a forgiving yet nevertheless pointed critique of politicians who promise a moral revolution in our public sphere through the "I'll-do-it-better" approach. However, this messianism is in many ways a trait we all share. Instead of rejoicing in and celebrating what unites us—numerous common cultural milestones, high points of our recent history, or pride in the achievements of our sports stars (which, in the case of Poland at the time of writing, would surely include Iga Świątek and Robert Lewandowski)—we love to despair over the differences that divide us and the supposedly inevitable demise of our national communities—communities, we should add, whose reconstruction we somehow always envision as involving "the others" agreeing with "us"!

A process of good constitutional design must steer us away from such unhelpful instincts. We hope that the efforts we have made over the better part of the past decade—together with this book, which outlines the fruits of our work—will inspire democratic constitutional designers worldwide to think differently about our constitutions, and, more broadly, about the relations between us. Not to convert or enlighten each other by force, but to find a way in which our democracies can accommodate us all.

Notes

1. Karl R. Popper, *The Open Society and Its Enemies* (Routledge, 1945).
2. Samuel P. Huntington, *The Clash of Civilizations and the Remaking of World Order* (New York: Simon & Schuster, 1996).
3. Maciej Kisilowski, "Constitutional Strategy for a Polarized Society: Learning from Poland's Post-revolutionary Misfortunes," in *Revolutionary Constitutionalism: Law, Legitimacy, Power,* ed. Richard Albert (Hart Publishing, 2020).
4. Mariusz Kolmasiak, "O szkatule z konstytucją Królestwa Polskiego: Z okazji 100-lecia rewidndykacji," *Mówią Wieki* 10, no. 753 (2022): 52. For the detailed description of the drafting process of the 1815 see Michał Gałędek, "The Monarchical Sovereignty and the Ministerial Responsibility in the Course of Works on the Constitution for the Kingdom of Poland, 1814–1815," *Giornale di Storia Costituzionale* 37 (2019): 153.
5. Krzysztof Persak, "Stalin as Editor: The Soviet Dictator's Secret Changes to the Polish Constitution of 1952," *Bulletin of the Cold War International History Project* 11 (1998): 149–154 .
6. Grażyna Skąpska, *From 'Civil Society' to 'Europe': A Sociological Study on Constitutionalism after Communism* (Brill, 2011), 81–100.
7. Michał Siedziako, "A Polish Invention or a Copy of the Soviet Model? Electoral Practices during Parliamentary Elections in Poland under the Communist Rule (1944–1980)," *Contemporary European History* 33, no. 1 (2024): 115.
8. Zofia Libiszowska, "The Impact of the American Constitution on Polish Political Opinion in the Late Eighteenth Century," in *Constitution and Reform in Eighteenth-Century Poland: The Constitution of 3 May 1791*, ed. Samuel Fiszman (Indiana University Press, 1997).
9. Id.
10. Jerzy Lukowski, "Recasting Utopia: Montesquieu, Rousseau and the Polish Constitution of 3 May 1791," *The Historical Journal* 37, no. 1 (1994): 85.
11. Richard Butterwick, *The Polish Revolution and the Catholic Church, 1788–1792: A Political History* (Oxford University Press, 2011), 209.
12. Jerzy Michalski, "The Meaning of the Constitution of 3 May," in *Constitution and Reform in Eighteenth-Century Poland: The Constitution of 3 May 1791*, ed. Samuel Fiszman (Indiana University Press, 1997).
13. Hugo Kołłątaj, *Uwagi nad pismem, którze wyszło w Warszawie z Drukarni Dusourowskiey pod tytułem: Seweryna Rzewuskiego Hetmana Polnego Koronnego o Sukcessyi Tronu w Polszcze* (Drukarnia Uprzywilejowana M. Grolla, Księgarza Nadwornego J.K. Mości, 1790), 71–2. (our translation)
14. See Butterwick, *The Polish Revolution and the Catholic Church, 1788–1792: A Political History*, 206.
15. Butterwick, *The Polish Revolution and the Catholic Church, 1788–1792: A Political History*, 248–249.
16. Paweł Cichoń, "Concepts of Local Government in the Polish Constitutions of the Interwar Period (1918–1939)," *Studia z Dziejów Państwa i Prawa Polskiego* 25 (2022): 150.
17. Andrzej Misiuk, "Police and Policing Under the Second Polish Republic, 1918–39," in *Policing Interwar Europe: Continuity, Change and Crisis, 1918–40*, ed. Gerald Blanley, Jr (Springer, 2007).
18. Dawid Michalski, "Constitutional Norms in the Polish and Finnish Constitutions of the Interwar Period," *Studia Iuridica*, no. 80 (2019): 240; Andrzej Ajnenkiel, *Polskie konstytucje* (Wiedza Powszechna, 1982), 314; Marta Marcinkiewicz, "O konstytucji kwietniowej raz jeszcze," *Pamięć i Sprawiedliwość.* 31, no. 1 (2018): 335–337.
19. Cichoń, "Concepts of Local Government in the Polish Constitutions of the Interwar Period (1918–1939)," 150–151.
20. Dagmara Jajesniak-Quast, "Polish Economic Circles and the Question of the Common European Market after World War I," in *Expert Cultures in Central Eastern Europe: The Internationalization of Knowledge and the Transformation of Nation States since World War I*, ed. Martin Kohlrausch, Katrin Steffen, and Stefan Wiederkehr (Fibre, 2010), 140.
21. Marcinkiewicz, "O konstytucji kwietniowej raz jeszcze," 318 (our translation).
22. Przemysław Olstowski, "The Formation of Authoritarian Rule in Poland between 1926 and 1939 as a Research Problem," *Zapiski Historyczne* 89, no. 2 (2024): 49–53.
23. Bruce Ackerman, *Revolutionary Constitutions: Charismatic Leadership and the Rule of Law* (Harvard University Press, 2019), 274.
24. "Konkordat, Konstytucja, Wierzący Obywatele," *Gazeta Wyborcza*, May 5, 1997.

25. Wiktor Osiatyński, "The Roundtable Talks in Poland," in *The Round Table Talks and the Breakdown of Communism*, ed. Jon Elster (University of Chicago Press, 1996); Paweł Kowal, *Koniec systemu władzy: polityka ekipy gen. Wojciecha Jaruzelskiego w latach 1986-1989* (Instytut Studiów Politycznych PAN, 2012); Jan Skórzyński, *Okrągły stół: wynegocjowany koniec PRL* (Znak, 2019).
26. Elżbieta Matynia, "Is Liberal Democracy Already History?" *East European Politics and Societies* 34, no. 3 (2020): 531–545.
27. Jadwiga Staniszkis, *The Dynamics of the Breakthrough in Eastern Europe: The Polish Experience* (University of California Press, 1991).
28. Michał Bilewicz, "Moving beyond the Past: The Role ofHistorical Closure in Conflict Resolution," *Social Psychological Bulletin* 14, no. 4 (2019): 1–10.
29. Antoni Dudek, *Reglamentowana rewolucja: Rozkład dyktatury komunistycznej w Polsce 1988–1990* (Znak, 2014).
30. Grzegorz Ekiert and Jan Kubik, *Rebellious Civil Society: Popular Protest and Democratic Consolidation in Poland, 1989–1993* (University of Michigan Press, 2010).
31. Maciej Kisilowski and Anna Wojciuk, "The Authoritarian Hangover," *Project Syndicate*, May 9, 2023.
32. Cf. Susan Rose-Ackerman, *From Elections to Democracy. Building Accountable Government in Hungary and Poland* (Cambridge University Press, 2005), 100–25.
33. *Samorządna Rzeczpospolita* (I Krajowy Zjazd Delegatów NSZZ "Solidarność", 1981).
34. Id.
35. Id.
36. Maciej Tymiński and Piotr Koryś, "Od socjalizmu do socjalizmu. Koncepcje reform gospodarczych w PRL po wybuchach społecznych w 1956 i 1980 r," *Dzieje Najnowsze* 48, no. 4 (2016): 125–140 .
37. Jerzy Regulski and Michał Kulesza, *Droga do Samorządu: Od Pierwszych Koncepcji do Inicjatywy Senatu (1981–1989)* (Wolters Kluwer Polska, 2009), 27–8.
38. Jerzy Regulski, *Życie splecione z historią* (Zakład Narodowy im. Ossolińskich, 2014), 438.
39. Antoni Dudek, *Od Mazowieckiego do Suchockiej: pierwsze rządy wolnej Polski* (Znak, 2019), 203–206.
40. Jerzy Bartkowski et al., *Droga do samorządności terytorialnej: Polska 1989–1990* (Instytut Studiów Politycznych Polskiej Akademii Nauk, 2016), 60.
41. Włodzimierz Wesołowski and Aneta Gawkowska, "Communitarian Motives in Polish Political Thought," *Polish Sociological Review* 145 (2004): 22–24.
42. Adrian Vermeule, "Echoes of the Ius Commune," *The American Journal of Jurisprudence* 66, no. 1 (2021): 90–22; Steven G. Calabresi and Lucy D. Bickford, "Federalism and Subsidiarity: Perspectives from Law," *Northwestern Law & Econ Research Paper*, no. 12-12 (2011): 5.
43. Regulski, *Życie splecione z historią*, 443, 50.
44. Regulski, *Życie splecione z historią*, 472–3.
45. See Maciej Kisilowski, "Poland's Democracy Is Crumbling," *Politico*, Dec. 24, 2015; Maciej Kisilowski, "Poland: A Country without a Constitution," *EU Observer*, Jan. 6, 2017.
46. See Maciej Kisilowski, "Poland's Point of No Return," *Politico*, Jul. 15, 2017.
47. Xero Floor w Polsce sp. z o.o. v. Poland, No. 4907/18 (European Court of Human Rights 2021).
48. Commission v. Poland (Disciplinary regime for judges), No. C-791/19 (Court of Justice of the European Union Jul. 15, 2021); European Commission v. Poland (Rule of law), No. C-204/21 (Court of Justice of the European Union Jun. 5, 2023); Reczkowicz v. Poland, No. 43447/19 (European Court of Human Rights 2021); Dolińska-Ficek and Ozimek v. Poland, No. 49868/19 and 57511/19 (European Court of Human Rights 2021); Advancs Pharma sp. z o.o. v. Poland, No. 1469/20 (European Court of Human Rights 2022); Wałęsa v. Poland, No. 50849/21 (European Court of Human Rights 2023).
49. European Commission, Reasoned Proposal in Accordance with Article 7(1) of the Treaty on European Union Regarding the Rule of Law in Poland: Proposal for a Council Decision on the Determination of a Clear Risk of a Serious Breach by the Republic of Poland of the Rule of Law, COM(2017) 835 final (Brussels 2017).
50. European Network of Councils of the Judiciary, "ENCJ General Assembly Voted to Expel the KRS," news release, Oct. 28, 2021.
51. Cf. Maciej Kisilowski, "How Poland Won Back Its Democracy," *Project Syndicate*, Nov. 6, 2023.
52. Gregorio Sorgi, "Commission's Budget Plans Endanger the European Project, Says Regions Chief," *Politico*, Oct. 8, 2024.

53. See e.g. Peter McCormick, "Social Contract: Interpretation and Misinterpretation," *Canadian Journal of Political Science* 9, no. 1 (1976): 63–76 ; Jeremy Waldron, "John Locke: Social Contract versus Political Anthropology," *The Review of Politics* 51, no. 1 (1989): 3–28.
54. Fritz Scharpf, *Governing in Europe: Effective and Democratic?* (Oxford University Press, 1999), 10–23; see also Peter L. Lindseth, *Power and Legitimacy: Reconciling Europe and the Nation-State* (Oxford University Press, 2010), 4–14.
55. For the analysis of commonalities between the social contract and deliberative democracy theories see Albert Weale, "Contractarian Theory, Deliberative Democracy and General Agreement," in *Justice and Democracy: Essays for Brian Barry*, ed. Keith Dowding, Robert E. Goodin, and Carole Pateman (Cambridge University Press, 2004).
56. See Jane Mansbridge et al., "The Place of Self-Interest and the Role of Power in the Deliberative Democracy," *Journal of Political Philosophy* 18, no. 1 (2010): 64, characterizing deliberative democracy as "traditionally … defined in opposition to self-interest."

Caption: Contributing authors. Front row, from left: Helena Chmielewska-Szlajfer, Mikołaj Herbst, Maciej Kisilowski, Wojciech Przybylski, Marek Tatała, Anna Wojciuk, Antoni Dudek, Sylwia Sysko-Romańczuk, Jakub Drożdż. Row 2, from left: Jan Smoleński, Alicja Pacewicz, Jacek Giedrojć, Ryszard Balicki, Marcin Zieliński, Tomasz Kaczor, Agnieszka Chłoń-Domińczak, Artur Wołek, Arkadiusz Radwan, Tomasz G. Grosse. Row 3, from left: Michał Żabicki, Paweł Dobrowolski, Fryderyk Zoll, Jarosław Gwizdak, Maciej Bukowski, Leszek Stypułkowski, Łukasz Rozdeiczer, Mirosław Granat, Jacek Sokołowski.

Photo by Olena Herasym

Index

For the benefit of digital users, indexed terms that span two pages (e.g., 52–53) may, on occasion, appear on only one of those pages.

Figures are indicated by an italic *f* following the page number.